Protestants

For Anita

Protestants

A History from Wittenberg to Pennsylvania 1517–1740

C. Scott Dixon

A John Wiley & Sons, Ltd., Publication

This edition first published 2010
© 2010 C. Scott Dixon

Blackwell Publishing was acquired by John Wiley & Sons in February 2007. Blackwell's publishing program has been merged with Wiley's global Scientific, Technical, and Medical business to form Wiley-Blackwell.

Registered Office
John Wiley & Sons Ltd, The Atrium, Southern Gate, Chichester, West Sussex, PO19 8SQ, United Kingdom

Editorial Offices
350 Main Street, Malden, MA 02148-5020, USA
9600 Garsington Road, Oxford, OX4 2DQ, UK
The Atrium, Southern Gate, Chichester, West Sussex, PO19 8SQ, UK

For details of our global editorial offices, for customer services, and for information about how to apply for permission to reuse the copyright material in this book please see our website at www.wiley.com/wiley-blackwell.

The right of C. Scott Dixon to be identified as the author of this work has been asserted in accordance with the UK Copyright, Designs and Patents Act 1988.

Library of Congress Cataloging-in-Publication Data
Dixon, C. Scott.
  Protestants : a history from Wittenberg to Pennsylvania 1517-1740 / C. Scott Dixon.
      p. cm.
  Includes bibliographical references and index.
  ISBN 978-1-4051-5084-2 (hardcover : alk. paper) 1. Protestantism–History. I. Title.
  BX4805.3.D58 2010
  280.4–dc22

                                    2010009543

A catalogue record for this book is available from the British Library.

Set in 10/12.5 pt Galliard by Thomson Digital, Noida, India.
Printed and bound in Malaysia by Vivar Printing Sdn Bhd

1 2010

Contents

Acknowledgments

Much of this book was researched and written while I was resident in Vienna, Wolfenbüttel, and Berlin, and I would like to take this opportunity to thank the scholars who helped to facilitate my stays in these cities. I am grateful to Martina Fuchs and Alfred Kohler for their friendly support during my time in Vienna, to Jill Bepler, for her years of kindness during my stays in Wolfenbüttel, and to Claudia Ulbrich, for helping to me to get on my feet in Berlin. I would also like to thank the following friends and colleagues who have answered questions, provided advice, or sent me unpublished chapters of their own work to help me on my way: Euan Cameron, Geoffrey Dipple, Martin Gierl, Kevin Gould, Mark Greengrass, Susan Karant-Nunn, Peter Marshall, Judith Pollmann, Penny Roberts, and Alexandra Walsham. I am also extremely grateful to the two readers who worked through the manuscript and provided me with such thoughtful and helpful reviews. None of these scholars, of course, is responsible for the views of this book or the errors that remain.

Both at the beginning of this project and at the end the assistance provided by the Alexander von Humboldt Foundation enabled me to undertake research in world-class libraries. It gives me great pleasure to record my appreciation in print for the generous help the Foundation offered during my time in Wolfenbüttel and Berlin. And finally I would like to record my gratitude to the Queen's University, Belfast for making it possible for me to live and work in two worlds.

C. Scott Dixon

Introduction
Law and Gospel

The law and the gospel is Scripture's immanent hermeneutic; it is a georgic of the mind, in which the central labor of a Christian is taught: the pious reading of and response to the Word of God embodied in the Bible.[1]

Protestants: A History from Wittenberg to Pennsylvania 1517–1740   By C. Scott Dixon
© 2010 C. Scott Dixon

Around the turn of the seventeenth century an anonymous German artist published an engraving of an imaginary church entitled *True Image of the Ancient Apostolic Church* (*Vera Imago veteris Ecclesiae Apostolicae*). German readers would have noticed the word "evangelical" in the vernacular transcription, but even without this interpolation there could be no mistaking its Protestant credentials. Almost entirely devoid of icons and images, and free of the choirs and altars that ordered sacral space in late medieval Catholic churches, the interior appears as a vast, unbroken expanse, with only the columns to mark out a sense of structure. Standing and sitting beneath the nave is the congregation of believers listening to a sermon being delivered by a clergyman from an elevated stone pulpit. On the margins of the illustration are depictions of the two remaining sacraments of mainstream Protestantism, baptism and Communion, being ministered to the congregation in smaller groups, each within earshot of the spoken Word of God. All of this could only lead to one conclusion. It is, as the artist suggests, a faithful image of the church as imagined by Protestants, a *vera imago* of the evangelical *and* apostolic church, for not only has it been reduced to the absolute essentials of the faith – Word, sacrament, and congregation – but in the sheer austerity and emptiness of the interior it reminds us that, even as late as the start of the seventeenth century, this was a people with an deep abhorrence of the Catholic past.[2]

There is another clue that this is a Protestant church. At the far end of the nave, facing down the congregation, the artist has included two rounded stone tablets next to an open book: tablet and text, the two symbols of law and gospel. And above both sits a clock, signifying that both are valid in the course of a Christian life. These were not uniquely Protestant symbols evoking a uniquely Protestant concern. Identifying the right relationship between law and gospel was a task as old as Christianity, as were the issues relating to faith and community raised by interpretation. But early modern Protestants were particularly absorbed by this theme, beginning with Martin Luther, who claimed that almost all of Scripture, and the whole of theology, depended on proper knowledge of the relationship between the two. For Luther, understanding this dialectic was "the highest art in Christendom," for it provided the believer with all of the knowledge necessary for salvation.[3]

In addition to the spiritual function of the dialectic, it also taught the balance appropriate to a Christian life, just how much weight had to be placed on precept and commandment and how much freedom inhered in the promises of the gospel. It was a complex issue, and one that placed the reformers in different camps, as was partially revealed in their approaches to Scripture. Luther, for instance, while claiming that the same merciful God ran through both testaments, nevertheless made sharp distinctions between the two, and he tended to stress the role of the law in its office of "sin and death," its main purpose being to reveal the depth of corruption and bring men to Christ as revealed in the gospel. Huldrych Zwingli and John Calvin, the founders of Reformed Protestantism, also made relative distinctions between the testaments, but both men thought in terms of a single covenant united in Christ and placed less emphasis than Luther on their antithetical natures.[4] And yet all of the reformers within the mainstream Reformation tradition, even if to different degrees, recognized the importance of the dialectic for Protestants, and not just for the concerns relating to individual salvation (though these were paramount), but for the issues relating to the Christian commonwealth as a whole. For when the reformers spoke of the law they did not just mean the Old Testament or the Mosaic law, but the law as it affects the heart, the conscience, civil society, and indeed reality as it "concerns every man as man."[5] Law and gospel were not separated by the two testaments: there was gospel in law and law in gospel, and it was the dialectical relationship between the two that made up the form and content of the Christian life. And it was not just a theoretical concern, but of the upmost importance for the soul in search of salvation.[6]

This study is based on the assumption that much of Protestant history in the early modern period can be understood by concentrating on the dilemma captured by these two symbols, tablet and text. The allusion to the law/gospel dialectic is not meant just in a theological or hermeneutical sense, but rather in a heuristic way as it applies to the problematic of Christian order that surfaced with the Reformation. For in challenging and ultimately rejecting the authority of Rome and the established truths of Catholicism, the early reformers not only opened up Christianity to new modes of theological analysis, they also subjected the entire Christian commonwealth to an extended exercise in critical reinterpretation. Just as urgent as the question of theological order was the concern with the nature of the secular order that would emerge in its wake. And at the very forefront of this concern was the question of how much latitude this order would grant to Christians and how much it would hold them in check. The Reformation was about many things, but few concerns ran so deeply or so broadly as that of freedom.[7] Of course, speaking in terms of freedom or constraint is not a distinction the reformers themselves would have recognized. Luther made this point at the very outset of the Reformation with his famous paradox of 1520:

> A Christian is a perfectly free lord of all, subject to none.
> A Christian is a perfectly dutiful servant of all, subject to all.[8]

But behind the theological paradoxes of this kind (which were common in Luther's thought) there was a rather more transparent historical dynamic at work fed by precisely the problems the paradox was designed to overcome. Namely, What shape should the Christian order take in this new Protestant world? What was the most godly political system or the most godly method of rule? What form should the god-fearing community assume, both inside and outside of the church, and who might belong? What were the main features of the Protestant society or the Protestant individual and how might they be realized? And encompassing all of these questions, How much restraint was entailed by godly order and how much liberty?

What follows is a study of the ways in which early modern Protestants ordered their secular lives in accordance to the true sense, as they saw it, of the Bible-based religion that originated with the Reformation. It is not a survey of the theological ideas that arose in the face of this dilemma or an exploration of the preconditions that made it possible (or indeed likely) that Protestants emerged to confront it when they did. Theology is addressed only in so far as it helps to explain social and political agency, and origins are examined only in so far as they contribute to an understanding of distinct strands of Protestant development. This is a sociological approach to spiritual history and is thus primarily concerned with public religion, which, to borrow the definition of a historian of American religion, we may characterize as "the religious expression and organization of a group of people who have constituted themselves, formally or informally, as a religious *community*. The life of each religious community, whether in early, more spontaneous stages or in later, more consciously organized form, creates normative patterns and expectations to which individual members are expected to conform."[9] In order to shed light on these patterns, the work is structured thematically, drawing on paradigmatic case studies grouped under broad headings and arguing general points. Thus the approach is selective rather than comprehensive, making its case by focusing on crucial episodes or profound transitions and using them as a sort of historiographical *camera obscura* to get an idea of the bigger picture. Being thematic, however, has not necessarily ruled out a narrative or diachronic dimension. The themes are approached historically, meaning that those in the latter parts of the book are generally indicative of the concerns of seventeenth- and early eighteenth-century Protestantism, while those at the start were ingredient to the age of Reformation.

But this is not a work that aims to capture the history of early modern Protestants in any comprehensive narrative sense, especially during the first century of reform, partly because the approach makes it impractical, and partly because the realities of the English-language book market make it unnecessary.[10] Rather, this is a history of Protestants that is concerned with a specific issue in historical context: the question of order. And it is fully in keeping with the spirit of the age and the dynamic of the Reformation and its aftermath to accentuate this theme, for historians have long recognized that the early modern period was an age out of joint, perhaps "the most shapeless in European history."[11] At precisely the time when the first reformers began to question the teachings of Roman Catholicism, many other familiar landmarks of social, cultural, and political life were starting to disappear, from the cosmologies, epistemologies, and methodologies of the intellectual world, the fixed orders of time and space, the hierarchies, ideologies, and expediencies of the political realm, to theories relating to the will, emotion, passions, and the "becoming" and the "being" of the individual man or woman.[12] As in macrocosm, so too in microcosm, the world was in disarray. All people during this period, regardless of religion, had to come to terms with these seismic shifts, but Protestants in particular were obsessed with the problem of order – and little wonder, given that they intended to make this world their own.

In the past, historians, and above all church historians, have portrayed Protestant history as something that occurred a few steps removed from the forces and contingencies at work in the profane world. This is no longer true of modern scholarship, and yet even in the most nuanced of recent studies the authors tend to write from the perspective of the theological ideas at the heart of the Reformation, speaking in terms of an intellectual or spiritual "revolution" that lifted Protestants out of their age and shaped their trajectories from the early modern to the modern period.[13] Describing Protestant history in this way, identifying a core of methods or precepts of thought, such as the biblical imperative or the priesthood of all believers, and abstracting from this a "fundamental Protestant principle of constant reexamination, reassessment, and restatement,"[14] may apply in certain contexts at certain times, but it does run the risk of overlooking some rather incongruous home truths when applied to the confessional age. During this period, mainstream Protestantism, viewed as a historical phenomenon, was an extremely conservative movement. It had very few revolutionary qualities about it. Confronted by the dilemma of its own making – that is, the need to determine what sort of order should replace medieval Catholic society – Protestantism inevitably chose to embrace and adapt the forms that were already in place rather than to build something new from the ground up. Given that the Reformation represented the most intimate religious dialogue with the social world since the days of apostolic Christianity, this is an important point, and not just with reference to the historical effects. In their origins as well, the Protestants of the magisterial tradition (Lutheran, Calvinist, Anglican) were conventional in their outer forms, tending to take the world as they found it.

Tracing the influence of Protestants on social, political, or cultural relations, which is the purpose of this study, thus means that close attention has to be paid to context and contingency. It also means that there is no point in looking for a single model of Protestant development, for different sociopolitical environments, joined together with a different range of aspirations, could give rise to different histories. From the very beginning, the Reformation was less the heuristic force implied by the use of the word "revolution" than an impulse that had to be cautiously accommodated within existing social and political patterns.[15] And indeed, as the following analysis will demonstrate, much of its internal dynamic was generated in its efforts to stave off the revolution that its own principles threatened to bring about.

Traditionally, histories of the Reformation have moved from a discussion of origins in Wittenberg, Zurich, or Geneva and followed developments in Europe to the point where, it was thought, Protestantism had either become an established historical phenomenon, which meant that there was a natural arc to the story, or the original impulse had started to lose its hold on the age, a point of transition often marked with reference to one of the peace settlements of the period, either the Peace of Augsburg (1555) or the Peace of Westphalia (1648), the latter often being equated with the shift from a confessional to a more secular age.[16] In contrast to this traditional approach, the following study works from the premise that the Reformation debate about order continued to shape Protestant history well into the eighteenth century, and thus that to comprehend *both* the Reformation *and* the history of Protestants in the early modern age, it is necessary to give equal weight to developments that occurred at the tail end of the period, namely the rise of the English Puritans, the Dutch and German Pietists, and above all the Protestants of America. This means that both ends of the spectrum, the rise of the Reformation in the German and Swiss lands and the initial waves of evangelicalism in the eighteenth century, are part of the same historical phenomenon, and that to understand why early magisterial Protestantism evolved as it did it is necessary to look beyond the sixteenth century to the forms of the faith it was trying to forestall. Equally, if we want to understand Protestant history in the age of awakenings and revivals, then knowledge of German and Swiss origins is crucial, for in many ways the developments in the early eighteenth century, particularly in America, were the denouement of tensions and forces that had been just beneath the surface since the first days of reform in Wittenberg and Zurich. This book is based upon the premise that the crucial arc of early modern Protestant history reaches beyond the dates traditionally ascribed to the confessional age. And it also argues that in order to comprehend this history, it must be approached as a transatlantic event.

In accordance with this line of thinking, more pages are devoted to events in Frankfurt, Halle, New Amsterdam, Boston, and Philadelphia than would normally be the case in a study of early modern Protestants, precisely because these were the historical locations, it is argued, where the order that surfaced with the Reformation took on new forms. This is not to suggest that after the early eighteenth century the idea of order was no longer a Protestant concern. Any survey of modern developments would quickly give the lie to such a claim. Rather, what is meant by this suggestion is that the Protestants during the age of Puritanism, Pietism, and early American colonialism had ideas of self and community that eventually led to the creation of new syntheses, new types of believers, and new types of congregations. Much of this will remain speculative, for the bulk of the analysis is devoted to a study of Protestantism in its magisterial mode; nevertheless, this history of Protestants ends with the gradual unraveling of the mainstream churches in the late seventeenth and early eighteenth centuries and the re-emergence of the radical tradition. One of the underlying arguments of the book is that the Protestant communities that were marginalized and persecuted at the start of the period resurface at the end – and indeed not just in terms of a physical presence, but in terms of spiritual and intellectual ideals.

Finally, a few words about names. Any mention of magisterial or radical Protestantism necessarily raises questions touching on definitions and types. Because so much of Protestant identity was relational rather than substantial, fashioned in opposition to a perceived false understanding of Scripture or through juxtaposition with adversaries such as Catholics or other Protestants, it is difficult to arrive at a definition that does not shift in some way with time and place. Theological principles such as faith alone (*sola fide*), Scripture alone (*sola Scriptura*), and grace alone (*sola gratia*) readily apply to the bulk of the mainstream tradition, but not all of the so-called radical groups accepted these principles on the terms understood by reformers such as Luther and Calvin, and indeed some rejected them altogether. Protestants, mainstream and radical alike, can also be understood historically as those Christians who traced their roots back to the Reformation and had some ontological claim to the events or the theological principles that followed on from Luther's protest. But this definition too is problematic, for not all Protestants thought of the Reformation in positive terms, and for many the events of the sixteenth century were secondary in importance to the events of the first century of apostolic Christianity, where they claimed the real roots of their faith were to be found. One other way to categorize Protestants is simply to refer to them as all those churches or bodies of believers who, viewing themselves as part of a historical continuum, had rejected the authority of the pope and separated from the Roman Catholic communion. This final definition certainly catches the most Protestants in its net, but it suffers from a lack of precision. It does not really tell us that much.[17]

One of the aims of this work is to explore this question of identity as it is evoked through the individual histories, to define Protestants against the background of time, place, and circumstance. However, it does use aspects of the above definitions for the basis of its analysis, including the idea that juxtaposition was crucial for Protestant self-fashioning and the conviction that certain core principles of theological thought were fundamental for development, even when they did more to divide than unite. But most important of all is the distinction made earlier between magisterial and radical Protestants, two categories common to modern historiography that owe much of their meaning to the theories of church types and sect types pioneered in the work of Max Weber and Ernst Troeltsch. Neither man thought of the terms as hard-and-fast categories, acknowledging that there was a lot of blurring in between, and in time Troeltsch added another type, mysticism, to accommodate a more nuanced scale of Christian forms of belief.[18] The distinction between radical and magisterial must be understood in similar terms, as a sliding scale with considerable blurring in between. Radical Protestants occasionally embraced some aspects of Reformation theology that were magisterial or "church-type" in nature, but in the general gist of their thought, and indeed in the use they made of these magisterial principles, the radicals represented an ongoing threat to the theological and societal foundations adopted by the churches of the mainstream tradition. It was precisely because the radical tradition was relative rather than a substantial, and more concerned with subjective perceptions than with objective forms, that it was such a threat to magisterial Protestantism, for in its relentless search for a pure, apostolic mode of Christianity it was constantly prepared to overturn the status quo. Radical in this context, as one historian has remarked, is less a referent to a noun than to "an adjectival quality, in other words, to a thoroughly consistent pursuit of a matter that seeks to go to the very root [*radix*]."[19]

In the century or so of scholarship that has passed since the works of Weber and Troeltsch appeared, scholars have refined these categories even further, and yet the basic insight remains just as valid as when it was first conceived: namely, that there was a scale of Protestant modality that moved between two types. The first type, the magisterial type, was based on fixed confessions with universal ideals, an objective church with a monopoly on grace and salvation, clerical authority, obligatory membership, orthodox modes of sacrament and liturgy, and a close affiliation with the structures of rule. The second type, the radical type, tended to reject traditional social and religious forms (especially when they were at variance with their own ideas of godly order) and gather together, voluntarily, as communities of the religiously qualified at some degree of separation from state and society. Religious order was based on a strict reading of the New Testament, read in the light of the indwelling Spirit, and salvation was sought through personal piety and ethical action rather than the ministrations of the public church.[20] These are the two ends of a spectrum, not fixed and formalized types, and the history of early modern Protestants is essentially a study of the dialogue between these two extremes as they came to terms with the dilemma of Christian order. And it was very much a *Protestant* dialogue based upon an inbuilt antagonistic duality. The first Protestants may have contrasted themselves with the histories of Catholic Rome when marking out their place in history but later generations within the Lutheran and Reformed traditions often evoked the history of Münster instead, the Westphalian city where the radicals established their first kingdom on earth.

1

Foundations

In his search for true Christianity, Martin Luther began with the soul, with his own soul, and the question at the forefront of his mind was as old as the church. How can humankind, so deeply and indelibly stained by sin, stand in a right relationship with God? In coming to terms this question, Luther laid the foundations of a theology that broke with medieval Roman Catholicism – with its emphasis on good works, earned grace, and a hierarchical church mediating between the sacred and the profane – and proposed in its place a form of Christianity that privileged the personal relationship between the believer and God and made salvation the unconditional consequence of faith in Christ as revealed through the Word of God. This breakthrough was held in place by a range of associated theological principles, primarily the so-called *sola* formulas, which later Protestant theologians would bring together in general syntheses and confessions. In addition to the central principle of justification through faith alone (*sola fide*), which was the foundation principle of all mainstream Protestant thought, there was grace alone (*sola gratia*), which taught that God is the source of all grace and salvation independent of earthly intermediaries, and Scripture alone (*sola Scriptura*), which emphasized the exclusive authority of the Word of God in the Protestant interpretation of Christianity. If not in substance then certainly in emphasis, each of these principles, as well as the articles of belief subsequently derived from these principles, represented a break with the thought and praxis of medieval Catholicism.[1] In its origins, the Reformation was a radical recasting of traditional Christian ideas, a theological revolution.

Yet this theological revolution will not explain the rise of Protestants as a historical phenomenon or the variety of forms they assumed in the early modern world. To do this, we have to place the Reformation movement in its historical setting and examine how it was that the reformers were able to muster so much support for their ideas among the public at large. How was it, for instance, that Luther, a relatively obscure professor of theology at a marginal university in Saxony, was able to turn his personal concerns about medieval religion into an issue that gripped the entire German nation? And similar questions can be asked of the other leading reformers of the mainstream Protestant traditions. How was it that Huldrych Zwingli, the founding father of the

Protestants: A History from Wittenberg to Pennsylvania 1517–1740 By C. Scott Dixon
© 2010 C. Scott Dixon

Swiss Reformation, was able to gather so much support for the new faith in Zurich and other parts of the Swiss Confederation that it ultimately led to open war? And how was it that John Calvin, the refugee reformer of Geneva, was not only able to transform the city in the image of his version of evangelical Christianity but contribute to the reform of whole territories and nations of Europe? The answer lies in the issue of order, though not in the sense of the order that grew out of the thought and energy of the Reformation, which will be the theme of subsequent chapters, but rather the social, cultural, and political order that initially embraced it. Within the geographical framework of the early Reformation – that is, the German and Swiss lands of central and southern Europe – the movement was successful because it was able to accommodate its theological principles within the traditional forms and notions of community and order. And indeed, during the early phase of the Reformation, when it appeared that these very principles might lead to an inversion of traditional relations, the reformers were quick to lend their support to the standard-bearers of the status quo. The first Protestant communities emerged remarkably quickly, and that was because in social, cultural, and political terms, the foundations were already in place.

Wittenberg and Rome

Leucorea

In the frontispiece of his massive anthology of the work of Thomas Aquinas, the *Conflatum ex Sancto Thoma* (1519), there is a portrait of Silvestro Mazzolini da Prierio (1456–1527), the first papal theologian to write against Martin Luther. Prierias (as he was known) appears in two different poses: on the left he kneels before an image of Christ, on the right he sits praying at his desk. And at the center of the frontispiece, suspended above Prierias, is a medallion with the likeness of Aquinas.

Given the course of Prierias's career, the image is uniquely appropriate. Born in the village of Priero in Piedmont, Prierias spent his youth and early adulthood in the Dominican order studying Aquinas. Later in life, he published a compendium of Catholic theology and dedicated it to the Medici pope Leo X. In return for his years of service, and in recognition of his academic achievement, Leo appointed Prierias to a chair of theology in Rome and elevated him to the status of Master of the Sacred Palace, an office which in effect made him the pope's personal theological counselor and head inquisitor of Rome. It was then that Prierias turned to the *Conflatum*, the work he had been planning since his student days in Bologna. Just at this stage, however, another matter was brought to his attention, the furor caused by a set of theses written by a German monk in the Saxon town of Wittenberg. Working through the final stages of the *Conflatum*, Prierias was not about to be distracted by the criticisms of an unknown monk. As a consequence, the first papal reaction to Luther, Prierias's *Dialogue Concerning Papal Power against the Presumptuous Positions of Martin Luther* (1518), was a cursory dismissal of the theses against indulgences shored up by an unyielding endorsement of papal infallibility – all of which, as Prierias himself boasted, took no more than three days to write.[2]

In fairness, Prierias can be forgiven for underestimating the importance of Martin Luther. There was no reason to assume that anyone from Wittenberg could possibly prove a threat to the unity of the Roman Catholic Church. Wittenberg, a small town in east-central Germany, built atop a hill of white sand near the banks of the river Elbe, did not even appear on the Vatican maps. It was, to cite the Nuremberg jurist Christoph Scheurl, "on the very borderlands of civilisation," with no more than 2,500 inhabitants, most of whom were pressed together in small cottages of wood, wattle, and daub. Friedrich Myconius (1491–1546), local historian and sympathetic eye, described it as "a poor unattractive town, with small, old, ugly, low wooden houses, more like an old village than a town." The Catholic controversialist Johannes Cochlaeus (1479–1552) was even less complimentary, speaking of its "unhealthy, disagreeable climate," its "dirty homes and unclean alleys," and the "barbarous people" who made their livings from breweries and taverns.[3]

Despite the apparent poverty of the old town, however, considerable improvements had been made. Wittenberg had become the residence of the electors of Saxony, and Friedrich the Wise (1463–1525), Luther's prince and patron, had initiated a building program in the town. University colleges had been built, as had a range of stone houses, a Renaissance town hall, and even a few large patrician residences, such as the quarters bought by the artist and apothecary Lucas Cranach, newly renovated for his move from Vienna. Scattered throughout the town were churches, ornate apothecaries, bath houses, a large market, as well as a Franciscan and an Augustinian monastery. Of particular interest was the castle church, adjacent to the Ernestine residence at the western edge of the town, recently rebuilt in a gothic style to house the elector's relics. When Luther posted his theses against indulgences, it was on the door of this church, behind which lay one of the most valuable relic collections in Germany, framed by works of art by Lucas Cranach, Albrecht Dürer, and Hans Vischer.

But the jewel of Wittenberg was its university, a foundation approved in 1502 by Emperor Maximilian and occasionally referred to by its Greek designation of Leucorea. According to the foundation charter, the university was established in order to honor God and bring benefit to the land and people of Electoral Saxony. These were noble sentiments, yet there was a degree of dynastic intrigue thrown in as well, for the elector had long been jealous of the fact that the neighboring duchy of Albertine Saxony (the other half of the twofold division of Saxony) had the renowned University of Leipzig while his lands had none. Friedrich set his stamp on the university from the very beginning, drawing on Tübingen for the particulars and the Italian universities for inspiration. Four faculties made up the pathways of study: the faculty of arts, and the higher faculties of law, theology, and medicine. Most interested in the study of the arts, this best reflecting his profile as the Saxon Maecenas, Friedrich made considerable efforts to recruit the leading humanist scholars. There was even a work written with this aim in mind, the *Dialogus* (1507) of Andreas Meinhardi, which portrayed the new university as a sort of classical wonderland and the town as the ideal setting for a Renaissance prince, a place where even the peasants spoke Latin.[4] Most of the original humanists came from Leipzig or Erfurt, unhappy, as was Martin Pollich von Mellerstadt, with the influence of the scholastic theologians in the ancient institutions. Others came because they considered it an opportunity to work in a less hidebound environment. Nicolaus Marschalk moved from Erfurt to Wittenberg for this reason, with a retinue of students and his own personal printing press in tow. Others may have had similar thoughts.

Whatever the reason, all of the faculty members would soon have noticed that Wittenberg was unique. No other university of the day was so institutionally adaptable, partly because of its size, and partly because of the influence of the prince, who had established a council specifically for the purpose of overseeing regular reform. It was more flexible, easier to modify, more open to change, and small enough to make it possible for ambitious individuals to dominate the faculties. It may not have occurred to Prierias, but in fact Wittenberg was the perfect setting for the rise of a reform movement, and the ideal environment for a charismatic scholar to make his mark.

Our theology

The origins of the German Reformation are located within a geometry of the theological vision of Martin Luther, the creative actions of the interpretative community that ordered and enacted his ideas, and the dialogue generated in the meeting between the perceived principles of the faith and the contexts of its realization. To speak of foundations thus evokes a complex picture, and one that requires different methods and angles of analysis. At this stage, the best place to start is with narrative, and the most appropriate setting is Wittenberg.[5]

In the late summer of 1511, Martin Luther (1483–1546) was transferred from the black cloister of the Order of the Augustinian Hermits in Erfurt to the Augustinian monastery in Wittenberg. The following year he was appointed to the faculty of theology, replacing the overworked vicar of his order Johannes von Staupitz (1460–1524). Aside from a few famous exceptions, such as his journeys to Augsburg and Worms or his enforced residence at the Wartburg, Wittenberg remained the backdrop of his life. As a professor of biblical theology, Luther was responsible for lecturing on the books of Scripture, something he did with great care, often having the pages of the Psalter printed on order and filling the empty spaces with interlinear glosses and cribbed marginalia. In addition to his university duties, Luther was a reader in the monastery and a preacher in the town church, where he held regular sermons from a pulpit surrounded by a frieze of the evangelists Matthew and John. Within the monastery he was director of general education, subprior, and ultimately district vicar of Meissen and Thuringia. It was a busy schedule, as Luther detailed it in a letter to his friend Johannes Lang, adding at the close, "Besides all that, I have to contend against the temptations of the world, flesh, and the devil. You can see how much leisure I have."[6]

Soon after his arrival in Wittenberg, Luther began to reflect on the traditional teachings of the Catholic church, not only from the perspective of a clergyman and theologian, but more dramatically from the viewpoint of an anxious and uncertain Christian conscience. As he later confessed,

> I did not love, yes, I hated the righteous God who punishes sinners, and secretly, if not blasphemously, certainly murmuring greatly, I was angry with God, and said, "As if, indeed, it is not enough, that miserable sinners, eternally lost through original sin, are crushed by every kind of calamity by the law of the decalogue, without having God add pain to pain by the gospel and also by the gospel threatening us with his righteousness and wrath!" Thus I raged with a fierce and troubled conscience.[7]

Eventually Luther arrived at an insight that released him from his torment and led him to a new formulation of the relationship between the human and the divine:

> At last, by the mercy of God, meditating day and night, I gave heed to the context of the words, namely, "In it the righteousness of God is revealed, as it is written, 'He who through faith is righteous shall live.'" There I began to understand that the righteousness of God is that by which the righteous lives by a gift of God, namely by faith. And this is the meaning: the righteousness of God is revealed by the gospel, namely, the passive righteousness with which merciful God justifies us by faith, as it is written, "He who through faith is righteous shall live." Here I felt that I was altogether born again and had entered paradise itself through open gates. There a totally other face of the entire Scripture showed itself to me. Thereupon I ran through the Scriptures from memory. I also found in other terms an analogy, as, the work of God, that is, what God does in us, the power of God, with which he makes us strong, the wisdom of God, with which he makes us wise, the strength of God, the salvation of God, the glory of God.[8]

Later known as the theological concept of justification by faith alone, this idea of passive salvation was the working hypothesis of the Reformation.

It is worth pausing for a moment to consider this breakthrough, for even though this book will not be exploring theology in any depth, there were some ideas that anchored Protestant development throughout the early modern period, and *sola fide* was fundamentally important in this regard. Not only was it the first point of departure in the evangelical turn away from Roman Catholicism; it was one of the few principles held in common (with some subtle distinctions) by the entire mainstream tradition. All of the first rank of founding reformers accepted some wording of the idea that the acceptance of God, and thus the bestowal of divine grace on sinful man, was not subject to causes or conditions but purely thanks to the grace of God through faith. This insight represented a radical break with the Catholic tradition, for it spoke of an outright promise of unconditional salvation. No reasons or provisions had to be met; there was no system of worship, no cycle of redemption by means of which God's grace was acquired. Justification, in Luther's famous words, was through faith alone, for the sinner had been given the promise of unconditional salvation through the redemptive work of Christ. As a consequence, there was no longer a process of renewal or an infusion of God's grace as was taught in medieval Catholicism. Righteousness was perceived as a state beyond ourselves (*extra nos*), essentially a new relationship with God, who sees mankind in light of Christ's righteousness, rather than a new quality inherent in man. That is why faith was so important for the Reformation doctrine of justification, "for faith is the means whereby man is led from his moral subjective existence into the final validity of the righteousness of Christ, in which he is preserved for salvation – outside himself, where God looks graciously on him."[9]

This had profound and immediate consequences for the meanings and the forms of Western Christianity, for the evangelical principle of justification left no place for the gradual climb towards salvation implied by medieval religion. God became the active element in the quest for salvation, the sinner passive; Scripture became the sole standard of religious truth and the only route to salvation; faith alone, not works, was now necessary for justification, for it led man beyond himself to the righteousness of Christ; and religion became a concern of the worshipping community, no longer the preserve of a sacerdotal elite.

Luther recalled his breakthrough on the idea of justification late in life in a preface to the Latin edition of his works (1545), claiming that his insight came to him during the time of the indulgence controversy and the subsequent conflict with Rome. As it was retrospective, colored by decades of dramatic events, historians have treated his recollection with caution.[10] Some have proposed a more gradual unfolding, beginning with his lecture exegeses (1515–17) as the more likely account, especially in view of the fact that many of the core features of his mature thought were already evident before his disputes with the Catholic authorities. Well before the posting of the theses, Luther had developed a pronounced sense of sin and a belief in the inability of fallen man to contribute anything to salvation without the grace of God; he had grown convinced that God was beyond human comprehension, and borrowed from the language of German mysticism to stress the necessity of total resignation before the majesty of the divine through faith, suffering, and the renunciation of earthly man; and he had developed a loathing for scholasticism, the theology of the schools, and the philosophy of Aristotle in particular. In contrast to the teaching of Aristotelian scholasticism, Luther had grown to believe that man could not earn grace without the participation of God. Humankind, he was convinced, did not have a natural love for the divine, and was ineluctably disposed to sin.[11]

Even as a young professor, Luther had an uncanny ability to draw people into the orbit of his ideas. He never preached to the birds in the manner of a medieval ascetic; he always sought out an audience, and he was a master at making the most of the means at hand. While in Wittenberg, he preached, lectured, circulated open letters, drew up theses for debate, spoke in confidence to colleagues, and defended his theological insights in public disputations – and to great effect. Within a few years, his ideas had become the subject of considerable interest at the university, and there was already a group of Wittenberg scholars who shared a similar approach to the faith.

First of the university intellectuals to join Luther was Johannes Lang (1487–1548). A former student from Erfurt, like Luther, Lang too had immersed himself in the study of Scripture and the Church Fathers and had grown critical of traditional authorities. One of the first traces of the reforming spirit can be found in Lang's work on the letters of Jerome, where he made the critical distinction between the language of scholastic theology and the purity of Scripture. Other sympathetic minds followed: Nikolaus von Amsdorf (1483–1565), a lecturer in Wittenberg before Luther arrived, who confessed to the sense of freedom he felt as he cast off his reliance on scholasticism and turned to the works of Paul and Augustine; Johannes Dölsch (d.1523), whose work *Defensio* (1520) charted his gradual drift away from scholastic teaching towards "the truth of Christ," and who also recounted how Luther had worked for years to break down his trust in scholasticism and bring him closer to the new teaching; and Andreas Karlstadt (1486–1541), perhaps the foremost theologian in Electoral Saxony before Luther's rise to fame, who, though at first resistant to the new teaching, was won over by his younger colleague and went on to become one of the most vocal and productive of the Wittenberg reformers, publishing a steady stream of diatribes and counterblasts against the scholastic controversialists.[12]

Others came from outside of Saxony, either to work at the university or to be near Luther. Philipp Melanchthon, Johannes Bugenhagen, Caspar Cruciger the Elder, Justus Jonas, and Georg Rörer, to name a few, became part of what Luther termed the "school of Wittenberg" (*schola Witebergensis*), and all became instrumental in the rise of the Reformation movement. Luther's celebrity has eclipsed the renown of those who worked beside him, but without the practical support of colleagues like Cruciger and Bugenhagen (the editors, the translators, the popularizers) or the emotional support from friends like Amsdorf and Jonas (the drinking companions, the extended families), or the intellectual guidance from men like Staupitz and Melanchthon (the mentors, the systematizers), Luther would not have become the reformer of the German Nation.[13]

Understanding the origins of the German Reformation requires a sense of the close-quartered community where Luther and the reformers lived and worked.[14] Despite a fairly sizeable student body, Wittenberg remained a small town. A local inhabitant could have walked through the entire intramural close from the Elster gate to the Coswiger gate in 10 minutes. There was little space separating the buildings or the inhabitants, and most locals would have been familiar with the workings of the municipal landscape. There must have been a strong sense of closeness and contingency in a setting on this scale. Certainly the early reformers thought in these terms, even if they moved at different levels in different spheres. Throughout his career, for instance, Luther maintained close relations with the Wittenberg authorities, and not just with advisors of the elector such as Georg Spalatin, but with lesser urban officials as well, some of whom stood as godparents to his children and wrote deeply sympathetic letters of consolation when they died. Men such as these became the technocrats of the Reformation. But even more important were the close relationships among the Wittenberg reformers themselves, with Luther remaining the dominant figure until his death. All manner of strategies and ties kept the constellations in place – emotional bonds, intellectual empathy, powers of patronage, force of will.[15] Philipp Melanchthon (1497–1560), who was the youngest of the first generation of reformers, had a deep emotional and psychological dependence on Luther. He never stopped believing that Luther was divinely inspired, that he was a prophet who had been sent to Wittenberg, the "New Jerusalem," to free the Word from its Babylonian captivity.

The Reformation thus owes its origins to a group of university men, joined in some measure by religious sensitivity, philosophical conviction, and hermeneutical acumen, who developed a vision of spiritual renewal while working together in Wittenberg. "In every age it must be remembered," remarked the humanist Willibald Pirckheimer (1470–1530) in 1520, "that the learned of Wittenberg were the first who, after so many centuries, began to open their eyes, to know the true from the false, and to distinguish the depraved way of philosophy from Christian theology."[16] Even in the beginning – indeed, especially in the beginning – the Wittenberg movement was monumental in its province, nothing less than rethinking the relationship between humankind and the divine. The main objective was to read Scripture in its proper light. Indeed, for many reformers, this was their central sin in the eyes of the Catholic authorities. "The Wittenberg theologians have begun to discover the truth by way of Holy Writ itself" was how Karlstadt put it in his *Apologeticae Conclusiones* (1518), "that is why they have been labelled heretics by those who, with Aristotle's help, interpret the Bible at their own discretion."[17]

It was this hermeneutical shift, this move away from a reliance on glossaries to a direct encounter with Scripture, that served as the foundation for the making of the *schola Witebergensis*. As the interpretative community began to expand beyond the walls of Wittenberg, however, the reform initiative no longer remained a type of contained experiment within a marginal university. Once Luther and the Wittenberg theologians began to engage the Catholic authorities outside of the town walls it took on the form and dynamics of a popular movement and turned into a sociopolitical event. But not before the theologians had the final word.

Theses, dialogue, and debate

When the conflict between Wittenberg and Rome began it was brought about by a longstanding and relatively trivial issue – the sale of indulgences. In October 1517 the Dominican preacher Johannes Tetzel (1465–1519) was traveling through the dioceses of Magdeburg and Brandenburg preaching the plenary indulgence proclaimed in 1515 by Pope Leo X. According to the instructions drafted for Tetzel by the archbishop of Mainz, the indulgence had the power to effect a complete remission of sins, including a diminution of their sentence for those loved ones languishing in purgatory. The indulgence worked as a kind of promissory note of divine grace: there was no sin too grave, as Tetzel reminded his audience, that might not be wiped clean by its salvific powers. "The claims of this shameful monk [Tetzel] were unbelievable," wrote the historian Myconius in his *Historia Reformationis*, "thus he said that if someone had slept with Christ's dear mother, the pope had power . . . to forgive as long as money was put into the indulgence coffer . . . He claimed that in the very moment the coin rang in the coffer, the soul rose up to heaven."[18]

As both a pastor and a theologian, Luther found the claims of indulgence peddlers like Tetzel shameful and misleading. For over three years he had been developing a theology based on the premise that sin was an indelible condition of humankind; it could not be wiped clean by the rites and rituals of the church. Any promise of automatic salvation (Tetzel's coin in the coffer), even if it had the imprimatur of the papacy, was a delusion and a betrayal of Christ. Fearing for the salvation of his parishioners, that they might place too much trust in indulgences and lose sight of faith, Luther forwarded 95 theses to the archbishop of Mainz on October 31, 1517 along with his critical thoughts on indulgences and his advice for reform. No longer just addressing local students or university colleagues, and no longer just confiding to members of his order, Luther spoke as a theologian to the congregation of the Christian faithful.[19]

In Wittenberg, despite the fact that Luther had (allegedly) posted a copy of the theses on the door of the castle church in the hope they would provoke debate, the theses fell flat. Outside of Wittenberg, however, interest was stirred. In this instance, a rarity in his career, Luther had had nothing to do with the dissemination of his work, as the theses had been taken without his knowledge, translated into German, and handed over to a printer. Reactions were mixed. Predictably, many humanists, Erasmus of Rotterdam (c.1466–1536) among them, welcomed another critique of the notorious practice of indulgence peddling. The papal theologians, in contrast, recognized the dangers lurking in the depths of Luther's theses and condemned them as heretical and a direct challenge to the authority of Rome. Tetzel went so far as to prepare his own set of theses in defense of indulgences and promised he would have Luther in a bathing cap – the traditional garb of a heretic chained to a pyre – within three weeks.[20] The papal theologians were less dramatic, but they too considered it a serious matter and issued a summons for Luther to appear in Rome.

After the posting of the theses the Wittenberg movement became the Luther Affair (*causa Lutheri*), a public event. Although Luther still spoke of "our theology," even after his meeting in Augsburg in 1518 with the papal legate Cardinal Cajetan (1469–1534), the first attempt at reconciliation with the Catholic authorities, by this stage he was clearly seen as the inspirational leader. And he had done much to fashion his fame. Within the university he had used every means available to get his ideas across – lectures, sermons, disputations, and a flood of German and Latin writings. Following the spread of his theses against Scholasticism and indulgences in 1517 he began to tailor his works for a wider public, writing both the *Resolutiones* and *A Sermon on Indulgences and Grace* (1518) in order to ensure that there be no misunderstanding about his position in the indulgence debate. He also emerged as a public figure, spreading his theological insights in lectures and disputations and impressing many onlookers with his powerful presence and his skills as a debater. Years after Luther's death the evangelical clergyman Martin Frecht would remember the Heidelberg disputation (April 1518) as the birthplace of the Reformation, for that is where Luther, speaking in front of Frecht and a host of other future reformers, first presented his theology to the world beyond Wittenberg.[21]

But it was Luther's appearance at the debate in Leipzig in 1519, where he came face to face with Johannes Eck (1486–1543), the premier scholastic theologian of the Holy Roman Empire, that made the greatest impression on the growing community of supporters. The debate had been called into being during a war of words between Karlstadt and Eck, the former thinking it necessary to meet the champion of the papal curia in Germany in order to defend the Wittenberg theology. "I have decided to endure war and tyrannical siege," wrote Karlstadt, "rather than a perverse peace at the price of disparaging the divine writings."[22] Staged by Duke Georg of Albertine Saxony (1471–1539), who would soon be revealed as Luther's most active opponent in northern Germany, the debate was viewed by papal controversialists as an opportunity to discredit the fledgling movement and pull it up by its roots. In the end, however, it was Luther and the Wittenberg party that emerged with the better hand. Once engaged in debate, Luther used every means at his disposal to sway public opinion, from the works he published before and after Leipzig to his hand and facial gestures in the lecture hall. And it had an effect. By the end of the debate Eck had no doubt that it was Luther alone who was responsible for the rise of the new teaching (*nova doctrina*) and called for his condemnation. Melanchthon, in contrast, expressed his wonder at Luther's performance ("his pure and Christian spirit"), thus anticipating the general cast of mind that turned Luther into a celebrity and his reform initiative into a religious movement.[23]

The public confrontation between Luther and Eck in Leipzig was the turning point of the early Reformation, both in terms of ideas and perception. Once the two protagonists met, each representing the opposite poles of the emerging divide, the points of disagreement came clearly into focus. For Eck the heart of the matter was papal authority. Either Luther recognized the divine foundation of the papacy and its primacy over the church or he did not. If he did not, then he was a heretic in the mold of the Bohemian Jan Hus (c.1372–1415), who had been burned at the stake in Constance for his teachings, and his sole aim was to undermine the faith and turn the church into an abomination, a *monstrum*. Luther defended himself by asserting that Christ alone was the head of the church. He agreed that the papacy had been founded according to the will of God, but disputed the claim that it enjoyed primacy over all Christians, Greeks included, and he expressed doubts over whether belief in the supremacy of the Roman church was necessary for salvation. To make his point, Luther even went so far as to defend views of the church associated with Hus, an utterance which shocked the onlookers, delighted Eck, and lifted Duke Georg of Saxony out of his seat. "A plague on it!" were his purported words.[24]

Questioning papal primacy was a dangerous theme, as Eck realized, but there was a deeper issue at stake. Luther held that Scripture was the ultimate arbiter of Christian truth. Other sources might offer insight, but no other source of knowledge or body of writing stood on the same level. For Luther, all other authorities were measured according to their proximity, historically and theologically, to Scripture. Eck, however, without disputing the primacy of Scripture, believed that recourse to other authorities (church fathers, canon law, conciliar decrees) was necessary in order to obtain certain knowledge. Proof was established through the accumulation of citations and witnesses in support of an idea. This was a traditional, and orthodox, approach to the faith. Luther thought that it failed to get to the heart of religion. He likened Eck to a spider on the water, just sitting on the surface of things.[25]

Leipzig was important in a more general historical sense as well, for it worked as a catalyst for public perception. Despite the fact that a record of the meeting had been carefully transcribed by notaries and sent to Paris and Erfurt, no swift judgment followed. Consequently, it was left to the intellectuals of Germany to carry on the debate.[26] This was the moment when the concerns at the heart of the reform movement in Wittenberg spilled over into the public realm. In this sense, Luther and Karlstadt had been the victors, for they had insisted at the outset that the themes of the disputation should be made available to everyone, not just professors and clergymen but equally to Christians with no claims to expertise in theology. The search for religious truth was no longer preserved for the papacy and the councils alone: it had become a debate, a dialogue, an exchange of ideas rooted in the higher concerns of Scripture in which laymen as well as clergymen had the right to take part.[27] Leipzig was also instrumental in drawing the lines of division. It pushed Luther out of the Catholic fold, confirmed Eck and the papal theologians in their suspicions of heresy, forced the theologians and the humanists to think in terms of contrasting and incompatible truths, and called on the secular authorities to act, either in support of Wittenberg or in support of Rome.

In 1520, partly in response to the findings of Eck, the papacy issued a bull of excommunication. Entitled *Exsurge Domine,* and like all papal bulls taking its title from its preliminary clause ("Arise, O Lord, and judge your own cause"), it expressed deep sadness that errors so "heretical, false, scandalous, or offensive to pious ears" should have arisen in the German nation, for the pope had always "held this nation in the bosom of our affection" and the Germans had "always been the bitterest opponents of heresies." It then went on to list the errors found in Luther's works, 41 in all.[28] The pope gave Luther 60 days to recant and submit to the judgment of Rome. Eck, along with Girolamo Aleander (1480–1542), one of the two nuncios commissioned by the papacy to disseminate the bull throughout the lands of Germany, managed to deliver it to the bishoprics of Meissen, Merseburg, and Brandenburg without difficulty, but in the cities the people proved more defiant. In Erfurt the students dubbed it a "bulloon" and threw copies into the river to see if it would float. In Torgau printed copies of the bull were torn up and scattered in the streets. In Ernestine Saxony the district officials were instructed to resist the bull and to rip it down should the parish priest post a copy on the church.[29]

In 1521 the circle of censure was brought to a close when Luther was condemned by the highest secular authority in the realm. On April 17, 1521, the reformer appeared before the Holy Roman Emperor Charles V (1500–58) and the imperial estates in Worms to answer the charges of heresy. The following day, in a larger hall where the hearing had been moved owing to the press of the crowds, Luther gave a defense of his writings. In reply to the demand that he stop dissimulating and give a clear answer ("without horns"), he offered a closing statement of his convictions:

> Unless I am convinced by the testimony of the Holy Scriptures or by evident reason – for I can believe neither pope nor councils alone, as it is clear that they have erred repeatedly and contradicted themselves – I consider myself convicted by the testimony of Holy Scripture, which is my basis; my conscience is captive to the Word of God. Thus I cannot and will not recant, because acting against one's conscience is neither safe nor sound. God help me. Amen.[30]

Emperor Charles V read out his answer to the Estates the following day. It was a summary rejection of Luther's reformist program and an unequivocal confirmation of his Catholic faith and the orthodoxy of his dynastic heritage. On May 26, 1521, the emperor issued the Edict of Worms, a decree which endorsed the papal bull of excommunication and placed Luther under the ban of the empire. Luther's life was no longer protected by the law, his theology was condemned, and his books were to be eradicated from the memory of man.

Despite the efforts of both the Catholic and the imperial authorities, however, the Wittenberg theology spread. From 1522 onward clergymen began to preach in an evangelical manner, which generally meant speaking critically of the Catholic church and its more obvious failings or emphasizing the need for faith and Scripture alone. Johannes Sylvius Egranus lectured in this fashion in Zwickau, as did Wolfgang Fuß in Borna and Nikolaus Hausmann in Schneeberg. Hundreds of other names could be added to the list. For their troubles these men were termed Martinians, evangelicals, or heretics and cited before the authorities, though they did not always think of themselves as representing a school of thought so much as preaching the Word of God. Egranus, for instance, who also railed against indulgences, the wealth of the papacy, and traditional rites and ceremonies, avoided direct association with Wittenberg. "We should not be divided into sects," he wrote, so that we say "I am a Martinian, I am an Eckite, I am an Emserite, I am a Philippist, I am a Karlstadter, I am a Leipziger, I am a papist" and whatever more sects there may be. I will follow Saint Paul and say that I am of Jesus Christ. I preach the gospel . . . In sum, I am a follower of the Gospel and a Christian.[31]

In the majority of cases, however, the local reform movements sought direction from Wittenberg and consciously emulated events in the electoral town. Altenburg, for example, secured an evangelical preacher by seeking Luther's intervention, while the difficulties facing the commune of Leisnig not only prompted the local authorities to write to the reformer but inspired Luther to publish a general tract in defense of local initiatives. Luther remained a tireless missionary in his Saxon homeland, embarking on a series of preaching tours in the early years, notably in Zwickau, Torgau, Erfurt, and Weimar, and dispatching letters of advice to sympathetic communities. And where Luther and his university colleagues were unable to intervene directly there quickly emerged a generation of clergymen who had studied at the feet of the reformers in Wittenberg and then taken the new theology back to their parishes and towns. As it would be tedious to relate too many examples, the following short histories will make the point: Gottschalk Kruse, a Benedictine monk from Braunschweig who journeyed to Wittenberg to get a grounding in the new faith and was awarded, through Luther's recommendation, with a preaching post in Celle; Johannes Briesmann, a Franciscan from Cottbus who sought out Luther in Wittenberg and stayed long enough to get a doctorate in theology, thereafter becoming an important figure in the spread of the teaching in Prussia; and the Basel Dominican Jakob Strauß who was forced to leave his native soil of Switzerland because of his evangelical preaching and made his way to Wittenberg to study, later planting the faith in Wertheim, Eisenach, and Baden-Baden.[32]

It was in this fashion, through this piecemeal crusade of committed evangelicals, that the early Reformation movement spread throughout northern and central Germany. And it soon threatened the very sovereignty of the Catholic church. Luther claimed that this early success was owed to the Word of God. Cochlaeus, his Catholic opponent, put the matter down to the devil. But surely both men must have been surprised by both the sheer speed at which the movement spread as well as the seeming ease with which it was aligned with the other concerns of the early sixteenth-century empire. It was almost as if the German nation had seen it coming.

Martin Luther and the German nation

With the publication of *Exsurge Domine*, the movement associated with Luther and Wittenberg was placed in opposition to Rome. And yet it was not this juxtaposition of extremes that gave Protestantism its early momentum or its initial shape. It was rather the seeming familiarity of the message that struck the crucial chords. In academic circles, the Reformation evolved as part of a "constructive misunderstanding," a misreading made by many humanists in Germany who viewed Luther as a fellow crusader against scholasticism and the Luther Affair as one in a series of conflicts between the forerunners of the new learning and the aged custodians of the old.[33] And there were good reasons for this association. Since its foundation, Wittenberg had been one of the leading centers of humanism in Germany. Its reform program was the most progressive of its kind in the empire, setting out to reduce the influence of scholastic theology and increase the profile of the *studia humanitatis*. Little wonder the German humanists at first considered Luther one of their own: he shared the same interest in language, the same *ad fontes* approach (which was the deep need to turn to the original sources in the search for truth), the same low opinion of scholasticism, and the same desire to preserve the distance between philosophy and theology.[34] He also touched on the same nerves: the nascent sense of nationalism, the mood of anxious presentiment, the prevalent anticlericalism, and the apocalypticism common to the late medieval age. Luther was lumped together with the champions of secular reform, his persecution at the hands of the papal theologians viewed as part of the same battle for the liberties of the German nation that had been waged by the humanists for over a century.

What this suggests is that the success of the evangelical movement was due in large part to the propitious intersection of common concerns. To borrow a metaphor that has been used to explain the rise of the new scientific paradigms of the age, Luther stepped into an already existing cultural and linguistic space. His ideas were close enough in kind to fill the void. The issue of national identity will make the point. When the Luther Affair first surfaced, two notions of German identity were in transition. On the one hand there was the concept of the *Imperium Romanum*, the sacral empire bequeathed to the German kings bound up with the superintendence of Christendom, and on the other the idea of the German nation, a secular community defined primarily by language, custom, history, and political pragmatism.[35] By the late fifteenth century, the two traditions were beginning to overlap and a vague sense of national identity was emerging. Early efforts were religiously inspired and antipapal in tone. From the work of Nicholas of Cusa and Gregor Heimburg to the Grievances of the German Nation (*Gravamina nationis Germanicae*), the underlying thread was the desire to invest the German church with its own legitimacy and remove Rome from national affairs. Typical of the type of antipapal invective was the sentiment expressed in the works of Conrad Celtis (1459–1508): "Resume, O men of Germany, that spirit of older time wherewith you so often confounded and terrified the Romans. Behold the frontiers of Germany: gather together her torn and shattered lands!"[36] In a similar vein, humanists such as Celtis, Sebastian Brant, Jacob Wimpfeling, and above all Ulrich von Hutten set out to rewrite the history of the German nation and return to its vernacular origins. Little wonder the *Germania* of Tacitus proved such a central text during this period. It was the ideal foundation text for the emerging notion of identity and its encapsulation of the supposed primal virtues of the Germanic tribes: virtue, honesty, a love of liberty, and an honest and untainted piety.

With the appearance of Martin Luther and the early Reformation, this dormant sense of community and expectation assumed both an immediacy and a point of focus. The Luther Affair worked as a catalyst for public perception, convincing people to believe that the time to act had finally arrived. In large part, this was down to Luther's own skills as a publicist. In his reforming tract *Address to the Christian Nobility* (1520), Luther wrote directly to the ruling elite of the German nation and outlined a program of reform that was little less than a manifesto for a national movement. Luther did not just list the grievances and hope for better days as did the authors of medieval tracts; he targeted the cause of Germany's misery (the papacy) and called for immediate action. The *Address* was a calculated step taken by Luther in order to transform his religious concerns into political action. And it was skillfully done. Source analysis has revealed that Luther drew on an unprecedentedly wide range of materials in order to equate his cause with the cause of the German nation. Borrowing from the traditional themes in the grievances and various conciliar tracts, he also seems to have made use of more radical medieval reforming works such as the *Reformatio Sigismundi* (1439). The final effect was to consolidate and crystallize the emerging sense of national or ethnic community and conflate its concerns with the agenda of Wittenberg.[37]

But the sense of expectancy and congruity ran deeper than a single text. Luther's words had resonance, not only because he was a writer of genius, but because they spoke directly to the long-forecast idea of a "great change" in circulation during the late medieval period. For those familiar with the prophetic traditions, it was not difficult to cast Luther as the long-promised *reformator* come to unite the German peoples or to see him as the fulfillment of the medieval prophecies. When Luther first appeared, many of his followers referred to him as the White Rider of Revelation, the herald of the last days; others spoke in terms of a prophet, a holy man, an apostle reborn or an angel sent by God. Necessarily, Luther as the figure or symbol of apocalyptical expectation had a powerful historical dimension. His appearance was both the confirmation and the final realization of a long tradition of medieval prophecies.[38]

Working within this framework of forecast and presentiment, Luther built on the sense of community by identifying the papacy as the Antichrist and insisting that the Germans represented, and had always represented, the opposite. In doing this he introduced two insights that broke with the past. First, he ignored the corpus of medieval apocalyptical speculation and located the proofs in Scripture – it was solely a theological or exegetical claim; and second, he made the Antichrist a collective rather than an individual threat. As he wrote in the *Babylonian Captivity*, the final antagonist was not a person but an institution located in place and time.[39] This had the effect of situating and pluralizing the enemy, creating a foil or a mirror for the fabrication of identity and making it possible to establish boundaries and frontiers.

The first attempt at visualizing the contrasts appeared in a series of woodcuts by the Wittenberg artist Lukas Cranach the Elder (1472–1553) entitled *Passional Christi et Antichristi* (1521). The images worked as a set of antitheses, pitching the evils of the papacy against the virtues of Christ. The following year, with the publication of Luther's New Testament translation, the eschatological dimensions of this division were further emphasized in the illustrations prepared for the Book of Revelation. The notorious papal tiara atop the Beast of the Apocalypse was perhaps the most shocking image, and the most direct proof that Luther was working behind the scenes.[40] This use of imagery was taken one step further with the appearance of Luther's Bible translation of 1534, which came with a series of woodcuts projecting this cosmic battle in nationalistic terms. Kneeling before the Babylonian whore were the figures of Emperor Charles, Archduke Ferdinand, Duke Georg of Saxony, and Johann Tetzel, all of whom were associated with Catholic resistance, while the cityscape of Babylon, based on the image of Rome taken from Schedel's *Weltchronik* (1493), was swallowed up by the earth. In contrast to this, Luther's patron, Elector Friedrich the Wise, appeared in the guise of pious kings of the Old Testament, while Luther himself played the role of a most sacred high priest.[41] Later editions of the Bible would develop these types of images, with woodcuts of Worms or Augsburg serving as biblical cityscapes and Germanic tribesmen standing in for Old Testament figures, thus further biblicizing German history and stressing the contrasts at the root of the conflict. Many readers must have reacted like Georg von Anhalt (1507–53), Lutheran bishop of Merseburg, who remarked how glad he was to be alive in an age when "the most holy David and the holy prophets speak to us so clearly in both words and meaning, as if they had been born and raised in our own mother tongue."[42]

Indeed, the German language in its written form is the most obvious "national" trait that evolved in a close dialogue with the Reformation, the most famous tribute being Jakob Grimm's later reference to High German as the "Protestant dialect." More than any other author of the age, Luther invested the vernacular with both the facility and the authority to serve as the language for a new sense of imagined community and bound the rise of early Protestantism with evolving ideas of culture and identity. He did this in two ways.

First, Luther used the vernacular much more effectively than ever before as a means of defining the boundaries of the community. Philologists no longer speak of Luther as the founder of modern German, but there is little doubt that he was the force behind the evolution of the language forged out of the various dialects in and around the lands of Saxony and middle Germany. From the very outset, especially after the appearance of the New Testament translation, Luther's use of German emerged as a model of proper style. The reformer even charged some of his Catholic opponents with having stolen "my language." It was soon enshrined in a wide range of publications – mandates, ordinances, tomes and pamphlets, poems and prose, and books of grammar.[43] Luther's vast literary output and his unprecedented ability to reduce and refine the vernacular to a level of general readability laid the foundations for a community empowered by a common printed language, much more aware of where the center and the peripheries lay. The Basel edition of Luther's New Testament (1523), for instance, came with a glossary of unknown Thuringian terms rendered into Swiss-German in order to enable the reader to follow the translation. It was a minor technical innovation, but the very attempt to connect the two vernaculars in the southern empire and elsewhere generated a sense of linguistic self-consciousness without precedent in German history.[44]

Second, and perhaps more importantly, Luther elevated the status of the language. Not only did he demonstrate that German could bear the burden of theological discourse, but his translation of the Bible entrusted the vernacular with the weight of God's Word. "I thank God," wrote Luther, "that I may find and hear my Lord in the German tongue in a manner which I have not experienced before, neither in Latin, nor in Greek, nor in Hebrew."[45] From this point forward, the way to God was through the vernacular, for with the appearance of the New Testament and its massive success, few people could now seriously doubt that a written language capable of speaking for the divine might not also mediate between the dialects of upper and lower Germany. Luther's Bible conveyed this idea to the German public, and ultimately it helped to create a sense of linguistic community. For centuries children learned the basics of grammar by pouring over this text – its style, rhythm, syntax, images, allusions, metaphors, and treasury of words. Some scholars consider the Luther Bible not just the crucible for the making of the language, but the early-modern German imagination *tout court*.[46]

In a less precise manner as well, Luther helped to create a common cultural language for the German nation. He was the ideal subject for the myths prepared by previous generations, and within a few years the Wittenberg reformer had become a symbol at play in the minds of the German people. A flood of publications followed the close of the Worms diet, compact narratives describing the reformer's journey from Wittenberg to Worms and his famous speech before Charles V. One pamphlet went so far as to depict the hearing as a repeat of the passion of Christ, with all of the participants taking on biblical roles. In the short period between the disputation in Leipzig and events in Worms, the iconography of Luther had been appropriated and reshaped under the weight of public expectation. He was portrayed as an Augustinian monk, a doctor and man of the Bible, and the saintly prophet of God shadowed by the Holy Spirit. Nor did it end there. After Worms, images of Luther entered the bloodstream of the body politic, the most striking being a woodcut designed by Hans Holbein the Younger (1497–1543) entitled *Hercules Germanicus* (1523), which has a tonsured Luther in his monastic habit wrapped in a lion's pelt and wielding a club against the enemies of truth. Vanquished at his feet are the scholastic figures of Aristotle, Aquinas, and Duns Scotus, while he grapples with his most recent victim (and real-life adversary) the Dominican inquisitor Jakob Hochstraten.[47] Here was the perfect composite image of the new German hero: a man wrapped in history and prophecy doing battle with the champions of Catholic Rome.

Emperor Charles V had issued the Edict of Worms with a view to preventing the spread of the Wittenberg movement beyond the walls of the university town. The mandate had not only been directed at the theological dangers posed by Luther's teaching but at its perceived threat to the social and political fabric as well. Once issued, however, as we have seen, the edict made little impact. Moreover, with the emperor absent from the German lands and the regency council pulled in different directions by the variety of ruling opinion, there was no effective political opposition to the spread of the early Reformation. Some princes moved to contain the movement, in particular Duke Georg of Saxony; but many if not most of the estates were rather noncommittal, preferring to wait until the emperor negotiated a settlement while allowing for the spread of the Word in their principalities. But those waiting for a swift political solution were waiting in vain. In the end, the problems raised by the evangelical movement were not really addressed until the publication of the recess of the Diet of Speyer on August 27, 1526. Even then the solution was ambiguous and provisional, but it granted just enough latitude to release reforming energies. The recess ordered the estates to pursue a policy in religious affairs mindful that they should "hope and trust to answer to God and his Imperial Majesty"[48] Although intended as a stop-gap interdict against further innovation, those princes and estates sympathetic to the movement interpreted the wording in a positive sense and viewed it as the political endorsement of their right to reform the territorial church. Against the actual intentions of the emperor and his imperial officials, the recess provided the German princes with legal and political legitimation for the spread of the faith.

Landgrave Philipp of Hesse was the first to act in a positive way to the Speyer decree, but it was the electors of Saxony, guided by the reformers Luther and Melanchthon, who provided the blueprint for the princely Reformation in Germany in the 1520s. The process and the timetable varied from territory to territory, but in general all of the Lutheran rulers took similar steps in order to fashion a Reformation church, beginning with the toleration of the preaching of the Word clear and pure, the appointment of evangelical clergymen, the change of the religious service, the publication of confessional statements (church orders, visitation orders, catechisms), and the construction of the territorial church. In the Lutheran variant this meant, as well as the establishment of regular visitations, marriage courts, and consistories, a range of new officials, starting at the level of the parish with the Protestant clergyman and reaching to the superintendents at the upper echelons of government. The first Lutheran Reformations of this kind occurred in the lands of Saxony (1522–28), Hesse (1526–32), Brandenburg-Ansbach-Kulmbach (1528–33), Braunschweig-Lüneburg (1526–27), Anhalt (1526), and Mansfeld (1525–26), and others would follow in Württemberg (1534), Brandenburg (1540), and Albertine Saxony (1539).[49] Later in the century territorial Reformations of Reformed (or Calvinist) Protestantism – sometimes known under the rubric "Second Reformation" – would intensify the process, as the German lands experienced the onset of religious division and the rise of the confessional dynamic.

Thus, when Charles V did return to Germany in 1529 following his coronation in Italy, his hair newly styled in the antiquated fashion of a Roman emperor, he was confronted by an alliance of princes and cities that thought of themselves as evangelicals (and later as Protestants), opponents of Rome, and supporters of the teachings of Wittenberg. Indeed, when Charles appeared at the Diet of Augsburg in 1530, the Lutheran alliance was consolidated enough to submit a joint confession of the faith prepared by Philipp Melanchthon that referred to the Catholic estates in German as the "other party" and detailed the principles of their own faith "and in what manner, on the basis of the Holy Scriptures, these things are preached, taught, communicated, and embraced in our lands, principalities, dominions, cities, and territories."[50]

Swiss Protestants

The gospel of Christian freedom

By the time Luther appeared before the imperial estates at Worms in 1521, preachers of the evangelical message had emerged throughout the German-speaking lands, and that included the region at the southern edge of the empire, the Swiss Confederation. The Swiss Reformation was guided by its own reformers and shaped by its own historical dynamic, yet the general formula was similar to that of Saxony. Here too we can see the centrality of the direct witness of Scripture against the assumed errors and inventions of Catholic tradition, the coming-into-being of religious awareness by way of dialogue and debate, and the strength of purpose that resulted when the early evangelical movement joined forces with the ideals of an imagined community. But there were significant differences as well, significant enough for historians to treat the Protestantism of the Swiss tradition as an independent phenomenon.

The Reformation in Switzerland traces its origins to the city-state of Zurich under the leadership of the stipendiary preacher of the Great Minster in the city, Huldrych Zwingli (1484–1531). Unlike Luther, Zwingli was not a university professor embroiled in a controversy with Rome, nor was he part of a community of like-minded scholars along the lines of the *schola Witebergensis*. Zwingli was rather closer to the type of disaffected parish clergyman that made up the first generation of evangelical preachers, driven by a private sense of religious mission. Born into a family of farmers in Wildhaus in the Toggenburg valley, Zwingli completed his primary and secondary education in Basel and Bern before attending university in Vienna and finishing a masters degree in Basel. With a relatively basic theological background, Zwingli was ordained into the priesthood in 1506 and took up his first post in the rural canton of Glarus, where he remained for ten years before moving on to the parish of Einsiedeln in 1516. His path to reform was more of a private journey than that of Luther. By way of letters and personal contacts, Zwingli was able discourse with "learned and excellent men" in Zurich and beyond, but his Reformation was never conceived in the same manner as Luther's. And indeed this holds true for the Zurich Reformation in general. Zwingli's success in Zurich was not so much due to his ability to see through an abstract theory of religious truth as his ability to provide biblical solutions to the religious problems revealed (and largely created) by the evangelical movement.

Much of Zwingli's early theological development occurred years before his arrival in Zurich while he was serving as a parish priest in Glarus and Einsiedeln. It was during the tail end of this period that he began to turn against the scholasticism he had learned as a student and embark on an intensive study of Erasmus's recent edition of the New Testament. Eventually, close study of Scripture led him to emphasize the same key principles that defined the German reform movement, including justification through faith and Scripture alone, both of which, in slightly altered form, emerged as core principles of Swiss Reformation thought. Zwingli always claimed that he came upon his insights independently of Luther, that he was a preacher of the gospel as early as 1516. By 1520, he conceded, he had become aware of the Luther Affair, but Zwingli never thought of himself as a disciple or a follower of Wittenberg, and he certainly did not think that the religion he preached owed its origins to a Saxon monk. "I will not bear Luther's name," he wrote, "for I have read little of his teaching and have intentionally refrained from reading his books . . . I will have no name but that of my Captain, Christ, whose soldier I am . . . yet I value Luther as highly as anyone alive."[51] Whatever the degree of influence, it is clear that by 1519, once Zwingli had taken up his post in Zurich, he was publicly preaching directly from Scripture and touching on the foundational themes of the early Reformation. In addition to his powerful anticlerical, or anti-papal, message (he once compared the pope to a sea serpent), he also emphasized the need for faith in place of a reliance on works and the absolute centrality of Scripture to the Christian life.

The Swiss Reformation began with an event.[52] In Zurich, on Ash Wednesday in April 1522, a group of evangelical sympathizers met in the house of the printer Christoph Froschauer and ate sausages, thus deliberately breaking the Lenten fast. Zwingli himself did not partake, but he published a sermon soon afterward that made it clear he did not think that Catholic laws such as those pertaining to fasts were crucial to salvation. The sermon was a turning point in the Swiss Reformation, for not only did it place the issue of evangelical reform atop the political agenda and thereby necessitate the intervention of the magistracy, it also spelled out the two central themes of Zwinglian theology: first, the nature of Christian freedom and its relationship to unnecessary laws; and second, the role of Scripture as the standard of religious truth. But the sermon was not the first time Zwingli had defended these ideas. Since 1520, he had been preaching against what he termed the "invented, external worship" of Catholicism, and that included devotion of saints, religious festivals, some forms of tithes, monastic orders, and clerical celibacy (indeed, he married a widow in 1522). In the *Apologeticus Archeteles* (1522), his first major statement of faith, Zwingli opened with an appeal to his countrymen to defend the freedom of the gospel against human doctrines and false prophets, whether they be bishops, popes, or general councils. The only certain guide was Scripture. Nor was Zwingli the lone voice of evangelical reform in Zurich. Leo Jud (1482–1542), who had been Zwingli's colleague in Einsiedeln and had translated some of Luther's Latin works into German, was also preaching against false laws and superfluous images, and in 1522 he performed a vernacular baptism in the Great Minster.

Both men were able to preach in this manner because Zwingli had the support of the city magistracy. The reasons for the close cooperation between the reformers and the council will be the subject of a subsequent chapter, but even at this early stage the point must be made that the Zurich Reformation was an archetypical magisterial Reformation, guided and enacted by the political elite. For its part, the council protected Zwingli from the declarations of the Swiss Diet, which demanded the suppression of Luther's books and associated teaching, and the commissions of the bishop of Constance, who as the ruling prelate of Zurich was responsible for religious affairs in the city. For his part, Zwingli promised to preach "the holy gospel and pure holy Scriptures" in line with the council's mandate and avoid issues that gave rise to unrest. As early as his fast sermon of 1522, Zwingli counseled restraint, advising his readers that since the practice was not bad or dishonorable, "one should peacefully follow it, as long and as much as the greater portion of men might be offended at its violation."[53]

By way of this incremental and closely managed process of reform, the Reformation took shape in the city. By April 1525, at which stage the Mass according to the Roman rite was abolished, the Zurich council, working together with Zwingli, had overseen the removal of religious images and statues from the city churches, secularized the monasteries and rechanneled the income, reduced the number of religious holidays and put an end to a number of traditional processions, suspended the jurisdiction of the bishop of Constance, established an independent marriage court, and instituted yearly synods for the regulation of the Zurich church and its dependent clergy. Zurich was the first fully reformed Protestant commune.[54]

In the manner of Luther and Karlstadt at Leipzig, Zwingli used a public disputation as a forum for the defense of his ideas. And the same convictions were at the core. Like the Wittenberg theologians, Zwingli preached that all Christians had the right, and to a certain extent the ability, to judge whether an idea or a practice was in line with the teachings of Scripture. He also believed that the best way to gather support for the movement was to address the laity directly, to make reform a public concern rather than a private quarrel. What was unique about the first disputation in Zurich (January 29, 1523), however, was that it was not instigated by the reformer but the city council. It was a judicial hearing, its main purpose being the preservation of civic order, and the reason it had been called into being was to deal with the charges brought against Zwingli by the bishop of Constance.[55] And yet it was not the bishop who would pass judgment on Zwingli but the council itself, empowered by the evangelical premise that a decision could be made by a lay tribunal if Scripture remained the final judge in all things, a point made with some symbolic force at the start of the disputation when three folio texts were placed before the assembly: a Greek New testament, a Hebrew Old Testament, and the Latin Vulgate.

In truth, the first Zurich disputation was something of a kangaroo court, for the Catholic clergy were little more than observers and the council had essentially decided before the event that unless it could be proved that Zwingli was spreading heresy it would allow him to preach the gospel "clearly and purely" as he claimed to have done to that point. For Zwingli, however, the disputation was a coup, for he was able to set the agenda with 67 articles outlining his vision of reform. With these articles the foundation ideas of Swiss Protestantism were put on full display, including the role of faith in justification, the primacy of the Word of God, the futility of good works in the search for salvation, and the church as a community of the faithful. The first disputation did not result in the introduction of the Reformation; many issues, such as those relating to the mass and religious images, were not dealt with until after a second disputation in October 1523. But the basic framework for the Reformation had been put in place, and the underlying rationale behind the initiative – with the council claiming it was acting "in the name of God in aid of peace and Christian unity" – never wavered.[56]

If there was one theological precept of the early Swiss Reformation that set it apart it from the movement in Saxony, where Luther's theory of justification was systematically dismantling late medieval Catholicism, it was the principle of Scripture alone (*sola Scriptura*). Though fundamental to all Reformation thought, and the first string in Wittenberg's bow at Leipzig, no reformer of the first order made such consummate *use* of the principle as Zwingli in Zurich. By the time of the Froschauer incident in 1522 he had already gone beyond his early humanist disposition to search for a greater clarity and truth in primary texts. Ancient authorities such as the church fathers might be drawn upon to confirm a point of theology, but the source of the faith must be Holy Writ, which was revealed to all men under the inspiration and guidance of the Spirit.

On the basis of this profoundly enabling idea, Zwingli was able to convince the Zurich council to intervene on the side of reform and provide the political support required for the preaching of the Word. Consequently, at a very early stage of reform in Zurich, the principle of *sola Scriptura* took on the function of civil law, thus making it a relatively straightforward matter for Zwingli and the magistrates to draw on traditional notions of order while placing limits on interpretation.[57] More difficult to control, however, was the meaning of the principle once it had been embraced by the parishioners, for many had taken to heart Zwingli's early declaration that "every diligent reader, in so far as he approaches with humble heart, will decide by means of the Scriptures, taught by the Spirit of God, until he attains the truth."[58] As Zwingli quickly discovered, the notion of religious truth meant different things to different people, particularly once the more radically minded evangelicals started to reassess traditional teachings on baptism, religious imagery, and the payment of tithes.

One reason why Zwingli attracted so many followers in so short a time was the broad appeal of his message. He was not just peddling theological concepts but the promise of freedom, by which he meant freedom of the gospel, or the gospel of Christian freedom (*evangelica libertas*). The basic point he was trying to get across was that the Christian is situated between two extremes: between those things that enslave him and ultimately damn the soul and those that liberate him and join him with Christ. Zwingli preached the latter, and at its most direct, it was fairly easy to grasp. The worship of God, as proclaimed by the evangelicals, liberates; the worship of the world, as practiced by the Catholic church, enslaves. This was a formula that could be appropriated in different ways. Freedom could be understood in a political sense as the freedom from tyranny and oppression, which was readily applied to Rome and its laws. Freedom could be understood in a spiritual sense as the emancipation of the individual soul by the preaching of the gospel. Or freedom could be understood in an anthropological sense, as in the ability to break free of the human tendency to worship false gods or observe false laws. Whatever the reading, the main message was the same: that the essential source of all freedom was Christ as the Spirit reveals him through the gospel.[59]

For Zwingli, even the law was a source of Christian freedom, though by this he meant the divine law, not civil law or ceremonial law. Unlike Luther, who drew a sharp contrast between law and gospel, Zwingli spoke of them as one and the same thing, which was nothing less than the eternal will of God. Indeed law, like the gospel, revealed the nature of the divine, which was why it was beyond the ability of fallen man to meet its demands. Only the saving intervention of Christ made it possible for men and women to honor (however imperfectly) the law. This is what Zwingli meant by freedom in this context. The Christian is liberated through faith in Christ to meet the requirements of the law and practice his "office and work."[60] From the viewpoint of the reforming party this was a profoundly enabling use of the notion of freedom as well, for it implied that the pursuit of godly order was in some form an act of liberation.

The revolutionary potential of these two pillars of the Swiss Reformation – namely the principle of Scripture alone and the appeal to Christian liberty – was revealed in the Swiss countryside. Numerous towns and villages had experienced considerable political and economic development in the late medieval period, to the extent that on the eve of the Reformation some local communities went about their business as if they were autonomous polities. Regional elites, like Zwingli's own father, managed local political, economic, and legal affairs, and in many instances this control extended to the church and its clergy. In these rural parishes, one of the few areas in Europe where the peasantry had the right to bear arms, the preaching of the reformers found a receptive audience, but not always for the reasons intended. Here, the appeal to Scripture and the promise of evangelical freedom tended to exacerbate deep-rooted resentments and play out in displays of anticlericalism and iconoclasm. Parishioners even vented their rage on the church itself, ripping down images and hacking up statues in an effort to free themselves from their recently revealed enslavement to the false idols of a false faith. But the message had a powerful positive impact as well. Feeding into the existing drift towards local autonomy, the early Reformation message made it possible for the rural parishioners to reorder the Christian world within the framework of the commune. According to Zwingli, or so the parishioners thought, the local congregations had the right to free themselves from the tyranny of the Catholic church without waiting on the authorities. They had the right to appoint a clergyman to preach the Word of God and have him put an end to previous religious abuses. They would judge this man and pay his salary, and in return they would act as good Christians, which meant in effect they would "hear the gospel and live accordingly."[61]

None of this was based on faulty logic. As the first in a long line of Reformed theologians, Zwingli had indeed preached the need to bring the world into conformity with the Word of God, and this necessarily implied transforming the local religious community under "the instruction and guidance of the Spirit" (to use his words). But in truth the parishioners' idea of freedom had little in common with Zwingli's theology of Christian freedom, and he was quick to take the side of the council and write against those who were taking reform into their own hands and causing unrest. As we will see, this was just the first phase of a turn towards radicalism that threatened to undermine Zwingli's vision of reform. He would face much more dangerous opponents in Zurich itself. But it was a significant example of the Protestant tendency to drag religion down to the level of the parish, and it was a very early glimpse of the variety of opinion that could arise on the basis on the principle of Scripture alone.

Zwingli's empowerment of the commune explains why historians often trace the roots of congregational Protestantism to the hinterlands of Zurich, but in fact his idea of evangelical freedom was much more ambitious in scale. Ultimately his intention was to unite all of Switzerland under the banner of evangelical liberty. Such thinking was natural for a Swiss intellectual, for the confederation itself owed its existence to the ongoing quest for freedom and autonomy. Its origins were located in the thirteenth century, when the first alliance between the rural territories of Uri, Schwyz, and Unterwalden came into being. Over the course of the next century these founding members were joined by urban powers such as Bern, Zurich, and Lucerne as well the rural cantons of Glarus and Zug. On the eve of the Reformation, there were 13 core states, in addition to associated territories such as Graubünden, Valais, and St Gall. In social and political terms, it was an incongruous mix, for it was not a single polity with a single head but a loose alliance of rural cantons and city-states ruled by urban patricians, old nobility, craft guilds, and wealthy peasants.[62] It had the rudiments of a constitution that provided the framework for a common defense, a federal diet (*Tagsatzung*), and the rule of law, which preserved the autonomy of the individual member states, but there was very little common purpose or mutual political interest. The only "national" agenda in any meaningful sense was the preservation of freedom from the tyranny of the monarchical states, a goal that had been successfully realized in the late fifteenth century in the wars against Burgundy and Austria. Thus when Zwingli, the humanistically educated son of a politically enfranchised peasant farmer of the Toggenburg valley, preached freedom, it was natural for him to extend it to the Swiss peoples in general – that is, as the humanists would define it, to the entire province of Helvetia in the land of Germania. No less than the hard-won political liberty wrested by the Swiss from the medieval tyrant-princes of Burgundy and Austria, the liberty to preach God's Word had to be won by the federated members in a battle with the foreign tyrant-pope. They were one and the same to Zwingli – *evangelica et publica libertas* – though the war that he was preaching from the pulpit was a matter of eternal salvation rather than worldly success.[63]

Outside of Zurich, the first areas to adopt the faith were Appenzell, St Gall, and the lower valley of Graubünden. St Gall had its own reformer of note in the renowned humanist Joachim von Watt or Vadianus (1484–1551), who had been preaching the faith and counseling others in small Bible groups as early as 1522. Vadianus soon secured the support of the guilds; in 1523 the council mandated the preaching of the gospel, and the first steps of evangelical reform followed, including the revamping of the welfare system, the removal of medieval images, the introduction of a new church order, and eventually an evangelical service. In Appenzell the council also legislated for the preaching of the Word in 1523, then held a disputation the following year to decide the fate of the church. Unlike in Zurich or St Gall, however, the authorities left it to each commune to vote on whether they would adopt the faith, a strategy that was also adopted by the council of Glarus. Next to Zurich, the two biggest gains for the movement were the cities of Bern and Basel, though both moved at a very cautious pace. Evangelical preachers were active in Bern in the early 1520s, and the council allowed for the preaching of the Word in 1523; but because Bern was so closely bound to French affairs to the east the magistracy had to act with care. Not until the disputation of January 1528, which had effectively been forced on the council by the strength of lay support, did the process of reform begin – images were removed from the churches, the diocesan jurisdiction was suspended, and a new service with a new liturgy was introduced. The history of events in Basel, the crossroads of ideas in Switzerland, was similar, though the city had its own reformer of European distinction, the humanist scholar and biblical exegete Johannes Oecolampadius (1482–1531), who left his distinctive stamp on the movement. Even beyond the boundaries of Switzerland proper the theology of Zwingli and his followers played its part in the early Reformation. In Strasbourg, Constance, and Augsburg, three of the most powerful cities in the south of the empire, reformers openly preached Zwingli's theology from the pulpit and printers published his tracts.[64]

Despite this early success, Zwingli's vision of a Switzerland united under the banner of evangelical freedom never became a reality. On the contrary, with the reform movement came a new type of confessionalized politics that tore the confederation apart. True to their medieval instincts, many of the states were wary of Zurich's recent conversion, their thinking being that the faith was little more than a pious cloak for imperialism. And this suspicion was even stronger among those member-states that remained Catholic. The result was a situation of constant tension that eventually erupted into open war. A early as 1524, the five inner states of Uri, Schwyz, Unterwalden, Zug, and Lucerne came together in a Catholic alliance. At a later stage they would be joined by Fribourg and Solothurn, and at the end of the decade they would ally with Habsburg Austria against Zurich. In 1526 a religious disputation in Baden further weakened the evangelical front when the Catholic party, whose speakers included Wittenberg's nemesis, Johannes Eck, prevailed and the subsequent diet condemned Zwingli and declared him banned. The results of Baden placed a further wedge between the evangelical and Catholic territories, even between the Catholics and the moderates such as Bern and Basel, for this was a clear judgment against the Reformation and a declaration of the Catholic states' desire to root out the faith from the land.

While the Catholics rallied, Zwingli and the magistrates of Zurich sought out allies. By 1528 the city had joined forces with Bern, St Gall, and Constance, and in 1529 it could count Biel, Mülhausen, Basel, Schaffhausen, and Strasbourg among its allies, later to be joined by Hesse. This was more than saber rattling; this was the build-up for war, a prospect Zwingli had entertained since 1525. The First Kappel War occurred in 1529, and the provocation was the preaching of the gospel in the mandated territories, those areas or common lordships that were ruled jointly by Protestant and Catholic states. In 1529 the canton of Schywz ordered the execution of the evangelical preacher Jakob Kaiser in just such a region, prompting Zwingli and Zurich to mobilize for war. The build-up ended in the First Kappel Peace (1529), brokered by Bern, a negotiated settlement that left it to the communes to determine their faith. The problems remained, however, and two years later Zurich once again went to war with the Catholic states, although this time it did come to a pitched battle ending in the defeat of Zurich and the death of Zwingli on the field of battle. The result was the Second Peace of Kappel (November 1531), which was a major setback for the Zwinglian movement. Not only was Zwingli killed and along with him the vision of a united Confederation fighting for the cause of the gospel, but the evangelical party within Zurich was pressed back. The peace imposed harsh conditions on the city, and from this point forward, in Zurich and elsewhere, the reformers and their supporters had to take a back seat to the moderates and the realists. After 1531, the idea of Christian freedom was not so much about liberation as it was paying heed to law and order. The point was brought home in a series of grievances submitted to the Zurich magistracy at Meilen after the defeat at Kappel, where it was made clear that Zwingli's close fit of law and gospel was not welcomed by all Christians. In the words of the fourth article,

> Gracious lords, it is our friendly entreaty and desire that preachers no longer be accepted in our city save those who are peaceable and generally orientated towards peace and quiet … Eventually, let the preachers in the countryside say only that which is God's Word expressed in both Testaments. Let the clergy, as already notified, not undertake or meddle in any secular matters either in the city or in the countryside, the council or elsewhere, which they should rather allow you, our lords, to manage.[65]

The Second War of Kappel put an end to Zurich's evangelical imperialism. The city had to renounce its alliances with foreign powers, it was forced to pay indemnities, and it was no longer able to influence the religious status of the mandated territories. In fact after Kappel, the Zwinglian Reformation in general lost much of its momentum, as powerful cities such as Bern, Augsburg, and Strasbourg moved towards Lutheranism and the Peace created a state of stalemate within the confederation. Switzerland had become, and would remain, a bi-confessional state, with some areas, such as Glarus, Graubünden, Thurgau, and Rheintal, holding both Catholic and Protestant services in the same churches. There were still substantial gains for the Reformation, especially in the west, where in the 1530s Bern began to expand into the Pays de Vaud and other French-speaking lands. But the vision once shared by Zwingli and his hard-core Zurich supporters of the expansion of the Reformation into all areas of the Swiss lands was no more. Indeed, Zwingli's successor in Zurich, the Aargau clergyman Heinrich Bullinger, once raised the possibility of dissolving the confederation altogether. The only sort of expansion Bullinger entertained was of the epistolary kind, the forward march of a network of Protestants joined together by thousands of letters.

These reverses were not only the result of events within Switzerland. By the late 1520s, the tide of reform had begun to turn in favor of the Lutherans of the north, a state of affairs confirmed by historical events, as when the evangelical princes and cities submitted their joint protestation to the estates at the Diet of Speyer in 1529 (hence the name Protestants) and then followed this up the next year with the first Protestant statement of common beliefs, the Confession of Augsburg (1530), which they presented to Emperor Charles V during a session of the diet in Augsburg. Realizing that the two early forms of magisterial Protestantism – Lutheranism and Zwinglianism – were starting down their own historical paths, Philipp of Hesse (1504–67), who was sympathetic to both variants, brought Luther, Zwingli and a host of other leading reformers together at his residence at Marburg (October 1529). His goal was to create a united Protestant front, strong enough to squeeze concessions out of the emperor. But it came to nothing. Ultimately the reformers were unable to agree and the colloquy ended without unity or resolution.

The central point of division in Marburg had been over the question of the real presence of Christ in the Eucharist, striking evidence of the extent to which abstract theological themes could impact historical developments.[66] While both Luther and Zwingli agreed, as all early Protestants agreed, that both the Catholic understanding of the Mass as a sacrifice and the scholastic theory behind the miraculous transformation of bread and wine into blood and body (which was termed "transubstantiation") were false, they could not agree about the meaning of Christ's words in Matthew 26:26: *hoc est corpus meum* – "this is my body." Luther understood it in a more literal sense than Zwingli. Without endorsing the Catholic doctrine of transubstantiation, he did maintain, however, that the body of Christ was "truly and substantially" present in the sacrament. Zwingli, in contrast, thought of the phrase "this is my body" as a figure of speech and rejected the suggestion (Lutheran and Catholic alike) that Christ was actually present in the elements. For Zwingli, the Communion was an act of remembrance, an attempt to "render present" Christ's act of sacrifice. As he described it, "the Lord's Supper, if it is not a sacrifice for the soul, is a remembrance and a renewal of that which once happened, which is valid for all eternity, and which is dear enough to render satisfaction to God's justice for our sins."[67]

This Protestant debate over the real presence would last the century and beyond. It was the main theological reason why Lutheranism and Zwinglianism went their separate ways, and it would play an important role in the marking out of Calvinism (or Reformed Protestantism) as well. However, we should not imagine by this that the early Protestants of Germany and Switzerland lined up neatly behind distinctive theologies of the Eucharist. Until the detailed confessional statements of the mid-century, evangelical teaching on the Eucharist, Communion, or the Lord's Supper (which was the preferred term) was open-ended. Local preachers, who were exposed to a variety of different opinions, mixed and mingled different teachings and preached fairly indiscriminately from the pulpit. A case in point is the city of Augsburg in the 1520s, one of the main meeting points of the different early strains of evangelical thought. During this period parishioners, were they so inclined, could hear sermons by reformers such as Oecolampadius, who spoke of Christ's body as both symbolic and present, or Urbanus Rhegius, whose shifting views on the theme eventually placed him in the Lutheran camp. Moreover, if they were literate, they could read through the range of opinions published by local printers, from Karlstadt's symbolic readings of the Eucharist and the writings of Lutherans such as Johannes Bugenhagen and Jakob Strauß to Catholic apologies and the works of Zwingli himself.[68]

Augsburg was fairly exceptional in the sheer variety of theological views making the rounds, yet there was in general a fairly rich and varied field of opinion in the 1520s as the movement gathered momentum. But it did not last long. In both the German and the Swiss lands, once Protestants had maneuvered themselves into positions of political and ecclesiastical power, they started to put their worlds in order.

Reformations

Order

The full effect of the Reformation on social and political relations first became apparent in the rural parishes of Switzerland and southern Germany. During the early 1520s, local clergymen and itinerant preachers began to take the ideas of Wittenberg and Zurich into the countryside. Naturally, a degree of accommodation was required; but if the run of printed sermons is any indication, central themes of the early movement such as anticlericalism (or anti-papalism), justification through faith and rejection of good works, the primacy of Scripture, and the recasting of relations between clergy, church, and congregation – including the empowerment of the laity in religious affairs – seem to have reached the ears of the local populace.[69] To the surprise of the reformers, however, evangelical theology was not always perceived in the same way that it was preached. Many parishioners were quick to embrace the movement, but in doing so they translated its message into familiar terms.[70] To use the language of the theologians, the parishioners read the message tropologically, that is, they applied its message to the social and political contingencies of communal life. Among the inferences drawn were the following: that Christianity was primarily about the preaching of the Word in the vernacular; that the commune had the right to appoint and dismiss the pastor, as well as the right to supervise his income and judge his teachings once he was in office; and that the gospel should serve as a guide for worldly relations.[71] The mainstream reformers were quick to distance themselves from this approach. Luther termed it a distortion of the Word and a deliberate perversion of law and gospel. In response, the parishioners (or, rather, their spokesmen) quite rightly pointed out that not only was their idea of Reformation in accordance with Scripture, it had been derived from the many evangelical sermons flooding the bookstalls.

In late 1524 and early 1525, as the wave of preaching and publishing reached its peak and visions of reform became increasingly radical, this communal movement passed over into revolution. The subject population took to the field in a series of extended sieges and regional battles historians have termed the Peasants' War of 1525, a period of unrest that swept through most of the German lands, including Alsace, Franconia, Thuringia, Upper Swabia, Switzerland, and Tyrol. In articulating their demands, the rebels used the same approach as the exponents of the communal Reformation: the same recourse to the Word, the same private and pragmatic readings, the same tropological cast of mind, though now with reference to "godly justice" as horizons broadened. Given voice in peasant manifestos, these new demands for "godly law" and "godly justice" worked as a type of rough-hewn ideology, and they were soon taken to extremes by militant reformers such as Thomas Müntzer and Hans Hut, who developed models of Christian society deeply rooted in subversive ideas of social and political justice. They even spoke of an end to feudal relations, imagining in its place a commonwealth based on the principles of communalism and egalitarianism.[72]

Despite their efforts, no new Christian society was called into being. Once the princes had mobilized, the rebellion was quickly defeated, and those parishioners who survived returned to a social and political system that was essentially the same as the one in place before the War. Worried about further unrest, the authorities granted some concessions. Some taxes were discontinued or commuted, in some instances marriage rights and inheritance laws were reformed, and in some territories the standing of the rural communes improved. Ultimately, however, it was a triumph of the princely state; and in fact the Peasants' War, because of its association with the evangelical movement, served to justify later attempts by the ruling elite to strengthen their control over the Reformation in the parishes. The end result was that "with help from the theologians, the rulers tried to restore their own legitimacy by turning the gospel squarely against the common man."[73]

Nevertheless, although short-lived and largely inconsequential, both the communal Reformation of the early 1520s and the Peasants' War of 1525 belong to the early history of Protestantism. For even though both Luther and Zwingli were quick to reject proto-congregationalism and peasant unrest, both reformers had popularized ideas that fed directly into the two movements. Before they were domesticated by the process of magisterial reform, numerous evangelical concepts could be drawn upon in defense of a program of reform undertaken by the laity at the level of the commune. The priesthood of all believers, appeals to New Testament ecclesiology, and Scripture-based vernacular religion readily endorsed libertarian interpretations that were never intended. Even the principle of justification through faith alone, when preached in the epigrammatic style of the evangelical sermon, could be interpreted as an argument in favor of freedom from the moral law on the basis of grace.[74]

In the beginning, even the most conservative of reformers used these ideas as theological battering rams to bring down the ramparts of Catholicism. Luther, for instance, called upon the priesthood of all believers in his repeated attacks on the Catholic clergy. In the early 1520s, he proposed that the congregation was no less empowered in religious affairs than a gathering of ordained priests. And soon after publishing his *Address to the Christian Nobility* (1520) he was encouraging the parishioners of Altenburg, Eilenburg, Magdeburg, Hamburg, Leisnig, Erfurt, and Leutenberg to initiate reform without waiting for the approval of the church. In his open letter to the community of Leisnig, Luther not only argued that, in light of the urgency of the times, the parishioners must act according to Scripture and call from among themselves an enlightened parishioner, but he added that it was their duty, on pain of damnation, to turn their backs on the Catholic authorities and take up reform.[75] With advice of this kind, it should not have surprised him when a year later the parishioners in the Franconian village of Wendelstein drew up a church order claiming that the local congregation had the right to install the preacher, assess his teaching, and dismiss him from post if he fell short of their expectations. Should he fail to meet their demands, they advised him that "we shall not only brand you as an unfaithful servant but shall also drive you as a ravenous wolf into the net and shall under no circumstances tolerate you in our midst."[76] Other congregational movements of this stamp emerged in the south-German and Swiss lands, from Zurich and its environs, where the villagers surfaced very early on as supporters of the movement, to Upper Swabia, where parishioners repeatedly demanded the right to appoint pastors to preach the Word of God, to the rural parishes of Salzburg, the Tyrol, and Alsace.[77]

The relationship between the Reformation and the Peasants' War of 1525 is more complex, not least because later generations went to such lengths to write it out of Protestant history. Yet here too we can see clear affinities. A brief survey of the main articles and manifestos published in the name of the peasant bands will make the point. Above all things the rebels demanded the preaching of the Word. As *The Twelve Articles of the Upper Swabian Peasants* (1525) made clear, the basis of all of their demands was "directed toward hearing the gospel and living according to it."[78] They wanted to be taught the true meaning of Scripture, free of the annotations of the Catholic theologians, convinced that this was not only their birthright as Christians but something that fell within their own powers of comprehension. Nothing separated the clergy from the laity in this regard, neither their standing nor their wit. Closely associated with this were the demands for the congregation to appoint and dismiss the pastor, for the church to be located and governed at the level of the parish, and for the clergy to be subject to the local authorities, a proposal partly derived from the long-term concern with clerical abuses such as absenteeism or the selling of offices. *The Merano Articles* (1525) made reference to these "evil abuses" and called for a new territorial ordinance to remedy the state of the church, while other regional manifestos projected a congregational solution to the general crisis. As the war gathered momentum, Scripture was called into service to justify and rearticulate ancient grievances about dues, fees, and feudal obligations. Indeed, some of the manifestos, such as *To the Assembly of the Common Peasantry* (1525), went so far as to challenge the entire fabric of the social and political order. By drawing on the so-called principles of godly law, many of which had close affinities to the first principles of evangelical thought, radical preachers began to reinterpret the world in revolutionary ways.[79] But this was a step beyond any sort of logical dialogue with the thought of Luther or Zwingli.

Neither the communal movement nor the Peasants' War shaped the theology of the reformers in any substantial way. Their importance was historical, in that they brought an end to the free rein and spontaneity of the early Reformation and turned it into a crusade for order. Of course, there were still episodes of localized and spontaneous reform, especially in the communes of northern Germany, but nothing that could be compared to the intensity or the profundity of the early phase, and certainly nothing that threatened to overturn the relations of power on the same scale.[80] Despite the encouragement he had given (and continued to give) to parishes to appoint evangelical preachers in the face of Catholic resistance, Luther never seriously thought of reform as something that could be left in the hands of the "common man." This conviction was confirmed in 1524 by events in Orlamünde, where, despite the opposition of the electoral officials and the threat it posed to the Wittenberg movement, the parishioners had come out in support of the liturgical innovations of his former colleague Andreas Karlstadt. These events, together with the disaster of the Peasants' War, convinced

Luther that the German parishioners (whom he now termed a *Pöbel*, "a mob") were still too "wild and crude" for independent religious enlightenment and would only come to an understanding of the faith through the traditional modalities of the secular and spiritual order. As he wrote,

> where God tells the community to do something and speaks to the people, he does not want it done by the masses without the authorities, but through the authorities with the people. Moreover, he requires this so that the dog does not learn to eat leather on the leash, that is, lest accustomed to rebellion in connection with the images, the people also rebel against the authorities.[81]

Zwingli too, though he always retained a strong communal element in his ideas of the visible church, moved away from the stress on the congregation to a stress on the magistrate and projected a vision of Reformation that was an act of corporate renewal, conceived by the clergy, enacted by the urban magistrates, and guided by a fixed corpus of belief. As he wrote, "we teach that authority [*magistratum*] is necessary to the completeness of the body of the church."[82]

This turn away from the communal dimension and the subsequent commitment to traditional forms of religious order meant that the German and Swiss Reformations, viewed in historical rather than in theological terms, were conservative movements. Luther in particular, while leaving it to systematizers such as Melanchthon and Bugenhagen to work out the details, was quick to stress the objective and institutional aspects of the new church, and he was generally willing to embrace the forms of the secular sphere as long as the essential role of the church – the preaching of the Word and dispensing the sacraments – was not obstructed. The end result was a church that was objective in its functions, in the sense that it served as a repository of salvation for all the baptized regardless of their own spiritual states; absolute in its religious claims, in the sense that it embodied the only forms of theological truth; and indispensable in its role, in the sense that it facilitated, through the ministry, the mediation of the Word and the sacraments and thus had a universal and all-embracing mission catering to the salvation of mankind. There were fewer sacraments, fewer clergy, and a closer fit with positive law, but otherwise it was a familiar idea. "It is the Catholic theory of the church, only purified and renewed."[83]

The characteristics of this mainstream or "magisterial" Protestantism were quickly revealed in Saxony, where Luther and Melanchthon presided over the making of the public church. Pressed by the need for more control over the parishes, Luther turned to the elector of Saxony and christened him an emergency bishop (*Notbischof*), thus investing the prince with the religious authority once exercised by the prelates. With this, a single vision of reform could be imposed on the principality. Electoral officials appointed evangelical clergymen, while troublesome Catholics were dismissed and dissenters expelled. Church teachings were standardized – theologically with Melanchthon's *Loci Communes* (1521), liturgically with Luther's *German Mass* in 1526, and then comprehensively with the church orders and visitation mandates issued under electors Johann (1468–1532) and Johann Friedrich (1503–54), all of which were to be followed as closely as possible by the local pastors in the parishes. Meanwhile the monasteries were gradually emptied and placed under the supervision of the state, the wealth being channeled into the common chests, which collected dues and alms, the buildings used for schools, churches, hospitals, or assimilated into the infrastructure of secular rule.[84]

But the main catalyst for reform was the visitation process undertaken in 1528. Claiming that the bishops of Freisingen and Naumburg had neglected this apostolic practice, the Saxon reformers revitalized the idea of a visitation, the literal parish-by-parish inspection of the state of religious culture by the higher church authorities, and turned it into one of the central modalities of ongoing reform. Its main purpose was to establish proper order: the visitors ensured that suitable clergy were in office, that the right ideas were being preached (to which end Luther's postils were introduced in 1525), and that the right conditions were in place to uphold the visible church. From this point forward, and at regular intervals for the rest of the century, visitations occurred in Saxony and other Protestant lands, with the reach of the Protestant church and the demands of the faith increasing from year to year in step with the relentless quest for unity and orthodoxy.[85]

Other princes followed the Saxon lead. Philipp of Hesse, for instance, borrowed from the Saxon model for his own Reformation, as did Ernst of Brunswick-Lüneburg, and Margrave Georg of Brandenburg-Ansbach-Kulmbach, all instigators of princely reformations. Indeed, the first wave of reform in the margravate of Brandenburg-Ansbach-Kulmbach was spent defining precisely what was meant by the idea of evangelical order. After the defeat of the Peasants' War of 1525, which the two ruling princes Casimir (1481–1527) and Georg (1484–1543) claimed was the outcome of a false understanding of Christian freedom, the margraves published a preaching mandate that quickly put an end to the initial phase of ungoverned theological discourse by targeting the clergy: "Where one or more is encountered (who has publicly preached, or can be shown to have preached, rebellion contrary to the holy Gospel and clear, pure Word of God), these should be arrested immediately and punished earnestly and remorselessly . . . or exiled from the land."[86] Leaving no room for further interpretation, Margrave Georg then issued resolutions that detailed exactly what was meant by a faith built on the "clear, pure Word of God." Any clergyman who refused to honor this understanding of the faith was dismissed from post. In order to enforce the religious changes in the parishes, the margrave and his higher clergy, working together with the imperial city of Nuremberg, saw through a visitation in 1528 and, once a few theological niceties had been ironed out, drew up the Brandenburg-Nuremberg Church Order (1533), one of the earliest syntheses of Lutheranism in Europe.[87] In all of this, as had been the case in Saxony, the new faith was simply poured into the existing ecclesio-political molds: there was one orthodox religion, inviolate and absolute, overseen by a trained ministry; there was one public church, held in place by a chain of command and superintended by a fixed hierarchy, though now with a different range of officers and institutions, and with the prince as *summus episcopus* instead of a bishop; and there was one route to salvation by way of the institutional church, a route mediated by the clergyman, and effected through the Word and the two remaining sacraments, baptism and Communion.

In an effort to restore what the reformers considered to be the practices of early Christianity the churches were cleansed of the unwanted remnants of Catholic religiosity, beginning with the erroneous ritual and ceremony that had grown up around the sacraments and extending to the physical surroundings of the church. In a

Lutheran environment the unacceptable attributes of Roman theology may have included candles, a few suspect altar paintings, the liturgical vestments, and the equipage of the Mass. In the Reformed setting, where Zwingli's thought held sway, a much more drastic process of purification may have entailed the removal of everything from cassocks and Communion napkins to statues and images and the overnight disappearance of Latin songs along with the traditional words of service and institution. In their place the evangelical authorities provided standardized orders of service largely devoid of ritual interplay with the congregation. The parishioners became the passive subjects of a Word-based offering of institutional sacramentality, with closely regulated sermons, hymns, prayers, admonitions, and commentaries on the catechism replacing the play of kinship and community and solemnized incarnations of the holy that characterized a late medieval Catholic service.[88] This reform of ritual provided an early example of the effect a typographical faith such as Protestantism would ultimately have on the anatomy of late medieval Catholicism. For while the latter was characterized by "God's extensive affinity" with both the social world and the sacral imagination of the local communities of worship, the former wanted to distance God from the vagaries of parish religion and, by capturing the essence of religion in words and turning it into something universal rather than personal or communal, closely regulate what the parishioners might believe and how they might come into contact with the divine.[89]

Where then was the common man in all of this, the peasants and townsmen who had been so receptive to the early movement? With the rise of the mainstream Lutheran and Zwinglian Protestant paradigm of order, the parishioners returned to their roles as passive members of a universal church and the lay initiative came to an end. In its place there emerged a religious culture built upon the twin foundations of confessionalism and clericalism, both of which were aimed at restraining precisely the type of religious enthusiasm that had proved so crucial for the reception of the early Reformation.

To get a sense of the shifting center of gravity we need look no further than the fate of the emblematical Bible-reading ploughman of the early years. With medieval scholasticism dismantled by the precept of *sola Scriptura* and with the Word of God now available in the vernacular it seemed only logical that the parishioners would have a greater say in what they believed. But in fact the opposite was the case. Once the various church orders started to emerge, it soon became clear that there was no room for deviation from the central teachings of the official church, whether derived from the thought of Wittenberg or Zurich. No less than the Catholicism it sought to replace, Protestantism kept its parishioners in close check, synthesizing, summarizing, and spelling out exactly what was meant by the Word of God and how it should be understood, while regulating both the timetables and the modalities of worship. On the main points, those that did not fall within the category of adiaphora (that is, things of no direct consequence for salvation), there was no room for negotiation. All parishioners were expected to acknowledge the same central beliefs and observe the same central rites.

Thus, while the reformers may have opened up Scripture to a greater number of individual *readers*, they did nothing to encourage a greater number of individual *readings*. The justification for this was partly political but primarily theological. Too great a Babel of opinions, it was thought, would lead to confusion and unrest – as the

Peasants' War had proved – and would disturb the equilibrium needed to maintain a Christian commonwealth. But more importantly, Scripture itself, while it could now be read by the many, could only be understood by the few, and in particular those few who had the training and the calling to take on the task of exegesis. Individual acts of interpretation, especially those that led to idiosyncratic readings of Scripture, were not encouraged by the reformers, nor was a homespun familiarity with the Bible considered a prerequisite for saving faith. It is worth noting that the authorities considered it a sign of subversive activity during the Peasants' War when people took to reading the Old and the New Testament within the privacy of their own homes.[90]

Having emerged as the liberators of the Christian conscience, the reformers were quick to stress that they would not coerce people into believing anything against their wills. Nor, in their pursuit of unity, would they confuse law and gospel and force the parishioners to believe in superfluous things. Luther made this point on a number of occasions in his disputes with the radicals, when he feared that the anxiety about order and uniformity might result in the distortion of the faith.[91] But this was written in the context of a discussion about ceremonies, external rites, and other matters considered peripheral to saving faith. When it came to questions of doctrine Luther was much less flexible, and while still touting the evangelical reluctance to force the Christian conscience, as he did in the *Large Catechism* of 1529, he made it clear that "if anyone refuses to hear and heed the warning of our preaching, we shall have nothing to do with him, nor may he have any share in the Gospel."[92] In this context, the "gospel" was equivalent to the Word as interpreted and taught by Luther and the Wittenberg reformers. None who wandered from this path had a place in the church.

This was not a distinctly Lutheran approach. The conviction that there was a single, orthodox corpus of religious thought and an established path of exegesis that made up a "true" reading of Scripture was one of the core principles of mainstream Protestantism. Substitute the name Luther with Zwingli, Calvin, Bullinger or any of the other leading reformers and the principle applies equally well. Protestants had a magisterium no less than the Catholics, the only difference being the fact that it was diffused throughout the confessional culture as a whole rather than seated in an office such as an episcopacy or a sacerdotal figure such as the pope. Despite its early association with the Bible-reading ploughman, once it became a social and political reality, the Protestant religion placed the same restrictions on lay interpretations of the faith as the Roman Catholicism it had supplanted. Much of its later history is a chronicle of the attempts made to resolve this inner contradiction.

The other casualty to emerge from the years of unrest was the parishioner as an active agent in the shaping of religious culture. The early leveling of the secular and the spiritual estates left many parishioners thinking, quite legitimately, that they were the partners rather than the subjects of the clergy, and that the open dialogue that had marked the early movement might be one of the constituent features of the new church. But the priesthood of all believers remained a spiritual rather than a social distinction: it was only valid *coram Deo*, that is, in the eyes of God. On earth, in the visible churches where the Protestants gathered, the clergy were still set apart from the parishioners and they still served as mediators between the congregation and the divine. Although no longer distinguished by the sacerdotal status of the medieval clergy, the Protestant pastor was still placed above his parishioners as the interpreter of Holy Writ and the minister of the remaining sacraments. Moreover, now that the church had formed such a close alliance with the state, new types of social distinctions began to elevate the Protestant pastor, not the least of which was the quality of education required in order to take up an office in the church. Unlike the vast majority of his parishioners, the Protestant pastor had been educated at a Latin school and a seminary or university; he had been trained at the highest levels in disciplines such as theology and philology, and thus thought and spoke in completely different terms; and he had gone through a collective process of self-development and self-fashioning in his formative years that left him with a unique sense of identity. He belonged to a caste of higher functionaries distinguished by background, status, and quite often family ties.[93] In some cities, certain families dominated church offices for generations – Fabricius in Nuremberg, Reuchlin in Strasbourg, Carpov in Leipzig. In many instances, the Protestant clergy-man had less in common with the congregation that his Catholic predecessor. He was just as distant, and just as doctrinaire and disciplinarian, as the medieval bishops and priests had been.

We should not conclude from this that the Protestant pastor was a uniformly oppressive presence or that the parishioners were completely excluded from religion affairs. In most parishes, urban and rural alike, the religious culture practiced at the local level was the product of dialogue and negotiation. Engaged laymen influenced the quality of faith, just as determined pastors shaped the secular world.[94] But in general it is true to say that in those lands of Germany and Switzerland where the magisterial idea of religious reform first took root, the laity remained subordinate to the clergy and the faith as practiced was the product of the theological and sacramental authority of the church rather than the faith or conduct of the parishioners. Any attempts to invert this relationship raised the specter of the radicals, and this was an entirely different idea of Protestant order.

Disorder

Order and disorder, of course, were relative concepts, for what Luther and the Wittenberg theologians considered out of synch with Christian teaching was not necessarily held in common by the Swiss reformers or the evangelical preachers in southern Germany. Nor did later Protestants necessarily agree with the notions of order and disorder established by Luther and Zwingli. John Calvin, for instance, associated the idea of disorder with things that were mixed up, polluted, or unpure, and this drew in a different range of considerations. But the emphasis on the ideal of order was common to all of the magisterial reformers, as was the stress on the dangers of its opposite, disorder, which they claimed was a defining feature of the emerging radical communities.

The first of the early reformers to move beyond the Wittenberg paradigm was Andreas Karlstadt. Soon after his abortive reform attempts in Wittenberg, he settled in Orlamünde, where he worked to resurrect the customs and forms of the apostolic church. Karlstadt became a man of the people; he went by the name of "brother Andreas," threw off his deacon's cope for the dress of a Saxon peasant, and discoursed on Acts from the pulpit. Indeed, in his conviction that interpretation was a collective endeavor, he became the first practical advocate of the later Puritan insistence that, read in the proper light, the meaning of Scripture was accessible to all Christians. This became a hallmark of the dissenter, though paradoxical in a way: the idea that God might speak to all men at all times. Another hallmark was the note of impatience and the associated readiness to sweep away old structures to make way for change. Karlstadt criticized Luther's reliance on tradition and authority and preached instead of how the true congregation "be it great or small shall make up its own mind what is right and shall do it without tarrying for any."[95] In pursuit of this idea, and not long after Luther counseled patience in his *Invocavit* sermons, Karlstadt published a work that argued for the reform of God's church without waiting on the weaker conscience. Reformation, in his view, could not be constrained by the timetables of man. God's churches must be returned to their original purity immediately, which meant (in the first instance) cleansing the interiors of all images and idols, eliminating pedobaptism, and driving out all remnants of the Catholic Mass.[96]

Two aspects of Karlstadt's thought are worth noting at this stage. First, from the very outset of his career as a reformer, beginning with his attempts to reform the church order in Wittenberg, and then in the following years when he served as pastor in Orlamünde, Karlstadt invested the congregation with the authority to see through the building up of the evangelical church. With the elimination of the Catholic Mass, the institution of the Lord's Supper in two kinds, and the end of aural confession, Karlstadt reduced the role and the authority of the clergy and instead turned to the parishioners themselves, those believers who had been seized by the power of faith. In such laymen, Karlstadt argued, lay the future of the church, and it was through their roles as readers and interpreters of the Bible, joined together in a congregation of equal members, that Christianity would renew itself. This version of the priesthood of all believers went beyond the teachings of Wittenberg, and it became a hallmark of the radical tradition. Second, while Karlstadt, like Luther, taught the centrality of faith and justification, he tended to place stress on the process of renewal. The main motif in Karlstadt's theology was Christ as an image or exemplar for the believer. A Christian life was spent in imitation of Christ, made possible by the indwelling Spirit. Here again we see Karlstadt moving away from Luther's stress on justification as a one-time act to an emphasis on justification as a lifelong process of sanctification.[97]

While Karlstadt was preaching to the Orlamünde parishioners, the clergyman Thomas Müntzer (1488–1525) was developing a similar vision in a crescent of Saxon towns to the southwest of the university town. Müntzer was also moving beyond the idea of reform as conceived by Luther, in both theory and practice. He devised the first evangelical liturgy for his parishioners of Allstedt, all the while advocating the need to return to the proper order of God. As with Karlstadt, Müntzer looked to Scripture for guidance; unlike Karlstadt, however, Müntzer privileged the inner resources, looking to the Spirit rather than the Word. "If a man had neither seen nor heard the Bible all his life," he wrote, "yet through the teaching of the Spirit he could have an undeceivable Christian faith, like all those who without books wrote the Holy Scripture."[98]

The other feature of Müntzer's theology that took it beyond that of Luther was the growing tone of apocalypticism, the conviction that the resurrection of the apostolic church would mark the beginning of the end time. In his mind, reform was not just a human impulse to modify the existing church, it was providentially and theologically scripted. Müntzer thus called on the elect friends of God, those "united in the poverty of the spirit," to withdraw from the existing churches and prepare the ground for the coming of Christ. More than just separation, this was vindication, the revenge of the elect for the betrayal of Christ. Müntzer saw himself as a prophet come to deliver the godly from the godless, and he began to speak openly of the need for violence in defense of this idea.[99] The high note was sounded in his *Sermon to the Princes* (1524), preached in the presence of both Duke Johann and the crown prince Johann Friedrich of Saxony. Evoking dreams from the second chapter of Daniel, Müntzer conjured an image of the German church that confirmed his apocalyptical forewarnings and emphasized the distance between the religion of his own day and the religion of Christ. Once it became clear that he would find no support among the ruling elite of Saxony, however, he turned to the parishioners and called on his fellow elect in Christ – the poor, oppressed, persecuted, powerless, and marginalized – to help him realize his vision. This was an idea of Christian Communion so far removed from traditional assumptions that Luther likened him to Satan.[100]

But the devil did not just reside in Saxony. Zwingli faced the same kind of opposition as he worked to see through the Reformation in Zurich. And like the situation in Saxony, the dissenting voices first emerged from within the ranks of his closest supporters, the main protagonist in the first instance being the recent convert Conrad Grebel (c.1498–1526), who began to preach reform in 1522. Even the initial grounds for separation were similar: Grebel came to disagree with Zwingli over his readiness to compromise the gospel in order to secure the cooperation of the magistracy, and he went so far as to suggest that Zwingli was willing to sacrifice the promises of the gospel on the altar of the law. "Zwingli," he wrote, "the herald of the Word, has cast down the Word, has trodden it underfoot, and has brought it into captivity."[101]

In contrast to Zwingli, Grebel and the other radicals held that Scripture could be understood by all men and women with faith. Bible exegesis was a collective endeavor – communal, dialogic, vernacular – and it was the responsibility of all Christians to seek constantly in the belief that the church could be restored with "the help of Christ's rule." As Zwingli charged them with literalist reading of Scripture and a stark legalism that lay behind the delusion in "supposing they would gather a church that was without sin," Grebel and his followers, speaking in similar terms, condemned the Zurich reformer for his betrayal of Christ.[102] Like Luther and Karlstadt before them, Zwingli and Grebel parted ways over the implications of their respective readings of Scripture for the actual process of reform. For Grebel, there could be no tarrying for weaker conscience; reform must be faithful to the Word, uncompromised and untarnished, and it must begin immediately. And he was not alone in his thoughts. In short order a number of like-minded reformers made their voices heard, among them Simon Stumpf, Balthasar Hubmaier, Wilhelm Reublin, and Ludwig Hätzer, who also began to challenge Zwingli's model of reform and call for a more thorough cleansing of the church.

Wherever dissenting or marginalized figures emerged, exclusion was as much imposed as it was voluntary. This was certainly true of Karlstadt and Müntzer, who were pushed out of the fold by Luther and the Wittenberg reformers. And it was true of Grebel and the later Swiss Anabaptists as well. But we should not let subsequent events obscure points of origin or deeper reasons for divergence. All of the evangelicals began with a common agenda; all were filled with the same desire to go beyond established practice and recover authentic apostolic religion.[103] What was different was the scale of renewal they had in mind.

The first Protestant dissenters, later termed "radicals" by historians, pursued an idea of Christianity that threatened to sweep away traditional order. It was not revolution for revolution's sake; the central issue was the working of the Holy Spirit, and to be precise, how the faithful might come under its affective influence. But unlike the magisterial reformers, the radicals did not hold that the Spirit *necessarily* had to be mediated by external forms or that it was bound to institutions or media. With the full revelation of the Spirit, as the Nuremberg prophet Augustin Bader put it, "all outer sacraments [would] be rooted out, and there would be no baptism but affliction, no altar but Christ, no church but the community of believing men."[104] This indifference to forms was not the same thing as an indifference to Christian history. No less than the mainstream reformers, the radicals understood their movement as part of the historic revelation. But when the radicals spoke about returning to the "pure church" and rediscovering the Spirit of apostolic Christianity they spoke in different terms to those used by Luther or Zwingli. What was required was a fundamental overturning of the old order. The church was to be resurrected in the image of the Spirit-filled gatherings of the first Christians, free of the proof texts and ceremonies that had since been heaped on the faith. For the radicals, there could be no checks on the Spirit, neither traditional convictions nor dogmatic restraints, nor indeed Scripture itself. What this means in historical terms is that any attempt to categorize the radicals has to remain an approximate science. The only constant was the desire to overturn the social and ecclesial status quo and put in its place a vision of godly order that did not cater (as they saw it) to the weaknesses of fallen man.

Fundamental to the dissident or nonconformist impulse was thus a readiness to seek a religious order that paid no heed to traditional forms. Even in their search for apostolic origins, there was no a priori paradigm of a church that guided the radicals on their reforming mission.[105] Nor was there a hierarchy of church leaders (even if certain charismatic preachers did amass followers over time), or confessions of the faith along the lines of the Lutheran or Reformed variants – a few gathered thoughts, but nothing as comprehensive as the later magisterial syntheses. It was this lack of fixed order, this seeming Babel of opinion, that first prompted Luther to refer to the radicalism of the Saxons as *Schwärmerei*, a word that evoked medical theories relating to "fluttering thoughts" that swarmed and stung the mind as well as divination, or more specifically the ancient opinion that the activity of bees, as Calvin put it, "had some portion of the divine spirit and have drawn some virtue from the sky."[106] Luther believed that the radical rejection of the externals of the faith, along with their presumed reliance on the Spirit, had led them away from the teachings of Christ. Similarly, he added, their aversion to traditional religious forms, whether sacraments, rituals, images, or ceremonies, had just pushed them in the direction of servility to a new set of external laws, though these were purely of their own making. The consequence, Luther believed, was a religion based on blatant subjectivity and willful invention, the only possible outcome being a denial of all earthly and spiritual realities.

There is exaggeration here, with a note of panic mixed in, for the radicals did not reject externals if they fell in with first principles; and in any event Luther was speaking about the Saxon movement, for the Swiss Brethren regularly referred to fundamentals "which are laid out in the Letter of Scripture and sealed with the blood of Christ and that of many witnesses to Jesus"[107] But Luther was right to emphasize their desire to resurrect perceived patterns of early Christianity that, if implemented, would have turned the world upside down. For the most part, they acknowledged Luther's "truths" only in order to see beyond them.

Ultimately, Luther's model of reform would dominate in northern and western Germany, but its rise was not as inevitable as later narratives might suggest. For every hard-line Wittenberg Lutheran there were men such as the patrician Gerhard Westerburg or the theologian Johannes Klopreiß, both of whom were sympathetic to the movement but saw no necessary contradiction in drawing together the thought of Zwingli, Erasmus, or Karlstadt and placing it alongside that of Luther. In numerous cities in the west and the north, from Dorpat and Reval, to the Hanseatic ports of Wismar, Stralsund, and Rostock, to large territorial towns such as Braunschweig, Goslar, and Celle, the early Reformation was inspired by a mix of influences, including Sacramentarianism, Zwinglianism, and the so-called enthusiasm of Karlstadt and Müntzer.[108] Thus it is misleading to speak of Lutheran uniformity during this period. Most reform-friendly clergymen would not have been preaching a distinct "brand" of the faith, but rather a syncretic grab-bag of evangelical ideas. Inspirited, emboldened, and often a bit punch-drunk from the sudden easy familiarity with Scripture, the early evangelicals of northern and western Germany were easy prey to the vagaries of interpretation. Different emphases might send the exegete in different directions. Too much Scripture might end in a bibliocratic church, for instance, while too much Spirit might remove the need for an institution altogether.

Historically speaking, the most profound diversity occurred in the villages near Zurich, where the men who had fallen out with Zwingli began to oversee local reformations. In the parishes of Höngg, Witikon, Zollikon, Tablat, and Teuffen, evangelical parishioners, often guided by wandering hedge preachers and former monks, gathered together in practicing congregations. The first step was active resistance to the Zurich paradigm, as when Stumpf, Reublin, and Grebel encouraged parishioners to stand firm against the collection of tithes, and this was soon followed by deeper criticism of the Zwinglian settlement, with the same men calling for a discrete church of believers, not yet fully separate but comprised only of "upright, Christian people." The religiosity of the radical Reformation will be discussed in a later chapter, but brief mention must be made here of some of the more profound changes that this entailed. Innovations included the abolition of the Catholic Mass and institution of a vernacular alternative; the purification of the church (which meant in essence the destruction of images and "idols"); the laicization of the office of pastor and the extension of the hermeneutic community; the introduction of adult baptism and communal discipline; and, following from this, the foundation of a voluntary church, a self-regulating, self-fashioning congregation of Christians. There may have been a practicing congregation of this type in the parish of Zollikon, where between January and June 1525 many of the essential traits of the radical tradition were put into practice, including communal readings of the Bible, commemorative celebrations of the Lord's Supper, adult baptisms, congregational discipline, and community of goods.[109]

Recognizing the threat to the status quo posed by such autochthonous reformations, the magisterial theologians were quick to react. Already by 1524 Luther had decided that no degree of charity would lead Müntzer back to the fold, and so he advised the elector to act against the reformer and his followers. He feared that the radical preachers were leading the parishioners to their own destruction, proof that the devil "intends through these emissaries to create rebellion and murder (even if for a while he carries on peacefully), and to overthrow both spiritual and temporal government against the will of God."[110] Rather than stigmatizing the Wittenberg church with the blood of so many "pious, holy, and blameless men" (as they were popularly perceived), Luther delivered the radicals to the secular authorities. With the destruction wrought by the Peasants' War of 1525 still fresh in mind, Luther began to draw a distinction between matters of conscience and instances of blasphemy, the latter being a public concern as it affected the entire electorate. After the publication of the *Instructions for the Visitors of Saxony* (1528), blasphemy or unrest (*Aufruhr*) was defined as anything that deviated from the faith as stipulated in the *Instructions*. As a consequence, the activities of the radical reformers, whom Luther considered to be preachers of blasphemy, fell subject to the secular arm as disturbers of the public peace. All religion that was not fully in accordance with the teaching of Wittenberg and its approved preachers became blasphemy and destructive of civil order. Melanchthon spelled out the crux of their concerns in a brief to Elector Johannes Friedrich, encouraging the elector be merciless in his use of the sword against Anabaptists, for their vocal condemnations of the ministry and conviction that salvation was possible without sermons or church service was no less destructive of public order than open rebellion.[111]

Faced with the same threat of disorder, Zwingli and the Zurich council reacted in a similar fashion. The first execution of an Anabaptist occurred in Zurich in 1526, with the victim being drowned in the river Limmat. Others followed in train. But this campaign against the radicals was not specifically Lutheran or Zwinglian. Throughout both Protestant and Catholic Europe, the authorities, encouraged and legitimated by the theologians, outlawed and persecuted the radicals, pushing them back to the dark corners of the land and uprooting them wherever they could be found. The death knell for the movement in its initial phase came in 1529, when the estates at the Diet of Speyer voted unanimously in favor of the law, rooted in the Justinian code, that rebaptism was a capital crime. Degrees of persecution varied, but most of the imperial estates were vigorous in the application of the law, with the result that those communities that were not disbanded or eliminated outright were forced into hiding. As we will see in a subsequent discussion, radical Protestants would look back on this period as an age of persecution and martyrdom, the crucible for the myths of origins cultivated by later generations. The martyrs hymn *How Costly is the Death of the Saints* (1526) relates something of the collective memory:

> To the forests depths we creep.
> With hounds they hunt us down.
> We're herded onward like dumb sheep,
> All tightly chained and bound.
> By everyone we're scorned and shunned,
> As would-be agitators;
> Given no quarter,
> Like lambs to the slaughter,
> As heretics and traitors.[112]

For moderate Protestants, the lingering memory was one of unease and anxiety, brought on by the fear that the radicals would rise again and turn the world upside-down. And indeed it did happen once. In 1534 Anabaptists took over the Westphalian city of Münster. The community was an outgrowth of the radical millenarianism fostered in parts of northern Germany and the Netherlands in the years following the defeat of the rebels in 1525. Foremost among its architects was the Swabian radical Melchior Hoffman (1495–1543), who had been preaching the coming apocalypse in the Baltic lands. Inspired by Hoffman's vision, and moved by the prophecy that Münster would be the site of the New Jerusalem, hundreds of Anabaptists made their way to the city and ultimately wrested control from the Lutheran council. By February 1534, the radical faction was in power. Catholics, Lutherans, Zwinglians, and all residents who would not accept baptism into the community were driven out of the city. Led first by the prophet Jan Matthijs and then by the self-proclaimed messianic king Jan Beukelsz, the Anabaptists worked to turn Münster into a theocracy. Inspired by the Spirit, a strict model of biblical rule was imposed on the commune, including government through 12 elders, an extreme form of community of goods, a harsh disciplinary code that punished without appeal transgressions of the Ten Command-ments and, once the reign of Beukelsz had reached its final phase, the reinstitution of polygamy as practiced by the patriarchs. In that year coins were minted in Münster heralding the arrival of the millennial kingdom with a verse that effectively summarized the ontology of the radical utopia: "The Word has become Flesh and dwells in us, One king over all. One God, one Faith, one Baptism."[113] In June, 1535 the kingdom came to an end when the town fell to the armies camped outside of its walls. In January, 1536 Beukclsz and his followers were tortured, executed, and their bodies were placed in steel cages and hung from the steeple of St Lambert's Church.

In the Swiss and German lands, the rise and fall of Münster was a turning point in Protestant history. Events in the city shocked the authorities into action, and there was a marked increase in persecutions after the defeat. For centuries, the memory of the radical utopia played on the Protestant mind, not only placing limits on the extremes to which the interpreters were willing to go in their search for the godly community, but also reminding them that the only thing separating their religion from the chaos of Münster was a reading of Scripture. Hence the rapid response of the Wittenberg reformers to the fall of the Westphalian city. Urbanus Rhegius wrote a work (prefaced by Luther) condemning the Anabaptists for their literal reading of the Old Testament and failure to understand it in light of the gospel. For Rhegius, the consequence of such an extreme misreading was clear to see: lust for power and worldly gain, all bound together in an earthly vision of the kingdom of Christ (*Reich Christi*).[114] Nikolaus von Amsdorf, Melanchthon, and a host of Hessian reformers wrote in a similar vein, as did other strains of Protestant commentators, from the Spiritualist Sebastian Franck, the authors of the *Chronicle of the Hutterites* (who referred to Münster as a "new religion"), to the later Lutheran Pietist Gottfried Arnold, who was willing to countenance Thomas Müntzer and a host of other radicals in his crusade against orthodoxy, yet dismissed Münster as an aberration.[115]

The ghost of Münster would long haunt the thoughts of the moderate Protestants in the German and Swiss lands. Whenever parishioners needed to be reminded of the dangers of religious enthusiasm the authorities would conjure the history of the kingdom of the Anabaptists. And the real fear was not so much the return of Münster as a specific historical episode as the realization that the ideas and the communities were still active in the world. They remained ever-present and very near, surfacing whenever the magisterial systems suffered a crisis or a period of disorder. Yet radicalism of this stamp was impossible to eradicate, for the threat of extremes was part of the Protestant condition, and to a large extent it was this "inner" anxiety, rather than the "outer" recoil from Catholicism, that would shape the magisterial tradition in the sixteenth century. Over the longer term, the radicals started to take on the role played by the papacy at the start of the Reformation: that of nemesis.

Geneva and Europe

The honor of Christ

A few months after the reign of the Münster Anabaptists reached its violent conclusion, a French scholar working in the Swiss city of Basel put the finishing touches on a work that came to be known as the *Institutes*, the most comprehensive and profound articulation of the idea of Protestant order to emerge out the Reformation. The author of the work was John Calvin (1509–64), traditionally viewed as the last of the first-generation triumvirate of Reformation founding fathers (along with Luther and Zwingli) and the consolidator of the Reformed tradition.

Born in Noyon in the French province of Picardy, Calvin was sent as a boy to study in Paris, where he read for an arts degree at the Collège de Montaigu. Details of his early life are in short supply, but it is likely that he was exposed to the same intellectual influences as any student in Paris at the time, which at the Collège de Montaigu would have been a mix of late-scholastic Aristotelianism, the Augustinianism of the "modern" school, along with the witches brew of theories that made up the *viae*, or ways, of philosophical thought. In 1525 or 1526, on the intervention of his father, Calvin transferred to Orléans to take up the study of law, a change of discipline that would prove invaluable for his later career as a reformer. It was equally important for his development as a thinker, for in Orléans Calvin was able to immerse himself in French humanism and its critical approach to medieval thought. It is not until 1533, however, in Paris once again, that we catch early signs of Calvin the evangelical reformer. Years later, much like Luther, he would speak in terms of a "sudden conversion" to the new faith. More likely, in the eyes of historians (again, as was the case with Luther), was a more gradual transition from a philosophy of Christian humanism in the mold of Erasmus and Jacques Lefèvre d'Étaples to an active anti-Catholicism, a private pilgrimage helped on its way by the clampdown on the early Reformation movement in France after 1533 and the persecution of so-called Lutherans and evangelicals that began in earnest after the Affair of the Placards in 1534. Like many of his reform-minded colleagues in Paris, Calvin was forced to leave France. In late 1534 he settled in the Swiss city of Basel, where he took on a pseudonym and prepared the *Institutes* for publication.[116]

No Protestant reformer of the first rank was as occupied with the issue of godly order as John Calvin. Everywhere Calvin looked, from the proverbial hairs on his head to the Alpine peaks that encircled Geneva, he saw the evidence of God's ordering hand at work. And yet it did not lead to a sense of equilibrium or security. On the contrary, it inflamed his state of anxiety, for it reminded Calvin of the essential contingency and ultimate incomprehensibility of the world. Everything had been created by God and was dependent on the divine will. The only thing that stopped the natural order from descending into chaos, he believed, was the grace of God. Without this grace, the waters, the lightest of elements, would flood the earth and the sun and the moon would crash into the earth. "God shows us as in a mirror," he wrote, "the frequent and sudden changes in the world which ought to awaken us from our torpor so that none of us will dare to promise himself another day, or even another hour, or another moment."[117] Humankind was perched on a precipice, perpetually, and the only thing that prevented the descent into chaos was the controlling hand of the divine.

Calvin often made the point with examples taken from the natural world, but his real concern was with religious order, or, more precisely, how Christian society could best serve the divine will on earth. As he wrote, "It is only when we live in accordance with the rule of God that our life is set in order; apart from this ordering, there is nothing in human life but confusion."[118] In working out this order, it has been remarked, Calvin tended to move between two related extremes: on the one hand he spoke of the dangers of the abyss, by which he meant the absence of order, forms, and boundaries; and on the other, he spoke of the labyrinth, a claustrophobic idea that played on the inability of Christians to free themselves from suffocating and alienating constraints.[119] This is a similar thematic to the law and gospel dialectic favored by Luther, and once translated into social and political terms it was concerned with the same dilemma of how much freedom and how much constraint made up the godly order. Calvin had no doubt that the answer to this question was in Scripture, which he spoke of as a type of "carpenter's rule" that clearly revealed the will of God. Unlike Luther, Calvin did not think that God tied up his thoughts in paradox.

Following the 1534 Affair of the Placards in France, which had been an attempt by the evangelical underground to win the sympathy of the French people by posting a series of notices against the "horrible, great and insufferable papal Mass" throughout the kingdom (including, it was alleged, on the door of the king's bedroom in Amboise), the Reformation movement was branded a threat to the sovereignty of the Crown and evangelicals became rebels. Converts were faced with two choices: either to remain in the land and risk persecution or to go into exile. Many chose the latter option and left for the French-speaking regions on the eastern borders of the kingdom, and in particular those areas drawn into the orbit of the Swiss Reformation, such as the county of Neuchâtel and the Pays de Vaud, which had fallen under the influence of the Protestant city of Bern. During the course of its expansion in the 1530s, Bern had also contributed to the spread of the Reformation in the neighboring cities of Lausanne, Solothurn, Fribourg, and Geneva. This proved fateful for the broader history of Protestants, of course, for Geneva was the place where the firebrand evangelical preacher Guillaume Farel (1489–1565) convinced Calvin that God had marked him out for the task of reforming the church, by which he meant the Genevan church. Calvin had intended to pursue a quiet life immersed in scholarship, but his sharp sense of providentialism impelled him to remain. In his own words, after he had explained to Farel his plans to devote himself to private study, "he [Farel] proceeded to utter a threat that God would curse my retirement, and the tranquility of the studies which I sought, if I should withdraw and refuse to give assistance, when the necessity was so urgent."[120] Later Reformed Protestantism would look to this union of the refugee French evangelical and the recently liberated episcopal city on the borders of the Swiss Confederacy as the historical point of origin of their religion as a providential coming together of prophet and place – much as Lutherans have often treated Luther's early history in Wittenberg.

In truth, for all of his theological and organizational genius, Calvin had a fair share of Protestant luck on his side. Politically speaking, Geneva, like most of the cities and territories where the Reformation first took hold, was predisposed to find certain aspects of the evangelical message appealing. Long under the dominion of the dukes of Savoy and the Genevan bishops, Geneva was in the midst of a struggle for independence when the first reformers arrived. Consequently, the sharp tone of anti-Catholicism and the evangelical message of Christian freedom, both of which were quickly appropriated by the preachers of political freedom, provided welcome support for the party of independence. Moreover, in order to defend itself against Savoyard aggression, Geneva had entered into an alliance with the Swiss cities of Fribourg and Bern. This enabled the Protestant magistracy of Bern to foster the rise of the Reformation in Geneva, especially after the alliance with Catholic Fribourg came to an end. Farel, for instance, had first come to the city under Bernese safe-conduct. Thus when Calvin arrived in 1536, there was no resident bishop to contend with, no powerful Catholic clerical presence, and an extant group of local patriots who readily associated the early Reformation with the struggle for local autonomy.

Once established in Geneva, Calvin was able to develop a system of church rule that adapted New Testament essentials to local circumstances. Not only did it empower the clergy to a greater degree than any other Catholic or Lutheran ecclesiology of the time, but with its emphasis on discipline, its fourfold offices of ministry, and its new institutions such as the Consistory and the Company of Pastors, it turned the church into a more effective means of binding the parishioners to the faith, both as the agents of church rule and as its subjects. Yet none of this was done at the expense of civil sovereignty. At no stage in Calvin's career did the church work independently of the state, and indeed it was never the intention to free the church from secular control, but rather to effect the appropriate balance (what Calvin termed *aequitas*) between the secular and the sacral.[121] No less than Luther, Calvin thought it essential – a matter of salvation – to get the balance right.

Calvin devoted his career in Geneva to this end, and it often brought him into conflict with the Genevan populace. His first stint in the city, from 1536 to 1538, was cut short after he, Farel, and other pastors fell out with the magistracy over the new church order. The sticking-point was the issue of excommunication and whether it should be placed in the hands of the magistrates or the clergy. Refusing to bend to the will of the council, Calvin was forced to leave the city and took up residence in Strasbourg, only to be approached in 1541 with the request for his return, sweetened with assurances that he could develop his model of church governance. Yet even after 1541, anti-Calvin and anticlerical factions were prominent in the city, often led by citizens of high standing. Until 1555, when the pro-Calvin party finally got the upper hand, the idea of *aequitas* seemed a very unlikely prospect. A threatening note directed against Calvin and posted in one of the churches gives something of the mood:

Gross hypocrite, you and your companions will gain little by your pains. If you do not save yourselves by flight, nobody will prevent your overthrow and you will curse the hour when you left your monkery. Warning has been already given that the devil and his renegade priests were come hither to ruin every thing. But after people have suffered long they avenge themselves ... We will not have so many masters. Mark well what I say.[122]

Over the course of his career in Geneva, Calvin had to face continuing resistance of this kind. And not all vented their wrath in anonymous notes. Among Calvin's more famous opponents the following usually have a place of prominence in his biography: Jérôme-Hermès Bolsec, the former Carmelite theologian and physician who challenged Calvin's teaching on predestination and was arrested and banished for his efforts; Ami Perrin, the Genevan nobleman and city magistrate who led the struggle against the power of Calvin and his pastors over issues of discipline and excommunication – he too was expelled; and, most famously, Michael Servetus, the Spanish theologian, whose views on the Trinity eventually led to his imprisonment by the Genevan magistrates and death by burning at the stake.[123]

Calvin was greatly influenced by Luther, and he held the Wittenberg reformer in esteem, but in his full-blooded theology he was a clear proponent of the southern German/Swiss variant of early Protestant thought. And he was more than just a latter-day synthesizer. Calvin's thought on predestination, the nature of the church, and the importance of discipline were no less significant for the shaping of Protestant history than Luther's theory of justification or Zwingli's appeal to Christian freedom. On many of the issues that divided Zurich and Wittenberg he took up a position that placed him outside both camps. Like all mainstream Reformation theologians, he taught justification through faith alone, and he rejected any suggestion that grace might be earned or mediated by a priest. But he was more inclined to speak of a "path" to justification than Luther was, thus stressing sanctification as well as justification, and he emphasized how the believer might participate in the grace of Christ and share in his benefits. Similarly, he adopted something of a middle way in the debate over the Eucharist. Calvin rejected Catholic teaching, yet he did not embrace Luther's notion of ubiquity, nor did he side with Zwingli and his symbolic interpretation of the sacrament. Instead, he taught that the bread and wine, though having no power in and of themselves as signs, raised up the heart and spirit of the faithful and thus, through the Word, brought them closer to the presence of God. Finally, again like all mainstream reformers, Calvin emphasized the importance of Scripture for knowledge of the faith and the pursuit of a Christian life. According to Calvin, the entire world was a "mirror of divinity" that could be perceived through the "spectacles" of Scripture. But he was quick to place restrictions on the liberties that the parishioners might assume with the sacred text. The final judge in matters of belief remained the clergy, those marked out by education and authority for the task (*doctores*). The laity might look to the Bible to clarify or confirm a point of teaching, but they were not to stray beyond Genevan orthodoxy.[124]

Calvin detailed his understanding of the faith in a huge outpouring of works over the course of his career, most of which were published by the Genevan printers Henri Estienne and Jean Crespin. Like Luther, he wrote in both Latin and the vernacular, and while his style was generally much more structured and formal than Luther's, he too showed great invention in the use of his mother tongue, sometimes creating new words in order to capture the meaning of complex Latin (such as the French verb *édifier* to relate the notion of building up, *aedificatio*). His most influential publication was the *Institutes of the Christian Religion* (1536), a text that was carefully crafted and re-crafted in multiple editions in order to capture the changing dimensions and emphases of his evolving thought. In the first edition, the *Institutes* was a fairly manageable compendium, just six chapters long, and written in the manner of a catechism (he had used Luther's 1529 catechisms as a guide). From the 1539 edition onward, the structure and the purpose of the work changed. It went from being a teaching tool for the inculcation of piety and doctrine to a compendium intended for a learned readership. By 1559, the Latin edition numbered 82 chapters in four books, the most comprehensive statement of Protestant theology of the sixteenth century, and the best guide to Calvin's thought on the nature of the Christian religion.[125]

The final edition of the *Institutes* (1559) was structured according to the following themes: the doctrine of divine creation and providence; the doctrine of redemption and sin; the application of this redemption to the faithful (faith, regeneration, justification, predestination); and the nature of the godly community – by which was meant the church, the ministry, and the sacraments. No single theological principle united the work, but it was clearly rooted in the idea that Christ, in both his divine and human aspects, was the key to salvation. In the final book, Calvin took up the matter of the church and consequently the issue of Christian order on earth. His views on this subject represent perhaps his most famous legacy, for here was the blueprint – in its general structural outline – for the most widespread form of ecclesiastical order in the Protestant world. In essence, Calvin's notion of the true church was the same as that of the other Protestant reformers: the church is where the Word is preached and the sacraments are properly administered. But in addition to this essentialist view, Calvin drew on Scripture to develop a practical guide for the ordering of the church in Geneva, all of which he spelled out in the *Ecclesiastical Ordinances* (1541). From that point forward, four offices comprised the body of ecclesiastical officials in Geneva: pastors, teachers, elders, and deacons. Paramount was the office of pastor, for these were the men charged with the preaching of the Word and the administering of the sacraments. Calvin never wavered in his belief that the office of pastor was the lynch-pin of the Christian commonwealth. "Neither the light and heat of the sun," he wrote, "nor food and drink, are so necessary to nourish and sustain the present life as the apostolic and pastoral office is necessary to preserve the church on earth."[126]

With a view to the history of Protestant order, however, the most significant office was that of elder, for these were the agents of the disciplinary process, the men charged to uphold what Calvin termed "the honor of Christ" by ensuring that the commune of Geneva became, and remained, Christian. That is why the issue of discipline was so important for Calvin and the churches that followed the Genevan paradigm, for proper faith did not just embrace understanding, it embraced conduct as well. Calvin was not the first of the reformers to stress the importance of discipline for the church. The Strasbourg theologian Martin Bucer, Calvin's patron during his period of exile, went so far as to consider discipline one of the marks of the true church. But Calvin was the first of the reformers to turn the pursuit of Christian conduct into a social and political dynamic.

The image of Calvin as the bearded puritan killjoy and Geneva as the laboratory for his experiment in godly discipline has had a long life in Reformation historiography. It first emerged during the lifetime of the reformer, and indeed the sheer wealth of firsthand testimony, popularized by Protestants and Jesuits alike, would suggest that there was truth in the idea: namely, that Geneva was a commune under the yoke of Scripture. The Lutheran Johann Valentin Andreae (1586–1654), for instance, who visited the city, claimed that the discipline of morals in Geneva was without parallel in Europe. "As a result," he wrote, "all cursing, gambling, luxury, quarreling, hatred, conceit, deceit, extravagance, and the like, to say nothing of the greater sins, are prevented. What a glorious adornment – such purity of morals – for the Christian religion!"[127] True or not (and Andreae would go on to write a utopia), the image, and the ideal, captured the Protestant imagination.

What turned the ideal into practice was the Genevan model of church rule, the prototype of the presbyterial–synodal system. With the introduction of the *Ordinances* of 1541, which was in effect the mandate of reform in Geneva, not only was the liturgy reworked, the number of holy days reduced, the sacraments pared down to baptism and Communion, the walls of the churches whitewashed and the pulpits repositioned, but a new form of church rule emerged to hold everything in place. Superseding the former episcopal hierarchy was the Company of Pastors, a body made up of the urban and rural clergy responsible for doctrine and clerical discipline. But even more important was the consistory. Comprised of 24 officials – 12 urban pastors and 12 lay elders, the latter representing the main councils of the city – the consistory was created in order to watch over Christian discipline. It did not mete out high justice, but as a method of overseeing the parishioners and elevating the importance of godly conduct it was extremely effective. Fundamental to its workings were the lay elders, whose remit was "to keep watch over every man's life, to admonish amiably those whom they see leading a disorderly life, and where necessary to report to the assembly [consistory] which will be deputized to make fraternal correction."[128] Research on the consistory records would suggest that the main concern was with crimes that threatened the family or sexual norms, such as adultery, prostitution, premarital intercourse, and rape. But it swept a wide range of sins up in its net, from drinking, dancing, and public violence, to superstition (which included Catholicism) and blasphemy. It was, in the words of its historians, "a remarkably intrusive institution."[129]

For the issue of Protestant order, Calvin's emphasis on discipline was a particularly important aspect of the Genevan Reformation, as this was a clear instance of the conflation of evangelical theology with social and political reality, a demonstration of how the religious ideals of the Reformation impacted upon the age. The concern with discipline was not new, of course; the late medieval church had been no less concerned with the moral order. But there was now a more explicit association between what a Christian should believe and how he or she should behave. This union of faith and morality runs throughout Calvin's theology. It is apparent in the stress he placed on the relationship between justification and sanctification, on the continuity between the laws of the Old Testament and the gospel of Christ, and on his insistence that faith would effect a moral regeneration. True believers would necessarily live in accordance with God's Word. Moreover, discipline was viewed as an earthly means of preserving the purity of the eucharistic community, a way to reunite sinners with God while preventing the "putrid members" from infecting the church. For Calvin, Holy Communion was the "primary order," a point he made as early as 1537 in the articles he drew up for Geneva:

> The primary order which is required and for which one should have the greatest solicitude is that holy Communion, ordained and instituted to join the followers of our lord Jesus Christ with their chief and among themselves in body and spirit, must not be defiled and contaminated by the communication of those who declare and make manifest by their wicked and iniquitous lives that they do not at all belong to Jesus; for in this profaning of His sacrament our Lord is greatly dishonored.[130]

As we will see, in Geneva and elsewhere in Europe, the extent to which the clergy watched over this order independent of the state was a matter for ongoing debate, particularly when it came to the question of excommunication. But, whatever the relationship between the secular and the spiritual, all of the later Reformed communities followed Calvin in emphasizing the necessity of discipline. The institutions that were established varied: there were consistories in France, for instance, but kirk sessions in Scotland and *Chorgerichte* in the Swiss lands. The nature of the officials varied as well: while elders were fairly ubiquitous, there were also "censors and captors" in Aberdeen and anonymous informers in Montauban. And the intensity of the disciplinary process changed with time and place. Few communities could match the godly ethos of Geneva during Calvin's ministry – perhaps St Andrews while Andrew Melville was preaching or Utrecht under Gisbertus Voetius – but at some level and in some form the moral imperative marked out all the Reformed churches of the sixteenth century.[131]

And yet, as important as the moral dimension of Christianity was to Calvin, his concern with discipline was the corollary of a more prominent theme: the sovereignty of God. On this subject, Calvin revealed his thoughts most dramatically in his discussions of providence and predestination, the latter being God's plan as it concerned the election and damnation of fallen man. Despite the importance of these two themes in later Reformed thought, they never had pride of place in the run of Calvin's published works. In the *Institutes*, for instance, the two concepts, so indelibly bound, were treated as separate subjects, partly because Calvin was reluctant to probe too deeply into mysteries he considered beyond human comprehension. Yet they were fundamentals of his theology, and both concepts were explicit illustrations of Calvin's teaching that God is the all-powerful primary cause, that he superintends the universe according to a "secret plan" beyond the comprehension of humankind, and that it is the duty of the faithful, in so far as it is possible, to devote their lives to living in accordance with this plan. For even though much remains hidden behind mysteries and secondary causes, all believers must do their best to "inquire and learn from Scripture what is pleasing to God so that they may strive toward this under the Spirit's guidance."[132]

Taken together, the twinned concepts of providence and predestination exercised a powerful influence on the history of early modern Reformed Protestants. Of course, both concepts were as old as Christianity, and in the essentials Calvin borrowed most things from the Thomist tradition. But no previous theologian had spoken about these mysteries in such unsparing terms before, and few theologians had used them to such effect in the body of their thought. Calvin's teaching on providence, for instance, proved a very effective ordering device, for it could encompass all other aspects of the faith within the folds of its logic. The question of sanctification could be illustrated with reference to God's secret plan, for just as God was assuredly "constructing, redeeming, and restoring" his kingdom on earth, so too was he sanctifying the souls of the elect. Similarly, Calvin's theology of the social and political order, which was essentially a conservative scheme, could be justified with reference to providentialism, for God worked his will *through* history, which meant that the rulers and the institutions of the day were part of the divine order and, unless they were explicitly violating God's Word, must be honored and obeyed. And, of course, the idea of predestination itself, which Calvin defined as "God's eternal decree, by which he compacted with himself what he willed to become of each man," not only helped to explain the place of the believer within the economy of salvation, it made it possible for the clergy to relate the essentials of evangelical theology to the spiritual and psychological dimensions of human experience. Election, it was claimed, was something that might be revealed in daily life, through an increase in charity, for instance, or a steady stream of brotherly love. God's hand was everywhere. "When we see that there is *some* order in the world," wrote Calvin, "we can see as in a mirror that God has not so let loose the reins to all confusion that he does not still show us some sign and token of his justice."[133]

For many parishioners, the justice of Calvin's theory of double predestination was difficult to grasp. The idea that some were born to salvation and others to damnation was not easy to reconcile with common sense. And it is doubtful there was much consolation in Calvin's insistence that God's willingness to save any souls from a stock of pure sinners was proof enough of his love, particularly for those who were more concerned about the damned than the saved. But just as a hanging, as Samuel Johnson once put it, will wonderfully concentrate the mind of a condemned criminal, so too did providence and predestination focus the minds of early modern Protestants. As a historian of providentialism in England has put it: "It was a set of ideological spectacles through which individuals of all social levels and from all positions on the confessional spectrum were apt to view their universe, an invisible prism which helped them to focus the refractory meanings of both petty and perplexing events."[134]

Speaking in general terms, two types of reaction might follow from the "terrible decree" of predestination. At one extreme, it could easily cripple the faithful and push them to the edge of despair. Damnation, after all, was the predestined lot of the majority, and for any soul already inclined to suffer doubt and anxiety in the face of the law this would have just stoked the (pending) flames. Later Protestants, as we will see, were inclined to dwell on the negative aspects of predestination, and indeed one of the underlying motives of the later revivalist movements was to break free from this decree. But there was another response to the doctrine, and it tended to have the opposite effect. For many Protestants, the doctrine of predestination was liberating. From a personal viewpoint, the idea that one might be among the elect was a very powerful conceit, for it marked out the believer (in his or her mind) as one of the predestined saints, one of God's chosen few. "I honour and glorifie my God," proclaimed a Puritan of the following century, "who hath passed by so many thousands as he hath done, and left them in their sins, and yet hath chosen me freely before the foundation of the world was laid."[135] But at a more general level as well, the notion that God had a secret plan, eternal and ineluctable in its course, and that there was a group of elect Christians who were in a special bond of fraternity with God, did much to contribute to the rise of Protestant identity. For it meant that men and women of pure faith (the elect) might think of themselves as advancing God's purpose, and that all laws and constraints that opposed or undermined this purpose were ungodly and had to be overcome.[136] What were customs and traditions compared to the divine decree? This sense of providential purpose, and this community of self-conscious saints and self-righteous actors, were important legacies of Calvin's Reformation in Geneva, and one of the main reasons why it was the Reformed Protestants, rather than the Lutherans, who became the first missionaries of the faith.

The Reformed matrix

Even before Calvin emerged triumphant in 1555, the different strands of Reformed Protestantism had started to gather together. The process dates back to the long tutelage of Heinrich Bullinger (1504–75), Zwingli's successor in Zurich, which eventually led to a rapprochement with Geneva and a joint theological statement, the *Consensus Tigurinus* of 1549. By way of an extensive network of correspondence, a prolific and successful career as an author, and an active community of like-minded scholars, Bullinger had been able to preserve and indeed expand the Zwinglian legacy. Calvin followed Bullinger's lead. In close cooperation with neighboring reformers such as Pierre Viret in Lausanne and Guillaume Farel in Neuchâtel, Calvin first built up a matrix of Reformed communes, then he turned his attention to international affairs. Like Bullinger, he corresponded with contacts throughout Europe and produced a steady stream of publications for an international readership, often directing his works at Europe's ruling elite in the hope that they might emerge as patrons of the movement.

But this Reformed matrix was not just reliant on Bullinger and Calvin. Other prominent reformers within the Swiss tradition also contributed to the creation of an international Reformed community, perhaps the best known being the clergyman John a Lasco (1499–1560), a Polish nobleman who had been trained for a career in the Catholic church before converting to Protestantism in the early 1540s. While serving as principal pastor of the city of Emden and superintendent of the church in East Friesland, a Lasco encouraged the planting of the faith in northern Germany close to the borders of the Dutch Republic and within the trade corridors of southern England. Emden became the "Geneva of the north," not only in the sense that it experienced a (slightly altered) Reformation in the Genevan mold, but also to the extent that it became an important nodal point on the growing network of Reformed communities and a place of refuge for the persecuted brethren in the north.[137]

By mid-century, Reformed Protestantism had surpassed Lutheranism as the most dynamic form of Reformation Christianity. Followers continued to congregate in urban sanctuaries such Strasbourg, Frankfurt, Aachen, and Wesel. Moreover, as we will see, the faith emerged as the public religion of a number of nations and territories, including the Palatinate, England, Scotland, the Dutch Republic, and parts of Poland-Lithuania and Hungary. Historians have come up with a long list of reasons why this may have occurred, ranging from the deep motives of religious psychology to the pragmatics of rule. Opinions vary, but what seems common to all of them is the emphasis placed on the transient nature of the faith. It traveled well. Although there were a few "perfect schools of Christ" like Calvin's Geneva, the majority of first-generation of Reformed Protestants did not belong to a public church but rather acquired their sense of community by way of the traffic of ideas, personal contacts, and shared experience. For an early convert such as the English churchman John Bale (1495–1563), for instance, who was forced to flee persecution in Ireland and find shelter among the refugees in Wesel in Germany, the mark of a Reformed Protestant was the experience of persecution and exile and the associated sense that the true church was not hedged in by any specific polity or place. The sheer experience of so much uprooted humanity in Geneva prompted to Bale to ask "is it not wonderful that Spaniards, Italians, Scots, Englishmen, Frenchmen, Germans, disagreeing in manners, speech and apparel, sheep and wolves, bulls and bears, being coupled only with the yoke of Christ, should live so lovingly and friendly ... like a spiritual and Christian congregation."[138] Born in part by this type of experience, the Reformed Protestants, more so than the Lutherans (though not as much as the radicals), were able to look beyond the distinctions of traditional Christian society and imagine themselves as members of a church united by the higher ties of faith. Moreover, in their search for religious purity, the followers of the Helvetic tradition were more prepared to reject or abandon society, community, or the state in order to pursue their ideal. The final goal was a sacral community fashioned and regulated by Scripture alone, and this necessarily meant that many of the Reformed Protestants were rootless and mobile, ready to displace themselves in the search for their own perfect school of Christ.[139]

These tendencies made Reformed Protestantism an extremely tractile and resilient tradition, as was borne out by the theological agreements of the sixteenth century, which were made possible by a mix of dogma and calculated ambiguity. Throughout Europe, believers could think of themselves as belonging to a universal Reformed community while teaching and worshipping in terms that were specific to a particular area or church. Different national groupings had different theological emphases, while the church structures, though similar to the Genevan system in their essentials, could vary from place to place, often using different names to describe institutions that were essentially the same. Even the experience of worship varied. In England, for instance, a parishioner was most likely to kneel to receive Communion from a clergyman in a surplice; in France, he or she would file past a minister who was dressed in a basic black gown; in Scotland or the Dutch Republic, the parishioners might be seated at a table and receive the bread and wine from the local elders.[140] It was this mix, part principle and part pragmatics, that made the faith take so readily in different environments. This point can be demonstrated with reference to two brief examples separated by circumstance and place: the spread of the faith in France to the west and Hungary to the east.

It was inevitable that Calvin, Noyon's own prodigal son, would turn his attention to France once his position in Geneva was secure. Despite the major setbacks of the 1530s – when the French king Francis I (1494–1547) began to persecute evangelicals and over-zealous humanists – the early Reformation movement had made some progress. By mid-century there was an active underground network, more Swiss than Saxon in its essentials, and numerous small Reformed communities throughout the kingdom, both in the countryside and in large cities, where the faithful would gather in homes, barns, sheds, and fields for clandestine services and Bible readings, often meeting with drawn swords and armed scouts just to be on their guard.

After 1555, Geneva became the main hub of a Reformed support system providing the French communities with a steady stream of preachers and publications for the spread and upholding of the faith. As a result of this initiative, most of the Reformed churches in France adopted the Genevan forms of the service and Calvin's interpretation of the faith. A particularly valuable export was the Genevan model of church rule, which in the typical Reformed manner was adapted to fit French circumstances. Since the state would not be the framework for reform in the manner of the Lutheran Reformation an ecclesiology had to be developed that could work independently of the secular arm. French Protestants achieved this by tweaking the Genevan model and devising the presbyterial-synodal system, a form of church governance that made all of the congregations (in theory) equal parts of a hierarchical scheme based on consistories, colloquies, and synods designed to oversee church affairs at the national and provincial level while pastors and elders administered to local congregations. On the basis of these foundations Reformed communities were able to emerge throughout the kingdom, and in particular in the crescent to the south of the kingdom linking the provinces of Dauphiné, Languedoc, Gascony, and Poitou. Reformed Protestantism attracted a considerable portion of the population – up to 10 percent by some estimates – ranging from artisans and merchants in major cities such as Nîmes, Montauban, and La Rochelle to members of the ruling family in Paris.[141]

The history of the Reformed community in La Rochelle, the French Atlantic port that became the "theatre of the French religious wars," offers some insight into the local dynamics.[142] Although a "bonne ville" marked out by special privileges granted by the Crown, the relations between La Rochelle and the royal officials were tense during the sixteenth century. Like all urban communes in this period, the magistracy sought greater autonomy, which in this case could only occur at the expense of the bishop of Saintes and the Crown. The ideas of the early Reformation, with the stress on liberty and communal forms of religion, had a natural appeal for a people attuned to the ideal of civic independence, and the movement soon found a ready audience. By the 1540s, the Parisian magistrates at Angers considered La Rochelle the foremost city of the new heresy in France. And with some justice. Throughout the 1540s and early 1550s Reformed clergy had been preaching the message and gathering supporters. After 1555, once Geneva intervened, the Protestants were substantial enough to establish a system of church rule, appoint Reformed preachers, and set up a consistory. Additional clergy arrived in the 1560s – there were four Geneva-trained pastors in the city in 1563 – and in short order a substantial community emerged. According to one estimate, up to 30 people per day were recruited to the faith. And while the membership increased, the clergy continued to preach, teach, and spread the message. In this they were given crucial aid in the 1560s when the Calvinist printer Barthélemy Berton set up shop in the town and published a steady stream of psalters, vernacular copies of the New Testament, catechisms, pamphlets, and works by Calvin and his successor Theodore Beza (1519–1605). By the 1560s, most of the ruling elite had converted to the faith, and that included a mayor and a royal governor, and La Rochelle was well on its way to becoming the bastion of the French Protestant cause during the Wars of Religion.

Indeed, it marked itself out for this role, establishing ties with the Huguenot grandee Louis, prince de Condé, in 1568 and quickly putting its defenses in order – which meant, among other things, building new fortifications, an undertaking that was partly facilitated by forced loans on Catholics and the use of their family tombstones in the stonework of the new defenses.

In Hungary, on the eastern edge of Europe, a similar process was at work. Close cultural and commercial relations with the German nation coupled with a fairly lax state of rule allowed for the spread of the evangelical movement into these multiethnic, multilingual lands in the early 1520s. Moreover, after the battle of Mohács in 1526, the kingdom suffered an additional breakdown of order and the consolidation of a tripartite division of rule that further opened up the land to innovation. The northwestern portion, termed "Royal Hungary," was in the hands of the Habsburgs and the central Danube plain fell under the sovereignty of the Ottoman Turks, while the eastern portion, largely comprising the eight provinces of the Partium and the principality of Transylvania, was ruled by the local magnates together with an elected prince. Protestants settled in all three areas, though the most developed communities emerged in the east.

Given the state of religious plurality in the land, Protestants of all stamps had settled, and yet it was the followers of the Swiss tradition that proved the most successful at adapting to the local conditions. By the 1570s, the Reformed Protestants of Transylvania had established an ecclesiological system based on the presbyterial-synodal model of France. There were synods, 7 provinces, about 450 congregations, articles of belief, and superintendents presiding over the church. Moreover, despite the barriers created by distance, history, and language, the Transylvanian communities were able to think of themselves as part of the broader European Reformed family of belief. This mindset had been cultivated from the very beginning through close connections with reformers such as Bullinger and Beza, and it continued into the early seventeenth century. And the same methods and modalities were used that joined the communities in France – shared statements of belief, an ongoing correspondence, the local printing and spread of texts, the exchange of pastors, the utilization of transregional systems of rule, and the general movement of people and ideas.

For the Transylvanians, one particularly important aspect of the broader Reformed community was the network of institutions of higher learning. It was not unusual for parents or patrons to send aspirant clergymen to study in France, Germany, the Dutch Republic, or England. This so-called *peregrinatio academica* not only prepared them for the church: it also cultivated the personal ties that kept Transylvania joined to the international matrix. The educational experience of the Reformed theologian and wandering scholar Albert Szenczi Molnár (1574–1634) will make the point. During his time as a student in the 1590s, Molnár studied at Wittenberg, Heidelberg, and Strasbourg. Along the way he met Theodore Beza, whom he termed his "father in Christ." With his education complete, he returned to Germany in 1600 and spent time at the universities in Heidelberg, Herborn, Altdorf, and Marburg. While there he corresponded with Johann Heinrich Alsted and Bartholomäus Keckermann, numerous Huguenot scholars, and a number of French and Flemish congregations, some of which he mentioned in his 1624 translation of Calvin's *Institutes*, thanking them for the assistance they had given along the way.[143]

These brief histories of the Reformed communities in France and Hungary shed some light on the sociological dimensions of early Protestantism, and in particular on how individuals and groups, although faced with social, cultural, and geographical barriers, could join together in communities that were inspired and maintained by the combination of an idealistic vision of what the true church actually was and a very practical and pragmatic approach to religious affairs. With reference to the making of early Protestants, it was a fundamentally important process. Yet it was not the experience of the majority of Protestants during the first century of Reformation. For the majority, it was not necessary to create a sense of order out of a matrix of sympathetic souls. Order was imposed from above, realized within the framework of early modern systems of rule.

2
Kingdoms

With the rise of the Reformation, religion took on a heightened ordering function in the political world. From the level of individual relations to the vast field of territorial sovereignty, orthodoxies began to inform the systems of power and the workings of rule. And it was not a side-effect of the reformers' Faustian bargain with the secular arm. There was an important political dimension to Protestant thought from the very outset. We should not conclude from this that reform was merely a handmaid to early modern statecraft or that evangelical theology was little more than a pretence for theories of political aggrandizement. Yet there is no doubt that early Protestant history is in large part a story about the search for a proper balance between the secular and the spiritual spheres, and one that was significant enough to precipitate a wholly new dynamic and establish a completely new phenomenon: confessionalized politics.

The story begins at the level of the urban commune, where the dialogue between evangelical ideals and civic culture made its initial impact, not only modifying the praxis and the theory of rule, but also shaping the nature of the theologies that went into the making of the Reformation city. At the level of the territory and the nation-state as well, Protestantism evolved as part of a political dialogue, and one that could work to the advantage of the burgeoning early modern state. With the synthesis of the secular and the spiritual dimensions of rule, aspects of sovereignty crucial for the intensification of power were now at the disposal of the ruling elite to a degree without precedence in European history. And while outcomes varied, the intention remained constant. For all of the mainstream traditions, the final aim was to create a domain "in which the symbiosis of new churches and states would bring forth new, more or less homogeneous societies."[1] The rise of religious identity in this period, which was often bound up with early notions of national identities and jingoistic narratives of chosen peoples, was one consequence of this process.

But it was not a unilateral process. Protestantism could work as a double-edged sword. Just as it provided the nation-state or urban commune with a sense of common vision or conviction, it could also empower other sovereign corporations to draw on

Protestants: A History from Wittenberg to Pennsylvania 1517–1740 By C. Scott Dixon
© 2010 C. Scott Dixon

religious thought to extend the base of their assumed rights and privileges – and often in order to resist the claims of their immediate overlords. The confessional state was never a seamless join of religious injunction and political order. Even in the German territories, where there was often such an organic relationship between the will of the rulers and the lives of the ruled, religious change had an ambiguous impact on the structures and relations of power. In some respects it clearly strengthened the systems of rule and consolidated political relations; in other respects the faith destabilized the frameworks of governance and brought with it a number of unforeseen effects with lasting implications. But whatever the end result, the basic trend remained the same: Protestantism evolved in a very close symbiotic relationship with the political world. From the very beginning, Protestants were by nature a political people.

Kings, Priests, and Prophets

Given the synergy of the secular and the spiritual in the late-medieval world, it was impossible for the Reformation to develop any degree of momentum and remain a purely religious affair. Moreover, given the vision of the Christian community developed by the reformers, it soon became clear that any reform of religion would necessarily bring with it a new matrix of earthly authority. Consequently, from the very outset the Protestant religion was conceived and articulated with a view to temporal relations. This is not to suggest that the first generation of reformers worked up fully-formed philosophies of rule. The earliest reflections on church and state were speculative and often contradictory, more quick thinking than systematic thought. Nevertheless, the movement raised questions about the relationship between the secular and the spiritual that had to be answered. And the two men who did the most to establish the early parameters were Martin Luther and Martin Bucer. Neither reformer developed an ideology in the modern sense, but in their different approaches we can see the basic tensions and configurations at the heart of all Protestant political thought.

Luther was reluctant to offer his judgment on politics, but when he did his ideas were always derived from the first principles of his theology, and two precepts in particular informed his thought from the earliest days. First, he held that secular authority was a divine institution and as necessary to the Christian life as spiritual rule. Behind Luther's formulation was his notion of justification through faith and the corollary that man was of two natures, flesh and spirit, and was thus both sinner and saved at the same time (*simul iustus et peccator*). This meant that man needed some form of earthly rule in order to discipline himself and his relations with other Christians.[2] Second, Luther never wavered in his belief that Scripture speaks to all aspects of human experience, including the social and political dimensions. Indeed, he even construed the Song of Songs to be an elegy of "political order, peace, and the present state of the realm" and read it as an anthropomorphic vision of good government, with the magistrates compared to flowers in the field, the state making up the body of the beloved, the church providing the legs, the common people the trunk, and the princes and the higher clergy forming the head, the two paired lips symbolizing law and gospel.[3]

In the *Address to the Christian Nobility*, Luther spoke directly about the need to reform the German church. Opening with an appeal to the emperor and the nobility, he set out to expose the wickedness of the papacy and to demonstrate how corruption had led to the perversion of the faith. Tailoring his text for his imagined readers, Luther conjured up the image of a fortress under siege and emphasized the need to break down the "three walls" that had traditionally safeguarded Rome in the hope that his words would "set free the Christian rods for the punishment of sin, [and] bring to light the craft and deceit of the devil, to the end that through punishment we may reform ourselves and once more attain God's favour."[4] With his first salvo, the idea of the priesthood of all believers, Luther struck at the sovereignty of the church (the first wall). By claiming that Scripture provided no support for the distinction between the secular and the spiritual spheres, he undermined the sacerdotal uniqueness of the clerical estate and placed church and state on the same level. "I say therefore," he wrote, "that since the temporal power is ordained of God to punish the wicked and protect the good, it should be left free to perform its office in the whole body of Christendom without restriction and without respect to persons, whether it affects pope, bishops, priests, monks, nuns, or anyone else."[5] Taking aim at the axiom that only the church in Rome had the right and the facility to interpret the Word of God (the second wall), Luther referred to the long train of "unnatural" ordinances that had prostituted the faith and dismissed the idea as an "outrageous fancied fable," just as he trumpeted down the third wall (the idea that the pope alone had the right to call a council) with references to the long history of error and misinterpretation and the need to restore the church to the rightful sovereign community, which meant in the first instance the temporal authorities.[6]

Luther never proposed to subject the church to the powers of the state. On the contrary, as he made explicit a few years later in his work *On Secular Authority* (1523), his main concern was to keep the secular and the spiritual at a distance.[7] Fundamental to Luther's notions of order was his conviction that mankind had a dual nature and thus stood in a double relationship with God. Fallen man was at once the subject of the kingdom of Christ, a member of the assembly of believers (*congregatio fidelium*) ruled by the Spirit through the Word *and* a subject of the kingdom of the Sword, the temporal realm, where law and reason held sway. Luther's main concern was the preservation of the boundaries between the two spheres. In part his anxiety was born of historical circumstance, as the Wittenberg movement began to suffer the trials of princely persecution as well as the rise of radical evangelicals looking to fashion the world in the image of God's Word. According to Luther, both were mistaken: the former for violating the kingdom of Christ, the latter for enlisting the divine law in the service of the state. It was crucial to keep the two realms distinct, for they served different ends and ruled according to different notions of righteousness and law. To confuse the two was to distort them (the devil's favorite trick). Recognizing the two kingdoms, Luther believed, brought the two natures of man into harmony: the inner, spiritual dimension remained inviolate and subject only to God, while the outer, corporal dimension assumed its public role and offered itself to the service of society through the offices and institutions of the state.[8] Governing the two realms also required different methods. In the kingdom of the Spirit, the Word alone held sway, for there was no need of force among Christians. In the secular kingdom, however, the dwelling place of mankind, the sword was necessary in order to maintain peace. The former relied on persuasion (it was an empire of the spoken Word, a *Hörreich*), the latter on coercion. But both honored God's purposes, both served salvation, and both kept Satan at bay.

Luther's idea of two separate spheres of existence represented a radical conceptual break with medieval tradition. Where there had once been theories of spheres and orders joined together, however unevenly, in an ontological whole, there were now two distinct realms, each with its own purpose and place in the divine scheme of things. It was not a political ideology in any meaningful or modern sense; and yet in its concern to maintain the balance between the secular and the spiritual, Luther's Reformation gave rise to a dialogue that was at the heart of political thought throughout the early modern period. No Protestant secular order could escape its categories, for the categories themselves corresponded precisely to the nature of Protestant man. Nor could fallen man avoid the paradox by residing in one or the other of the realms, as his very nature – *simul iustus et peccator* – necessitated dual residency. This did not mean, of course, that all Protestants would share the same visions of the secular order. Different views on sin, atonement, righteousness, or the meaning of religious freedom would lead to different ideas about how the two kingdoms should sit in relation to each other. But since both spheres were the basic setting for Christian existence, and as both were required in order to lead a Christian life, it necessarily gave rise to a dialogue between the theologians and the ideologues about ecclesio-political relations. And more than just good order was at stake. Without the proper balance, salvation was at risk. Hence Luther's warnings that the authorities stay clear of matters that touched on conscience, and hence his rising concerns about the radicals and their projections of New Testament Christianity. "If anyone attempted to rule the world by the Gospel," he warned, "and abolish all temporal law and sword . . . he would be loosing the ropes and chains of the wild savage beasts and letting them bite and mangle everyone."[9]

But not all reformers thought in terms of antipathies. According to the Strasbourg clergyman Martin Bucer (1491–1551), perhaps the most profound of first-generation reformers to take up the theme, the only sure solution was to refashion the world in the image of the divine, and this required bringing the secular and the spiritual into harmony under what he called the "kingdom of Christ."[10] In his short work entitled *One Should not Live for Oneself Alone but for Others* (1523), Bucer illustrated how all earthly relations, including those between church and state, ultimately derive from the Word of God. All things have been created by God to serve a purpose. From the sun to crops to insects – each completes the natural order by serving something else. Man, however, because of the Fall, sits outside this order, neither participating nor really understanding, and instead of serving others serves only himself. In this sense he is unique, with only the devil as company. Yet this state of affairs can be transformed through the preaching of the Word, and it could be realized in human terms by the formation of the authentic Christian community. And at the very heart of this community was the principle of brotherly love, for this was the pure teaching of Christ and the means by which mankind could participate in the divine order. Serving one's neighbor, Bucer concluded, was the calling of a Christian man, and all earthly relations, secular and spiritual alike, should work in close union to make such a moral compact possible, for each was bound to honor the same Word of God.[11] Here, in the thought of Bucer rather than the later syntheses of Calvin, are the foundations for the Weberian notion of the Protestant ethic considered so consequential for the development of modern Europe. "God willed the social achievement of the Christian, *because* it was his will that the social structure of life should accord with his commands and be organized in such a way as to achieve this purpose."[12]

As the resident of an imperial city, Bucer naturally looked to the civic authorities to realize this vision. Like all Christians, the secular authorities were compelled to honor the divine order and, Bucer concluded,

> ought, therefore, to direct all their abilities, as God in his law has commanded and as the Spirit of Christ himself teaches and urges in all whom he leads, to the end that through their subjects God's name be hallowed, his Kingdom extended and his will fulfilled – so far as they can serve thereto by virtue of their office alone.[13]

There was more than just a sense of civic duty behind the union. Bucer's reference to God in his law speaks of the sacerdotal dimension underwriting the marriage of church and state. All men were bound to obey both tables of the Decalogue, to the point that they must be enshrined in the inner and the outer constitution of the Christian community. In place of the two kingdoms as described by Luther, Bucer thought in terms of two churches – one purely spiritual, the other earthly – sitting parallel in a world totally subordinate to the teaching of Christ.[14] As we will see below in the section of civic Protestantism, little separates this vision of a godly commune from the more explicit covenantal theocracies of Zwingli and Bullinger, or indeed the Old Testament motif of a people or nation standing in a special relationship with God.

Like other German reformers of his generation, Bucer spent his life searching for the proper relationship between flesh and spirit. Late in his career he moved from Strasbourg to Cambridge, where he prepared his final work on the theme, *De regno Christi* (1550). Dedicated to the English king Edward VI, Bucer projected his final vision of a Christian community.[15] Sovereign over all was Christ; he alone reigns through the Holy Spirit. In this sense, it was not an earthly realm at all, but an unseen empire of justification, grace, and salvation, known only to the elect. Christ reigns through his earthly instruments, and above all through the clergy, who have been commissioned by the Holy Spirit to see through the divine will. In order to ensure that the clergy fulfill their mission and spread the Word, the secular authorities have been invested with the responsibility of creating and maintaining the conditions that will allow for the kingdom of Christ (*regnum Christi*) to come into being. Hence Bucer's approach to the second part of the work, which is a discussion of the measures needed to fashion the Christian commune, ranging from the reform of churches and schools, the safeguarding of proper worship, the transformation of public welfare and social relations (from the poor law to marriage), to the need to create a land of active and industrious subjects and the improvements needed in both law and governance. In all of this, the presiding power was the Word of God. Bucer believed that once the nature of rule had been conformed to the teaching of Scripture, the Spirit would effect a transformation of the realm and the kingdom of Christ (or at least the closest thing possible on earth) could be realized. The Christian remained a sinner, of course, but there was a new awareness, a new sense of perception, which affected the entire being and would in the end create a community of true Christians marked out by faith and the spirit of brotherly love.[16]

Bucer died before *De regno Christi* was published, and ultimately the work had little impact on secular and spiritual relations in England. This was a common enough fate for a work of this kind. Theology was essential for providing the secular authorities with a justification for the break with Catholicism, just as it provided a basic framework for the dialogue between church and state. But, in following the advice of the reformers, few Protestant authorities kept as close to its letter as men like Luther and Bucer would have liked. Instead, the rise of the Protestant polities in Europe was determined as much by circumstances and traditions as the abstractions of evangelical theology. In this sense, Bucer's *De regno Christi* captured something essential about the rise of the first Protestant kingdoms: namely, that the Word of God could effect a transformation. However, he had overlooked a force of equal strength, the *regnum mundi*, the kingdom of this world.

Civic Protestantism

Theaters of reform

Although it has become something of a historiographical commonplace, it remains true to say that the history of Protestants begins in the Swiss and German cities. A certain affinity was predetermined. There was a clear correspondence between the values upheld by the urban populace and the values preached by the early reformers. There were also ways in which people thought of social relations that made the new religion seem logical and familiar. But above all it was the ongoing need to resolve antagonisms, the need to reconcile contradictory perceptions of community – between horizontal and vertical models of association, between allegiance and obedience, between the individual and the collective – that made the evangelical message take so readily to local conditions. Reformation ideas quickly appealed to a wide range of urban interest groups, and they seemed to have moved between the secular and the spiritual without losing relevance or suffering too much distortion.[17]

Viewed from the perspective of late-medieval political culture, the common ground between evangelical theology and the ideology of the urban elites is not difficult to grasp. Within the field of political discourse, the most cherished values were those that were seen as contributing to the common good (*Gemeinnutz*), a concept that could mean different things to different people, but essentially referred to the range of ideals that best preserved harmony and unity. The values underwriting the myth of community were thus those that placed collective welfare above the interests of the individual, and these usually included concord, unity, justice, love, peace, and charity. The greatest fear was fear of discord.[18] Sitting alongside these secular ideals, and if anything lodged even deeper in the urban psyche, were the spiritual values that bound the community together, imparted through sermons, liturgy, and ritual, and further confirmed through the habitus of rule as the communes embraced more and more aspects of local ecclesiastical life. Many urban parishioners in late-medieval Germany and Switzerland had begun to think of religion in collective terms, imagining the city as a type of sacred society, a body of Christian believers (*corpus Christianum*) bound together in a common quest for salvation.[19] Over time, the two spheres had drawn closer and closer together, with the secular authorities taking on many of the powers and functions that once belonged to the church. The point to make is not that religion had become a handmaid to the powers of local rule, but that the urban mind had grown accustomed to conflating the two realms and anticipating their full development within the framework of the commune. The city had become a total environment, a place where both secular and spiritual values could be fully realized.

Given the complexity of the political landscape in Germany and Switzerland, there is no single historical example that illustrates this process. Each region, sometimes each city, had its own pattern of reform. In many of the Hanseatic towns of northern Germany, for instance, the Lutheran faith was embraced by the guildsmen and the influential burghers of the cities, those men whose prosperity (real and imagined) was best preserved by the principles of communal rule. Against them were ranged the Catholic oligarchs, those men whose claims to legitimacy were based on hierarchy and privilege. Further to the south, in the imperial cities of Franconia and Swabia, the evangelical faith quickly found a niche in a wide range of political communities, in the guilds above all, but also among the laboring classes and the merchant elite. These southern imperial cities were also the home to the most important plutocrats of the early Reformation, the councilors, jurists, and city secretaries such as Lazarus Spengler, Jörg Vögeli, and Jacob Sturm, who embraced the teaching of the reformers and took the practical steps to make the Protestant church a reality.[20] Yet even in cities of high-profile evangelicals such as these, where the movement had the support of both the ruling elite and the subject population, the faith was not introduced without making political waves. In both Nuremberg and Strasbourg, for instance, two cities where the Reformation was effectively an act of state, the change of religion had a lasting impact on the constitution. In Strasbourg, the discord that erupted between the radical evangelicals, the moderates, and a minority of conservative aristocrats, eventually brought about the decline of the city's Catholic elite as a social and political force.[21]

The most obvious and immediate effect of Protestantism on the urban landscape was the assault on the outward constitution of the church. With the secularization of the monasteries and the liquidation of the foundations, thousands of church offices were abolished, patronage networks collapsed, wealth was confiscated, and a way of life, so central to civic relations, fell away. In capturing a sense of this vanishing world, we must remember that medieval religious culture was in large part a material culture, and much of its meaning was typified in objects such as chapels, altars, paintings, retables, shrines, and church windows. Thus in its attacks against the fabric of the church, the Reformation also launched an attack against the symbolic forms and material substance of power. Family masses were discontinued, chapels were pulled down, gravestones were defaced, and epitaphs of the city's leading families were destroyed. Some cities went so far as to abolish the practices associated with the interring and memorializing of the dead according to their earthly rank within the confines of churches, and even the most honored men as well as their common co-citizens were buried in outlying cemeteries. Faced with this sudden assault on their symbolic world, the elite reacted in different ways. In Strasbourg, the patrician Mathis Beger, fearing further insult to his family honor, gathered together his father's bones from the Carmelite convent and reinterred them at his chateau in Geispolsheim.[22]

In general, however, the Reformation strengthened the position of the ruling elite. For although they invoked ideals of community and corporation, most urban councils governed as *Obrigkeit* – that is, as a closed oligarchy with exclusive powers of rule. Inheriting the right to superintend the urban church extended both the range of council sovereignty and the instruments of its rule. This development was already evident in late-medieval Germany, but the Reformation accelerated the trend.[23] After the introduction of Lutheranism in Esslingen, for instance, the city councilors were invested with the right to watch over almost every conceivable aspect of communal life, from the administration of the parish churches and the supervision of the clergy to the policing of local morality and the general welfare system in the city. All of this required considerable innovation in the methods of governance, and this in turn led to the creation of new institutions such as marriage courts and consistories, orphanages, hospitals, workhouses, schools, and even local libraries.[24] And while it was spiritual in its motivation, it was secular in its effects. Indeed, now that the magistracy could justify rule by drawing on the Word of God, political discourse became "biblicized" as the language of power turned to theology. There was a considerable history at the root of this sentiment, as we have seen, for there had long been a tradition in the imperial cities of projecting the commune as a type of a sacral corporation (an important fiction if not a historical fact). The Reformation revived this vision, though now with the added elements of a theology that emphasized the themes of the common good and "brotherly love" and made little practical distinction between the secular and the spiritual spheres.[25] Evangelical theology became the idiom of public sovereignty, while the process of reform forced through a functional assimilation of church and state.

The rationale behind this synthesis of the sacred and the profane was captured in the thought of the Nuremberg city secretary Lazarus Spengler (1479–1534). Long in the service of the council (*Rat*), Spengler was thoroughly familiar with the ideals at the heart of urban governance. In particular, he was alert to the emphasis placed on communal ethics and the need to nourish a system of rule that validated the council's role as the custodian of the common good. However, he was also aware that power was in the hands of the few, and he had a systematic knowledge of how this power had been extended through the years, how it had gradually embraced more and more aspects of civic culture and reached into the workings of the church. Thus, when Spengler first encountered the ideas of Luther, the new theology not only enabled him to view his own relationship with God in different terms, it also provided him with the language and ideas needed in order to articulate his understanding of the reformed Nuremberg polity as a *corpus Christianum*. In the evangelical idea of brotherly love, he saw the divine analogue of the common good; in the Word of God, he abstracted the mandate for the *regnum Christi*; in the salvation of the individual, he perceived the grounds for the salvation of the whole. And he also recognized, aided by the Nuremberg theologian Andreas Osiander (1498–1552), that the responsibility for both the foundation and the maintenance of this Christian community had been placed in the hands of the secular authorities. As Osiander put it, within its proper bounds, all authority was the instrument of God's will.[26]

Ideologically, this was not a radical break with the medieval past; instrumentally, however, it was little short of a revolution. And the net result was one part liberation and one part oppression. In so far as the lately born evangelical commune had been released from its self-perceived Babylonian captivity, the magistracy could portray the change of religion as an act of emancipation. No longer subject to Rome, the city was free to realize the models of evangelical reform. For the subject parishioners, however, this could prove an oppressive legacy. Common to all of the spokesmen of the early Reformation in Nuremberg was Luther's deep sense of sin and human depravity. "Man's heart, reason, temper, sense, and power," wrote Spengler, "in other words his entire nature, have been so corrupted by the primal serpent poison of our first parents that no deed he performs out of his own resources can be anything but sinful."[27] Long disposed to believe this, but now empowered by the proofs of divine sanction, the ruling elite stepped in to compensate for the Fall and thereby increased their control over the citizenry by abstracting a religious compact between the rulers, the ruled, and Holy Writ. No Protestant city, not even Geneva, ever became a theocracy; but by the same token, no medieval city had ever experienced so close an interweave of the secular and the spiritual as the early Protestant communes.

In those cities where theology and ideology harmonized, the very symbolism of sovereignty might change. The town hall of Regensburg is a case in point. Before the Reformation, all deliberations in the main chamber had taken place within sight of a painting of the Last Judgment. The image was meant to signify at least two things: first, the close relationship between earthly and divine judgment, and second, that those who judge must judge according to conscience, for at the End of Days all earthly deeds would be called to account. After the introduction of Lutheranism, the iconography of the chamber was reworked to reflect the shift of emphasis away from Christ as Judge to the evangelical theme of Christ as Savior, and it projected an image of God as the loving father who would accept the guilty despite their inability to meet the requirements of the law. The iconography incorporated this aspect of paternal love. Moreover, as Lutheranism had severed the causal relationship between justice in this world and the prospects of salvation in the next, it was a reminder of the increased importance placed on the pursuit of good government, for government had been established by God to realize his will on earth. And with temporal authority now set in its separate sphere, notions of justice and sovereignty could be captured by both traditional profane concepts such as *Justitia*, *Caritas*, *Pax*, and *Fides* (allegorized in female form) and joined by episodes and parables taken from the Bible. As we know from surviving architectural drafts of the Regensburg town hall, the outer façade of the building was saturated in scenes taken from both Roman and biblical history.[28]

The objective was to underscore the idea of an urban constitution derived and preserved by both classical civic values *and* the principles of Holy Writ and thus supremely humane in its workings but divine in its purpose. In Protestant cities throughout Germany and Switzerland, symbolic representations of urban rule were refashioned to accentuate this idea. In Lutheran Ulm, the town-hall facade was renovated to integrate antic maxims and biblical themes, in effect an artistic synthesis of *De officiis* and Genesis. In a chamber of the Lüneburg town hall the painter Daniel Frese finished a series of allegories depicting the godly relationship between the secular and the spiritual, a visual sermon on how the magistracy had been invested by God to rule in his stead on earth. In some Reformed cities, such as Danzig and Thorn, the range of good government depicted in the public ornamentation began to extend deeper and deeper into the province once preserved for the church.[29]

Of course, there were cracks beneath the façade. In many cities where the rhetoric of civic Protantism was at its most effusive, there was an equally thriving understory of clerical discontent. And it was significant, for even after the first flush of Reformation, the pulpit remained the most effective medium for the spread of opinion. Town-hall symbolism might momentarily engage, but words convinced and converted. Over time, a well-ordered and self-aware Protestant clerical estate emerged, with a developed sense of calling, and a powerful conviction that there should be divisions between the secular and the spiritual realms. Necessarily, this often led to conflicts, for the danger inhered in evangelical thought. From the very outset of reform, active clergymen such as Johannes Bugenhagen had projected a social and political system grounded in the ethics of brotherly love and legitimated in the Word of God. The main duty of the pastor was to watch over this order and defend the interests of the Christian commune against any possible abuses of the ruling elite.[30] Similarly, in his work *The Shepherd* (1524), Zwingli wrote of the prophetic role of the urban clergyman. The minister of God must preach the gospel and he must speak to both the inner and the outer constitution of the faith, even though it may draw the wrath of an ungodly ruler. There were, after all, no lack of Old Testament precedents: Samuel rebuking Saul, John the Baptist defying Herod, Elijah denouncing Ahab. And the result, Zwingli was quick to add, would not be a fall into chaos but rather the safeguarding of order: "O happy rulers, cities, and peoples, among whom the Lord speaks freely through his servants the prophets. For thus religion can increase, innocence return, justice reign, without which what we think [are] kingdoms and governments are robbery and violence."[31]

But prophets did not always bring blessings down on the city-state, as was particularly evident in some towns and cities of the Netherlands. Faced by the mix of republicanism, Erastianism, corporatism, mercantilism, and the budding ideologies of liberty and autonomy nurtured during the struggle against the Spanish Habsburgs, the Calvinist preachers of the Dutch Republic were often obstructed in their designs by the magistrates and regents. That the Reformed religion was the religion of the nation was not in question; the magistrates supported the church and guaranteed its monopoly over public worship. What was disputed was the extent to which the faith might influence the civic constitution, not only in the sense of the extent to which it might see through its vision of the external church, but also how far it might intrude upon the urban conscience. For many magistrates, the answer was clear: the secular authorities alone had the right to determine the nature of religious culture in the city. As the jurist Hugo Grotius pronounced in 1613, "nobody has the right to decide on the faith of the church inasmuch as it is public, except for him in whose hand and power all public bodies lie."[32] Rather than drawing on religion to biblicize urban governance and pursue the type of sacral commune imagined by men like Zwingli and Bucer, the regents tended to keep the church at a distance – or at least prevent it from reaching the stage where it could threaten the type of civic culture favored by the magistracy, which was, relatively speaking, liberal, tolerant, multi-confessional, even a-confessional, and, when pressed to reveal itself, more worldly than otherworldly in tone.[33]

A particularly instructive example of this type of balancing act is offered by the dispute between the Calvinist clergy and the town corporation (*vroedschap*) of the city of Leiden. As in other Dutch towns, the Reformation in Leiden owed its origins to events at the national level; unlike other towns, however, Leiden had the history of the siege of 1574 and the revealed proofs of its native courage, fortitude, and ingenuity, as well its particular place in the divine scheme of things, to provide the locals with a unique perspective. Hence, when the Calvinist clergy pressed for a local church built on the model of Geneva, or at least in the image of the 1578 Dordrecht synodal ordinance, they met with opposition. The city fathers, who thought the purpose of religion was to maintain "good Christian" order largely dependent on the magistracy and more or less coterminous with the entire urban commune, proved resistant to any notion of community that divided congregants or shared power. Ultimately it led to open conflict over spheres of rule and how the consistory, the diaconate, and the Rijnland classis stood in relation to the powers of the *vroedschap*. In 1580 the elevation of the quarrel to a national issue led to the intervention of William of Orange and a temporary solution was found. But this did not remove the differences. The magistracy continued to advocate a model of public religion that, while Reformed in its general outlines, was inclusive enough to accommodate all but the most contentious individuals. In the view of the city fathers, there was one church and one community with one civic polity that subsumed them both. Individuals could worship in private as conscience dictated, and the Dutch Reformed Church could claim unopposed primacy as the public religion, but neither should make claims that threatened civic peace.

The local dynamics varied, as did the place of the commune in the overall config-uration of reform, but generally speaking the familiar refrain about the Reformation being an "urban event" holds true.[34] In the Swiss and German context, where the movement first evolved, the urban environment was vital for development. But this was also the case, to different degrees, for all regions where Protestant communities appeared, whether the Reformed congregations of the Netherlands, the Lutheran churches of Sweden, the Anabaptist communities of Moravia, or the English Calvinists of Massachusetts Bay. The advance of Calvinism in France, for instance, would not have been possible without the conurbations of the "Huguenot crescent," an area which took in substantial cities such as La Rochelle, Nîmes, Toulouse, and Montauban, as well as the numerous smaller towns of the Dauphiné valleys.[35] It would not be difficult to write a history of Protestants solely from the perspective of the city. What needs to be stressed in the context of this discussion, however, is not just that the urban commune was a crucial setting for the rise of the faith, but that the Reformation first became an agent of historical change within the context of the urban environment and, as a consequence of this, the city itself and its notions of power and community contributed fundamentally to the shaping of the faith. Some general trends have been touched on already in the discussion of the German lands and the Dutch Republic. An even closer perspective is offered through a study of the dialogue between the reformers and the magistrates in one city of central importance for the making of Protestants: Zurich.

Commune and covenant

Huldrych Zwingli began his ministry in Zurich by adopting the so-called *lectio continua* method, which entailed working through the books of the Bible without relying on preaching aids for style or substance. Zwingli believed that preaching the Word would effect a godly transformation and that Zurich would be the cradle of this Christian rebirth. To cite his celebrated formulation, "When the Gospel is preached and all, including the magistrate, heed it, the Christian man is nothing else than the faithful and good citizen; and the Christian city is nothing other than the Christian church."[36]

Two things are worth noting here, both well established in the historiography. First, Zwingli recognized both the importance of the communal setting and the civic magistracy for the process of religious reform. Without the support of the secular authorities there could be no Christian city. And second, he realized that the Christian church and the Christian commune would be built on the basis of dialogue – or more properly put, on the basis of preaching: the clergy would sermonize and the citizenry would heed. Zwingli had no doubts about the critical role of the preacher in this relationship. In his work *The Shepherd* (1524), he drew on numerous Old Testament examples to illustrate how the prophets of the past had opposed the princes of their day whenever they believed that the Word of God had been violated or deserted.[37]

But the relationship between the clergy and the Zurich magistracy was more nuanced than a reading of Isaiah might suggest. From the very outset, the Reformation had been reliant upon the laity, and in particular the ruling elite, for its development. This secular involvement was consistent with Zwingli's ideas of the Christian community and how faith and practice together led to sanctification. In this, his approach to theology was essentially the inverse of Luther's, for while the Wittenberg reformer built, as it were, from the center out with theorems and abstractions, Zwingli started at the periphery, with the subsidiary themes of the Christian life, and worked inward toward the eternal truths of the faith.[38]

Zwingli came relatively late to the evangelical principles that defined the Wittenberg movement. Instead, he spent the early years preaching and writing against so-called secondary issues such as clerical corruption, images and idols, tithes, and excommunication. There was, however, a theological method behind this approach, one that developed and legitimated his ideas within a triangulation of perspectives. Zwingli's reformation was an act of hermeneutical negotiation between the city council acting in its role as an executive authority, the Word of God as judge (as interpreted by the clergy), and the parishioners themselves, the "brothers in Christ" who made up the body of the church. It was a three-way dialectic, the best examples being the two public disputations of 1523. In both instances the debates were under the control of the council, but Zwingli used the disputation as a means of situating and legitimating his teaching within the commune, for not only did he win the support of the council with his appeals to Scripture and the associated language of peace and the common good, he drew the people to his cause, and their personal convictions to his faith, by claiming that a town hall full of Zurich parishioners was every inch as qualified to judge Scripture as the bishop of Constance.

Zwingli consistently let his theology speak to the themes that were most important and familiar to the city magistracy and its citizens. When he referred to Catholicism as a form of idolatry, a false religion that placed the selfish, fleshly desires of the individual above the universal, spiritual truths of the evangelical faith, there was a strong awareness of the urban ideals of the common good and order beneath the surface; when he spoke of the correlation between faith and regeneration and the need for good works to bear out belief, he was evoking the medieval idea of the sacral city and the moral dimensions of salvation; when he counseled patience, distinguished between anathema and adiaphora, and judged it beyond the gifts of mankind to separate the wheat from the tares, he was in part tailoring his theology to match the realities of power in the Swiss commune.[39] Even his attacks on the Swiss mercenary system were tailored to suit the policies of the Zurich council, for in 1521 the decision was taken to reject the traditional alliance with France and stop the flow of young Swiss men into French service. Zwingli did not only play up the economic and moral harm this caused Zurich; he preached an evangelical theology of war that condemned the trade because it was not Christian. Unlike the early Swiss wars, which were waged to secure liberty from tyrants and protection for families, the mercenary trade was purely for worldly gain. It was the traffic of the devil, and it had no place in the confederation, which Zwingli compared to the House of Israel.[40]

The Reformation in Zurich is thus a powerful example of the importance of place in the rise of Protestants. Christianity had become bound up with a specific horizon of perception and expectation. This was a step beyond the localization or communalization of parish religion of the late-medieval period, for it was not just the cultic aspects of the faith that had been appropriated (such as devotion to a saint or the patronage of a church) but religion as a heuristic force. The theological foundations for this way of thinking were articulated in Zwingli's early work, and in particular in his ideas on the relations between the secular and the spiritual. Although he made a very clear distinction between the things of God and the things of this world, Zwingli was convinced that both types of law were essential for the existence of a Christian community. Whereas the spiritual laws informed the inner life, the temporal laws, in so far as they had been derived from Scripture, were crucial for the outer forms. As Zwingli projected it, the godly community would necessarily effect the right balance between law and gospel, not because order had to be imposed on Christian society but because faith would naturally lead the Christian man to honor the law. In his words, "the law is a Gospel for the man who honors God."[41] This was a much more positive understanding of law than that developed by Luther, and one considered crucial by Zwingli, for no set of social or political relations devised by men relying on reason (*ratio*) alone could be in harmony with the divine order.

Zwingli believed that God had revealed his universal truths to the people of Zurich and that the conclusions reached by the disputations and the assemblies spoke for the entire Christian church. Of this he had no doubt. In response to the objections raised by opponents like Johannes Fabri, the vicar-general of the diocese, Zwingli simply pointed to the prophetic stamp of local events. Zurich was in a covenant with God. And as it was beyond human ability to identify the elect, this meant that the entire commune was in effect the church. Overseeing its livelihood was not the pope or the bishop of Constance but the city magistracy, whose highest purpose was to preserve a form of rule that would govern outer behavior in harmony with Scripture and divine law. Only this type of godly order would liberate mankind from the constraints of an earthly morality and allow for complete Christian freedom, by which Zwingli meant the freedom of the gospel expressed through the law. In this type of polity, secular government assumes an important and positive function in the *corpus Christianum*: not only does it minister the laws that govern human justice, but by deriving such laws from Scripture it makes possible the pursuit of divine righteousness.[42] The end product would not be the kingdom of God on earth but rather a community of imperfect Christians awaiting the end time. "For we do not have a city here, in which it is given to remain perpetually," were Zwingli's words to Myconius: "we seek a future [city]."[43]

Even before Zwingli lost his life on the battlefield at Kappel, the synergism of evangelical preaching and political culture had begun to transform the city of Zurich. In line with early Reformed ideas on idolatry, the council commissioned teams of workmen to remove the statues, crucifixes, images, altars, and votive lamps from the parish churches and whitewash the medieval murals. In 1524 the civic officials seized the property of the monastic houses and forbade the taking of vows. Virtually overnight the monasteries, for centuries islands of privilege and prerogative, were integrated into the urban constitution, the wealth diverted to fund schools and hospitals or parceled out to the deserving poor. The council handpicked men in each of the parishes to oversee the collection and distribution of the funds, with each official working on the premise that the wealth had to benefit the commune as a whole. A year later the council suspended the jurisdiction of the episcopal court, setting up in its place a marriage court (*Ehegericht*), an autonomous assembly that gradually extended its range of competence to include a broad range of moral offences and public conduct. Reserving the former ecclesiastical penalty of excommunication for themselves, the city authorities effectively absorbed the powers of discipline once exercised by the bishop.[44]

The reformers who came after Zwingli were more realistic about the place of the ministry in the Christian polity and less ambitious in their expectations of reform. Moreover, the climate had changed after Kappel, with the magistracy now convinced that the clergy should stay clear of matters of state. And so, when Heinrich Bullinger arrived as Zwingli's successor in 1532, he was immediately faced with the decree that henceforth preachers were forbidden to pronounce on political issues from the pulpit. Bullinger resisted and worked out a compromise that granted the clergy the right to submit private memos to the council; but it was clear that the magistracy was not willing to relinquish its authority over the church.

Nevertheless, Bullinger preserved much of Zwingli's legacy by drawing on the same ecclesiological principles. Indeed, with his extreme emphasis on covenantal theology, Bullinger effectively collapsed all lines of discontinuity between church and state and made every baptized member of the Zurich commune equally subject to the conditions imposed by the covenant. "The summary of all laws," he declared, "is the love of God and the neighbour."[45] Despite warnings that too much compromise would endanger the church, he continued to argue in favor of greater civic involvement, especially in matters touching on education and poor relief. Together with Leo Jud, he drafted a new set of ordinances for the synod. Much more detailed than anything written by Zwingli, the ordinances gave a full account of the Reformed church in Zurich. Presided over by both secular and spiritual authorities, the two main figures being the head of the church and the acting mayor, the system of church government described by the ordinances detailed the close cooperation between the secular officials and the clergy. Furthermore, in 1532 Bullinger created a joint committee of magistrates and ministers to oversee the territorial church, an initiative based on the premise that the best secular laws are those that "according to the circumstances of every place, person, state, and time, do come nearest unto the precepts of the ten commandments and the rule of charity."[46] Bullinger was able to preserve, and partially augment, the standing of the clergy during his period in office (he more or less dominated the joint committee, for instance), but in the end the commanding sense of covenant that ran through his theology drew the state even closer to the church.

The model of church and state relations that emerged in Zurich was in many ways unique to the city. It was difficult to transplant in other settings, even in the Swiss lands. It failed to take in Basel, Bern, or Schaffhausen, for instance, in large part because Bullinger's synodal system granted too much power to the resident clergy. Nor was its close fusion of the secular and the spiritual to the tastes of Calvin, who proved a less rigid decalogist in this regard, preferring to keep politics and positive law at a distance from the religious sphere. Nevertheless, the process in Zurich was paradigmatic of the synergism between evangelical ideas and political culture. Relations of power shaped theology, while the norms and the values of the faith provided a foundation for a new biblicized language of rule. It was the first stage in an ideological transition that would reshape the cities and states of Protestant Europe. But in its further development it would not remain an urban phenomenon. Even as the first generation of reformers established Protestant churches in the towns and cities of Germany and Switzerland, a new force was beginning to pull the movement into the gravity of its political orbit. By the late 1520s, the state was beginning to absorb the energy of the early Reformation movement.

The Politics of Faith

Protestant polities

The architects of the first Protestant polities were theologians, men devoted to the glory of God but bound on earth to the service of secular rulers. And they were quick to place the Reformation in the hands of the state. According to Philipp Melanchthon, whose overlord was the Elector of Saxony, the ruler had been invested by God with this charge, not because he stood apart in any sacerdotal sense, but because as "chief member of the church" (*praecipuum membrum ecclesiae*) it was his duty to watch over the Christian community. He was God's agent among men, put in office to rule over the visible church just as he ruled over the state.[47] And more than this: Melanchthon believed, as did Erasmus and many commentators before him, that the state itself was a Christian entity with a religious purpose. Without usurping the authority of the ministry or offending the glory of God, and without trespassing on theological terrain, the state and its sovereign had the duty to preserve the earthly church and oversee the faith. That not only meant creating the conditions for proper worship and the preaching of the Word, but ensuring that the state was ruled in accordance with the divine ordinance.

The theoretical framework that enabled Melanchthon to invest the prince with *de facto* rule over the church was Luther's two kingdoms dialectic. But there was a difference. Whereas Luther considered the rule of the prince over the church a temporary measure, witness to the urgency of the times, Melanchthon granted the secular authority a more positive and permanent role in maintaining the balance between the two spheres. Melanchthon was convinced that extending secular power even further into the realm of religious affairs would result in greater security for the church. In the 1535 edition of his *Loci Communes*, he argued that the secular authorities, as "gods" and "guardians" of the church, had the obligation to uphold true religion and watch over both tables of the Decalogue, not just the final seven commands dealing with worldly relations but the first three as well, those which concerned the externals of the faith and the proper public worship of God. In his view, Christian rulers were "obliged to accept the holy gospel, to believe, confess, and direct others to true divine service."[48] This was a full endorsement of the prince's right to reform the church, and it was adopted by other reformers who helped to construct the Protestant state, prominent among them Johannes Bugenhagen, Johannes Brenz, Thomas Erastus, and Richard Hooker. With some of these men, the conviction that the secular powers had the duty to intervene grew so intense it led them back to the root language of the faith, projecting models of the territorial church while speaking in terms of redemption and sanctification.

This model of reform was not an inevitable corollary of Protestant thought. Other evangelical thinkers, working within the same framework as Luther and Melanchthon, drew the opposite conclusions. In the teaching of the radical Protestants, and in language just as elemental, the conviction arose that the Reformation would not be brought to completion until temporal interference in the affairs of the church and the kingdom of the Spirit had been abolished. This was as much the result of historical circumstance as it was of theological principle, as the initial phase of marginalization and persecution soon convinced many of the radical groups to move from a philosophy of qualified acceptance of the state to passive resistance and finally, once it became clear that the aim of all governments, Catholic and Protestant alike, was to root them out, to separation and rejection. This latter stance is usually associated with the early Anabaptists, and in particular with the Swiss Brethren and the revolutionary leaders of the Peasants' War. The radicals acknowledged that the state was a divine creation and necessary for sinful man, but because they believed that sanctification was possible during this earthly life, they tended to place strict boundaries between the two spheres and counsel separation, lest the purity of the pure congregation be compromised. Magisterial reformers like Melanchthon condemned this schematization, claiming that the idea of a worldly kingdom of Christ was a "Judaic dream and an odious error" and would only lead to confusion and damnation.[49] But the radical alternative continued to tempt Protestants long after Luther first framed the discussion in *On Secular Authority*. It would surface again in milder forms in places as far apart as Moravia and New England.

The first Protestant polities to assume a historical form were built in the image of Lutheran ecclesiology and were closely allied with the state. Indeed, it is worth noting the ease with which the faith adapted to the circumstances of rule. In Germany, the princes already enjoyed a considerable degree of control over the church. By exploiting rights of patronage and guardianship, both of which were legal expedients, territorial rulers had been able to exercise influence over local ecclesiastical affairs. In terms of actually determining the teaching or constitution of the church, however, the most a medieval prince could lawfully enforce (and often only with papal dispensation) was a reform of the monasteries or the supervision of finances. This would change with the Reformation and the idea of the right of reformation (*ius reformandi*) formalized by the Peace of Augsburg (1555), when the Lutheran princes of Germany were awarded the right to determine the religion in their lands and oversee the workings of the church. Among the rights confirmed were the prerogative to introduce religious reform, the right to determine the religion of the subject population (either Catholic or Lutheran), the right to maintain the church property in their possession, and the suspension of all diocesan jurisdiction.[50] All of this was different in terms of the quality and the intensity of secular involvement; and yet this should not disguise the fact that the Protestant polities were the natural outgrowths of their medieval predecessors and borrowed substantially from these pre-Reformation states.

A case in point was the Protestant use of canon law. Although Luther condemned canon law for being the midwife of so much papal corruption, once reform was underway and it became apparent that the freedom of the gospel had given rise to chaos, confusion, and the threat of tyrannical civil authorities, Luther and the other reformers began to look to canon law as a means of restoring order. Naturally, the evangelicals were wary of the medieval codices and tended to draw only on the most ancient sources. And yet as Melanchthon confessed, there must be *some* divine wisdom in a corpus of law that had been around for so long. Provided canon law was kept within the proper sphere – that is, alongside natural law and civil law – there was no reason why it might not provide a foundation for earthly relations.[51] As a consequence, once the Lutheran territories of Saxony, Hesse, Brandenburg-Ansbach-Kulmbach, Württemberg, and Brandenburg began to build up the new church, both the jurists and reformers borrowed freely from the *Corpus Juris Canonici*, the compendium of canon law.

Any number of princely Reformations would illustrate the rise of the Protestant polity, but perhaps the most exemplary Lutheran Reformation occurred in Denmark, where the faith remained the official religion throughout the sixteenth and seventeenth centuries.[52] As in many lands in northern Europe, the movement found its first footings during a period of political unrest, initially under Frederik I (1471–1533), when towns such as Viborg and Malmø adopted the faith, and then under Christian III (1503–59), whose victory in the civil war and subsequent accession to the throne brought with it the formal introduction of the Reformation. While ratifying a range of constitutional changes, Christian also transformed the Danish (and subject Norwegian) church. Catholic bishops were removed from office, replaced by superintendents (also termed "Christian bishops") under the direct control of the king; diocesan jurisdiction was usurped and the monasteries sequestered; episcopal patronage was expropriated along with one-third of the tithes formerly earmarked for the bishops; and in 1537 a new church order was introduced that effectively made the king the supreme authority over the church. As King Christian declared on the occasion of his coronation, he would serve his subjects in both capacities, that is "with the gospel and the sword."[53] All aspects of church governance now fell under the exclusive control of the monarch, from former prelatic prerogatives such as the supervision of visitations and the reform of marriage and education to the more ambiguous areas of parish discipline and church finance. From this point forward, all clergy had to render an oath to the Crown.

This Protestant order remained in force long after the death of King Christian, who after all had been a zealous evangelical and regular correspondent of the Wittenberg reformers. Both Frederik II (1534–88) and Christian IV (1577–1648) continued to cultivate close relations between church and state. Christian IV in particular, whose motto was *regna firmat pietas* ("piety strengthens the kingdom"), presided over a move towards an even more uniform Lutheran state. With the help of the Bishop of Zealand Hans Poulsen Resen (1561–1638), Christian IV purged the land of crypto-Calvinists,

Catholics, and other dissenting sects and imposed a rigid orthodoxy on the land, a course of action Resen celebrated in 1617 with a centenary publication entitled *Lutherus Triumphans.*

Contemporaries recognized that a change had taken place. In the first volume of his *Danmarks Riges Krønike* (1595), the Danish historian Arild Huitfeldt drew comparisons between the reign of Christian III and that of the Roman emperor Constantine. Both oversaw the conversion of their dominions and (as Huitfeld saw it) led their subjects from paganism to the true faith. Both were Christian monarchs carrying out a divine commission. And if we push the analogy further, we might even say that King Christian also had his own early Christian bishop in the figure of the Wittenberg reformer Johannes Bugenhagen, who took up residence in Copenhagen and was instrumental in drafting the mandates of reform, including the 1537 Lutheran church ordinance. Divided into two sections, the ordinance distinguished between that of God's order and that "our" [King Christian's] order. God's order touched on the fundamentals of the faith, such as preaching, teaching, and sacraments; while "our" order dealt with the external form of the church, all earthly aspects of the faith that did not impinge on the content or ministration of the faith. Or as Christian III's great grandson Frederik III formulated it in the King's Law (1665), the king was supreme head of the church, exercising *jus circa sacra* ("jurisdiction in ecclesiastical matters") but not in matters that touched on salvation.[54]

Christian III's claim to be God's agent on earth did not set him apart from Catholic rulers, nor did the emphasis placed on the eminence of the monarch within the church. The essential difference was the extent to which the Protestant prince was both an active participant in the shaping and defending of the church and, as a consequence, the degree to which he could draw on religion to legitimate and consolidate his rule. By way of analogy, in medieval Catholic thought, kingship was defined against the backdrop of two cognate traditions, that of the mystical corpus of the church and the living corpus of the secular realm. Out of this dualism arose the theory of the two bodies of the king. In the Protestant scheme, with the sacral dimension abolished and religion bound so closely to the secular in the compact of the territorial church, the two worlds were united in the person of the prince. There was a single corpus.[55]

Bugenhagen made this point in his coronation sermon for the king of Denmark. Although little of the liturgy had been changed for the event, he stressed that the royal consecration had no effect in the sense of a sacrament. The significance of the rite was symbolic, a means of making sensible the sovereign's pledge to uphold the trust placed in him by God. The ruler was a man like any other; there was no sacerdotal distinction between him and the most lowly of his subjects.[56] This did not have a direct impact on the standing of the German princes, as they were never objects of a sacramental rite of coronation, and yet the explicit desacralization of the rite – and, by implication, rulership – undoubtedly contributed to a shift in perception. As we will see, this would have important implications later in the century once Reformed Protestants in France, Scotland, and England began to challenge the notion of the divine right of kings. In Germany, however, at least during the first century of reform, rather than weakening the standing of the prince, it tended to invest him with even greater authority. Heirs of a divine commission, Protestant rulers began to develop their own notions of godly sovereignty, speaking in terms of the majesty and the charisma of kingship and stressing their unmediated proximity to the will and the Word of God. If no longer sacred, the body of the king now became the living embodiment of the church teachings on conduct and order, a type of personified "theatre of royal virtue," that functioned as an exemplar for the rest of his Protestant subjects.[57] In this sense the standing of the Protestant prince outweighed that of his medieval predecessor, for he did not just represent a sacramental instance of divine favor. The prince had become the broker of the divine covenant, entrusted with the enforcement of his laws and the preservation of his honor, and all with a view to the sacral welfare of the land.

Calvin did not depart in any fundamental way from the political theology of the Wittenberg theologians, though he did go beyond Luther in some minor respects. Although Calvin maintained that all forms of government were divinely ordained, he preferred a slightly modified or popular form of aristocracy, though less *sui generis* than because it best compensated for the failings of republics and absolute monarchs. Like Bucer and Zwingli, he was willing to draw on Scripture as a guide to the construction of a Christian polity. In doing this, however, his purpose was not to construct the kingdom of God on earth, an idea which Calvin considered "Judaic folly," but rather to create the type of order that would best serve the church and keep fallen man in check.[58] This is where the famous biblical casuistry of Calvin the theocrat finds its point of origin, but in fact he never endorsed specific biblical guidelines for rule, just the basic, catholic truths of Christianity, which he thought were already written in the hearts of men and inscribed in natural law. And like Luther, he too believed it was the task of the godly authority, God's legate on earth, to watch over the visible church. To cite the *Institutes*,

> Civil government has as its appointed end, so long as we live among men, to cherish and protect the external worship of God, to defend sound and pious doctrine and the position of the church, to adjust our life to the society of men, to form our social behaviour to civil righteousness, to reconcile us with one another, and to promote general peace and tranquility.[59]

Within the context of the state, the political theology of Reformed Protestantism is usually associated with Thomas Erastus (1524–83), professor of medicine in Heidelberg and physician to Elector of the Palatinate, Friedrich III (1515–76), first of the German princes to embrace the faith. Erastus's endorsement of secular intervention in religious affairs was so pronounced it has become proverbial, though when his ideas are examined at close quarters he seems an unlikely candidate for the first of the secularists. To begin with, most of his thought was derivative, cobbled together from the views of Zwingli, Melanchthon, Bullinger, and Wolfgang Musculus (1497–1563), the reformer of Basel. Second, Erastus was not a public intellectual in the mold of the reformers. Up to his death, his opinions only circulated in manuscript, and thus he never really shaped policy in the manner of a Melanchthon or a Bugenhagen. He wrote to a specific historical purpose: to counter the claims of the Heidelberg partisans of Geneva who argued that discipline, and in particular excommunication, should be exercised by a consistorial system independent of the state. His main concern was to preserve the realm of faith from the corruption of the temporal world. Thus, when Erastus invoked the two spheres of Christian existence (which he termed the internal and the external), he reserved all matters relating to the use of discipline and force to the external church (*ecclesia externa*), which, as it was an earthly institution, was subject to secular law and stood within the power of the state.[60] The internal kingdom of Christ, in contrast, was ruled by faith alone. By the simple default of the human condition, the prince assumed responsibility for watching over all things relating to the visible church, including excommunication. Friedrich made some concessions to the Genevan consistorial system, but the Reformed church in the Palatinate remained a territorial church (*Staatskirche*) and the process of reform was even more intense and comprehensive than in the Lutheran lands.

The rise of the Reformed faith in the Palatinate heralds the start of a second stage of Protestant state-building.[61] Unlike the initial phase of reform, this was a historical process orchestrated from the top down, and often against the will of the subject population, which in the majority of instances was made up of recalcitrant Lutherans. And while the underlying ideology was derivative, the dynamic was unique, primarily because by mid-century the historical setting had changed so dramatically. When the Reformed powers started to emerge, continental Europe was already divided between Lutherans and Catholics. It was a confessionally volatile environment. Thus the states that adopted the Reformed faith tended to be more aggressive than the Lutherans, for as neither the Catholics nor the Lutherans recognized the legal or theological legitimacy of their religion they converted at double the risk. Little wonder that Nikolas Krell, chancellor of Reformed Saxony, turned to the resistance theories of the French Huguenots for support, or that the Calvinist prince Wilhelm von Hesse was so eager to employ clergymen like Urban Pierius, who "understood matters, and will stick with us [Wilhelm] against the papists and others ... and will resolutely defend our Christian religion against the Jesuits and their like."[62] It is easy to exaggerate the martial character of the Reformed state, especially as the latter sixteenth century was in general such a bellicose period; and yet there was a combativeness to the Reformed polities that was not evident in the second- and third-generation Lutheran states. It is no accident that in 1616 the first modern military academy was opened in Siegen by the Calvinist count Johann of Nassau, nephew of Maurice of Nassau, captain-general of the Dutch Republic.

But the distinction between the Lutheran and Reformed reformations was not just the result of political circumstance. There were inherent differences as well. To a greater extent than the Lutheran tradition, Reformed Protestantism held that God exercised his sovereignty in every sphere of human experience. All aspects of earthly life were subject to divine commandment, and this meant that the entire social and political order had to conform to the teachings of Scripture. The Word was viewed as a blueprint for the making of a Christian commonwealth, with particular emphasis on the reform of morality. As a consequence, the subjects of Reformed rulers were exposed to even closer scrutiny by church and state as the prince and his ministers sought to realize the Christian order and uphold the covenant with God. In the Palatinate, for instance, the clergy and the lay authorities, under the guidance of the elector, worked together to implement the changes. Churches were purified of images, monasteries were emptied and inventoried, the schooling system was reformed, church discipline was restructured, and the poor laws were redrafted and the methods of alms-giving placed under state supervision. The Palatine subjects were given constant reminders that they were bound to the upkeep of a Christian society. Alms collections occurred on Sundays in the church as well as Wednesdays and Fridays in the public squares, offertories were gathered in guildhalls, alehouses and inns, while God's Penny was collected at weddings, burials, and feasts.[63] Politically, this idea of a godly commonwealth resulted in an increase in the control exercised by the sovereign, for despite the founding of synods and presbyteries and the evocation of early Christianity, in practice, at least in the German lands, the turn to Reformed Christianity represented an amplification of princely power and a corresponding retraction of the sphere of sovereignty once preserved for the church. Calvinist princes, no less than Lutheran princes, were reluctant to share power with the clergy. On the contrary, responsibility for the faith, as Friedrich IV (1574–1610) of the Palatinate put it, was "the foremost part of our rule as elector and the basis of all temporal and heavenly welfare."[64]

However, before we conclude that the adoption of Reformed Protestantism repre-sented a shortcut to the strengthening of secular rule, it is necessary to consider the broader dimensions of the movement. During the second half of the sixteenth century and into the early decades of the seventeenth, a wide range of states (or significant factions within states) adopted the Reformed faith. On the continent, the crucial conversion was that of the Palatinate Elector Friedrich, who not only attracted many leading theologians to the University of Heidelberg, thus creating something of a bulwark for the religion in the German lands, but also issued a church order and a catechism in 1563 that served as symbolic texts for the tradition. With the faith established and (reluctantly) tolerated by the imperial estates in 1566, other German princes followed Friedrich's lead and introduced the Reformed confession. Most of the German territories were modest in scale and significance, fairly minor enclaves such as Nassau-Dillenburg, Hanau Münzenberg, Sayn-Wittgenstein, and Hesse-Cassel, though in the final decades of the century the rulers of Electoral Saxony (albeit briefly), the duke of Anhalt, and eventually the margrave of Brandenburg converted to the faith. The real gains were made outside the empire, as the Reformed religion also became the dominant form of Protestantism in Scotland, England, France, the Dutch Republic, Hungary, Bohemia, Transylvania, and even the Habsburg lands to the south. At one stage late in the century, the Heidelberg court preacher Abraham Scultetus (1566–1625) thought that the faith would sweep all before it. As he wrote: "We imagined that *aureum seculum*, a golden age, had dawned."[65]

The political repercussions of Calvinism in these lands varied considerably, for the model of ecclesio-political relations common to the Reformed tradition, which favored a synodal or presbyterial system of church rule, did not always translate into an increase in the powers of the state. A case in point is the Reformation in the Dutch Republic. Having emerged as the "public church" after the revolt, the Reformed church in the Netherlands had been closely reliant on the secular authorities from the outset. Yet many of its ecclesiological ideas had been transplanted from the independent con-gregations of England, France, and East Friesland, where church governance was largely in the hands of the local congregations and there was little political interference. Ultimately, this conception of a system of church governance based on national synods, provincial synods, consistories, and local *classes*, had to yield to the political realities of the republic, where power was shared between the States General, the provincial states, and the local cities and towns. And while relations varied from city to city, in most matters relating to the governance of the church, the secular authorities held sway, and that included matters touching on funding, the censorship of theological debate, the content of synodal debates, the appointment of ministers, and the disciplining and excommunication of the parishioners.[66]

These antithetical notions of church and state relations gave rise to serious tensions. In the beginning, the clergy were relatively compliant, grateful for secular patronage. As the church evolved over the years, however, the Reformed ministry became less conciliatory and more determined to preserve the spheres of ecclesiastical rule. One of these disputed areas was the issue of clerical independence, for while the civic magistrates in towns such as Leiden, Gouda, and Hoorn continued to act against unsuitable candidates (by which they meant disturbers of the public peace), the ministers and synods resisted the intrusions of the state. Another was the issue of discipline. Integral to the ecclesiology of Reformed Protestantism was the idea that discipline was fundamental to the faith. The godly ministry must have the exclusive right to exercise this function at the level where it intersected with the worshipping community. But in this as in other fields, the secular authorities aimed to monopolize the exercise of power, the States of Holland going so far as to suggest that a body of four lay commissioners should take on the function of the consistory. None of these issues was quickly resolved, with the consequence that relations between church and state remained precarious throughout the sixteenth century as both sides worked to map out kingdoms of the spirit and kingdoms of the world. And by mid-century, there was a variety of polities to choose from. The clergyman Gaspar van der Heyden, for instance, while preparing for coming battles with the authorities, looked to Geneva for guidance, remarking in a letter to a fellow minister (July 8, 1575) that "there are those who spread the views of Erastus so as better to oppose the discipline. Therefore I would like to have the response of [Doctor] Beza, if you have a copy."[67]

The revolutionary aspect of the political theology of the Protestant reformers was not in its vision of order, which was in its essentials medieval, but in the dialogue it provoked. Neither Luther nor Calvin thought about the state in systematic terms. Their political ideas were derived from their theology. But this was an ideal formula for rethinking the social and political world. The best evidence of theology's creative power was the extent to which the two kingdoms schematic could be problematical in settings where abstract themes such as the nature of Christ, the distinctions between imputed and infused grace, or the relationship between active and passive righteousness were contested. Drawing lines between the church and the state necessarily raised questions about how the Christian was best led to Christ, and the only way to answer questions of this sort was by way of discussions about faith, grace, and charity. Yet all of the magisterial reformers agreed it was necessary to have these lines. As Calvin advised in the *Institutes*: "Now these two [realms], as we have divided them, must always be examined separately; and while one is being considered, we must call away and turn aside the mind from thinking about the other. There are in a man, so to speak, two worlds, over which different kings and different laws have authority."[68]

The issue of order was central to the making of the Protestant polity, but it was equally important to the Protestant individual, as Calvin makes clear, for each Christian existed at once in these two worlds. Yet this synergy of godly state and godly subject raised an additional dilemma. What should a believer do if he or she felt that the state itself, or perhaps an external power, was trespassing into the kingdom of the spirit? At what stage might the defense of Christian freedom move from theology to ideology?

Conscience and authority

In the beginning, the evangelicals gathered in defiance of the Catholic authorities, a state of civil disobedience they frequently justified with reference to the apostolic injunction to obey God before man. But as Protestants grew in strength and numbers, it became necessary to develop more sophisticated arguments in defense of their right to exist. The problematic was not conceived in terms of the private conscience versus public authority, but the "true church" as a whole as defended by the authorities and guided by the theologians. And the dilemma was two-sided: on the one hand, how to challenge the authority of a God-given sovereign without taking on the role of a rebel; and on the other, how to invest their religious conversions with a semblance of public legality.[69]

The first Protestant theories of resistance were conceived by jurists in Hesse and Saxony in the late 1520s when it became clear the Catholic emperor posed a fatal threat to the movement. None of their ideas was new. The themes of allegiance and defiance reached as far back as the works of Cicero, and there was a rich heritage of medieval thought, especially the corpus associated with conciliarism, which helped to guide and substantiate evangelical arguments. Drawing from this tradition, the Hessians formulated a model of constitutional resistance, contending that Charles V did not reign as an absolute monarch but rather shared sovereignty with the imperial Estates. In persecuting evangelicals, Charles had overstepped his office and violated the agreement between the German nation and its elected king. The Saxons, building on theories of private law, claimed that when an authority went beyond the bounds of his office he was no longer a rightful judge but a private citizen. In this case, the emperor was abusing his office by legislating in matters of belief, thus proceeding outside of his lawful jurisdiction and inflicting a notorious injury (*notoria iniuria*).[70]

Taken together, this was the first theory of Protestant resistance, even if largely based on a mix of Roman and canon law and scholastic ideas. What was significant, and distinctively "Protestant," was the religious teleology. The Lutherans felt justified in their resistance because, as Luther taught, it was the essential purpose of the secular order within its sphere to maintain the true church (which in this context meant the church as conceived by Wittenberg), and hence every magistrate of the realm was, as Andreas Osiander put it, "no less ordained of God" to resist evil than the emperor. No magisterial reformer of the first generation granted the private subject the right to oppose a legitimate ruler. Resistance could only be in the hands of the magistrates or, in extraordinary situations, the heads of households or other "patriots" of the realm. But once in the heat of battle it was not much of a stretch to move from godly magistrates to godly individuals. Even Luther's assurance in his *Warning to his Dear German People* (1531) that he would not reprove anyone for defending himself against the unwarranted attacks of the "murderers and bloodthirsty papists" anticipates the role that private conscience would assume for future generations.[71]

The first grand act of Protestant rebellion was mounted in 1546 by the princes of the Schmalkaldic League when they took up arms against the Catholic emperor. When the war finally came, however, it amounted to little. The emperor defeated the Lutheran princes within a year. The significant event occurred some time after the defeat when, because of its ongoing resistance, the Lutheran city of Magdeburg was placed under siege by imperial forces. The siege was the setting for the appearance of the *Magdeburg Confession* (1550), the first systematic defense of Protestant resistance. Published in both German and Latin, it was in large part a synthesis of the theories developed by the Saxon and Hessian jurists.[72] But certain aspects of the argument had been advanced. The gloss on Romans makes the same appeal to the authorities to protect the good and defend against evil, though now speaking quite openly about how the lesser magistracy is required by divine injunction to resist a superior power who rules contrary to the ordinances of God. There was also a more sophisticated framework for understanding how this "ordinance of God" should be conceived, a scheme largely Lutheran in its design, from the idea of vocations and proper spheres of rule to the later theory of three orders. Moreover, the authors of the *Confession* were now more explicit in their assertion that any figure of authority who threatened the existence of a community built in the image of the true faith was necessarily in the grip of the Antichrist, perhaps "even the Devil himself."[73]

The Schmalkaldic War and the publication of the *Magdeburg Confession* represent the highpoint of Lutheran resistance. In the second half of the century, with Lutheranism legalized in the empire, the issue of conscience versus authority became the preserve of Calvinism. In order to survive, the Reformed communities had to adopt the same strategies as the Schmalkaldic princes, which meant justifying their acts of disobedience while undermining the legitimacy of their Catholic opponents. But times had changed. Given the historical circumstances and the threat posed by the reinvigorated Roman church, Calvinist resistance theory went beyond anything developed to that point by the Lutherans, not only in the sophistication of its arguments, but in the extent to which the religious discourse fed on the political dynamic.

The first blast of Calvinist resistance was sounded by the Marian exiles John Ponet (1514–56), Christopher Goodman (1519–1603), and the Scottish reformer John Knox (1503–72), all of whom had spent part of the 1550s in Europe preaching and publishing diatribes against the French regent Mary of Guise and the Catholic monarch Mary Tudor, the latter considered an "open idolatress" and "horrible monster Jezebel." All of these men were casualties of the Catholic counter-advance, and like all disenfranchised prophets much of their thought was devoted to the search for new forms of legitimacy. And they were angry, prototypes of a Protestant specialty – "the saint-out-of-office, the oppositional man, the political radical."[74]

Despite their Reformed backgrounds, however, most of their thought reflected Lutheran theory. Insisting, as Knox did, that the primary duty of secular government was to create the conditions for the preaching of the Word, that the purpose of all earthly rule was to protect the "good" and promote the glory of God, or that all rulers who opposed this order were serving the interests of the Antichrist and could be resisted with good conscience, was to invoke the Lutheran tradition. Yet there were additional aspects as well, even if more shifts in emphases than sharp breaks.[75] Confirming Paul's declaration that "there is no power but of God," by which he meant only "such power as is His ordinance and lawful," the exiles were able to add a further argument in defense of resistance by claiming that tyrants were against the ordinance of God and thus did not warrant obedience. Another advance was in the social spectrum of resistance. When speaking of the magistrates who might legally resist the rule of an ungodly king, Ponet drew on the example of the ephors of ancient Sparta, elected officials who were thought to have represented the will of the populace and served as constitutional checks on the ruler. What was revolutionary was not the use of the example (both Zwingli and Calvin had used it), but the suggestion that the "ephoral" authorities served both the will of God *and* the people. Once assumed, it could be argued that if the authorities did not act themselves, then God, as Goodman proclaimed, "gives the sword into the people's hand."[76]

These Marian exiles revived the dialogue, but the most influential body of Reformed writing on resistance emerged in France, where the sudden death of King Henry II in 1559 set off a struggle for power. What gave the conflict an added edge was the fact that the antagonists were also separated by religion. Roughly speaking, the ruling elite was split between a Catholic faction gathered around the House of Guise, a party of Protestants (or Huguenots, as they were termed) associated with the Bourbons and the Montmorency clan, and a grouping of moderate Catholics and *politiques*, who were anxious to avoid extremes.

French Protestant resistance literature generally gravitates around the work of François Hotman (1524–90), Theodore Beza (1519–1605), and Philippe Duplessis-Mornay (1549–1623). All were active during the French Wars of Religion (1562–98), and all were deeply affected by the Saint Bartholomew's Day massacre of 1572, when Catholic forces slaughtered thousands of French Protestants in the streets of Paris within the full gaze of the Crown. "How can there be any majesty in such a monster [as Charles IX]," asked Hotman after the event, "and how can one accept as a king a man who has spilled the blood of 30,000 persons in eight days?"[77] In search of the answer, the Huguenot authors drew on many of the arguments already synthesized in the *Magdeburg Confession*. What was especially innovative in the French tracts was the detail relating to *who* might resist a tyrannical monarch, a shift of emphasis that pushed the theorists more and more in the direction of popular sovereignty and elective kingship. In the *Francogallia* (1573), for instance, Hotman argued that in ancient Germanic culture sovereignty had been shared between the kings and a public council. French kings had been elected, with power bestowed on them by the representatives of the people. Beza struck a similar chord, stressing how inferior magistrates such as the ephors of Sparta or the imperial electors could unseat rulers if they broke the conditions of rule of their election capitulations and coronation oaths.[78]

But most emphatic in the power he invested in the lesser magistrates was Philippe Duplessis-Mornay, the likely author of *A Defence of Liberty against Tyrants* (1579).[79] Unlike Hotman, who located popular sovereignty in an obsolete public council, and Beza, who looked to the cumbersome assemblies of the Estates-General, Duplessis-Mornay was quite explicit in his contention that sovereignty was shared between the monarch and the magistrates, the latter having been invested with a perpetual right by the people to watch over the king and ensure that he governed within the constitution and the laws of God. Rulers who did not honor these conditions violated both the covenant with the people and the covenant between God and the inferior magistrates and could be resisted and removed from office. And Duplessis-Mornay listed the types of magistrates he had in mind: those in the direct service of the kingdom, such as constables, marshals, peers, and palatines, and those who served a province, city, or part of the realm, such as dukes, marquises, earls, consuls, mayors, and sheriffs. As all of these officials had been called to arms by the civil wars, there is little doubt that most readers grasped the revolutionary implications.[80]

In Huguenot resistance theory the compact between the rulers and the ruled was described in primarily secular terms. In an effort to appeal to a broad audience, moderate Catholics included, the authors employed the more neutral language of natural laws, moral obligations, and mutual political rights. The result was a corpus of thought with the latitude of a political ideology, the best proof of this being the use made of it by the French Catholics, who pushed the arguments even further than the Huguenots were willing to go. Having recognized this, however, we should not overlook the fact that these works were conceived primarily in order to protect and preserve the Protestant religion. Writing "politically" was a rhetorical strategy whose very success has often led to the eclipse of the central concern.[81] Fundamental to all of the Huguenot theories was the query posed at the outset of Duplessis-Mornay's *Defence*: "The question is, if it be lawful to resist a prince violating the law of God, or ruinating the church, or hindering the restoring of it?" The answer returns us to the primary grounds for resistance:

> In short, if the king on the one hand and God on the other were to summon us to do service, who would not decide that the king should be abandoned in order that we might fight for God? So not only are we not obliged to obey a king commanding something contrary to God's law, but also if we should obey, we would be rebels.[82]

The deep logic remained religious, not only the biblical precept to obey God before man, which was a commonplace of the day, but the conviction that the main responsibility of the ruler was to preserve the realm in line with the laws of God as understood by the Protestants. The *Defence* presupposed that all true Christians were in a covenanted relationship with God and had the duty to wage war against the Antichrist and preserve the church of Christ. Hence the reference to "rebels" in the passage above, by which was meant those who failed to honor the covenant. This note was sounded at the outset of the civil war with the call to stand firm against the "violence and efforts of the enemies of the Christian religion who hold our King and Queen captives," and it was just as dominant in the work of Duplessis-Mornay, who structured the *Defence* around a series of leading questions about whether resistance could be justified in the case where a prince acts against the laws of God and the "true religion" (*vraye religion*).[83] Taken to extremes, as it frequently was in times of crisis, the defense of *vraye religion* led to theories that sanctioned regicide (or rather tyrannicide), placed the right of resistance in the hands of the subject population, and even suggested that a prince without proper religion had no right to rule. In such an instance, sovereignty might devolve to the common man, as it had in the Swiss Confederation.[84]

French Protestants did not set out to overturn the state. From the very outset the Huguenot leaders stressed their obedience and respect for the Crown, repeatedly protesting their loyalty and belief in royal justice. The main reason given for resistance was the perceived need to save the kingdom from the usurpation of foreigners. Yet even when theory was not taken to extremes, there was by necessity a state of tension, contradiction, and incompatibility built in to the relationship between the Huguenots and the French monarchy, a mixture of militancy and loyalty.[85]

We can catch soundings of this unease through the various editions of the *Institutes*, as Calvin oscillates between confirmations of secular authority and references to intermediaries with the divine warrant to resist and oppose tyrants.[86] But no degree of casuistry could disguise the fact that Reformed thought had revolutionary implications. Even the Reformed theology of the Eucharist and associated rejection of sacramental religion struck at the heart of the monarchy. For what would a Calvinist population think of a king whose authority had been invested in a coronation ritual termed a *sacré* that elevated him to the level of a mediator of God's grace on earth? And where would France's most Christian king be situated in a religion that recognized no sacral distinctions, cut all ties between the earthly hierarchy and the spiritual realm, organized the church on a local and provincial level, and shared an understanding of the Lord's Supper that absorbed all individuals equally into a broader notion (active and memorative) of Christian community?[87] Nor should we forget that Huguenot resistance continued well into the seventeenth century, and that the ultimate suppression of the radical wing had as much to do with pure military might as with the realization among the Huguenots themselves that the best way to secure the future was by professing and demonstrating their collective loyalty.[88] In the end, although the ideas of the French thinkers had limited impact, the political settlements did not exorcise the fundamental contradictions. Resistance theories would surface again after the Revocation of the Edict of Nantes, and particularly among the refugee scholars of the Low Countries, who would go so far as to suggest that, with the annulling of the edict, Louis XIV had forfeited his right to rule. There was no quick answer to this dilemma of liberty and law.

There were analogous histories in other parts of Europe. Calvinist resistance theory was put to use in the Netherlands during the war against Spain (1572–1648), in the German Empire as part of the resistance movement that fed in to the Thirty Years' War (1618–48), and by the Puritan opponents of Charles I in England (1640–49), where the king was opposed by a mixed bag of theological and constitutional arguments, some of which drew on Ponet and Goodman. The example of France has been discussed because it is particularly illustrative, partly because of the rich vein of theory inspired by the conflict, partly because of the sheer dynamics of the war. But in one important sense it comes up short: France remained a Catholic country.

In Scotland, in contrast, resistance theory played an important role in turning the nation towards the Reformed faith. Following events from his vantage point of Geneva, John Knox provided Scottish Protestants with a discourse of civil disobedience that justified and ultimately legitimated the rejection of the French regency and the overturning of the Catholic church. This had not been the original intention. Knox's first works were directed at the England of Mary Tudor rather than the Scotland of Mary of Guise, the former nation being different in kind, he believed, because it had already entered into a covenant with God under Edward VI and thus stood condemned of blasphemy for its return to Catholicism. Scotland was not yet in league with God.

Once the faith had made headway among the civic burgesses and lowland lairds, however, Knox began to tailor his message for the Scottish situation, eventually visiting his homeland in 1555 and embarking on a preaching tour. While in Scotland, Knox managed to secure the support of a number of noblemen, making such an impact they wrote to him in Geneva two years later with the pledge that they were now ready to risk their lives and their possessions for "the glory of God."[89] Knox obliged with a series of works in defense of resistance, the most significant for the Scottish Protestants being his *Appellation* (1558), a work that essentially synthesized the thought of the *Magdeburg Confession* and placed the right of resistance in the hands of the aristocracy. Although Knox did not intend this to be a call to arms, there were enough blurred lines and ambiguities in his language to make the *Appellation* a manifesto for revolt.[90] And while there was more behind the events of 1559 than just theology, there was clearly a powerful undertone of Knoxian resistance theory in the public statements of the Lords of the Congregation and the first Protestant communities in towns such as Perth, Montrose, Stirling, St Andrews, and Edinburgh. Nor was it totally absent from the sentiments of the Lords who saw through the Reformation in 1560, once the regency of Mary of Guise had been "suspended" and the Catholic church replaced by a Reformed alternative. Indeed, once covenanted, the rhetoric of resistance reached an even higher pitch, Knox himself thundering with regularity against Mary Queen of Scots and her idolatrous Mass.

In one sense, it was relatively easy for men like Duplessis-Mornay and Knox to develop theories in defense of the Protestant conscience for they had a number of high-profile Catholic antagonists to serve as straw men (and straw women) for their ideas. But the issue would not be so straightforward for future generations of theorists as, by the seventeenth century, the question of religious tolerance and rights of resistance would be asked by Protestants ruling over a Protestant people. What would be the relationship between conscience and authority now that rebels had become rulers? This dilemma would not be fully explored until the following century, and the most thoughtful answers would come not from Europe but from the New World. In the sixteenth century, most of the magisterial thinkers were still too busy combing through passages of Scripture looking for the proofs of divinity behind the rise of the Protestant nation.

Scripture and identity

There was nothing uniquely Protestant about singling out a people as the new nation of Israel or claiming that a territory or a homeland was the dwelling place of God. Any early modern nation with a sense of common identity had at some level a myth of divine origins that helped to plot and preserve its own narrative of growth. Indeed, the genealogy of modern nationalism itself reaches back to the age when the nation was imagined in terms of a sacred communion and the destiny of its people predetermined by a covenant with the divine.[91] Throughout the sixteenth century, for instance, the Catholic kingdom of France claimed to be the one true nation of God. Not only did its many apostolic foundations and sites of early Christianity testify to France's pedigree as the most Catholic land of Europe and seat of the *Rex Christianissimus*, but the history of the faith in the land was portrayed as the one unadulterated line of descent that extended from Christ.[92] Other nations could, and did, make similar claims. And yet it was the Protestant lands of the sixteenth and seventeenth centuries that proved particularly proficient at drawing on Scripture to give meaning to their myths and histories of origin. The first Protestants were profoundly influenced by a scriptural idiom that fashioned, by way of rhetoric, allegory, analogy, metaphor, illusion, typology, as well as bare biblical example, a sense of Elect Nation, all of which helped to order contemporary experience and give deeper meaning to the present. Before it had run its course it proved powerful enough to convince men that some nations are called to their destiny "by God as Judah was," as Oliver Cromwell said of his own nation of Englishmen: "A People of the blessing of God; a People under His safety and protection, a People calling upon the name of the Lord; which the Heathen do not. A People knowing God; and a People fearing God. And you have of this no parallel; no, not in all the world."[93]

Protestant nationhood began with the allegories and figurations of the Lutheran princes of Germany, who drew on the common stock of Christian imagery to distinguish themselves from their Catholic rivals. At the Diet of Speyer (1526), for instance, both Philipp of Hesse and Johann Friedrich of Saxony arrived with the letters VDMI(A)E (*verbum domini manet in aeternum* – "God's Word remains in Eternity") stitched onto the sleeves of their livery. Within a few years this slogan had spread throughout the Protestant camp in a variety of media (clothes, banners, coins, swords, powder flasks, horse muzzles, cannon bores, and halberds) and was quickly identified with the evangelical cause. In the art and imagery of the courts as well, symbolism changed. From portraits to theater to music, the Protestant princes began to privilege explicitly biblical themes or exploit motifs associated with the Reformation.[94] More to the point, Protestant rulers began to incorporate Christian imagery in order to distance themselves from traditional Catholic history, often evoking figures or types from Scripture to sanctify local events, such as the Old Testament studies commissioned by Elector Moritz of Saxony (1521–53) for the walls of his loggia, or the more personal visual histories of the Ernestine princes devised with a view to their heroic struggle against the forces of the Antichrist in the early years of the Reformation. The new sense of Protestant identity that evolved in Saxony was meticulously fashioned, and it was nothing less than an attempt to re-imagine the recent past within the framework of sacral history. Hence, in a range of paintings and engravings, Johann Friedrich, defeated and imprisoned by Emperor Charles V after the Battle of Mühlberg, becomes the wounded Protestant warrior, the scar on his cheek as stigma and biblical verse on the edge of the portrait testifying to his role as the new Daniel. More direct was the series of woodcuts depicting the baptism of Christ in the Elbe, with the Ernestine princes and their families, joined by Martin Luther, bearing witness to the event.[95]

In Protestant lands, the biblical turn led to a rethinking of the imagined community. Propagandists began to use Scripture as a type of mirror for the self-imaging of the emerging state. Memorialists of the Elizabethan Empire, for instance, constantly drew parallels with Old Testament histories in order to mark out England's place in the world. The primary proof of election was purity of faith. "Why else was this Nation chos'n before any other," asked Milton in *Areopagitica* (1644), "that out of her as out of *Sion* should be proclaim'd and sounded forth the first tidings and trumpet of Reformation to all Europe?"[96] But authenticity of doctrine alone was not the only testimony to the nation's election. As generations of English Protestants learned from the pages of John Foxe's *Book of Martyrs*, much of the England's religious past had to be understood within the grand Christian narrative – battles between good and evil, captivities and martyrdoms, sufferings and resurrections.[97]

Similar in kind was the language of national identity developed in the Dutch Republic. If anything, the Calvinists of the northern Netherlands were even more profuse in their mimesis of Scripture, drawing on every possible biblical allusion and allegory in order to give some sort of meaning and structure to the newly founded Republic. Of course, much of the typology was conventional, as in the use of Elisha to represent altruism, Potiphar and Joseph innocence, or Job and Tobias fortitude. But there was also a flood of new associations that were distinctly Dutch in provenance – William of Orange as David or Moses, for instance, or the military general Duke of Alba and Philip II as Pharoah – that helped to personalize, and naturalize, familiar stories.[98] The Dutch and the English were especially prone to this cast of Hebraic self-fashioning, but all Protestant communities tended to see their own reflections when they looked into the pools of Holy Writ. For those communities that felt the very existence of the faith was under threat, no doubt this type of association helped to strengthen resolve. Perhaps that is what the Calvinist speaker of the diet was trying to convey when Gábor Bethlen (1580–1629) was elected prince of Transylvania in 1613: "Your Grace is given to us today by God, as he gave David after Saul, or Hezekiah after Ahaz, and we ask that as of old God blessed holy kings from amongst his people, David, Solomon, and Hezekiah, he will bless and sanctify Your Grace with wisdom, truth and bravery."[99]

What made biblical patriotism such a powerful force in the Protestant lands was the sheer ubiquity of Scripture and references to Scripture in the culture. It was bound to take root at some level. This not only had implications for the individual religious conscience, but also for ideas of national identity and collective self-understanding. Once again, the Dutch Republic provides an ideal example. From the beginning the faith was bound up with the history of the Republic. Even if Calvinism could never claim to be the exclusive religion, the fact that it was inseparably linked to the start of the Revolt and the struggle against Spain meant that the views of the church and the rhetoric of the *predikanten* shaped the first accounts of origins. There were other influences as well, notably the antique chronicles and the humanist histories of the modern age, but it was the idiom, imagery, and logic of Scripture that left the most profound impression. There seemed to be too many parallels for simple coincidence. The same plotlines that structured the history of the tribe of Israel helped to account for the Dutch, from captivity and persecution to exodus and rebirth. The cast of characters did not only include William of Orange as Moses, Solomon, David, or a captain of Judah with Philip and Alba in their forementioned roles of Pharaoh as well as the king of Asyria, Goliath, or Saul; the Spanish nation itself was reconfigured as hordes of latter-day Egyptians, Amalekites, and Philistines, while the Republic became the new Zion. Moreover, there was recent history itself, replete with sieges and floods and the crossing of great waterways. Little wonder that Adriaen Valerius (circa 1575–1625) drew such close parallels between Israel and Holland in the closing prayer of *Neder-Lantsche Gedenck-Clanck* (*The Netherlands Anthem of Commemoration*) of 1626:

> O Lord when all was ill with us You brought us up into a land wherein we were enriched through trade and commerce and have dealt kindly with us, even as you have led the Children of Israel from their Babylonian prison; the waters receded before us and you brought us dry-footed even as the people of yore, with Moses and with Joshua, were brought to their Promised Land.[100]

This was more than just an exercise in type and countertype. As the Zeeland minister Maximiliaan Teellinck observed in 1650, the sacral history of the republic implied principles of rule that had to be observed now that the special relationship with the divine had been revealed.[101] The nation and its people were bound to act in a particular way.

Standing in a covenantal relationship with God thus had implications for national development. Not only did it have an influence on how the land portrayed itself, it also shaped the expectations of its public elite. For just as the Children of Israel had to meet the conditions of the Mosaic covenant, so too did the Dutch and the English have to observe the laws lest they forfeit God's favor. This idea was also voiced in the *Gedenck-Clanck*, where Valerius conceded that "when we have not heeded you [God], you have punished us with a hard but Fatherly force so that your visitations have always been meted out as a children's punishment."[102] In the first Protestant nations, a conditional covenant of this kind could work as a powerful force for self-construction. God's favor was contingent on Christian conduct, and this not only required initial moral renewal but constant vigilance, constant scrutiny. And for most self-proclaimed Chosen Peoples, the main struggle was not with modern-day Midianites and Amalekites but with themselves. But there was a flipside as well: when times were good, all evidence of prosperity, expansion, or success in politics and warfare might be read as signs that the ways of the nation and its people had been pleasing to God. And more than this, it could confirm an Elect Nation in its conviction that it was a light for other peoples with a divine commission to expand beyond its own borders. This cast of providentialism was most readily associated with New World expansion, but it played a role in European politics as well, not least during the confessional warfare of the mid-seventeenth century, when both Lutheran Sweden and Anglican England felt that their status (respectively) as God's last bulwark on earth obliged them to intervene on the Continent and come to the aid of the faith, the latter in particular believing that it was the "sanctuary of all the Christian world."[103]

Much of this remained pure rhetoric, of course, and the historian would need a steady hand to tie the various threads of scriptural patriotism to the actual politics of the day. But we should not overlook the extent to which this rhetoric could affect public opinion. In Elizabethan and Jacobean England, it was commonplace for clergymen to discourse on the special relationship between the nation and God. "You are at this day, and long have beene, the astonishment and wonderment of all the world," declared Thomas Sutton in *Englands Summons* (1612) in a typical sermon. "God hath opened the windowes of Heaven wider, and offered more grace unto you ... then to all the Nations under the canopy and roofe of heaven."[104] Protestant England held itself up as the replica of Israel, meaning that it too would fall from God's favor if the nation did not first take stock of its own great sins and prepare to remedy them. Reflecting on the nation in this way does move a bit closer to the modern sense of national identity, for it tends to imagine the community in more impersonal terms, the peoples being joined by a species of contract rather than dynastic or personal bonds.

More important (and easier for the historian to identify) was the shift in the way public figures started to speak about the English nation, stressing its unique place in the world while pointing up the proofs of its election – not the least of which was the fact that it was ruled by a woman, clear testimony of God's paradoxical favor.[105] Above all else there were the constant reminders of the relentless sins of the nation and the wrath of God that was sure to follow. In England, the main forum for the Protestant Jeremiad was the pulpit, and in particular the open air pulpit at the churchyard at St Paul's in London. But the discourse found its way into more popular media as well – pamphlets, street ballads, songs, plays, pageants, even puppet theater – and became a cultural mainstay. Whether it brought mass repentance is doubtful, but what does seem certain is that the very idea of England as the elect nation conditioned the people to think of the country as a whole rather than its parts. Even those parishioners against whom the sermons (to cite Sutton one final time) "proved but like paper bullets shot against a brazen wall" had to sharpen their own ideas of nation in order to reclaim it.[106]

But where Scripture and patriotism formed the most effective union was not in the impulse of self-imaging but rather in the studied fabrication of an image of "the other" – that is, an image of those open enemies of the faith. As a foundation, Protestant communities could draw on the dialectics of the Antichrist discourse. This rhetoric had already done most of the legwork, having conditioned evangelicals to think of Catholics in terms of opposites, inversions, and extremes. Once applied within the context of national identity, however, the idea of Antichrist did not just refer to the Roman church as a whole but to a Catholic nation in particular.

Protestant England offers a final example of the process at work. Disdain for foreigners was nothing new; late-medieval Englishmen already had a stock of stereotypes and prejudices to call on when characterizing Europeans. But by the late sixteenth century the distinguishing mark of a country had become its faith, with the exemplary "enemy nation" in England's case being Catholic Spain, viewed by many as even worse than the Papacy because its religion was masked by dissimulation. As one Englishman remarked, "The Spanish were, and are, little better than Atheists, only making use of the Pope for their own particular ambitions and ends, as to confirm and establish him in unlawful monarchies, and under the colour of Religion to make Subjects become Slaves."[107] Of course, typecasting all Spaniards as shallow in faith and deep in guile said more about the English than the Spanish. It enabled the propagandists to highlight the virtues of the English nation against a backdrop of assumed Spanish deficiencies – English piety versus Spanish guile, English tolerance versus Spanish fanaticism, and so on. But more than this, once placed within the master narrative of the true faith versus the Antichrist (or papacy), now available in Bible translations and recounted in detail in Foxe's *Book of Martyrs*, enemy nations such as Spain assumed a much more threatening profile. As the dangers mounted throughout the Elizabethan era the godless Spaniard and his Jesuit henchmen started to assume extraordinary powers, sometimes described as having the sharpened instincts of animals or the ability to deceive the senses in the manner of a thaumaturge.[108] Only a truly great nation could resist the onslaught of such a formidable foe, a nation that had been chosen by God to do battle against Rome and its Spanish and Jesuitical minions.

Thus, despite the language of crisis and pending doom, the Antichrist discourse could actually work to compose and console the English nation, for not only did it draw attention to the enemy within and point up the manifold proofs, it allowed for the various Protestant groupings to join together in common resistance. Even those Puritans whose consciences chafed at the thought of the Elizabethan settlement could unite with the nation in its war against the Antichrist. To an extent, it was the externalization of the Protestant psyche as reflected through Scripture and applied to national development, the journey from anxiety and despair finding succor in the Word and ultimately salvation and election.[109]

It is easy to make too much of the role of Scripture in the self-imaging of the Protestant state, largely because the states themselves made so much of Scripture. Nevertheless, it remains true to say that Protestant nations such as the Dutch Republic, England, and the German territories were unique in the extent to which they put Holy Writ in the service of the national narrative. But recourse to Scripture did not always lead to the consolidation of the national community, nor was it always meant to. Quite often, even in the work of patriots like John Foxe, the idea of the godly nation was not conceived in the literal sense. Foxe and many other like-minded Calvinists often spoke of the universal church, not the national church, and thus reached beyond profane distinctions such as English or Dutch or German. This meant that the notion of belonging to the true church was not necessarily tied to place of birth, and that not all people within a Protestant land were necessarily part of the godly nation. Naturally, this could contribute more to discord than to unity, as a breakaway group (the elect) within the body politic began to think of itself as distinct from the rest of the realm.[110] And more than this, on occasion their reading of Scripture might lead them to believe that the very nation itself was in the grip of ungodly rulers, and that the only proper conduct for a Christian subject was to resist the state and go beyond the existing church in search of religious purity.

3

Communities

With the rejection of Roman Catholicism and its centuries of tradition and authority, Protestants had to come up with an alternative model of the *corpus Christianum*. And this raised profound questions. What form should the Christian church take and to what extent did it embrace the visible world? Who should belong to it? How might it be gathered? These were issues that touched on age-old questions about the nature of religious community, and to solve it the reformers often reworked medieval arguments while citing the parable of the tares (Matthew 13:30 and Luke 14:23), the two most important proof texts, in order to make their respective positions clear. Either the church should be like the ark, clean and unclean joined together, or it should be a community of saints, a new elect in the New Jerusalem.[1]

When the issue first surfaced in the Reformation, it was with reference to the threat posed to the emerging magisterial paradigm by the Anabaptists and the Spiritualists. All of the mainstream reformers (and the Catholics as well) concluded that the radicals were tares in the garden of the faith. But the dilemma facing Protestants as a genus was that the radicals themselves believed just as passionately that they had no place in the church as it was conceived by men such as Martin Luther, Huldrych Zwingli, or John Calvin. Indeed, some of them, Thomas Müntzer above all, drew on the parable of the tares in order to turn the tables on the magisterial reformers in openly rejecting the churches of Wittenberg and Zurich. In different tones and in different language all of these thinkers were addressing the same concern, namely the nature of true Christianity, and it was not long after the Reformation had begun that individuals and communities surfaced that rejected the schemes offered by the prevailing religious settlements. These were the radicals.

Because the names given to the radicals were imposed on them by others they generally varied according to time and circumstance. In the German lands, the early Lutheran reformers referred to them indiscriminately in terms such as *Schwärmer* (enthusiasts), fanatics, Anabaptists, Sacramentarians, heavenly prophets, or just *Sekten und Rotten* (sects and gangs). In later decades, as both the mainstream Protestants and their opponents acquired greater theological definition, the nomenclature grew more

---

Protestants: A History from Wittenberg to Pennsylvania 1517–1740   By C. Scott Dixon
© 2010 C. Scott Dixon

nuanced. In seventeenth-century England, for instance, the Anabaptists, Brownists, and separatists of the Elizabethan period were joined by dissenters and nonconformists, with each of these groups further divided into smaller units depending on the reasons for their opposition to the established church and the degree to which they were willing to create an alternative. Indeed, many of the English dissenters remained within the church while distancing themselves from a specific point of theology or a particular liturgical practice, often in the hope that an earlier state of purity would return. But underwriting all of the name-calling was the same dynamic of thesis and antithesis: there were always some Protestants who thought that the existing church was not Protestant enough. This search for further purity and authenticity led to the creation of alternative communities, first within the lands of Europe, where they became the foil of the mainstream churches, and then, more successfully, in the lands of the New World, where Protestant communities would emerge that reshaped the nature of the faith.

Biblical Utopias

In early Protestant culture, on a scale without precedent in Christian history, Scripture began to shape and stimulate the religious imagination. Lutherans, Zwinglians, Calvinists, and radicals began to project their personal notions of the faith in visionary terms and imagine utopias fashioned in the image of the Word. Unlike the Renaissance utopias, which generally envisioned a world that was better and more just but nevertheless within reach, the utopias inspired by Reformation thought did not seek to redeem humankind in moral and spiritual compacts. The conviction of sin was too overwhelming. Protestant utopias were designed as worlds where sin and corruption could provisionally be held in check, where fallen man might be contained and, in essence, kept from himself. This was true of both the magisterial and the radical tradition. Only the urgency and the agency separated the two visions of perfect order. No Protestant thinker of any substance imagined a world where God and man were reconciled in full. Only death could do that.[2]

The first reformer to publish a vision of an alternative society based on early Protestant thought was Johann Eberlin von Günzburg (circa 1465–1533), a Franciscan monk who began preaching evangelical sermons in 1521 while based in Ulm.[3] Quickly converted, Eberlin left both his order and the city in the same year, dividing the rest of his life between itinerant preaching and pastoral duties. During the period immediately following his departure, Eberlin wrote his account of the utopia of *Wolfaria* as part of a cycle of pamphlets entitled *The Fifteen Confederates*. Much of the work is medieval in inspiration and eclectic in its approach, but it is an accurate reflection of the outlook of the early evangelicals, and it does reveal at its core the same concerns with the human condition that preoccupied the Protestant mind in later centuries.

In its discussion of the secular order, *Wolfaria* offered little beyond what could be found in late-medieval reform manifestos. In his vision of Wolfarian religion, however, Eberlin was more visionary and his influences more obviously evangelical. In the statutes of Wolfaria, the monastic orders were dissolved, the cloisters emptied and used as schools and hospitals, and the monks turned into citizens. (Eberlin was less temperate with the mendicants, whom he placed under penalty of death.) Church practices were reformed in line with the teaching of early Lutheranism. Marriage, the Mass, and funeral ceremonies were reformed and simplified, the sacraments were reduced in number (though to five rather than Luther's two), and emphasis was placed on the centrality of faith and prayer. Although it is too early to speak in terms of a distinctly "Protestant" utopia, much of this chimes with early Wittenberg thought, including the idea of the priesthood of all believers, the Pauline insistence on faith, the attack on indulgences and good works, and the emphasis on brotherly love. Moreover, in the sections touching on conduct and morality, Eberlin went beyond the rote sermonizing of the early movement and hinted at the later Protestant obsession with the perversions of fallen man. Aware of the immensity of sin and its consequences, the people of Wolfaria were subject to a very rigid moral regime. Adulterers and murderers were put to death, chronic drunks were drowned, and swearing was punished with beatings. Public pastimes were closely monitored and a watch was kept on both the household and the classroom. Sumptuary ordinances regulated styles of dress, beards, and haircuts along with the outward appearance of streets and houses. Even in the churches, the regents of Wolfaria did all they could to mitigate the temptations of the flesh, including the enactment of a statute preventing the use of three-dimensional or over-elaborate images, lest the seeming verisimilitude seduce the viewers and turn them away from the faith.[4]

Wolfaria was prophetic of the Protestant mission of later centuries devoted to fashioning a community in the image of the Word. It was also prophetic of the tensions that would result, pulling between the desire to impose a Christian order and the conviction that the Word alone must do the work. In theological terms, there was nothing the Protestant faithful could do to contribute to the salvation of the community. It was neither a world in the making nor conceived in terms of a holy experiment leading to collective sanctification. *Wolfaria* was primarily a projection of the reality of the human condition (and thus reflected nature rather than artifice) and the purpose of the exercise was to imagine the best possible way to come to terms with sin. Necessarily, there was a strong element of millenarianism in projections of this kind, for the utopian order was not viewed as an end in itself but a final stage in the preparation for the coming of Christ.

Representative of a more equitable notion of utopia was the *Christianopolis* (1619) of the Lutheran pastor Johann Valentin Andreae (1586–1654), written a century after *Wolfaria*. Andreae spent much of his life imagining Christian communities in which relations reflected as far as possible the teachings of Christ. The idea never left him: from Tübingen, where he gathered students and scholars together in pious fellowships, to his deaconate at Vaihingen, where he continued to speculate on the nature of true Christianity in letters and drafted his contributions to the Rosicrucian movement, to the parish of Calw, where in his efforts to witness "faith active in love" he established smaller societies of mutual aid and assistance. Polymathic in his range and an early Pietist in his leanings, Andreae drew on his learning and his pastoral experience to devise in Christianopolis the most comprehensive Protestant utopia of the age.[5]

As in similar works, Andreae adopted the device of a first-person narrator who recounts his tale of having landed on an uncharted island where he had been granted access to a utopia. In scale, however, Christianopolis is closer in kind to a monastic institution than a polity or a city. Indeed, so precise, symmetrical, and harmonious is the layout that, in an act of reverse anthropometry, it has the same mathematical proportions as the human body. In social and economic terms, there is little in *Christianopolis* that could not be found in other utopian works of the day. Labor is communal, housing is modest and identical, money is superfluous, property is minimal. There are no distinctions of birth, the only distinctions being those marked out by God. The seat of government is located at the center of the community, where the ruling triumvirate watch over justice, religion, and learning by ensuring that the laws of Christianopolis, enshrined in two tablets on the walls of the college, are honored by all citizens. In his tour, the narrator visits the various laboratories and lecture theatres where the young are "moulded and shaped to God, nature, reason and the public good" as well as the temple of worship at the center of the complex (thus confirming the christological architectonics of Andreae's vision), all of which provide the institutional setting for the intellectual and religious constitution of the community.[6]

What does *Christianopolis* reveal about the ideal Protestant community? Despite the precision of its layout and the rigorism of its social order, *Christianopolis* was not meant to be read as a blueprint for a future society. It is theological myth of a kind Andreae used throughout his career in his efforts to relate higher truths about the nature of man and the teaching of Scripture. It was utopian in the sense that it represented a projection of the ideal (Lutheran) Christian existence, the perfect balance between the reality of earthly life and the teachings and promises of Christ. It was the embodiment of the world of faith that Luther developed in his idea of the two kingdoms, where he first drew the distinction between the kingdom of the spirit and the kingdom of the flesh. And it was also a faithful reading of the New Testament's views on the kingdom of God: not a call to reform, but a summons to prepare.

In Christianopolis, there is no need for the law in the traditional sense. The community is regulated by the Word to the same extent as Campanella's *Civitas solis* is regulated by the cosmos. Each citizen fulfils his role in the godly compact by assuming the office marked out for him. At the same time, however, there is a recognition that humankind will never reach a state of Christian perfection. *Wolfaria* had a similar message to relate, though Andreae was naturally more attune to the passive role of the believer in the Lutheran compact than Eberlin had been, and he was also representative of the later generation of reformers, men such as Calvin and Bullinger, who were less concerned with the possibility of transforming society and rather more focused on keeping it in check. Andreae was thus much more emphatic in stressing two essential features of the ideal Lutheran world. First, that it was not a community that sought to establish the kingdom of Christ on earth through human enterprise. The only precondition was absolute faith. Inspired by the Holy Spirit, the social and political order would follow from faith, a point Andreae alludes to by reference to the method of instruction in the Theater of Music: "For they very frequently remind the students that they should serve the Creator in relation to their fellow men in the same way as the hand serves the musician, responding to inner commands or external notes by moving, raising and lowering the fingers."[7] The second point follows from this, that the final purpose of Christianopolis was not to create the conditions leading to the complete sanctification of man. Rather, as the chancellor confesses at the end of the work, "Since everything human is imperfect, we have not been able to show you anything beyond our human lot. Nevertheless we have, as we hope, mitigated the burdens of our mortality in the ways which we have shown you."[8] For Andreae, this was the essence of the Protestant utopia: to mitigate the burdens of our mortality. It was all about balance.

Both *Wolfaria* and *Christianopolis* were indicative of the magisterial tradition, less concerned with exposing man to grace than necessary order. Different in kind were the utopias of the early Anabaptists and the radical reformers, and in particular the works written by men who had been caught up in the Peasants' War.[9] Much more than the Lutheran tradition, the utopian vision of the radical Protestants evolved out of an intimate dialogue with the social conditions of the day, projecting a world or a community actively transformed by the Spirit. In the thought of men such as Hans Hut, Hans Hergot, or Thomas Müntzer the moral compact that Andreae presumed would result from faith was the precondition of the utopian order. Many of the radicals spoke in terms of rebirth, purification, and renewal, and they rooted the realization of a collective utopia in the regeneration of the individual soul. These utopias were meant to be realized on earth, fully divine in their origins but brought to fruition through the renewal of the individual. Hence Balthasar Hubmaier's experiential call to arms: "brothers, make your salvation."[10]

Necessarily, this had implications for the type of biblical utopias imagined and developed by the radical tradition of Protestant thought. In his work *On the New Transformation of the Christian Life* (1526), for instance, the early Anabaptist Hans Hergot (d.1527) wrote of the transformation of society that would follow the influx of the Spirit. It was a complete overturning of the status quo. Hergot's ideal community, shaped by a rigid biblical morality, was a land where wealth and privilege had been leveled by Christ's saving sacrifice. Property and goods were held in common, hereditary privilege had been abolished, and brotherly love provided social cohesion. But it was more than just a projection of "right" belief in the mold of *Christianopolis*. Hergot, working within the tripartite schematic of Joachimite millenarianism, held it to be a stage in the unfolding of the divine plan – the first phase being that of the Old Testament, the second of the New Testament, and the third of the Holy Spirit. Utopia was the realization of the final stage. Its coming into being would bring about the active transformation of social relations, not just the model of passive faith described by Andreae. Utopia was not conceived as allegory or alternative, but as destiny.[11]

The spiritual founder of the radical tradition of the Protestant utopia was Thomas Müntzer. In contrast to Luther, who looked to the Word of Christ, and in contrast to Zwingli and Calvin, who looked to the laws of the Father, Müntzer declared true religion a matter of the Spirit. Once the outer man had been broken though suffering and resignation, the Spirit would enter, purify the inner being, and effect a transformation. In large part this was the teaching of medieval mysticism; and yet there was an additional dimension as well, and it was this that enabled Müntzer to adapt his ideas of inner transformation to a vision of the kingdom of God on earth. To begin with, Müntzer did not restrict the effect of the Word to a cloistered elite. On the contrary, he came to believe that it was the peasantry who would inherit the kingdom of God – for it was the common man, rather than the cleric or the scholar, who suffered the most in his earthly existence. Moreover, Müntzer taught that once the Spirit had entered it would not only bring about a transformation of the inner man but also effect a change in the nature of social conduct. What made Müntzer's vision so radical in comparison to a vision such as *Christianopolis* was his conviction that the kingdom of God had to be actively established on earth by mankind. Utopia was not a community of the faithful waiting passively for the final hour. Utopia was willful preparation for the coming of Christ. And what is more, in the view of Müntzer and many of the radical thinkers, the final hour was not just approaching, it had already arrived. As he declared to Nikolaus Hausmann in 1521, *Jam est tempus Antichristi* – "the age of the Antichrist is upon us."[12]

Influenced by Müntzer's life and works, a number of visionaries actually set out to recreate the apostolic church on earth, communities of the godly separated from the mass of mankind.[13] As with the work of Müntzer, there was an overwhelming sense of eschatological urgency, especially in the early efforts, joined to the related conviction that it was necessary to conform as closely as possible to biblical precept before the Last Days. For contemporaries, one feature in particular seemed to set off these communities. Basing their views on a literal reading of Scripture (above all, Acts 2:24–37), the authors of the radical utopias envisioned societies where, as in the age of the apostles, all property and wealth would be held in common. For the most part, this remained in the realm of literary trope. Historically, most of these communities were short-lived, the majority suffering the fate of the Anabaptists in Zollikon, who, as described by the chronicler Johannes Kessler, "broke the locks from their doors, chests and cellars, and ate food and drink in good company without discrimination. However, as in the time of the apostles, it did not last long."[14] As we will see, some of these utopian communities were able to endure over the longer term. For centuries, the Anabaptists of Moravia, the Hutterites, and the Mennonites preserved and realized, to different degrees, the ideals of community, harmony, equality, and holiness projected in the radical utopias. But in most instances, at least during the sixteenth century, their histories were brief.

The Pursuit of Purity

Wheat and tares

Generally speaking, when speculating on the nature of the church and the extended *corpus Christianum*, the magisterial reformers followed the same line of reasoning as Augustine and the majority of the later scholastics: it was a mixed body, both wheat and tares. But not all agreed. Some Protestants began to question and ultimately to challenge the vision of Christian community projected by the leading reformers and the prevailing religious settlements. This impulse to judge the world according to the gospel or the Spirit and reject all compromise with laws and institutions led some spirits away from the mainstream reform paradigms and in the direction of more individual and subjective forms of faith. It also fostered a general resistance to the idea that grace was to be found in formal institutions or hierarchical priesthoods, thereby laying the foundations for the type of religiosity wherein the order of salvation was a personal matter between the believer and God.

Historically speaking, the point of separation between the magisterial vision of Reformation and the radical variant occurred in Zurich within the first few years of the movement. It began with the boycott of the tithe in 1522, was further confirmed by the disagreements over the abolition of images and the Mass in 1523, and was finally sealed with the introduction of adult baptism in 1525. In the beginning, the debate was not about the external characteristics of the church or how it should sit in relation to the city-state, but whether grace was manifest on earth. Huldrych Zwingli, following the teaching of most medieval authorities, did not think it was within the power of mankind to identify the elect. God alone could do that. The church was a mixed body, saints and sinners, wheat and tares. Conrad Grebel and the radicals thought otherwise, however, and it was the conviction that the Word, when encountered at its source and in its purity, could effect a fundamental transformation of both the believer and the community that set them on alternative trajectories. For the radicals, there had to be a conformity of faith with works; there had to be visible signs of affinity with Christ that distinguished the elect from the body of time-serving Christians. Felix Mantz (circa 1478–1527), the first martyr of the cause, explained what was meant by tying the new birth and new life to the Anabaptist understanding of baptism:

> upon one who having been converted through God's Word and having changed his heart now henceforth desires to live in newness of life, and Paul clearly shows in the epistle to the Romans, the sixth [chapter], dead to the old life, circumcised in his heart, having died to sin with Christ, having been buried with him in baptism and arisen with him again in newness of life, etc.[15]

What set the radicals on this alternative course? Above all things, it was their fidelity to Scripture that separated them from the mainstream reformers, their readiness to overturn order and tradition in the search for religious truth. The most significant literal reading of the New Testament was the rejection of infant baptism in favor of the water baptism of adults, a corollary to the conviction that faith must precede admittance to the worshipping community. This was a reading of Scripture that implied both a spiritual and a social passage: once infused with the Holy Spirit, those baptized as believing adults would necessarily seek fellowship beyond the fold. It was also a reading that explicitly rejected one of the main foundations of traditional Christian order, the unity of the *corpus Christianum* created and confirmed through child baptism, and replaced it with a form of baptism based on an individual and voluntary decision. Not all of the radicals were Anabaptists, but for their opponents this quickly became a blanket term for the whole phenomemon.

This same searching biblicism that led to rebaptism also led to the rejection of other aspects of traditional Christianity, and it eventually drove the radicals beyond the bounds of the communities established in Zurich and Wittenberg.[16] From their denial of the small tithe and all of the outer ceremonials of the medieval church to their radical re-readings of the meaning of the Eucharist and the make-up of the worshipping congregation, the spiritual heirs of men like Müntzer and Grebel pushed the first principles of Protestantism further than the mainstream reformers were willing to go. Ultimately this pursuit of purity and fidelity in the reading of Scripture would lead to secular consequences, as many radicals found evidence in the Bible to refuse to swear public oaths, to place bans on the carrying weapons and violence of any kind, and to adopt a marked simplicity in worldly things (clothing, housing, personal possessions), and even new modes of greeting and habits of speech. The underlying logic was a resolute commitment to the revealed truths of Scripture. As Grebel declared, "what we are not taught with clear scriptural examples shall be to us as if it were forbidden, as if it were written not to do."[17]

The biblicism of the radical movements quickly exposed the perils and paradoxes inherent in the Protestant discourse of law and gospel. From one standpoint, the aversion to traditional Christianity prompted some interpreters to repudiate ceremonials altogether and project a clear break between the New Testament and the Old. In response to the talk of accommodation voiced by Wittenberg, Zurich, and eventually Geneva, some radicals proclaimed that the Word brings with it the "freedom of the spirit that comes with the new covenant pertaining unto the children of God through Christ."[18] Yet from another standpoint, too literal a reading could easily be seen as a turn towards Hebraic legalism and a renewed trust in the works of men. Luther made this point in his quarrel with Karlstadt over the iconoclasm of the early Wittenberg movement. There is little difference, he wrote, between this type of religion and the teaching of the medieval church:

> Both are enemies of Christian freedom. The pope destroys it through commandments, Dr. Karlstadt through prohibitions. The pope commands what is to be done, Dr. Karlstadt commands what is not to be done. Through them Christian freedom is destroyed ... on the one hand, when one commands ... what is to be done, although it is not so commanded by God [that is, the new traditions of the pope which lack a biblical basis], and, on the other hand, when one forbids ... doing that which is neither prohibited nor forbidden by God [Karlstadt's rejection of allegedly neutral religious practices].[19]

In their attack on the externals of worship and their ideas on the indwelling of the Spirit and the consequent rebirth or regeneration of fallen man, the radicals, Luther charged, had turned the gospel inside out. According to their teachings, salvation was no longer reliant on the external intervention of Christ, but rather on a type of reconfigured works-righteousness of introspection and self-analysis that subjected faith to the fulfillment of the law and turned Christ into a moral exemplar. To Luther, men like Karlstadt were replacing the gospel with their own mad fantasies about the order of salvation and the Christian ascent to God.[20]

Perhaps even more threatening to the magisterial reformers than the perceived legalism of preachers such as Karlstadt was the emergence of individuals who had been inspired by the evangelical movement to speak of a direct relationship between the believer and God and the need to do away with the external forms of religion. Luther had this aspect of the radical tradition in mind when he spoke of the enthusiasts (*Schwärmer*) who surfaced in Wittenberg and the surrounding villages of Saxony. But the rise of the Protestant Spiritualists was not limited to the lands of the Lutheran or the Zwinglian Reformations. The historian Sebastian Franck (1499–1543), himself a Spiritualist, considered it the fourth and final strand of the Protestant family:

> There already are in our times three distinct faiths, which have a large following, the Lutheran, Zwinglian, and Anabaptist; and a *fourth* is well on the way to birth, which will dispense with external preaching, ceremonies, sacraments, bann and office as unnecessary, and which seeks solely to gather among all peoples an invisible, spiritual Church in the unity of the Spirit and of faith, to be governed wholly by the eternal, invisible Word of God, without external means, as the apostolic Church was governed before its apostasy, which occurred after the death of the apostles.[21]

What was especially threatening to the magisterial reformers was the nature of the Spiritualist claims to knowledge and truth. Religious understanding was not mediated by words or rites but by deeply subjective modalities such as dreams and visions. Few ideas could have been more antithetical to Luther, who could not imagine the Spirit divorced from the external Word.[22] The tone had been set by Müntzer in the 1520s with his claims to divine insight and heaven-sent dreams, and the magisterial reformers were quick to act. Luther claimed the age of prophecies had passed and put their visions down to the devil's work (while demanding external proofs as well, just to be safe); Bullinger drew on the discourse of humors and melancholy and declared them mad; while Calvin rejected the Spiritualist epistemology, pointing out that true faith was "well regulated" and witnessed by a piety that "gathers itself in its limits," while the thought of the radicals was chaotic, disorderly, and nurtured in "great licentiousness," this latter trait being the first seedbed of superstition.[23]

Numbered among the prominent Spiritualists of the sixteenth century were Caspar von Schwenckfeld (1490–1561), who began as an early supporter of Luther before turning inward in the quest for the rebirth of Christ in man; the itinerant physician and occultist Paracelsus (1493–1541), who rejected all association with the churches of his day, claiming that "it is a sin against the Holy Ghost to say: the Pope, Luther, Zwingli etc. are the Word of God, or speak to us from Christ"; and the German pastor Valentin Weigel (1533–88), theologian, philosopher, and mystic, whose spiritualist writings circulated widely in manuscript and influenced generations of readers with their focus on religious individualism and the need for the old Adam in man to die before Christ might be reborn. None of these thinkers influenced Protestant development in the sixteenth century to any significant degree. Their followers remained scattered and tended to gravitate around principles and aspirations rather than communities of belief. If there was a center of Spiritualist activity in the sixteenth century, it was probably the imperial city of Strasbourg, the entrepôt of the magisterial and radical traditions in the southern empire, where some of the more extreme evangelicals began to preach and write against the Constantinian settlement, the conclusions of the early church councils (including the Nicene council), and traditional teachings on Christology and the Trinity. Both Schwenckfeld and Melchior Hoffman, for instance, speculated on the divinity of Christ while resident in the city.[24] But the Spiritualist influence would first emerge as a powerful force in the seventeenth century, and in particular when the works of Franck, Paracelsus, and Weigel were rediscovered and interpreted for later generations by Johann Arndt (who, as we will see in a later chapter, was one of the founding fathers of German Pietism).

Even after the fall of Münster, the radicals remained a presence in the parishes of Europe. Experts at the art of subterfuge, they had to suffer the fate of all people in the early modern period who challenged traditional ideas of order and community: ostracization, persecution, or death. Both the methods and the intensity generally varied from territory to territory. Some rulers, such as Ferdinand of Austria, were willing to ride roughshod over traditional liberties to root out suspect Anabaptists, while others, Landgrave Philipp of Hesse being a notable example, were very reluctant to persecute any of their subjects purely on the basis of belief. There was thus a large degree of discrepancy and variation in the enforcement of the laws, even if there was a general consensus that they could not be accommodated within the magisterial order.

In southern Germany and the Swiss lands persistent Anabaptists and suspect radicals, and in particular previous offenders or those who actively contributed through baptisms or teachings, occasionally suffered death as a consequence of their beliefs, whether through burning, beheading, or drowning in the local rivers. Other forms of punishment included mutilation of the body – cutting the tongue, branding the cheek, chopping off fingers and ears – imprisonment, either for a predetermined period or until there was a full retraction and conversion, exile or temporary expulsion, usually preceded by a whipping through the streets and followed by a confiscation of all earthly goods. The imposition of a fine was also a possibility, though it could be set at such a high rate that the victim could not pay and ended up incarcerated anyway. And there were less formalized, more subtle methods as well, including the prohibition of public meetings, the creation of a furtive police force to roam the streets, and the schooling of the local population into habitually informing on their radical fellows. The Lutheran theologians of Tübingen went so far as to advise that known radicals be forced to wear wooden boards hung around their necks painted with wolves, snakes, or imagined monstrosities, to warn those within proximity of their bodies of the dangers that lurked within.[25]

The Lutheran Church was particularly relentless in its harrying of the radicals. It mounted a campaign that stretched well into the seventeenth century, no doubt the result in large part of the close cousinage of the two movements, historically and theologically, in the early years. No one knew the dangers of seduction better than Philipp Melanchthon, one-time benefactor of the Zwickau prophets, who warned his parishioners against the false promises of these wandering sects. "Do not let yourself be deceived by the comportment of the Anabaptists," wrote Melanchthon in 1536, "by their lifestyle, and by their willingness to become martyrs for their faith. All their revelations are lies, their humility is pretence, so is their great brotherly love, their patient endurance of suffering, and the audacity and stubbornness with which they approach their death. All these are tricks of the devil."[26] Moreover, in the eyes of the Lutherans, the so-called enthusiasts and dissenters had none of the traits that characterized a magisterial confession – no church, no dogma, no rule – unlike the Calvinists and Catholics, who had clearly defined theologies and institutional shapes (and were therefore familiar, if inverted, images of themselves).

Thus the campaign against the radicals was not a religious conflict in the traditional sense, not the same sort of cold war that Wittenberg was waging against Rome or Heidelberg, for there was no clearly defined enemy and no clearly defined corpus of ideas. Instead, the danger was thought to be lurking *within* the church, a threat considered so real and so profound that the Lutherans argued it would result in the end of all social and religious order if it were not contained. In his 13-volume compendium of the heretical (or radical) tradition, the *Catalogi Haereticorum* (1597–99), Conrad Schlüsselburg (1543–1619), the superintendent of Stralsund, described the followers of Schwenckfeld as belonging to a sect that had no affinity with Christianity, for there was no finished corpus of teaching that spelled out the nature of proper faith. Instead, the typical Schwenckfelder chose to "creep in his corner" and spread confusion and division.[27] This type of thinking was also behind the clause concerning the radical tradition in the *Formula of Concord* (1577), which warned against the many sects that had arisen since the Reformation, "some of which teach many errors, others teach fewer. But in general they profess doctrines of a kind that cannot be tolerated either in the church, or in the body politic and secular administration, or in domestic society."[28]

Despite the best efforts of the magisterial reformers, the radicals remained a living presence. And yet even though persecution did not root them out, it did substantially reduce their numbers and marginalize the communities, all of which makes it difficult for historians to recover their early histories. Having no overarching identity of their own, the radicals generally went by the names given to them by others – sacramentarians, enthusiasts, heavenly prophets, Spiritualists, Anabaptists (*Wiedertäufer, wederdooper*). Moreover, in view of the disparate nature of the radical tradition, both in terms of origins as well as intentions, it is difficult to map out clear patterns of migration and dispersal. Nevertheless, as there were clearly some traditions joined by teachings or charismatic leaders, it is possible to detect the movements of the main groupings.

The heirs of Karlstadt and Müntzer tended to exercise the most influence in the lands of south-central Germany and Habsburg Austria. Because the exchange of ideas with the Swiss tradition was not uncommon, sharp lines are difficult to draw, but the Germanic strain did have certain features that set it apart. In particular, there was a greater emphasis on the role of the Spirit and a heightened apocalypticism. Much of its revolutionary force was thus fed by a deep and volatile subjectivism that readily translated into radical programs of reform. The main missionary in the south-German lands was Hans Hut (1490–1527), once a close follower of Müntzer who, having escaped the battle of Frankenhausen, where huge numbers of rebels were slaughtered by the princes, embarked on a life of preaching and baptizing in Franconia, Thuringia, Austria, and Moravia. With Hut we can identify a line of continuity reaching from the Saxon Anabaptists back to the revolutionary armies of the Peasants' War. Nor was he alone. Other prominent Anabaptists in southern Germany included Balthasar Hubmaier, Hans Denck, Melchior Rinck, and Hans Römer, all of whom had played a prominent role in the Peasants' War before taking up a life in the service of the faith, moving from parish to parish preaching and baptizing and gathering souls.[29] Of particular importance was the company of Anabaptists in Strasbourg. Their brand of sacramentalism had a direct influence on Melchior Hoffman, and it was Hoffman who would spread the message in north Germany and the Netherlands, his millenarianism eventually providing the foundations for the rise of the Anabaptist kingdom in Münster.

Swiss Anabaptism evolved separately, even though the Zurich radicals drew inspiration from Karlstadt and Müntzer. If south-German Anabaptism was distinguished in large part by its spiritualism and its heightened apocalypticism, the Swiss variant was equally unique in its profound biblicism, its belief in the necessity of separation, and its faith in the fruits of sanctification. There is also a much more thorough narrative of origins to Swiss Anabaptism, which to an extent is the story of how the search for purity as conceived by Grebel and his followers gradually took them beyond the Zurich settlement, progressing from opposition to tithes and images to the mass and finally to adult baptism. Not long after the second disputation (1523) the radicals began to disperse, many gathering supporters in the dependent rural parishes, as, for instance, Wilhelm Reublin did in Witikon. Prominent figures such as Grebel, Felix Mantz, Georg Blaurock, and Johannes Brötli became hedgerow preachers, moving through the parishes of north Switzerland, Alsace, South Tyrol, and Swabia, as well as large cities such as Basel and Bern, teaching their version of apostolic Christianity and baptizing followers. In a few instances local congregations formed. But most bands were quickly rooted out by the authorities and forced to disperse, some traveling eastward to Silesia and Moravia, others heading north to East Frisia or the Low Countries.[30]

However, most Anabaptist success was not registered in the Swiss or south-German lands but to the east in the frontier kingdom of Moravia, where a unique constellation of political and historical conditions made it possible for Anabaptist churches to lay down roots. First to gather were the followers of Hubmaier and Hut in the town of Nicolsburg, where communities developed that practiced believers' baptism and strict congregational discipline. Following a quarrel over the theme of resistance and non-resistance, a group moved on to Austerlitz, and it was from there that Jacob Hutter, founder of the Hutterites, would catch word that "God had gathered a people . . . to live as one heart, mind and soul, each caring faithfully for the other."[31] A combination of overcrowding and infighting gave rise to schism and effected a further migration to the settlement of Auspitz, where, under the leadership of Philipp Plener, refugees from Swabia, the Palatinate, and the Rhineland were able to gather a substantial community until it was scattered by renewed Habsburg efforts. Numerous histories of this kind could be told.[32]

In the vast majority of instances, the first Anabaptist congregations were short-lived and isolated experiments in apostolic Christianity, scattered by persecution and divided by theological opinion. Even during those brief interludes when the threat of persecution was at a minimum, they tended to remain disparate rather than parts of a whole. When the Italian weaver Marcantonio Varotto (Barotto) visited Austerlitz in the mid-1560s, he was struck and somewhat confused by the sheer multitude of opinions and the lack of unity. As he wrote on his return to Venice:

> I left Moravia because during the two months I spent there I saw so many faiths and so many sects, the one contrary to the others and the one condemning the others, all drawing up catechisms, all desiring to be ministers, all pulling this way and that, all wishing to be the true church. In one place alone, and that small enough, called Austerlitz, there are thirteen or fourteen kinds of sects.[33]

This was a fractured Christianity, a religion without a church.[34] The radicals tended to meet in small conventicles, sometimes in houses and farmsteads but also in cellars, gates, wayside shelters, clearings, water towers, forests, meadows, or "windstill zones," border areas where jurisdiction was contested. Once gathered, they would work through readings of Scripture under the guidance of men marked out for the task (readers, shepherds, servants of the Word) who would also oversee a service that relied on lay participation in the rites and rituals rather than just imputing their effects. In St Gall, for instance, lay-led Bible-study groups first met in private houses, took over the butcher's hall when the group grew too large, and then moved to the church of St Lawrence when the hall (with a capacity of 1,000) no longer sufficed. "For the first time," remarked the chronicler Johannes Kessler, "against the old custom, common people read or taught in the church."[35] Indeed, the magisterial reformers frequently commented on the extent to which the movement was made up of the common people, by which they meant the disenfranchised, men and women without substantial property or power whose stake in society inhered in the multitude. And they were more or less right. The vast majority of the followers of the Anabaptists and radical preachers were unlettered craftsmen, day-laborers, and rural peasants. The very demographic makeup of the movement represented a threat to established order. Its members were largely masterless, transitory rather than resident, with little property and therefore little to lose; many of them were willing to pack up and leave a village home in an instant (sometimes leaving wives and children behind) if a charismatic preacher convinced them of the need. It is telling of their general social condition that the authorities tended to identify them with reference to the shape of a hat, the color of a shirt, or the cut of a beard, as if their limited personal effects formed a more dependable description than any reference to residence or employment.[36]

A lay preacher of southern Tyrol by the name of Wölfl (Wolfgang) was a typical radical of this description. Originally an illiterate shepherd in the mountains of Tyrol, Wölfl was taken by the preaching of the evangelicals and converted to the cause. After an Innsbruck schoolmaster taught him how to read print so that he "might defend himself with the gospel and the Word of God," he became a colporteur of evangelical pamphlets, eventually preaching the message himself to the peasants and miners in the Tyrol. He traveled extensively, preaching, teaching, and debating with parish priests in the parishes of Inzing, Oberperfuss, Kematen, Füssen, Innsbruck, Hall, Gufidaun, and Bozen, eventually moving through the Puster Valley as well, before he was finally arrested in Brixen in 1527. When the inquisitors pressed him on his religious views, which had gradually become more radical over the years, he confessed that he believed the New Testament sufficed for the essentials of the faith. Of the outer forms such as the Mass, the church, the saints, the canon laws relating to marriage and fasts, even objects of worship such as the crucifix, which he compared to "sticks thrown at dogs or used to heat stoves," he thought very little. Only Scripture, which was open to all men, spoke of God's design.[37]

With the appearance of the dissenting or radical Protestant a new type of early-modern Christian community evolved. Voluntary rather than coincidental or pro-prietorial, it was made up of people whose search for purity had inspired them to reject the existing confessions, separate in part or in whole from the *corpus Christianum*, and adopt a set of beliefs and associated practices that were shaped to a large extent by inner convictions rather than institutional or orthodox fiat. It was thus an "exodus from history," but only because the magisterial churches could not accommodate their vision of a return to early Christianity, this turning back of the eschatological clock far enough to effect a restoration (*restitutio*) of the apostolic age. Persecuted by the secular authorities, rejected and cast out by the magisterial reformers, it was natural for these sects to gravitate towards isolation. And once it became clear that the mainstream Protestant movements would not accommodate them, the radicals no longer thought in terms of a church that encompassed the pure of faith under the guardianship of the state (though the evidence would suggest that this had been the initial idea); instead, they set out to recreate a community of apostolic Christianity separate from the impurities of the world. Suffering became one of the marks of the true church.[38]

The character of a community inspired by thought of this kind is best illustrated by one of the success stories of Moravian Anabaptism: the Hutterites. Followers of Jacob

Hutter (circa 1500–36), the Hutterite communities were conceived as tangible demonstrations of the conviction that faith brings with it a transformation of the Christian man, that true religion entails a graduation from understanding to rebirth (or as the theologians put it, from *fides historica* to *fiducia*). The first substantial synthesis of Hutterite belief was written by Peter Riedemann (1506–66), one of the men who took over after the death of Hutter. In a work entitled *Account* (1540), drafted while he was in prison, Riedemann summarized the essentials of the faith. Paramount was the idea of separation, a notion in keeping with Hutter's sense of mission as well as his tendency to think of himself as an apostle of the latter days "whom [God] has established as watchman, shepherd, and guardian over His holy people, over His elect, holy, Christian congregation."[39] It was thus natural that Riedemann would act on this sense of election, calling on the community of saints to break away from the world in order to preserve the true church from corruption. God's covenant with the nation of Israel provided the faithful with a prefiguration, but for the Hutterites more than just law was at issue. Riedemann believed that the community itself was the outward expression of inner sanctification. According to Riedemann, the Old Testament covenant had been replaced by the covenant of the Spirit, restored by Christ. The elect, those few who had been renewed by the Spirit, were guided by Christ alone and would necessarily behave in a Christian manner.[40] Hence the importance of separation and community: both were manifest proofs of the eternal covenant with God.

For the Hutterites themselves, the most profound demonstration of their election was the practice of community of goods. The idea itself was not new. The well-known references in the Acts of the Apostles had been the foundation text for a number of medieval experiments. Moreover, the communalization of goods and the redistribution of property had been one of the main demands of the revolutionary manifestoes of 1525.[41] Despite the associated hazards, the idea surfaced again in some Moravian communities and ultimately became the distinguishing feature of the Hutterite religion. It followed logically from the notions of faith and sanctification defended in works such as Riedemann's *Account*. What better proof of the living faith wrought by the Spirit than the ability of men and women to live together in harmony without desire or need for worldly goods? That is why God had established community of goods, argued one sixteenth-century apologist, "for in a just community there is no place among its people for the sinful tokens of finance and swindle, buying and selling, egotism and stinginess, usury and the excesses of vain creatures, and other and sundry unholy works."[42] This was the ultimate testimony to the radical ideal of renunciation and the indwelling effect of the Word. It also confirmed and preserved the idea of separation, for those who could not meet the demands of such a community of saints – in other words, those who were lacking in the Spirit – did not belong. It was a self-confirming, eternal covenant, for faith created the community and the community facilitated faith, and over the course of the century it became dogma, a precondition for salvation. It also gave rise to a dynamic religious culture. Historians have identified up to 120 Hutterite settlements (*Brüderhöfe*) in this period, each having between 200 and 400 residents, living, working, raising families, and worshipping together in a communal environment.[43]

In many of their particulars, the Hutterites mirror how the radical communities of the sixteenth century perceived both themselves and others within the narrative of

Christian history. Yet they were part of a religious tradition that is difficult to circumscribe. The radicals did not comprise a unified confessional community. There was no fixed corpus of ideas or sanctioned orthodoxy binding them together as there was with Catholics or Lutherans. Nor were the German and Swiss radicals anchored in place and time to the same extent as the members of these churches. *Restitutio* was not a concept that cultivated close ties with the present. Historically, the religion of the radicals was shaped less by formal thought than by aspirations; their rejection of traditional Christianity was not captured in lengthy dogmatic treatises but registered through gestures, rituals, actions, and language. The unavoidable outcome of a religious culture that placed so much stress on inspiration and conscience at the expense of forms was heterodoxy. As Müntzer put it, closing up the distance between God and the believer had opened the mouths of believers, unstopped their ears, and enabled them to converse with "heavenly voices."[44]

The radical tradition was thus rich, and continued to be rich, in disagreement, contradiction, and speculation. But all of this just reminds us that the very notion of radical was in the eye of the beholder. One man's enthusiasm was another man's religion. To seek further purity or authenticity remained the prime objective of the radicals throughout the confessional age, and it would be profoundly articulated in the late-seventeenth and early-eighteenth centuries with the rise of revivalist movements in continental Europe. But even before the radical spirit was reawakened in the homelands of the Lutheran and Reformed traditions, the dialogue resurfaced in England, where Puritan critics of the Elizabethan and Jacobean settlements began to breathe new life into the Protestant discourse of purity and essence, with some of the most pressing of the Puritans taking up themes that had not been discussed in any substantial sense since the defeat of the first-generation of radicals in Saxony and Switzerland.

Godly people

To an extent the Puritan episode in England was simply the reenactment of the debates and developments that had shaped the Lutheran and Reformed communities in Europe: the same dialogue deferred. But there was a difference, and it proved fundamental for the making of seventeenth-century Protestants. For nowhere in continental Protestantism had the dialogue ever been so personal or so charged with a heightened ethical and psychological dimension, to the point, indeed, where the future of the church really did turn on the pricking of conscience. And nowhere else in Protestant Europe had the implications of belief for daily life ever been probed so deeply, and so publicly, by so many minds, and in large part because what separated the Puritans were less issues of principle than questions of degree. For all of the main protagonists could agree that religious truth was only to be found in "things necessary."[45] What they could not agree on was what that meant in practical terms. How much formal religion should there be? And how much liberty?

Calvinism as a state religion came with the accession of Edward VI (1537–53), whose reign marked attempts to implement further reform, partly by targeting the traditional forms and gestures of worship and partly by introducing Reformed theology into the confessional statements of the English church. The central architect was Archbishop

Thomas Cranmer (1489–1556), whose close contacts with continental scholars not only led to an influx of leading reformers to Oxford and Cambridge but also laid the theological foundations for English Protestantism, which from this point forward was derived from the Swiss rather than the Saxon tradition. The main vehicles for the spread of these ideas were the two prayer books of 1549 and 1552 as well as the Forty-two Articles of 1553. With the relaxation of Henrician censorship, the theology was taken to the parishes in texts, sermons, and acts of state, such as the 1547 visitation of the parishes and the repeal of the heresy laws. This was the first sustained attempt to fashion the English church in the image of Reformed Protestantism, and not all people welcomed the change. Writing from the vantage point of the reign of Edward's successor Mary, the London stationer Miles Huggarde thought this period had opened the gates to religious chaos:

> O devilish liberty, I would to God Germany might have kept thee still: so England had never been troubled with thee. I would to God thou haddest had all our English beer to drink drunk with Hans and Yacob in Strassburg, upon condition London had never retained thee. I would to God thou haddest remained in Swicherland a conquerer, so that thou haddest never had conquest in England.[46]

But the seeds of religious liberty had been sown, and with the martyrdoms of the Marian interim having heightened the evangelical purpose, there was a profound sense of expectation when the Protestant Queen Elizabeth I assumed the throne in 1558. "We have a wise and religious queen," wrote John Jewel in a letter to Bullinger, "and one too who is favourably and propitiously disposed towards us."[47]

With the Acts of Supremacy and Uniformity (1559), the stage seemed to be set for the making of Europe's most powerful Protestant kingdom, but because Elizabeth pursued the letter rather than the spirit of early Edwardian reform, her church settlement, at least in the eyes of the "hotter" sorts of Protestants, remained a half-hearted compromise. Most of the clergy remained within the church and integrated without too much fuss, claiming it was better to accommodate than to resist and brushing off criticisms with reference to adiaphora. A very small number separated. But there were others who, though remaining within the church, continued to criticize the Anglican settlement, its "unprofitable ceremonies," and its likeness to popery. These were the Elizabethan Puritans, a group of men and women who were hypersensitive to the forms or formalities of traditional Christianity that had no obvious ancestry in Scripture.[48] Unlike the dissenters in continental Europe, the majority of Puritans remained within the magisterial church: they were beneficed clergymen, Cambridge professors, even bishops. And unlike the Lutheran and Reformed settlements in the empire, there was a sense of ambiguity in the Anglican settlement and a latitude of clerical opinion that left the Elizabethan Reformation "open" long after other Protestant powers had started to close up and confessionalize.[49] So, while the Lutheran clergy began to consolidate the church and its teachings in Germany and Sweden, the Puritans of England railed against the remnants of popery in the church and pressed for further reform.

Among the "abuses" Puritans set out to eradicate were the following: chancel ornaments, overly elaborate ritual, liturgy, and music, the cross at baptism, and the act of kneeling at Communion. One of the main flashpoints arose over the question of clerical dress, for the English clergy were still expected to wear the vestments of the pre-Reformation era. This so-called vestiarian controversy, while a fairly insignificant matter in the eyes of many (including the Swiss reformer Bullinger), was in fact an issue that touched on the fundamentals of religious order. Though less concerned with theology than ceremony and symbolism, the critics of clerical dress raised the same issues as the early Reformation movement, including questions relating to the role of the state in relation to the church, the right to force beliefs, and the justice of tallying for weaker consciences, and thereby reopened debates about the relationship between order and freedom.[50]

In their pursuit of further reform, some Puritan communities were able to realize quasi-presbyterian forms of rule similar to the French model – wholly voluntary associations, using church wardens or sidesmen as elders, stipendiary preachers as doctors, congregations of ministers that acted in effect like classes, and a hierarchy of synods held together by correspondence. It was an imperfect system and varied in form from parish to parish, but the end result generally moved the congregations closer to the Puritan ideals: namely, enhanced clerical control over religious affairs and a public faith, as the Puritan bill of rights of 1572 put it, that was situated "more nearly to the imitation of the ancient apostolical Church and the best reformed churches in Europe."[51] With no real possibility of replacing bishops with duly elected elders and deacons, most Puritans gathered instead in smaller groups within the parishes, the so-called *ecclesiolae in ecclesia* (which means "little churches within the church"), and practiced their brand of pure and simplified Protestantism together with like-minded believers. In some instances this could result in a revised or adapted service, with Puritan clergymen drawing on the Genevan *Forme of Prayers* for direction and placing emphasis on sermons, psalms, and prayers rather than ceremonies. In other instances it might mean meeting in voluntary associations such as prophesyings, lecture sessions, covenanting groups, or simply falling back on private devotions in the household. The essence of the movement was the "adaptation and domestication of Calvinism to fit the conditions of voluntary Christians,"[52] an approach to the faith that most first-generation continental Reformed theologians would have condemned.

Whatever the solution to the Puritan critique of the church, the dilemma remained the same: more religion, or at least more New Testament religion, proved corrosive of traditional order.[53] For not only did it challenge the forms and ordinances of the Elizabethan settlement, it challenged, directly or indirectly, the idea of the church hierarchy *tout court*. This was the heart of the matter in the presbyterian debate sparked in 1570 by Thomas Cartwright (circa 1535–1603), Lady Margaret Professor of Divinity at Cambridge. The true church, as Cartwright reminded his Cambridge colleague John Whitgift, at the time one of the most outspoken champions of the Elizabethan settlement, must not stoop to accommodate the secular order; rather, civil government had to take its lead from the church. To do otherwise, Cartwright insisted, "is as much to say, as if a man should fashion his house according to his hangings, when as indeed it is clean contrary, that, as the hangings are made fit for the house, so the commonwealth must be made to agree with the Church."[54]

The lengths to which the Puritans were willing to go in order to tailor the hangings to fit the house was revealed during the reign of King Charles I (1600–49), a monarch who ultimately lost his throne to an army that paused to sing Psalms before going into battle. Already during the reign of King James I (1566–1625), the Puritan faction had grown increasingly disaffected with the Stuart tenancy over the church, especially in light of the fact that James had traveled south as the king of a presbyterian land and yet still refused fundamental reforms. Yet James had managed to keep most of the religious tensions in check during his reign. His son and successor Charles I, however, was less successful, largely because he pursued policies that threatened ideas of purity and community shared by extreme and moderate Puritans alike. First among his mistakes was his perceived patronage of the Arminians, and in particular his elevation of William Laud, who would become Archbishop of Canterbury in 1633. This set the seal on the period of growing discontent, a phase when Laud and other like-minded clerics began to downplay the doctrine of predestination, elevate the episcopacy, attack Sabbitarianism and the preaching ministry, and introduce liturgical and ceremonial changes – such as replacing wooden communion tables with stone altars or enforcing the use of the Prayer Book and the surplice – that were seen by many as the first steps on the return to Catholicism. In addition, many of the radical Puritan preachers were suppressed, as were the lectureships and unlicensed preaching. In essence Laud's notion of "decent order" in the church touched on gesture and ceremony rather than doctrine. Yet it gave the impression that the entire Protestant religion was under threat.[55]

In the absence of a formal confession, the Puritan polemic against "false religion" was the most effective way to foster a shared sense of identity. This was the tried-and-true method of Protestant self-fashioning: whatever type of Christian you are, we are not. But it was especially important for the Puritans, since there were no fixed theological boundaries between the moderates and the radicals, just a sliding scale of Calvinist thought. The Puritan sense of community was thus based on mutual conceits rather than a common creed, but it was substantial enough for the pious to believe that they belonged to a select (and elect) group of people who had been set aside by God to fulfill his designs. One of the indicators of this was the Puritan habit of giving children names that marked them out as among the visible saints. Favored appellations included Above-Hope, Praise-God, Flee-Sin, Tribulation-Wholesome, Much-Mercy, More-Fruit, Perseverance, Deliverance, and Return. But there were other seemingly trivial ways in which they could give expression to their sense of uniqueness and election, including walking around with the Bible in their hands, over-pronouncing words (especially loaded words such as "liberty" or "brother and sister"), cutting their hair short, wearing simple, colorless clothes, and rolling their eyes theatrically when they prayed.[56] Contemporaries, even sympathetic contemporaries, were often irritated by the Puritan manner and the ostentatious piety they affected, and this more hostile perception of the godly people was constitutive of their sense of identity as well. Precisionists, "busy controllers," over-zealous biblicists, Scripture men, enthusiasts, Anabaptists – all these and similar terms were imposed on them by others.[57]

The point to make is that there was no fixed idea of what a Puritan actually was, neither among the Puritans themselves nor among those who labeled them. The term took on different meanings according to the context of perception. All that could be said with certainty is that Puritanism was a movement animated by the search for a past purity or truth (a type of myth of origins) and that its exponents, moving along a scale that ran from conservatism to radicalism, disagreed with the existing religious settlement and wished to bring it in line with a proper reading of Scripture. The laws of God, not man, were the foundation of the church.

English Puritans, no less than German and Swiss Protestants, looked to the towns in order to establish their godly communities. English towns were generally less autonomous than the imperial cities, but if the local officials were sympathetic to Puritanism, there were similar possibilities for the establishment of the type of *regnum Christi* envisioned by Bucer a century before. As early as the reign of Queen Elizabeth, dissenters and non-conformists had tried to push through Puritan reformations in towns in the southern and eastern counties, where some clergy, supported by Justices of the Peace and local magistrates, effectively set up presbyterian systems within the episcopal framework. Puritans thought of these "little Genevas" as the theaters for religious change they were not able to effect at the level of the state, "small zions" where godly reform could be imposed on the commune through the joint efforts of the secular and the spiritual authorities.[58] As in Zwingli's Zurich, it was a symbiotic relationship: magistracy and ministry, as the Ipswich preacher Samuel Ward put it, were the "principal lights," the "two optic pieces" through which godly order was perceived and realised.[59]

Godly order meant transforming the town into a haven of pious, charitable, and sober people whose conduct and beliefs were in absolute accordance with the teaching of Scripture and the model of Christian community expounded in sermons throughout the week by the Puritan preachers. In practical terms, this meant the elimination of traditional urban customs such as May Day festivities, mystery plays, religious processions, charivaris, morris dancing, church ales as well as a miscellany of games and sports; it meant the rooting out of moral indiscretions such as swearing, drunkenness, premarital sex, idleness, dancing, thievery, and adultery; and it meant the enforcement of regular attendance at church, more rigorous and effective local education, more exacting methods of discipline, and improved systems of poor relief and charity. The central purpose, as the Puritans of Dorchester worded it, was to "[reduce] the town into order by good government," which in this context essentially meant government by Holy Writ.[60] These were the men caricatured by the London playwrights as killjoys and zealots, the two most memorable creations being Shakespeare's Malvolio and Jonson's Zeal-of-the-Land Busy, whose only abiding passion was to uproot all "cursed mirth" from the land.

But the Puritan search for order reached beyond the towns and cities. Zealous Puritans wanted to reform the entire realm, starting with the Anglican church and then moving on to the failings of the social and political spheres. Here, as in all Protestantism, it was a question of degree rather than design. There was a wide spectrum of opinion running from Presbyterian Moderates to Separatists and Independents. Perhaps the best way to illustrate the Puritan challenge is by way of the thoughts of a conservative such as the theologian Richard Hooker (1554–1600), a man who viewed the Elizabethan settlement, with its magisterial matrix of monarch and episcopacy, its comprehensive Calvinism, and its enriched liturgy, ceremonials, and sacramental forms, as not only a wholly reformed church but, in its basic Christian philosophy, a *Weltanschauung* that held law and gospel in harmony.[61] Hooker wrote *Of the Lawes of Ecclesiastical Politie* (1594) in response to the challenges directed against the church by the Puritans, and in particular by the Presbyterians, for he believed that the drive to invest the world with too much religion would lead to unrest, division, and chaos. Hooker thus spoke of the need for an essential balance between reason, Scripture, and politics, and he also distinguished between what was strictly necessary to the faith (the essentials) and what was not (the adiaphora).[62] The more pressing types of Puritans, he believed, unsettled this balance with their restless search for verities and their mistaken conviction that the world had to be reformed in the image of the Word.

Hooker's arguments would prove convincing for later generations of English Pro testants, but the *Lawes* did little to quell the growing radicalism of the early seventeenth century. During the reign of Charles I, as attitudes hardened, Puritan opponents of Laud and his fellow Arminians began to preach openly against both church and state. As Samuel Brooke, Master of Trinity College, Cambridge, saw it, "Puritanism [had become] the roote of all rebellions and disobedient intractableness in parliaments etc. and all schisme and sauciness in the countrey, nay in the Church itself."[63] Evangelicals had objected to state churches before, of course, but no Protestant realm had ever experienced resistance on this scale, and certainly nothing so openly mutinous or so unreservedly contemptuous. In effect, the Puritan clergy had become ideologues, condemning the status quo as ungodly and openly resisting the will of both the monarch and the law with reference to a higher authority. "Let them chant while they will of prerogatives," wrote Milton in 1641, voicing a common conviction, "we shall tell them of Scripture; of custom, we of Scripture; of acts and statutes, still of Scripture."[64] Thus, even though it was rooted in a deeply spiritual malaise, the Puritan challenge was inescapably political, and inescapably revolutionary, in its effects. In the rant and cant of the preachers, with their pulpit vitriol, their air of confidence and calling, and their sense of distance to the society they wished to uproot, the Puritans on the eve of revolution are reminiscent of the German radicals on the eve of the Peasants' War of 1525. And indeed, two fundamentally *Protestant* dilemmas were at the heart of both revolutions.

First, the rise of radicalism was a consequence of the evangelical antipathy to Catholicism and the revolutionary potential that inhered in the idea of Protestant identity. Both Stuart monarchs pursued policies that fed into suspicions that England would soon be overrun by "popery," especially after the defeat of the Bohemian rebels and the subsequent success of the Counter-Reformation in the Habsburg lands in the 1620s. The Stuart failure to countenance the "general discourse of Europe" and take up arms against Catholicism did more than just spread anxiety among the faithful. By the seventeenth century, decades of Protestant self-fashioning had invested the idea of popery with a range of attributes that stood in direct opposition to the values of every sound Englishman. Whereas the faith of English Protestants (so ran the logic) was based in freedom, liberty, godliness, and responsible and representative government, the faith of Catholics was ineluctably bound up with papal tyranny and arbitrary rule.[65] Even if Charles and Laud had not politicized the spiritual realm, and even if the Puritans had not been such a powerful force in the Commons and judiciary, the rise of religious discontent was unavoidably political. Second, Puritanism could not avoid issues that touched on methods of governance or claims to power. And it need not be in the form of radical resistance to perceived tyranny. Because it placed such emphasis on the Fall of mankind and the inability of man to overcome sin and corruption through his own efforts, the Reformed church required a system of rule that could contain sin and make the world safe for Christians. There must be two kingdoms, properly disposed. The just polity, as Calvin wrote, was as necessary to humankind as "bread and water, light and air." Without an accurate balance between the secular and the spiritual, Fallen Man would remain alienated from God *in perpetuum*.[66]

It was thus inevitable that the overthrow of the monarchy would work as a catalyst for the gospel of social unrest. Europe had not experienced religious controversy on this scale since the rise of the Swiss and German radicals, and in fact there was a line of continuity and a genealogy linking the movements that historians have yet to trace in detail.[67] And as in Saxony so too in England, fundamental to the rise of radicalism was the Protestant impulse to recover the purity and essence of Christianity, the need to go beyond the forms and formalities of the existing church and resurrect a religious order that, as the Lord Mayor of London Isaac Pennington put it, made Christians subject to "one above man."[68] There was no general agreement as to what this meant; Presbyterians, Congregationalists, Independents, and radical Separatists, to name just the main parties, were polarized in their opinions. But they were united in the conviction that the solution had been revealed by God and that this truth, once understood and effected in the Christian community, had the power to transform the world.

Soon the more pressing preachers of the social gospel began to announce their visions of godly order and what this entailed for the English nation. The London merchant William Walwyn (1600–81), for instance, by abstracting universal patterns from his private affliction over the struggle between law and gospel, claimed that the essence of Christianity was love, and that this love would overcome the injustices and inequalities of man; John Lilburn (1614–57), also known as Freeborn John, spoke in similar terms, writing of the great social inequalities that plagued the common man and the need for godly righteousness to reign in England, a state of affairs that would lead to equality of wealth, power, and social standing; and Gerrard Winstanley (1609–76), who preached of the need to re-establish the apostolic community on earth, calling on those who wished to follow this divine ordinance, "they that are resolved to work and eat together, making the earth a common treasury, doth join hands with Christ to lift up the creation from bondage, and restores all things from the curse."[69]

To the moderate Puritans, it seemed as if every possible permutation of Protestantism had now taken shape in the land, particularly once the leitmotiv changed from reform to liberty. In his work *Gangraena* (1646), the clergyman and heresiographer Thomas Edwards (1599–1647) bewailed how England "is become already in many places a chaos, a Babel, another Amsterdam ... and in the high way to Münster." Edwards claimed to have counted up to 16 different sects sharing 271 theological errors between them.[70] But headcounts of this kind tended to play up the divisions while overlooking the historical fact that this was a Protestant movement within a Protestant state. Indeed, this sibling rivalry is what invested the episode with its multivalence. All sides (all sides, that is, this side of Catholicism) shared a common language, a similar framework of perception, expectation, and consensus, and a lingering confidence that the sects would one day reconcile. Puritanism, like all of Protestantism, moved along a sliding scale, and it also had the same paradox at its core: the Pauline paradox established by Luther in his work *The Freedom of a Christian Man*. Puritans spoke of freedom and liberty in this vein, by which they meant not freedom per se but rather the freedom from the laws and conditions of a false religion and the resultant liberty that could only be found in total and absolute subjection to Christ. But with no constraints or orthodoxies to observe, this proved a formula for the rethinking of all aspects of secular and spiritual life. "The formall world is much affrighted," remarked the radical Joseph Salmon in 1651, "and every form is up in Arms to proclaim open wars against it self."[71] Among the new liberties announced by the radical Puritans during the period of revolution were the entitlement of women to hold forth openly on religious matters, freedom from the demands of king and parliament (including taxes and laws), emancipation from the clergy and the symbolic texts of the Church of England, and deliverance from ignorance, magic, and the blind forces of the world. The world was breaking free from its vassalage to the "gross, carnall, visible evidences and material beams" of the previous dispensation and entering a new age.[72]

Speaking of how a Christian might prepare for the Last Judgment, John Bunyan declared that the question of Christian freedom was no less than "the principle as well as the practice that shall be enquired into . . . whether the spirit from which you acted was legal or evangelical."[73] And there was no shortage of men and women in England during the revolutionary period that had come up with answers, some so radical that all of the traditional restraints of magisterial religion were undermined. In their doctrines of free grace and election, for instance, radical sects such as the Levellers, Ranters, and Grindletonians expressed doubts about the reality of sin. On the basis of similar ideas, the Muggletonians and Fifth Monarchists cast doubt on the reality of Hell. Seekers and Ranters, extreme anti-formalists, raged against sin, Hell, and the Sabbath, allegorized the Bible to suit their spirit-filled visions, and claimed a true "freeman of Christ" had no more concern of the law than the laws of Spain should concern England.[74]

This was the type of chaos feared by men like Thomas Edwards, the "highway to Münster" that followed from a religion based purely on grace and released from the constraints of a magisterial church. As a presbyterian pamphlet remarked in 1647: "Remove once the shaking of these rods [the Decalogue] over their heads, then we open a floodgate to all licentious liberty."[75] This was the tension at the heart of all Protestant communities, and England did not escape its polarizing effects. In the words of one historian, "The deepest contradiction of all was that between two contrary principles, always held together in tension within English Puritanism – the principle of a godly and imposed rule and discipline and the contrary principle of religious liberty, requiring the toleration of sincerely held religious differences."[76] Of course, not all was chaos. Most of the dissenters lived piously and peaceably next to their neighbors, and some groups had long histories ahead of them. But for the majority of the radical sects that surfaced during the Interregnum, the Puritan experiment proved a short one.

Quakers and Baptists suffered the most after the war, many being fined and imprisoned, others exiled or transported. Presbyterians did rather better, either returning to the Anglican fold or, like Richard Baxter, conforming outwardly while observing a deeper faith at home. In truth, the persecution that followed on the publication of the Clarendon Code was rarely imposed to the letter; there was too much latent sympathy and leniency in the parishes of post-revolutionary England for that. But to the radicals, the measures were a harbinger of the very "kingdom of darkness" they had foretold over 20 years earlier. Most of the radical leaders and their followers, having been harried out by Cromwell and the army, faded into the background of Restoration England. William Walwyn turned to the Quakers, who survived the post-war persecution by practicing their faith in seclusion, and took up medicine; Gerrard Winstanley also became a Quaker, assumed the offices of waywarden and chief constable, and eventually returned to London to practice his former trade as a corn chandler; Abiezer Coppe changed his name to Dr Higham, practiced medicine, and served as an occasional preacher. Others, however, did not go as quietly. John Rogers spoke of the coldness, cowardice, and carelessness of his former brethren, while Christopher Feake, the Fifth Monarchist leader, advised his followers to lay low and become a "peculiar people," waiting for the word of command from God "to execute the vengeance written against Babylon."[77]

Others looked for alternative explanations, suggesting that the cause had been undone in Parliament or on the field of battle, or that the failure of the radicals was part of God's greater plan. And still others, such as George Fox (1624–91), the founder of Quakerism, claimed that the problem lay not with the army or the parliament but with the Godly themselves. The land and its people had not taken up the commission. As Fox and others started to realize, England was not the place where the gospel would overcome the constraints of the law. That honor was reserved for America.

New World Protestants

The holy commonwealth

Protestantism's most important exports were the Puritans of New England, both the separatists and the semi-separatists. The famous Pilgrim Fathers who settled Plymouth in 1620 were of the former stamp, being spiritual descendents of the Swiss Brethren of the early Reformation. They devolved from the Puritans of Scrooby, who had sought exile in Leiden in order to escape the growing corruptions of the English Church under King James I. Finding the liberties of the Netherlands equally corrupting, however, they set sail, via Southampton and Plymouth, for the New World. There, under the leadership of William Bradford (1590–1657), chief architect of the Mayflower Compact, the Plymouth congregation became a fully separatist, covenanted Protestant church. Smaller groups of émigrés followed in the 1620s and settlements emerged in Weymouth, Quincy, and Beacon Hill, but the most substantial congregation took root in Salem, where among other things the parishioners ordained their own ministers, thus making it de facto a separatist undertaking. By far the most influential Puritan colonists, however, were those who landed in Massachusetts Bay in 1630 and went on to develop the "New England Way" under the leadership of John Winthrop (1588–1649). Although congregationalist in form and spirit, the Bay Puritans were not full separatists but rather semi-separatists, or non-separating congregationalists, who saw no necessary contradiction in speaking of the Church of England as "our dear Mother" while setting up a covenanted church with additional requirements for membership.[78]

To third-generation Bay Puritans like Cotton Mather (1663–1728) there was only one noteworthy reason why the Puritans had set out for the shores of America: religion, the planting of the true church in a virgin land. Indeed, it was not really a question of human choice at all, but of fulfilling God's will. As Mather wrote in *Magnalia Christi Americana* (1702), it was God who chose Massachusetts, "the spot of *earth*, which the God of heaven *spied out* for the seat of such *evangelical*, and *ecclesiastical*, and very remarkable transactions."[79] Here was an "open door of liberty," where the true church could flourish free of persecution or impediment. In England, by contrast, not only did it seem that Archbishop Laud and his backbench of Arminians were gradually infecting the church with ever-increasing papal errors, but with the Thirty Years' War at the height of its murderous powers, the whole Protestant world seemed to be in flames. Having said this, we should not overstress the providential dimensions of the Puritan errand into the wilderness. In actuality, there were plenty of non-religious motives to explain why men and women migrated to New England, ranging from the difficult social and economic conditions in England, the disease, bad harvests, and agrarian unrest in the countryside, and simply the "sudden undigested grounds" that were doubtless good enough for a fair number of people to take the step.[80]

But most of the Bay colonists would have agreed with Mather's retrospective conclusion: religion was the rub. And it was not just because Puritans were habitual wayfarers, ready to abandon the solid ground of forms and ordinances if a greater chance of Christian freedom seemed just over the horizon. Many of the first-generation emigrants were extremely reluctant to leave England despite its seeming slide into godlessness, not least John Winthrop, the multi-term governor of Massachusetts, who only took up the special commission after much soul-searching and dry deliberation. Always favoring a steady course, Winthrop faced a uniquely Puritan dilemma. As parliament failed and popery crept, as oppression, immorality, and ostentation gained the upper hand, and as the Protestant powers of Europe struggled for their very survival, was this not precisely the time for English evangelicals to remain firm in defense of the church? Should not the faithful stand and fight? Exactly so, concluded Winthrop, and that is why he set sail for America.[81] For the central purpose of the pilgrimage to America was to preserve Protestantism from its final destruction. This is what was meant by Winthrop's famous declaration that the colony would be "a city on a hill" for all to see. It was not conceived as a final destination or a lasting utopia, but as a temporary refuge and a beacon for the faithful, a gathering of the elect that would return to the land of origin, fully cleansed and with a surfeit of grace from what Edmund Spencer termed "fruitfullest Virginia," once the dangers had passed.[82]

Lacking even the ruins of an ecclesiastical order, the Protestants of Massachusetts Bay had to build a church from the ground up. And it was more than just a church within a church in the sense meant by the non-separating Congregationalists and Presbyterians of Stuart England. In America, there was no existing institutional or theological *mater ecclesia* within which local congregations might configure themselves. And yet in at least one respect the colonists were well-placed, for as the Massachusetts Bay Company had been granted independent powers of sovereignty and ownership, simply relocating its place of meeting from London to the colony enabled the leaders to remove the Company from the control of the Crown and thereby establish the framework for a self-governing Protestant polity. But this still left the problem of order, and they solved it by conflating the traditional two-kingdoms framework. The Cambridge minister Urian Oakes (1631–81) described the solution as follows:

> According to the design of our founders and the frame of things laid by them the interest of righteousness in the commonwealth and holiness in the Churches are inseparable . . . To divide what God hath conjoined . . . is folly in its exaltation. I look upon this as a little model of the glorious kingdom of Christ on earth. Christ reigns among us in the commonwealth as well as in the Church and hath his glorious interest involved and wrapt up in the good of both societies respectively.[83]

Although Oakes spoke of "both societies," in truth the secular arm was the dominant partner. The clergy might preach and admonish, but the actual exercise of power was in the hands of the commonwealth officials. Likening it to Calvin's favored polity, the Boston minister John Cotton (1585–1652) spoke of the system as a type of "mixt aristocracie,"[84] with more than a casual allusion to Huguenot resistance theory. Indeed, even more than the prototypical ephors of Zwingli and Calvin, the secular authorities of the Bay colony were the guardians of the faith, for the central function of the Massachusetts government was not to uphold political liberty; rather, its purpose was to preserve *Christian* liberty – by which was meant moral liberty, effected through complete subjection to godly law – and thus to a greater extent than any ecclesio-political settlement in Europe the oversight of religion was in the hands of the magistrates, the "nursing fathers" of the church. Theoretically, the magistracy could not trespass on the Christian conscience; but as the entire polity was in place in order to bring into being a sinless society (or its closest approximation), the lines of division were necessarily blurred. Godly politics would make for a godly church and vice versa. To the early modern mind, New England society was a godly republic in the complete sense, for not only did the extension of the vote to the freemen mean that the colony was ruled by a species of representative government, but because political office was limited to members of the church – the so-called visible saints – religion remained the central pillar of rule and the guarantor of order. As the Boston clergyman John Cotton remarked, "purity, preserved in the church, will preserve well ordered liberty in the people."[85]

But this well-ordered liberty was precarious. No other Protestant community had ever been so finely balanced at the interstice between law and gospel as the Puritans of Massachusetts Bay. On the one hand it was a community bound by its special commission to uphold the commandments of God, to live according to the dictates of Scripture, and serve as a beacon for the rest of the Christian world, a charge that prompted some men to wonder whether it might uncover "more sins than (as yet is seene) God himselfe hath made."[86] On the other, it was a commonwealth brought into being in defense of religious liberty, empowered by the discretion of the individual conscience, and driven by the conviction that no man had the right to impede the soul in search of the true church. This latter impulse was able to flourish in the congregational system adopted by the Bay Puritans, which not only created a network of autonomous churches, each with its own sense of election, but also required of its members that they continually assess and reassess their own faith and the faith of their neighbors. How then did the Bay Puritans manage to institute a church without it dividing and subdividing and splintering into a multitude of inspired flocks? How did this final experiment in the magisterial Reformation keep its shape in the American wilderness?

In order to square the circle of contradictory impulses at the heart of their faith, the leaders of the Bay colony tailored the idea of a covenant to fit local circumstances – or rather, two main covenants, the covenant of works and the covenant of grace.[87] By doing this, by devising a framework that could reconcile apparent opposites, they made room for voluntary religion *and* a fixed and orthodox order in the church. The New England Way was thus based on a paradox, for it was conditional and absolute at the same time. The Staffordshire theologian Thomas Blake (circa 1597–1657) summed it up: "Ministers should perswade, and people improve endeavours as though they were Pelagians, and no help of grace afforded. They should pray and beleeve, and rest on grace as though they were Antinomians, nothing of endeavour to be looked after."[88] And yet, despite its inner contradictions, the covenantal paradigm was an extremely effective way of ordering a new church in a formless wilderness. Not only did it temper the near-despotism of the Calvinist God as taught by the high-priests of predestination, whose severe theories of election and damnation had a tendency to push people away from orthodoxy and into the embrace of "enthusiasm," but by emphasizing the importance of the covenant of works it invested the believer with an active role. To secure salvation, Bay Puritans had to meet the conditions laid down by the teachings of the church, just like the Protestants in London, Zurich, Wittenberg, or Geneva.

The covenantal (or federal) theology of New England was derived from the dissenting tradition of Elizabethan and early Stuart Puritanism. Early separatists such as Henry Barrowe and Robert Browne, whose ideas were further refined by Henry Ainsworth and Henry Robinson, spoke of the need for the church to take shape as a voluntary organization of believers who could demonstrate that they were a "faithful and holie people" and chose to be part of a new covenanted church. Originally, demonstration required some knowledge of doctrine; but by the time the separatists had settled in the Netherlands the trial had become more rigorous, to the point that membership required signs of saving faith, which was nothing less, as Robinson put it, than the need to prove that one was "visibly, and so far as men in charity could judge, justified, sanctified, and entitled to the promises of salvation, and life eternal."[89]

And yet, as exacting as the Leiden Puritans had become, no separatists or semi-separatists to that point had developed a covenantal theology with the sophistication or comprehension of the New England Way. It was, as the historian Perry Miller remarked, nothing less than "a scheme including both God and man within a single frame, a point at which, without doing violence to their respective natures, both could meet and converse."[90] Theologically, it was a gratifying solution, for it taught that the covenant of works was still in effect through a voluntary act of divine intervention, and since the observance of the law was proof of the "sweet concurrence" of nature and grace, it made it possible for individuals to believe that their actions, though not meritorious of themselves, were somehow declarative of a choice they had made to follow the ways of Christ. For those concerned with church order, it was equally expedient, because the proofs of election were to be found in the created order – in the scriptures, sermons, teachings, and sacraments – which meant that the faithful were still subject to the church, for it was the clergy who determined the means, methods, and morphology of sanctification, while the church and its sacraments facilitated and sealed the covenantal promise.[91] Nor was that the outer limits of the bond. Because in New England the secular sphere intruded so closely on religious affairs, the ecclesiastical order was necessarily reflected in, and indeed upheld by, the civic order. The believer was bound to the Christian polity no less than he was bound to the church; and indeed, given that it was the obligation of the authorities to facilitate proper devotion and due obedience, it is not too much to say that citizenship was one of the conditions of salvation. Speaking in terms reminiscent of Luther in his work *Freedom of a Christian Man*, Boston's John Eliot considered it a small price to pay: "it is no impeachment of Christian Liberty to bow to Christian Lawes."[92]

Thus, in essence, the New England Way was a conservative system, maintaining its shape by using a variable geometry of prescribed rules, trained interpreters, political authority, and congregational order (which included the rather more tangible supports of a general tax and judicial prerogative). Although it had rejected some of the teachings and ceremonies of the Church of England, Bay Puritanism still belonged to the magisterial tradition, preserving an "equilibrium of forces" by way of a balanced application of Scripture, doctrine, reason, and force.[93]

We can get a sense for this by piecing together the experiences of the prototypical visible saint. A full religious life in the church required membership, and this was first attained by approaching the elders with a request to join. At this point the aspirants would be examined by the original members, and once they were satisfied that there was sufficient evidence of grace, the candidates would appear before the congregation to provide a narrative of their spiritual history and proof that they walked in the ways of Christ. Following this, a vote was taken and, if found worthy, they were admitted to full membership. All churches in New England worked in this way. Degrees of intensity might vary from place to place – it was less rigorous in Connecticut, for instance, and more severe in New Haven – but in each case there was a fixed protocol that was applied to all potential members regardless of station. "Crook not God's rules to the experience of men," was how the minister Thomas Shepard (1605–49) summed up the general philosophy, "but bring men unto rules, try men's estates by that . . ."[94]

Of course, there were no sure proofs of election, neither for the individual nor for the congregation. Notwithstanding the number of inkwells that had been drained by theologians to explain its workings, the morphology of grace remained an extremely inexact science. Only the logic was precise, the general order of salvation that led a believer from sin to Christ within the confines of a "deeply penitential *via purgativa*" that had much in common with medieval modes of worship.[95] But for the individual believer there was no certainty. They could look for the "signs" that spoke of grace, such as a strengthening of faith, acts of love and charity, or renewed industry, especially when spent on pious pursuits such as prayer or meditation. But they could never really know.

Pieced together by a very public coming together of theological minds, the New England Way was all too obviously a human solution to the Protestant dilemma, and it was not long before other Puritans began to doubt its validity. Among the first to object were the clergy themselves, and not just the Presbyterians in England, who published critical tracts in London and Oxford against the works of John Cotton, but a number of close associates as well. Peter Hobart and James Noyes, for instance, questioned the authenticity of the affectionate divinity proposed by the Bay theologians, while Thomas Hooker and Roger Williams, both of whom left Massachusetts as a consequence of their spiritual unease, feared that the unremitting "duties and performances" expected of the faithful was legalism in another guise.[96]

But there was a deeper level of dissent as well, as there always was, one that surfaced with the appearance of the antinomians in the colony, men and women who rejected all teaching based on the need for covenants, conditions, works, threats, penalties, holy duties and holy zeal, and spoke instead of free grace and the possibility of sainthood without conditions or obligations. In New England, the most profound of these preachers of free grace was Anne Hutchinson (1591–1643), the pious daughter of a dissident clergyman in England, who, having been drawn to John Cotton's preaching of the Spirit while in Boston, Lincolnshire, followed him to the New World. Once in the colony, Hutchinson became a spiritual advisor, holding conventicles in her house and prophesying without clerical supervision. Eventually, convinced that the church order in Boston was built on outward forms and superfluous duties and conditions, she began to condemn what she saw as the legalism of the New England Way and spoke of the need for the Spirit and the sudden rapture of free grace. And she called practical divinity and Puritan casuistry into question. Can we really measure grace through signs, dispositions, or works? Hutchinson had no doubts about her own grasp of the Spirit, however, once claiming that "if she had but one halfe houres talke with a man, she would tell whether he were elect or not."[97] In 1638, Hutchison was brought to trial and over 90 of her ideas were condemned as errors. Soon afterward, she was disenfranchised and banished. Settling first in Rhode island, Hutchinson ended her days in Pelham Bay, at that time (1643) part of New Netherland, where she and her children – save her youngest, Susanna – were slaughtered by the local Indians.

Hutchinson's eloquent defense of free grace exposed the central weakness of the Bay synthesis. And the most dangerous part of it was the fact that it was an internal rather than an external threat. Hutchinson had not been wrong to consider Cotton a teacher of free grace, for he had often elevated the Spirit above the moral covenant in his sermons, especially in the mid-1630s, when he came to think that many of the colonists were in effect sleepwalking their way through the regime of duties and conditions and turning Puritan religiosity into a "bone-idle art." The line between Christian freedom and Christian accountability was very fine – so fine in fact that when governor Winthrop drew up a document explaining why the thought of Hutchinson was wrong, Thomas Hooker advised him against publicizing it, fearing that it may give too much encouragement to the Arminians, the very party he was writing against.[98]

But this was not a uniquely Puritan or American predicament. It was the Protestant condition in general. And the authorities in New England reacted in the same fashion as the theologians and theocrats of Europe. Following the expulsion of Hutchinson, the congregational churches of Boston and its environs became more rigorous in the policing of the faith and the preserving of orthodoxy. The clergy grew less flexible and ambiguous in their teaching, with Cotton, Shepard, and Hooker distancing themselves from their earlier forays into enthusiasm, while others, such as Edward Johnson, published apologies of New England intolerance, explaining that true liberty required a strong hand "to keepe the truths of Christ pure and unspotted."[99] The status quo was confirmed by the Cambridge Platform of 1648, with the churches formally integrated into a system that included de facto synods and councils. The power of the authorities, secular as well as spiritual, was increased in order to prevent that type of heterogeneity that arose with the antinomian crisis.

Governor Winthrop captured the mindset of mid-century New England Puritanism with his declaration that "men may not alter the kind or Form of Church, which Christ hath Instituted, but must preserve inviolate the Laws, Administrations, Privileges, and Church-Government ordained by him, without Addition, Diminution, or alteration."[100] The officers of the church now assumed a higher standing than the parishioners, sitting apart from the congregation on raised benches and meeting on weekdays in closed councils to draw up the church agenda. Boston's leading divines claimed a monopoly on exegesis and prophesying, and indeed some went so far as to allege a pseudo-sacramental power to heal the sick or probe the mind of God. According to Cotton Mather, the Boston preacher John Wilson once altered the trajectory of an arrow in the war against the Pequot Indians purely through the power of an impromptu prayer.[101]

As with the first Reformation, so too with the last. Ultimately, appeals to grace, gospel, and the errand of Protestant Christians to stand before God with a Bible in hand gave way to a religious culture articulated through orthodoxy, clericalism, and the forms and institutions of the magisterial mode. Even in the face of the decline in piety that set in with the second- and third-generation of New England colonists the Puritan authorities were reluctant to loosen the ties that held the holy commonwealth together. Only when it became unavoidably clear that more and more of the younger colonists were unable, and indeed unwilling, to meet the demands of membership in the covenanted churches did the authorities began to rethink the New England Way. The solution was the half-way covenant, devised by the clergy at an assembly in 1657 and then formalized at a synod in 1662. From that point forward, in those churches that chose to adopt the half-way covenant, the children of full members were members in their own right, which meant they were subject to discipline and could baptize their own children, but without taking part in Communion or voting in church affairs. The need to provide evidence that one had experienced saving grace, the distinct mark of New England Protestantism, was no longer a condition. Needless to say, both clergy and congregations reacted differently to this innovation. In some churches it was welcomed and quickly adopted; in others it was resisted, and often for the reason given in New Haven, that "the children of strangers uncircumcised in their heart shall bee brought into God's sanctuary to pollute it."[102]

But it was a necessary adaptation given the times, and one that remained largely faithful to the overall idea, for even though it allowed for greater accommodation it did not abandon the original principles. There was still a system that regulated membership, there was still a trained priesthood that judged degrees of right understanding, and there was still a level of faith expected from the parishioner, even if under the half-way covenant it was a historical rather than a saving faith. Without these basic conditions, most New England divines believed, the Protestant religion would simply fall away. John Cotton made this point in his dispute with the antinomians. "I know not how you can build up either church or commonwealth on the Holy Spirit alone," he wrote, "for it would then be 'an house without a foundation.'"[103] But some American Puritans had no difficulty at all looking to the Spirit alone for the upbuilding of a church. Indeed, Roger Williams, Cotton's former colleague, who had preached in Boston and Salem before venturing deep into the American wilderness, came to believe that the only true faith was *precisely* that faith free of the trappings of church and commonwealth.

The ways of providence

In 1636 Roger Williams (1603–83) obtained a verbal agreement from two Narragansett sachems to the grant of land that served as the foundation for Providence, Rhode Island. Like other Puritans before him, Roger Williams went into the wilderness in search of the "pure church," the original apostolic Church of Christ. Unlike the men of Massachusetts Bay, however, he came to believe that this was not possible as long as the faithful remained in fellowship with the Church of England, and indeed ultimately

Williams grew convinced that this would not be possible until Christ sent apostles in advance to prepare for his return. Since his arrival in America, there had been a gradual shift in his thinking from a search for sanctity in communal purification to the belief in election through isolation and resignation.[104] German Anabaptists and English Puritans had said similar things before, but what distinguished Williams was the extent to which his ideas of separation cut ties with Protestant precedent and enabled him (and later like-minded men and women) first to imagine, and then to establish, a religious culture in the American wilderness that moved away from the magisterial tradition. Rooted in the ideals of liberty of religious conscience and separation of church and state, Rhode Island took as its founding precepts ideas in direct opposition to the principles of community that had nurtured development in Europe. In place of orthodoxy, there was religious plurality, indeed a disdain for religious absolutes; in place of an established church watched closely by secular magistrates, there was a lack of formal ecclesiology, a separation of church and state, a charismatic clergy, and little formal worship.[105]

Williams prefigured much of the dialogue that shaped American Protestantism by taking an extreme position on two issues of lasting debate: freedom of conscience and relations between church and state. On both counts, Williams opposed the notion that there was an archetype or a pattern that had to be honored on earth. On the contrary, in the absence of an apostolic church, the only pure faith was a faith that was seeking. The Christian had to be free to prepare for the coming of Christ. In his public conflict with John Cotton, for instance, Williams made it clear that he believed the coercion of the New England Way was contrary to the teaching of Christ. Who had been given the commission to found the apostolic church? What man could do so free of sin? Who among us can influence the destiny of another soul? This was an understanding of the Christian conscience that sat in opposition to that of Cotton, who held that the average believer could come to recognize religious truth within the span of one or two admonitions. To sin against conscience, wrote Cotton, was to sin against these manifest truths. Religious freedom was the freedom to accept them.[106]

Underwriting the extreme notions of "soul liberty" that set Williams off from the thought of New England divines was the divide he built between church and state. While recognizing the need for civil order, and recognizing as well that the temporal power had been instituted by God, he refused the state any claims to power that touched on the spiritual realm. His objections were threefold. First, based on his reading of Scripture, he denied any line of association joining Israel of the Old Testament and the nations of the modern day; second, following from this, he refuted the vision of a national covenant and that there might be a people or a church invested with the authority to superintend the Church of Christ; and third, he rejected the claim that religious error might cause harm to the integrity of the civil order – or indeed the flipside, that in order for a state to be morally sound it must necessarily be Christian. In short, Williams called for a wall of separation between the spiritual and the secular, between the "garden of the Church and the wilderness of the World," not only to ensure that the earthly sphere was not overrun by the ambitions of a false church, but to ensure that religion was not hindered or molested by the ambitions of the state.[107] This was the same two-kingdoms equation first developed by Luther over a century before in order to find a place for the emerging Protestant church within the framework of rule in

Electoral Saxony. And the same concern sat at its core: how to reconcile liberty of religious conscience with the laws that hedged in fallen man.

For many Protestants of New England, the religious experiments of Rhode Island conjured up the ghost of Münster, a fear that the type of secular and spiritual chaos that surfaced a century ago in the Westphalian city had been replanted in the New World. Münster was brought to mind whenever the New England patriarchs sensed the dangers posed by the type of radical utopianism expounded by local groups of Anabaptists, Gortions, Quakers, and Baptists.[108] In general, the Bay colonists tended to view Rhode Island as a refuge for radical sectarians, an asylum for the hotheads and heretics of New England. And these accusations were not without foundation. Strict adherence to the principle of freedom of conscience and the separation of church and state had created the conditions for the rise of a pragmatic and somewhat anarchic Protestant community. No two towns worshiped alike, and as there was no model of reform or magisterium the colonists tended to let their conscience follow the arguments and proofs that best confirmed internal convictions. The only shared tenets were those that fostered plurality, ranging from the defense of the conviction that "all men may walk as their consciences persuade them" (to cite an edict of the General Court) to the precepts underwriting visions of an apostolic, voluntary, and charismatic church. As a consequence, from Providence to Portsmouth, Newport to Warwick, variety reigned – a point made by a royal commission in 1665, which observed that the parishioners could not even agree on a common meeting place and tended instead to alternate between their scattered homes.[109]

Although Roger Williams and the other Rhode Island colonists were the first to develop a "lively experiment" in religious liberty, the issue of tolerance was not new to Protestantism. In taking up this theme, Williams was transplanting to American shores a dialogue that had shadowed developments since the rise of the Reformation. Freedom of belief had never been a central tenet of Protestant teaching. Despite his own experience, Luther had limited tolerance for religious dissent, as did Melanchthon and Calvin, both of whom actively encouraged the rooting out and execution of Spiritualists and Anabaptists. The first principled defense of tolerance began with the French Protestant Sebastian Castellio (1515–63) in his work *Concerning Heretics* (1554). Written with the recent execution of the Spiritualist Michael Servetus in mind, it anticipated many of the later lines of argument taken up by Williams, including a similar tendency of relativizing religious truth, the use of Pauline morality to condemn persecution, and the conviction that belief was beyond the remit of earthly authority. Similar views would also surface in the early seventeenth century in the Dutch Republic, Europe's most liberal land, where a number of prominent voices weighed in on the side of tolerance during the debates surrounding the views of Jacob Arminius, among them Hugo Grotius and Simon Episcopius.[110]

Williams took up many of these themes and borrowed from previous arguments, and in particular the hermeneutical approach of Castellio, who made the typological distinction between the vengeful sword of the Old Testament and the spiritual sword of Christ. But the most profound influence on Williams' thought, and the context for understanding the tenor of his own ideas, was the debate raging in England during the Civil War. As soon as he returned to England, Williams published *The Bloudy Tenent of Persecution* (1644) and immediately became one of the major protagonists in favor of religious toleration.[111] Historically and symbolically, this was an important moment. The English toleration debates joined both sides of the Atlantic in a common discourse, conflated Old World Protestantism with the New, and enabled men such as Roger Williams and the Newport Baptist John Clarke to draw from American experience in order to rethink traditional Protestant convictions.

And yet as important as this transatlantic dialogue was for the development of the faith, Protestant culture in America was not only shaped by theological ideas. Just as significant, especially with reference to the themes of tolerance and plurality, was the setting itself. Never before had there been so much neutral space available for the evolution of a church, and while the sheer scale offered clear advantages for the march of the Protestant vision, it also worked to enervate and divide. Where was the dialogue, the tension, the juxtapositioning, the close-quartered Christianity that had shaped the European movements? American Protestantism, by its very nature, had to rely on the energies and the ideas of the individual believer to a much greater extent. There were too few parishioners and too much space in between. Equally as unique was the sheer diversity of peoples and religious cultures, the scale of the racial and ethnic landscape. No Anglican parishioner in Britain, for instance, ever experienced the same range and variety of neighbors as an English settler of the Middle Colonies, some of whom worshiped within earshot of Dutch Calvinists, Scottish Presbyterians, Swedish Lutherans, native Americans, and African slaves.[112]

In the beginning, pluralism was as much the result of practice as theory, and thus it was crucial that the Dutch Republic played such an important role in the establishment of the Middle Colonies, the settlements to the west of Rhode Island, where there was a similar range of religious diversity. Not only were the Dutch an extremely practical people, they were also habituated to a religious culture that professed the virtues of tolerance and had learned to live with diversity. Roger Williams himself conceded that the idea of tolerance was first widely put into practice in Amsterdam, for God had raised up "that poor *fisher-town*" precisely because it had shown mercy to the "*distressed* and *persecuted* consciences who fled there."[113]

The Reformation in the Dutch Republic had begun as a fragmented movement and it remained fragmented even after the Reformed confession had been declared the official faith. Lacking in political patronage, and pressed into isolation by Habsburg religious policy, the early movement quickly revealed two characteristics that cultivated plurality: a tendency to dissimulate and a talent to conceal. Both grew out of the experience of the years of persecution, and both helped to point the religious culture in the direction of accommodation. Contemporaries noted the relative liberalism of the land, remarking, as did the English statesman and essayist William Temple (1628–99), that the Republic seemed "to favour no particular or curious inquisition into the Faith or Religious Principles of any peaceable man."[114]

While this was certainly true to an extent, the practice of Dutch toleration was more complex than it seemed on the surface. Very few public figures actually defended the idea of open tolerance. Isolated voices emerged with the Arminian crisis in the 1620s, but in general what the Republic preserved was freedom of private conscience rather than freedom of practice. Minority religions might be observed in the household or even in covert Catholic chapels built into private dwellings (the *schuilkerken*, for instance), but they could not infringe on the public realm. It was not religious tolerance in the philosophical sense, but a type of dissimulation or connivance (*conniventie*) that had been fostered by the experiences of the Revolt and sustained by an urban culture that valued its civic freedoms.[115] It was vague, pragmatic, and opportunistic, and it would be the source of continual conflict between the Reformed orthodox clergy, who wanted to extend the influence of the church, and the "libertine" regents of the cities, many of whom, with political power and the interests of trade in mind, favored a non-dogmatic, laissez-faire approach. This tension between the spokesmen of the Reformed church and the ruling elite remained a mainstay of Dutch culture throughout its golden age. In the eyes of the orthodox clergy, the freedoms, the liberties, and above all the tolerance so prized in the Republic had brought nothing to the land but the shame of the whore of Babylon.[116]

This culture of tolerance and coexistence, as well the tensions and the fault-lines that had developed in the observing of it, was transplanted to America by the Dutch as they settled New Amsterdam in 1624. Religion was not overlooked by the Dutch West India Company, and in fact most of the Amsterdam directors tended towards the more rigid form of Calvinism. Similarly, the first servants of the Dutch church in the New World, from the first lay comforter of the sick (*krankbezoeker*), Bastiaen Janz. Krol, to the ministers Jonas Michaëlius, Everhardus Bogardus, and Johannes Megapolensis, were all orthodox Calvinists bent on maintaining and creating a church that mirrored the institution at home. Jonas Michaëlius (1577–1638), the first ordained clergyman sent to the colony, for instance, requested that all synodal acts of Amsterdam be shipped to the colony as soon as they were issued. But religion was never the first priority of the Company, and in any event the sense of spiritual union was always unsettled by the "stealthily tolerant" attitude of Dutch merchant society.[117]

As in the Republic, the only public religion was the Dutch Reformed; but just as in the Republic, the authorities included the proviso that no man should be persecuted for his faith. What was completely lacking in New Amsterdam, however, was the structural framework that made it possible for the Reformed church to maintain its dominance despite the freedoms granted to individual conscience. Although subject to the Estates-General, the church in America was effectively under the control of the Company's board of directors in Amsterdam. The classis of Amsterdam might approve clergy for appointment and submit appeals but ultimately it was the Company and thus the director-general that had power over the church. Michaëlius tried to establish more precise spheres of rule during his tenure, in the hope, as he wrote in a letter home in 1628, that he might thereby "separate carefully the ecclesiastical from the civil matters which occur, so that each one may be occupied with his own subject."[118] But his efforts, and the efforts of the clergymen who followed him, came to little. Religious affairs continued to reflect the fairly relaxed and broad-based heterogeneity favored by the regents at home.

Repeatedly during the period of Dutch rule, attempts made to impose a rigid form of orthodoxy or sharpen the boundaries between confessional communities met with stiff opposition. By way of example, in his efforts to impel the director-general Willem Kieft to maintain a stricter code of morality in the colony (public and private), the minister Everardus Bogardus (1607–47) fulminated from the pulpit, rallied the parishioners in their homes, and forwarded appeals to the Amsterdam classis. In response, Kieft boycotted his sermons and discharged cannons during the hour of service.[119] A few years later, as the rigid Calvinist director-general Pieter Stuyvesant set out to coordinate a sense of common confessional purpose his attempts were consistently undermined by the Company directors. His efforts to restrict the growth of the Lutheran community, prohibit open services and conventicles, and block the appointment of a minister were reined in by the Company directors. The directors took a similar line with regard to the Jewish settlers. But perhaps even more significant was the resistance offered by the locals themselves in the town of Flushing of Long Island, who viewed Stuyvesant's ordinance against the Quakers as both a violation of the "freedom from molestacon" clause in their charter and contrary to the teaching of Christ, by whose example Christians should learn to love all men regardless of faith and turn away from persecution.[120] This was the so-called Flushing Remonstrance (1657), the earliest theoretical defense of toleration to emerge in New Amsterdam.

Thus, from the beginning, the communities that took root in the Hudson River Valley were more tolerant of religious diversity than Protestant communities in Europe. In New Netherland, it was impossible to maintain the close functional association of church and state that characterized magisterial Protestantism in Europe. Not only was the ecclesio-political structure piecemeal and precarious, but the parishioners were drawn in so many different directions it was difficult to maintain any stable sense of religious community. As late as the 1660s the minister Johannes Polhemius was complaining about the lack of ecclesial coordination in the colony and the poor quality of education in the parishes. At the first scent of freedom, the children abandoned the schools, while the communities, if left untended, followed passing whims. To add to this, no other colony in America had such a multiethnic, polyglot population. In the patroonship of Rensselaerswyck alone, local inhabitants included men from the south Netherlands, Amsterdam, Norway, Germany, Sweden, France, Denmark, and England. When the Jesuit Isaac Jogues passed through New Amsterdam in 1644, he was told there were 18 different languages being spoken in the town.[121] Throughout the period of Dutch rule, the Reformed clergy noted with mounting alarm the growth of religious plurality, pointing to the rise of substantial communities tolerated by the Company, first the Lutherans, then the Jews, then the Quakers. With the arrival of the Jewish settlers, the clergyman Johannes Megapolensis wrote to the Amsterdam classis expressing his fear that the Reformed Church would soon be pressed out altogether.[122] Once again the Company counseled accommodation.

Colonial America was a religious land, and not just in the Puritan theocracies of New England or the epicenters of Anglican influence but Rhode Island and the Middle Colonies as well. Despite the great variety of cultures and religions, most people identified with a Christian confession and organized their life according to its calendrical rhythms. European Protestants did not become American atheists, even though in the darker days some of the Reformed ministers may have thought this was the case. What happened in America, and paradigmatically so in the Middle Colonies, was that the architectonics of the faith – that is, the ties between belief and community, and so between inner and outer faith – began to fall away. In Europe, religion was conceived and expressed in terms of organic community, a close association of the secular and spiritual, with the confession of the faith providing a foundation for both the institutional and the intellectual edifice. In colonial America, this synchronicity did not exist on the same scale, and this proved lethal for magisterial Protestantism. No longer pulled between the interests of the state and the interests of the church, religious beliefs in the New World were caught up in a tug-of-war between personal conceits and sacral community, between the institutional and the spiritual, and between order and enthusiasm.[123]

As we will see, these would be the main pressure points of Protestant development in the early eighteenth century, but they first came to the surface in the two contexts that particularly encouraged the rise of pluralism: the "lively experiment" in religious liberty in the colony of Rhode Island and the "stealthily tolerant" outpost of Dutch merchants in New Amsterdam.

4

Dominions

Orthodoxy was an axiom of early Christianity, derived from Paul's injunction to avoid division within the community (1 Corinthians 1:10). The Protestant Reformation did not suddenly introduce this ideal into religious culture; and yet with the rise of religious division in sixteenth-century Europe, the sense of urgency placed upon the need for an established orthodoxy or magisterium reached a level without precedent in recent Christian history. Confessional division threatened ancient, embedded assumptions about the church, while the sheer variety of voices began to challenge the self-evident truths of traditional religion. It was a problem that occupied all of the magisterial Protestant traditions, and they all responded in more or less the same way. The theologians argued that there could only be one true church and one faithful corpus of belief and that all deviations from orthodoxy dishonored God and led to the damnation of the soul. Confessional Christianity did not offer any latitude on this point: the best one could expect was a temporary stalemate before unity was restored.[1]

Thus, unlike developments in America, where the communities faced the danger of falling apart in the absence of magisterial control, in Europe the danger was the opposite, in the sense that some feared that too much order might extinguish the very lifeblood of the evangelical religion. Recently, historians of the German Reformation have captured this preoccupation with order in the paradigms confessionalism and confessionalization, all with a view to illuminating the interlocking and overlapping religious dynamic that shaped the culture of the age. Indeed, so fundamental is the process thought to have been that all of the main magisterial confessions, Catholicism included, are said to have been affected by it. Of course, there were distinctions according to time and place, and it was never a linear process. The strength of local resistance often contributed as much to the dynamic as the normative intentions of the state. Nevertheless, during the confessional age, and primarily from the Peace of Augsburg (1555) to the Peace of Westphalia (1648), theology emerged as the central rationale and religious habitus as the main means through which Protestants ordered the world around them. Using the resources recently placed at their disposal, from the symbolism and texts of public religion to the methods of control and indoctrination

Protestants: A History from Wittenberg to Pennsylvania 1517–1740 By C. Scott Dixon
© 2010 C. Scott Dixon

bound up with education and church discipline, Lutherans and Calvinists were able to piece together what the church historian Thomas Kaufmann has termed a "matrix for a mental world."[2] Protestants were starting to think and act as Protestants.

Bonds of Communion

Under the cross

The first Protestants thought of themselves as the direct heirs of the apostles, the descendants of a lineage of Christian men and women who had devoted themselves to God and suffered for it in their earthly lives. Proving this claim became a chief preoccupation of the first generation of reformers, and no one set to the task with more energy and learning than the Lutheran Matthias Flacius Illyricus (1520–75), author of the *Catalogus Testium Veritatis* (1556) and the *Magdeburg Centuries* (1559–74), who once neatly summarized his approach in a letter to an acquaintance. Flacius described how

> in a certain order and in sequence it would be demonstrated how the true church and its religion gradually fell off the track from that original purity and simplicity in the apostolic time because of the negligence and ignorance of teachers, and also partly through the evil of the godless. Then it must be shown that at times the church was restored by a few really faithful men, and why the light of truth sometimes shone more clearly, and sometimes under the growing darkness of godless entity it was again more or less darkened – until, finally at our time, when the truth was almost totally destroyed, through God's unbounded benefice, the true religion in its purity was again restored.[3]

But to be convincing as proof of election, histories of this kind had to do more than just trace the fall from apostolic Christianity or draw up lists of proto-evangelical "faithful men." They had to unite the Protestant present with the Christian past. As late as the eighteenth century Cotton Mather was still insisting on the need to commune with the Christian past: "The *First Age* was the Golden Age," he wrote, "to return unto That, will make a man a *Protestant*, and I may add, a *Puritan*."[4] There were different ways of doing this. Some scholars turned to historical exegesis, some to biblical prophecy, others to the methods used by Flacius, which entailed sifting through church histories looking for previsions of Protestant thought. But the most effective approach, at least in the early period, proved to be the genre of martyrology.

Four major martyrologists emerged from within the magisterial tradition: Ludwig Rabus, Adriaen Cornelis van Haemstede, Jean Crespin, and John Foxe. Although each man worked within a specific confessional or ethnic community, their martyrologies were similar in style and purpose, the authors themselves having similar personal histories and often moving in the same circles. Granted, there were differences in approach – Foxe wrote narrative histories, for instance, Rabus tended to compile – but the rationale behind their works was essentially the same. All four wrote histories of the Protestant church from the perspective of suffering and persecution. The schematic was Augustinian, cast as a struggle between light and darkness, and the intent was to shed light on the providential history of God's people. Moreover, all four authors recognized the rhetorical function of their works. Projecting Protestants as innocent victims not only invested their histories with the ready-made Christian moral of the triumph of the meek, it transfigured Catholics into villains and thereby turned centuries of Catholic historiography on its head. This was history with a clear purpose: to confirm Protestants in their faith and to turn skeptics into believers.[5]

Since many of the Protestant communities of the Reformation era began as victimized or ostracized minorities there were ample histories of adversity to relate, even if historically some groups suffered more than others. The early history of the Anabaptists, for instance, was little more than one chapter of exclusion and persecution followed by another. Within the magisterial tradition, the followers of the Reformed faith suffered the most, many communities sharing the same fate in their own homelands of France, England, and the Low Countries as the radicals did in exile: discrimination, displacement, and persecution. What follows is a study of one group of Reformed Protestants, the Huguenots of France, and their experiences as an oppressed and persecuted minority. Needless to say, no one history can stand for all others, but it will relate something of the role of persecution in the shaping of the faith.

The chief memorialist of Huguenot suffering was Jean Crespin (1520–72).[6] Having fled from France in 1545 because he was suspected of Lutheranism, Crespin eventually took refuge in Geneva and set up a publishing house in the city. There, while producing among other things works of Protestant church history, including French translations of the German historian Johann Sleidan, author of the *Commentaries* (*De statu religionis et reipublicae, Carolo Quinto, Caesare, commentarii*), and of Bullinger, he compiled and published the *Histoire des Martyrs* (1554), a compendium of martyrdom that began in the medieval period and continued up to the present day. Regularly revised and expanded by Crespin during his lifetime, and further reworked by the Genevan minister Simon Goulart after his death, the *Histoire* went through numerous amended editions until the appearance of the definitive version in 1619. Along with the Bible and the Psalter, this was one of the foundation texts of French Protestant identity. Memorized, vocalized, fetishized, even elevated to the status of liturgical text (in Normandy, it was regularly read from the pulpit during the service), the book itself became an object of devotion.

In the manner of its composition and the general tenor of the text, the *Histoire des Martyrs* says much about the place of adversity in Protestant self-perception. As the Wars of Religion raged, the text was revised and expanded to accommodate the reports of massacres and executions in cities such as Vassy, Sens, Nîmes, Tours, and Paris. The result was a work that served as both a record of the thoughts of the victims and a flesh-and-blood enactment of the religious struggle. Thus, like all of the martyrologists, Crespin could do two things very well: elicit sympathy and proselytize. While offering covert assurances to the Huguenot faithful that, although they were victims at present, ultimately they were on the winning side, Crespin also made it clear that the Catholics could look forward to a fate similar to that of the Egyptians or the Sodomites. False religion and the persecution of the godly would bring down the wrath of God. To make the point, Crespin was not beyond reworking the individual episodes in order to provide a more dramatic biblical backdrop or adding theological precision to the last words of a victim. Nor did he hesitate to depart from the traditional image of the martyr who went passively to his or her death. Huguenot martyrs often died with weapons in hand – no less innocent than the docile saints of the *Golden Legend*, but more in the mold of the victims of injustice described by Duplessis-Mornay and Beza. It was a text that spoke directly to a community under siege, moving backward and forward in time in order to make sense of the desperate struggles of the present.[7]

Pressed back by the Wars of Religion, the Huguenots naturally tended to withdraw into their own social and spiritual worlds, building dominions hedged in by the faith. Unlike the forced retreat of the radicals and the Anabaptists, this did not result in the continual uprooting and near extinction of the church. By the end of the first decade of the war, the population of France had become roughly 10 percent Protestant. This works out to just under 2,000,000 people worshipping in as many as 1,240 Reformed churches. This was a substantial number of Protestants living in the midst of hostile Catholics, and consequently it was necessary to develop social and institutional bonds to hold the community in place.[8] In the beginning, the Huguenots tended to group according to ties of kinship and patronage. At the apex were the Huguenot grandees and their provincial clientele: those in Picardy gathered around Condé, those in Normandy around Coligny, those in Poitou around La Rochefoucauld. But the associations cut through the entire social and political order, drawing in the rural nobility, royal and provincial officials, *parlementaires*, the complex sovereign bodies in the cities, and even the handworkers and artisans of the urban communes.[9]

Connecting, and indeed overseeing, these networks of believers was a church structure modeled on the presbyterial system of Calvin's Geneva. By the late 1550s the French Reformed church functioned on a federal level, its first national synod taking place in Paris in 1559, where the clergy drew up a confession of faith. With Geneva, the Pays de Vaud, and Neuchâtel dispatching clergy as well as catechisms and liturgical works, the churches in France soon had all the attributes of the Reformed system. Consistories, colloquies, and synods oversaw church affairs at the national and provincial level, while pastors and elders administered to local congregations in various spiritual, legal, administrative, and caritative roles.[10] Well before the Edict of Nantes (1598) secured the French Protestants the right to exercise their religion in public, the Reformed church was already a powerful presence in the realm.

The Edict of Nantes granted the Huguenots the same civil rights as Catholics and, under a set of strict conditions, a framework for public worship, but like the Peace of Augsburg, there was a large gap between the letter of the law and its application. From 1598 to 1685, that is, from the year when the Edict was issued to its revocation by King Louis XIV (1638–1715), the history of the Huguenots in seventeenth-century France is essentially a narrative of exclusion and withdrawal.[11] Louis XIII placed restrictions on political assemblies, suppressed places of refuge, and razed fortresses. Huguenot schools were closed down, churches were demolished, the clergy were harried out of the realm, while the gradual march of the Bourbon *reconquista*, aided in part by the Jesuits and the Oratorians, drew on all manner of techniques – from proselytization to bribes and rewards – to win back Huguenots to the Catholic fold. With the accession of Louis XIV and the application *à la rigueur* of the various restrictions on the exercise of the faith, the pressure intensified, the most effective and direct method being the increased surveillance and the billeting of troops in Protestant households in order to bring about forced conversions. Over time, the Reformed church was reduced to a shadow of its former self. As early as the fall of La Rochelle (1628), the exiled Huguenot poet Théodore-Agrippa d'Aubigné (1552–1630) feared that a new age had dawned, and it was little less than apocalyptic. "The storms which roll over our heads, the gulfs which open, one after another, before us – in a word, the three scourges of God which overwhelm us together . . ."[12]

How did the Huguenots react to these conditions? How did they order their world? One response, as we have seen in the discussion of the Protestant conscience, was the militancy of the sixteenth century. But this was politics. If we shift our focus to faith and religiosity we see different trends. The most notable feature was the tendency of the Huguenots to turn in on themselves, to adopt a siege mentality and rely on their own resources. This has been termed a process of "interior emigration" with reference to individuals such as Theodore de Mayerne and d'Aubigné, both of whom managed to compromise with the Catholic world while preserving, inwardly, their own values and traditions.[13] Most French Reformed lived a life of this kind, balanced between outer formalities and inner convictions. The Huguenot magistrates of Castres and Pau, for instance, solved the problem by drawing a distinction between the public and the private: husbands conformed to Catholic expectations when in the workplace, while the wives preserved the faith at home. This was a thoroughly pragmatic solution to the demands placed on the conscience, and one that had earned the opprobrium of Calvin in his tracts against the Nicodemism of the more cautious (or casuistical, as he saw it) of the early French evangelicals.

In terms of a general or a collective response, the natural reflex was to close ranks and seek closer union. This did not necessarily result in Huguenots avoiding contact with Catholics or seeking purity in separation. In Caen, the poet Jean Renaud de Segrais (1624–1701) described how "Catholics and Protestants lived in good understanding, eating, drinking, gambling, amusing themselves together, and with a friendly leave-taking went off on their separate ways, some to Mass, some to the *prêche*."[14] But as the Bourbon campaign of persecution gathered momentum, the Huguenots tended to place less stress on social forms and fell back on an "inner fraternalism" bound by the intimate and emotive ties of faith, family, and shared remembrance. Within the church, this gradual retreat into a type of inner refuge, both personal and collective, "created a dominant mentality of defensiveness and stoicism, and the need to rely on its collective resources."[15] Thus, while the public world of Protestantism atrophied, and as the numbers declined and the Huguenot presence in the kingdom fell away, a heightened sense of community and a deepening of personal faith began to compensate for the forms, structures, and outward display of the militant period. Whereas the heroic figures of the previous century had been depicted as little less than warrior-saints, the heroic Huguenots of the late seventeenth century were rather in the mold of those described by the historian Élie Benoît (1640–1728): "women and children . . . armed with all the passages of Scripture that could serve to explain the true doctrine."[16] Well into the eighteenth century, groups of believers continued to gather in dark places with their psalters and Bibles to sing psalms and hear sermons and readings from the Word. As ever, the one sure place of refuge for Protestants suffering under the law was the gospel.

For many others, the refuge was literal: exile in foreign lands. With the Revocation of the Edict of Nantes (October 18, 1685), Louis XIV sounded the death knell for organized Protestantism in France. Huguenot temples were destroyed, public worship was forbidden, further restrictions were placed on entry into offices, clergymen were forced into exile, and schools were closed. Huguenot children had to be baptized in the Catholic faith; if the parents resisted, or refused to convert, the children could be taken and placed in Catholic custody. Understandably, many chose to go into exile. But this too was fraught with danger. With the exception of some high-ranking officials and provincial nobility, no Huguenot subjects were granted the right to emigrate. If captured, they faced imprisonment, or even a stint in the galleys. And yet tens of thousands preferred to take the risk and head for Protestant lands. Calculations vary, but perhaps as many as 20 percent of remaining Huguenots decided to abandon the realm (up to 170,000 people).[17] Shepherded by guides, often in the dark of night along labyrinthine routes, frequently disguised as peddlers, pilgrims, beggars and peasants (faces darkened with polish), or even rosary-bead sellers, they made their way to temporary sanctuaries in Switzerland before moving on to settle permanently in England, the Dutch Republic, the principalities of northern Germany, Sweden and Norway, and even as far away as the New World. Next to the trade in slaves, it was the largest forced migration of the age.[18]

There was a sense in which transience suited the Reformed faith of the French Huguenots better than other forms of corporate Protestantism. The post-Zwinglian Helvetic tradition was not as deeply rooted in ethnic or dynastic tradition as Lutheranism or Anglicanism, and in fact one of the distinguishing features of the Genevan church was the extent to which it was conceived and peopled by foreigners. In his desire to renew Christianity without conceding any essentials, Calvin was in effect picking up where Bucer had left off with his ideas of the *regnum Christi*. The Genevan church *was* a church of the afflicted, gathered in exile in order to see through the vision of Christ's reign on earth.[19] There could be no compromise, no indulgence, and no essential ties to any particular place. It might have been Strasbourg (say) if not Geneva, and in any event Calvin always believed that once the French king had come to his senses, the final frontier would be the state. But this did not happen. Instead, Geneva remained the first city of Protestant refuge, its streets crowded with men and women from France, England, Scotland, the Low Countries, even Italy and Spain.

But Geneva was not the only safe harbor. As the religious persuasions of rulers changed, so too did the direction of the flow of refugees. While, during the reign of Mary Tudor (1553–58) in England at least 800 of the queen's opponents sought refuge in centers of Protestantism such as Strasbourg, Zurich, Frankfurt, Emden, and Geneva, the latter being the place which John Knox famously termed "the most perfect school of Christ,"[20] in more welcoming times, exile communities took root in England as well as the northern Netherlands, East Friesland, and the Protestant lands of Germany. Southern England, first under Edward VI and then under Elizabeth I, became a sanctuary for the persecuted Protestants of Catholic and imperial Europe. Peter Martyr, Martin Bucer, and John a Lasco were only the most prominent of the early exiles, and they were followed by a steady stream of lesser-known French and Dutch refugees, most of whom belonged to the communities gathered around the stranger churches in

London, though many others also settled in the smaller settlements of Sandwich, Colchester, Canterbury, or Southampton.

Thus, when the Revocation of 1685 set off the final Huguenot diaspora, well over a century of Protestant exile and *sociabilité à distance* had prepared the ground for their reception. A network of émigré French Protestants was already in place, with vast amounts of correspondence maintaining lines of communication. Crucially important in the early days was the advice dispatched by reformers such as Calvin, Beza, and Bullinger, the latter alone having written thousands of letters to Reformed congregations throughout Europe. These networks, both formal and informal, not only created a "community in the know," joined by the same general beliefs and the same sense of purpose and place, they also upheld the structural integrity of the exile churches. Requests for pastors, schoolteachers, church funds, and liturgical texts were regularly forwarded to the synods and men and books were dispatched in response.[21] And this sense of community was not just confined to national or linguistic groups. By the late sixteenth century, Reformed Protestants began to think in terms of a church that embraced all of the persecuted members of the fold. We can gauge the vitality of this imagined community by looking at one of the most hard-to-reach corners of human empathy: the money purse. Hearing of the massacres of the Huguenots during the Wars of Religion, for instance, the kirks of Scotland repeatedly took up collections for their fellow Calvinists in France. In Edinburgh, the amounts might reach from the 130 pounds of a wealthy merchant to the 4 shillings of Bessie Murdoch. During the Stuart age, the stranger churches of London raised funds for the Protestants of the Valtelline valley, the Bohemian Brethren in Poland, the Calvinists of the Palatinate, and the Irish Protestants of the 1640s. In a similar manner, the pastors of the Emden refugee communities frequently imposed fasts for the distant "communities of God" facing persecution at the hands of Guise or Habsburg hirelings.[22]

But it was the personal rather than the formal ties that invested international Calvinism with its vitality. Bound by faith, family, local loyalties, and shared histories, both imagined and real, the Reformed congregations in exile drew on the strength of their senior members for cohesion. The polymath Samuel Hartlib (1600–62) is an example of this type of refugee. Having left Prussia to escape the forward march of the Habsburg armies, he took refuge in London and established a newsletter service that became a clearing house for the commonwealth of learning. Exploiting his contacts with scholars and scientists throughout Europe, Hartlib frequently came to the aid of Reformed communities in Germany, Bohemia, Moravia, and northern Italy, whether through charity, intelligence, or hospitality, in order to assuage their suffering and prepare the ground for the "planting" or the "sowing" of refugees throughout the world. He spoke of it as "spiritual husbandry," and his efforts must be understood as part of his pansophic vision of the total reformation in preparation for the Last Days.[23] Of course, the risk in a life spent devoted to a community *in absentia* was that many of the émigrés might never really integrate into their new surroundings. Theodore de Mayerne, for instance, enjoyed great success in England as first physician to the Catholic queen, Anne of Denmark, but his personal world remained that of continental Calvinism. Wives, sons and brothers-in-law, personal confidants, doctors, apothecaries, amanuenses, agents – all were Protestants, and most were émigré Huguenots.[24]

On the whole, though, the history of the Huguenot exiles in foreign lands is largely a narrative of social and economic success. But it did require some measure of subterfuge, a willingness to skirt certain themes or speak in a vague or evasive way, and this tended to give rise to suspicions that their hearts and minds were elsewhere. The point was made in the charges brought against the Reformed theologian Jacques Bernard (1658–1718) in 1714. In eyes of his calumniator, Bernard was too quick to bend to orthodox consensus, certain proof that he was "one of the number of the Orthodoxo-politici, or Politico-orthodoxi, a type which, *entre nous*, displeases me; I think more highly of a man who is in error and who speaks according to his conscience, than of these people who skew and disguise their true sentiments."[25] But this was perhaps expecting a bit much from Bernard, even at this relatively late date. For even in the lands where Protestants went in search of sanctuary (such as the Dutch Republic, where Jacques Bernard practiced his alleged duplicity), there was constant pressure to conform to the orthodoxies of the public faith. Close in kind was rarely close enough. Indeed, Protestants often experienced the greatest degree of intolerance when they mixed among themselves.

Confessional culture: the Protestants of Germany

Generally speaking, historians consider the period spanning the mid-sixteenth century to the mid-seventeenth the high point of the confessional age. During this period, roughly speaking from the 1560s to the late 1640s, the tensions and disputes that had been brewing came to the surface in persecution and open wars. Paramount was the Thirty Years' War (1618–48), a conflict that pitched the Protestant and Catholic powers of Europe against each other in a struggle for religious hegemony, but there were other disputes on a similar scale, above all the Dutch Revolt (1572–1648) and the Civil War in England (1642–49). These conflicts were symptomatic of a broader dynamic, itself the sum of two related parts: first, the rise of religion as the rationale of private and public affairs, and second, the associated impulse to enforce religious uniformity, to unite the land and its people under the banner of a single, orthodox, uncontested faith. Throughout Europe, this determination to consolidate a public confession came to play a determining role in the fashioning of collective purpose and identity. This happened everywhere to varying degrees and with different levels of success in both Protestant and Catholic lands.[26] In the German context, however, the native soil of the Reformation, the process was particularly intense, not least because there were so many different confessional states in such close proximity. For this reason, and for the purposes of illustration, the following analysis will take German events as a paradigm of the general process.

For the German Protestants of the seventeenth century, the pope-as-Antichrist discourse had lost none of its urgency. The same dialectic used by the original reformers was now taken up by propagandists of the third and fourth generation, and in fact the discourse become so pronounced that many Jesuits considered it a novelty of the age. One Catholic author claimed it was ubiquitous: "The children in the household; the burgher in the street; the women at the dinner table; the students in the schools; the professors in the disputations; the preachers from the pulpit; the writers through their quills: all cry in unison, the Pope is the Antichrist, Antichrist, Antichrist!"[27] As familiar as this may sound to an ear attuned to the rhetoric of the early Reformation, there were differences. To begin with, it had become a much more complex science, as clergymen and theologians probed deeper and deeper into the prophecies. Although arcane, this antichristology was an important exercise in the making of confessional culture for it enabled interpreters to find a place for second and third generation Protestants in the Christian scheme of things and make sense of the trials and misfortunes of the present.[28] To add to this, the propagandists of the seventeenth century had integrated a new range of adversaries into the discourse. No longer just pitted against Rome or the German emperor, the Protestants of the confessional age had to deal with super-powers such as Spain and the Austrian Habsburg empire as well as Catholic leagues in France and Germany. And most threatening of all was the rise of the Jesuits, opponents so dangerous they might have been a mirror image of Protestantism's younger selves: mobile, militant, eloquent, and highly schooled, these men from Munich, Ingolstadt, and Mainz had all of the devotion and missionary zeal of the early evangelicals.

In light of the dangers, it is little wonder that Protestant right of resistance arguments resurfaced in the seventeenth century. By 1617, the year of the Reformation centenary, most German Protestants considered war with the Catholics an inevitability. Serious stand-offs had already occurred in Cologne (1583–88), Strasbourg (1592–1604), Donauwörth (1607), and Cleves-Jülich (1609–14), and on each occasion the likelihood of a general war drew closer. Thus, when the estates of Bohemia rebelled against the Catholic emperor Ferdinand II (1578–1637) in 1618, Protestant Germany was not surprised. Nor was Ferdinand in much doubt about who was responsible. The emperor blamed it on the Calvinist schools in Heidelberg, Geneva, and Basel, where many of the Bohemian nobles had been educated in their youth, having read while there, among other things, the works of Duplessis-Mornay and Beza, and thereby "imbibed the spirit of rebellion and opposition to lawful authority."[29] In actual fact, Ferdinand may have misread the rhetoric, for there was more constitutionalism than confessionalism to the Bohemian defense. But he was correct to suggest that the resistance arguments of the previous generations still had a presence in Protestant culture.

Most authors drew on the discourse in a half-hearted way, but others were more direct. The Calvinist philosopher and theologian Johannes Althusius (1557–1638) spoke openly of the covenant with God and the need for the magistrates to take up the sword in defense of the faith. Similarly, the Lutheran Johann Gerhard (1582–1637) drew on both the *Magdeburg Confession* and the *Vindiciae* of Duplessis-Mornay in arguing that a ruler forfeits his power when he abuses the laws of the realm, one of which is preservation of the true church. But even when the authors avoided any direct reference to resistance theory by couching their arguments in secular or constitutional language (and it was now that the word *politia* started to appear regularly in titles), the deeper purpose of the defense was essentially to protect "our true Christian religion," by which they meant either the Lutheran or the Reformed church of their fatherlands. Indeed, by this period the very idea of fatherland, which was at the heart of the arguments in defense of constitutional, customary, and ancient rights, had essentially become a Protestant trope: the defense of the nation, *defensio patriae*, implied the defense of the faith, *defensio religionis*.[30]

The full measure of religious anxiety was revealed in 1630 when Gustavus Adolphus (1594–1632), the Lutheran king of Sweden, landed with his troops in northern Germany and began marshalling a defense against the Habsburg advance. In the flood of propaganda that followed we can make out some of the dimensions of confessional culture during this period. Above all Gustavus was welcomed as the champion of Protestantism, God's chosen ruler of Christian men who would finally release them from persecution and captivity. But he was also projected as the new Constantine, the "Lion of the North" come to do battle with the seven-headed beast of the apocalypse, the prophesied savior, Judas Maccabeus redivivus, the Swedish Hercules, and a type of sacral figure whose image had the wonder-working qualities of a medieval saint. The Augsburg Catholics mocked this aspect of the Protestant reverence, claiming that Lutheran weavers nailed his pictures to their doors and prayed before it, "Dear Swede, help me!"[31] After his death the typologies continued. In mourning ceremonies from Helmstedt to Strasbourg, his corpse was likened to that of Caesar and Alexander, German heroes such as Arminius and Tuiscon, and biblical figures such as Daniel, David, Samson, and Solomon. In short, this figuration of a heightened Protestant consciousness had been embraced by all levels of cultural symbolism, from high classicism to popular religiosity, and appropriated by a broad range of social actors from professors to weavers.

It is worth noting that Gustavus Adolphus took on these roles as a *Protestant* hero, embraced by both Lutherans and Calvinists. The Swedish king's intervention in the Thirty Years' War raised the possibility once again that the two sides might unite in a single church. In this, little substantial progress had been made since the meeting in Marburg (1529), but the magisterial Protestants continued to address the issue of union from time to time, and there were instances when theological disparities had been overcome, especially when political circumstances favored a common defense. Examples of multilateral confessional statements would include the Tetrapolitan Confession (1530), the Wittenberg Concord (1536), the Consensus Tigurinus (1549), a joint declaration of the faith that effectively unified Swiss Protestants, the Second Helvetic Confession (1562), a symbolic work adopted by Reformed congregations in Scotland, France, Hungary, Poland, and the Netherlands, the consensus of Sendomir in Poland (1570), a formula that briefly brought together Lutherans, Calvinists, as well as the Bohemian Brethren, and the decision of the synod of Dort (1618/19).

Colloquies continued as well. Maulbronn (1564), Mömpelgard (1586), Leipzig (1631), Kassel (1661), and Berlin (1663) are just some of the more prominent meetings that placed union on the agenda. Hopes were so high at Leipzig that even the Lutheran controversialist Matthias Hoe von Hoenegg (1580–1645), who once confessed that he would rather seek common cause with Rome than the Reformed, opened the proceedings with an offering of peace.[32] But Leipzig, like the other attempts at theological unity, fell at the final hurdles, in this instance the differences over christology and the Eucharist. In the end, the only successful settlements were either based on an acceptable degree of ambiguity, such as the Tetrapolitan Confession and the Wittenberg Concord, or close credal cousinage, such as the agreements reached among the Helvetic Protestants.

The notion of a closer theological union, even the possibility of forming a single Protestant church (the radicals not included, of course), was never completely abandoned. The first of the reformers to argue in favor of union had been Martin Bucer, who stressed the continuities between the ancient church and the new. For Bucer, there could only be one church under Christ, and thus he spoke of the consensus of the apostolic community and set this as a common denominator for both evangelicals and Catholics. A similar line of argumentation was developed by the Helmstedt professor Georg Calixtus (1586–1656), one of the most eloquent and influential voices of ecumenicity in later Lutheranism, who turned to irenicism during the 1620s when the fortunes of German Protestantism were at their lowest ebb. Like Bucer before him, Calixtus believed that the theological disputes of his era could be overcome by reducing the arguments to the essentials, by which he meant those Christian tenets requisite for salvation. Calixtus termed this the ancient consensus (*consensus antiquitatis*) and he found its traces in the apostolic creeds, in the symbolic works of the fathers, in the councils, in tradition, and the history of the early church – the first five centuries – when the pure teaching of the apostles still hedged in the faith.[33] But Calixtus had little influence on his age. His brand of irenicism would not find a substantial following until later in the century. In his own day his ideas were generally rejected by both Protestants and Catholics alike, and he spent the final years of his life defending himself against the charges of being a syncretist and a nicodemite.

In the confessional culture of seventeenth-century Protestant Germany, it was extremely difficult to draw a line between details and essentials. For the *consensus antiquitatis* of Calixtus to have had any real meaning, religion had to be conceived in abstract and universal terms, detached from the contingencies of the present. As a historical phenomenon, however, magisterial Protestantism was the complete opposite of this: its history was contingent, its forms and configurations were contextual, and in the absence of a centralized and overarching magisterium, its corpus of beliefs was closely tied to time and place. Moreover, it is important to remember that the divisions among magisterial Protestants did not run between Lutherans and Calvinists but *types* of Lutherans and *varieties* of Reformed Protestants, the latter alone falling into categories such as Rhenish, Dutch, French, East Friesian, and Danubian. In short, the dynamic at work behind the growth of the Protestant churches along the Wittenberg–Zurich–Geneva axis did not cultivate toleration, inclusion, or ecumenicity. On the contrary, any religious community with a social or political presence was moving towards greater exclusivity within their respective domains.[34]

German Lutheranism, for instance, although it began as a fairly amorphous movement united by a few specific principles of belief and general loathing of the Catholic church, soon began to define itself more precisely in church orders and confessional statements. Luther's two catechisms of 1529 provided a point of departure, but it was the *Augsburg Confession* of 1530 that became the foundation charter of the church. This was the first substantial confession or public statement of Protestantism in history, a synthesis of the faith that defined what its members should believe. But this was not the final word. As the internecine debates heated up after Luther's death, both the Philippists, the Wittenberg faction that grouped around the writings of Melanchthon, and the Gnesio-Lutherans, a party of precisionists who claimed to be the sole custodians of Luther's pure ideas, recognized that staking a claim to being the legitimate heirs of the *Augsburg Confession* was the strongest argument in defense of religious truth. While the early reformers had drawn their arguments primarily, if not exclusively, from the pages of the Bible, later theologians worked more from symbolic confessions and epitomes stamped with the imprimatur of one of the leaders of the church. The disputes continued for much of the century, and it was only with the *Formula of Concord* (1577) and the *Book of Concord* (1580) that the Lutheran church (or the larger part of the church) was reconciled in its teachings. By that stage something essential about magisterial Protestantism had been confirmed: that the churches of Lutheranism and Calvinism had become as dogmatic and scholastic as the Catholicism they had set out to displace.[35]

This campaign to enforce orthodoxy and orthopraxis gave rise to a secular dynamic. It was an inescapable consequence of the place of religion in the social and political world. Few commentators at the time could imagine a temporal order without a uniform set of religious beliefs at its core. Without a stable and singular faith to bind society together, the state would descend into chaos. This was not just a Protestant conviction, but one shared by Catholics as well. The French *parlementaire* Étienne Pasquier (1529–1615) thought in the same terms as any mainstream Lutheran or Calvinist when he declaimed that "the general foundation [of a state] is principally dependent on the establishment of religion, because the fear and reverence of religion keeps all subjects within bounds more effectively than even the presence of the prince. Therefore the magistrates must above all other things prevent the mutation of religion or the existence of diverse religions in the same state."[36]

Unity of belief was an axiom of the confessional age and a core principle of magisterial Protestantism. Heterodoxy was equated with chaos and anarchy, orthodoxy with a fixed and unassailable order. And by the late sixteenth century it was the guiding logic of societal development in general. To borrow a metaphor of the age, the pursuit of orthodoxy had become the *primum mobile* of universal change, sitting above the other spheres of existence and exercising its influence at a distance through sermons and texts, confessions and articles of belief, catechisms, hymnals, new forms of music, art, and literature, as well as forms of ritual, symbolism, and material culture. Once translated into historical terms, this effected a phase of social, cultural, and political transformation with two related effects. First, the church and the state began to move closer together, with ministers often performing the same functions as secular officials and vice versa, presiding over the same organs of governance and watching over the same modalities of rule (discipline, public welfare, education), many of which had previously been the exclusive province of the church. And second, the state was invested with a providential purpose; it became a chosen nation, while the ruler became little less than a quasi-sacral figure in the mold of the heroic kings of the Old Testament.[37]

In the German lands, this development followed naturally from the Peace of Augsburg (1555) and the right of reformation: *cuius regio, eius religio,* "whose the region, his the religion." But there was a deeper impulse at work than just the letter of the law. Generally speaking, all social and political energies of the age were spent on the enforcement of order, and this included the religious sphere. The mainstream Protestant churches demonstrated the same sort of tendencies we associate with the making of the absolutist state, including the monopolization and centralization of power, policies of exclusion and circumscription, increased censorship and ideological inflexibility, and a tendency towards a closed rather than an open society. Translated into historical terms, this meant that Protestant Germany was made up of a collection of middling- and large-scale territories, petty princedoms, and city-states, each of which had its own unique conspectus of the faith (if based on symbolic texts) and its own local church magisterium. And more to the point, each of these territories sat in a symbiotic relation to the next. Not only did Protestants and Catholics share borders, but Lutherans and Calvinists as well. The result was a complex confessional landscape where the various churches worked to consolidate their own identities while staving off the threat presented by alternative faiths.

Thus, by the early seventeenth century, the magisterial Protestants of Germany not only defined themselves against the teachings of the papacy and the radicals but against each other as well. Indeed, if anything, the antagonism between the Lutherans and Calvinists was even sharper than that between Wittenberg or Heidelberg and Rome. Religious ideas were at the heart of the conflict, and in particular the doctrines relating to the Lord's Supper, predestination, and the nature of Christ. But there were more mundane reasons as well. Put simply, the rapid expansion of the Reformed faith threatened the continued existence of the Lutheran churches in northern Europe. Calvinism had not only become the public religion in Hungary, England, Scotland, and the Netherlands, but in lands closer to home. Moreover, with the conversion of Brandenburg and the intervention of the Dutch in the Cleves-Jülich crisis (1609), the possibility of northern Europe turning Reformed at the expense of Lutheranism was very real. It was thus the political resourcefulness of the Reformed church as much as its theology that lay behind Lutheran contempt. Lutherans rankled at the seeming Machiavellian ease with which it spread. The result was a deeply engrained sense of distrust among Lutherans whenever they were faced with Reformed appeals for unity or closer understanding. Even when the Reformed claimed to be fighting for the "Protestant" cause, as they did at the start of the Thirty Years' War, Lutherans such as Hoe von Hoenegg could not rid themselves of the suspicion that the Calvinists were up to something, perhaps waging a pyrrhic war against the Habsburgs in order to bring the entire Augsburg edifice crashing down.[38]

For the Lutheran theologians of the early seventeenth century, it was almost a rite of passage to publish a tract against some aspect of Reformed theology. The famous Johannite trio of the Lutheran University of Jena – Johann Gerhard, Johann Major, and Johann Himmel – set the standard, Himmel alone publishing 10 disputations against the Calvinists in 1627 that took aim at Reformed teachings on christology, predestination, and the Lord's Supper. But writing a polemical work against the Calvinists was a fairly common practice for theologians of Württemberg and Saxony as well. And despite the gravity of the themes at issue, the language of choice was German and the tone was polemical, the authors recognizing that it was necessary to reach the broadest readership possible using the most homespun terms the arguments could bear. For this was more than just the dry systematization of thought. When the Lutherans attacked aspects of Reformed teaching on Communion or predestination, their arguments were couched in terms that made it seem as if the entire fabric of their faith was at threat. As one anonymous Lutheran pamphlet of 1607 put it, the Calvinists had "a whole pile of such horrible atrocities, through which the entire foundation of Christendom is turned upside down and mankind's hope of salvation brought to naught . . . They deny the omnipotence of God and turn him into the creator of sins. In sum, the Devil has a stronger belief in God than the Calvinists."[39]

Needless to say, the Reformed authors answered in kind, denouncing the Lutheran idea of the Real Presence by referring to them as flesh eaters, blood suckers, and gormandizers of the Lord, some authors going so far as to ask how much of the divine flesh stuck between their teeth. The Lutherans Hoe and Himmel thought it sufficient just to publish edited (but unaltered) versions of such polemical attacks in order to win the sympathy of the reader. This polemical campaigning not only worked to mark out the two confessions, it also contributed to the further consolidation of the respective faiths. It was the relentless Reformed criticisms, for instance, that prompted the Wittenberg professor Nicolaus Hunnius (1585–1643) to compose a digest of Lutheran theology in 1625. Written in German for a lay readership and over 1,000 pages long in its final version, Hunnius outlined in precise terms the beliefs necessary for membership in the church.[40]

The full range of theological differences would only have been understood by a minority of engaged readers, many of whom were employed by the Protestant church in some capacity. However, it does seem that the polemics filtered through to the parish mind at some levels. A case in point is the Lutheran reaction to the introduction of the Reformed service. In many of the lands where a Calvinist ruler sought to introduce "further reform" according to the teachings of Zurich, Geneva, or Heidelberg, the local populations resisted the changes. It ranged from the open opposition of the various estates (from nobles, clergy, and burghers to peasants) in Brandenburg, Anhalt, Hesse-Kassel, and Albertine Saxony to the furtive defiance of the Lutheran parishioners of Ysenburg, who locked up the churches in order to obstruct the Reformed clergy. In Albertine Saxony, the parishioners voted with their feet, preferring to stay away from church altogether until the Lutheran service had been restored. Eyes misting over with crocodile tears, the Jena professor Georg Mylius (1548–1607) described the state of the Saxon church after the introduction of a Reformed liturgy:

> The churches were emptier than they had ever been in this land . . . There are quite a few who had not heard a single sermon in a year, some not even for several years. In many localities there were children who had not been baptised even though they were several months old . . . People had such contempt for their new [Reformed] pastors, that they compared them to Jews or Turks . . . and named their dogs after them.[41]

In some territories confessional antagonism was brought on by a sudden change in worship, as happened with the introduction of the Reformed service in the Berlin Cathedral on Christmas Day in 1613, or it might be the result of tensions that had been simmering for decades, as in Saxony, where the late-century fear of Calvinism had its roots in a quarrel between Gnesio-Lutherans and Philippists (Crypto-Calvinists) that reached back to the 1560s and 1570s – a controversy that ended in the imprisonment of the Philippists and an effigy of Calvin hanging from the gallows.

In the realm of enacted or embodied religion – that is, in the parish churches – distinctions of belief were marked out by ritual and symbolism. Theology provided

the rationale. Calvinists accepted fewer adiaphora than the Lutherans and believed a
further purification of the faith was required in order to cleanse the churches of the
"vain papal relics." Consequently, when the Reformed service was imposed on a
Lutheran community it often resulted in the purging of the church interiors and the
liturgical equipage. But the main crucible for both religious ideas and symbolic
actions was the Eucharist. Rejecting the corporeality of Christ, the Reformed preachers introduced the ritual of the *fractio panis* into the churches, the literal breaking of
the bread before its distribution. Few gestures could have been more disturbing to the
Lutheran psyche, a sacral sensibility that still held (if in modified form) to the idea of
the Real Presence. For the Calvinists, this act marked out the community. The plain
white bread pulled in pieces in basic surroundings and distributed by the minister was
symbolic of the Reformed ideas of the Eucharist: elemental, unadorned, and communal. For the Lutherans, in contrast, the *fractio panis* was above all an act of
sacrilege, a dismembering and profanation of Christ's body, and a reminder that the
Calvinists were (to cite Christoph Fischer) "inspired by Satan and misled by blind
reason when they claim that Christ cannot be truly present with his body and blood in
the holy Eucharist."[42]

   Even accounting for its centrality in Protestant thought, it is remarkable how much
symbolic weight the Eucharist was forced to bear. When the Lutherans viewed a
Reformed communion, they condemned it for its profanation of the elements, its
misreading of Scripture, its reintroduction of Hebraic legalism, and its denial of
Christ's saving sacrifice. Making similar points but overturning the analysis, the
Calvinists charged that the Lutheran service demonstrated a lack of faith and a failure
to appreciate what Christ had accomplished on the cross. The *fractio panis*, wrote the
Berlin preacher Johann Bergius (1587–1658), "provides the believing communicant
with the highest and most powerful comfort, namely that the Lord's body most
certainly was crucified for each and all truly penitent Christians."[43] If the Lutherans
are ill at ease with the idea of the *fractio panis*, so the argument ran, this was just
further testimony to how deeply rooted the papal idea of transubstantiation still was in
their hearts. It is the same sort of reaction that might be provoked in a witch by
pricking her mark with a pin.

   By the early seventeenth century, the main German Protestant traditions had
developed confessional cultures that were not only distinguished by theological
differences but marked out by distinct attitudes of thought and perception. This
did not exclude other forms of identity. In early modern Europe, as today, most
people and the communities they associated with had multiple levels of self-understanding. Nor did it necessarily mean that the confessional culture itself was uniform
and uncontested. The very process of consolidation that marked out magisterial
Protestantism could work to divide as well. The best example of this is provided by the
various theological feuds that plagued Lutheranism after the mid-century, the most
significant being the conflict between the Gnesio-Lutherans and the Philippists, but
there was a half-century of smaller-scale quarrels that fed in to the *Formula of
Concord*.[44] Another misconception would be to assume that thinking confessionally
necessarily meant thinking in fixed religious terms or that it inevitably resulted in an
arid or dogmatic type of culture. One of the remarkable features of both Lutheran and
Reformed culture of this period was the way in which the churches adjusted to

changing circumstances, and not just to historical conditions but to shifts in intellectual discourse as well. The problems facing the Lutherans of the seventeenth century, for instance, were different in kind to those that confronted the first few generations. Not only was the church under siege by Catholics, Calvinists, radicals, rationalists and "epicureans," but it seemed as if fortune itself (or rather the wrath of God) had been turned on the church in the form of wars, dearth, inflation, and decades of climate extremes. In response, the Lutherans began to develop a type of piety that best responded to the demands of the times, which meant less dogmatics and more personal piety, hence the flood of hymnals, prayer books, catechisms, pastoral tracts, and the further turn towards eschatology.[45]

How deeply the common understanding of this confessional culture reached will be an issue for Chapter 5. At this juncture, if we are content with taking as our measure of impact a vague sense of imagined community, then it does seem safe to say that German Protestants were thinking in confessional terms. Indeed, to find support for the notion, the historian need look no further than the urban household. By the end of the century, much of the material culture within the domestic setting had been transformed by the reformers' assault on the *memoria* of Catholic religiosity. Older objects remained, among them candles, crucifixes, images of saints, even sacramentals, but now they were joined, and partly overwritten, by a new range of artifacts and motifs, the leitmotiv being the centrality of the Word of God.[46] Vernacular religious texts, from Bibles, prayer books, hymnodies, pamphlets, catechisms, to church orders and published confessions, lay stacked on tables, cabinets, and windowsills. And where the Word could not be encountered, as it were, in its natural habitat, it was symbolized and objectified in wall hangings, broad sheets, biblical paintings, and citations from Scripture. By way of example, it was not unusual for Lutheran noblemen to have passages from the Psalms painted on the walls of their country residences, the meaning and the message of the citations designed to guide the viewer on a type of pilgrim's progress from one room to the next. Duke Ludwig of Württemberg (1560–93) had an entire cycle of pictures painted in his Stuttgart summer house, specifically conceived by the theologian Lukas Osiander in order to capture the essence of orthodox Lutheran teaching on the theme of Christology.[47] In less exalted settings as well, other objects and motifs conveyed similar confession-specific messages. Pictures of the great reformers such as Luther and Melanchthon were common, as were woodcuts of heroic Lutheran rulers such as Johann Friedrich or Gustavus Adolphus. Biblical themes, the most popular being the distinction between law and gospel and Old Testament histories, were portrayed on ceramics and stoves, carved into cabinets and chairs, and even stitched onto clothing.[48]

This profanizing or vulgarization of the faith, this willingness to capture belief in "the gravity of things," was a corollary of Luther's belief that the mind, at least the mind that had no claims to prophetic insight, needs to be prepared in order to grasp religious truths. To do this it relied on external stimuli. Paramount was the use of its visual memory, but faith could be aroused by other modes of perception as well, including touch, smell, and emotion, for the true Christian was a man or a woman whose faith ruled over his or her thoughts, whose modes of thinking and feeling were captive to the Word. Protestants were Protestants mind and soul.

Christian Subjects

The pansophic mind

Irrespective of religion, early modern intellectuals generally agreed that fallen man had but a small share of the knowledge once enjoyed by Adam. Although he had lacked the requisite understanding of sin, in all other fields Adam's knowledge had been perfect. Adam had been endowed with the powers of the divine, able to perceive and understand the world without suffering the distortions of the flesh. Longing for perfect knowledge of this kind, early modern scholars spoke of his encyclopedic range, his ability to see long distances without the help of spectacles or telescopes, and his capacity to view the minuscule without the aid of a magnifying lens. Having described Adam as a born philosopher who could perceive essence in accidents, forms in properties, and consequences still dormant in their principles, the Anglican Robert South (1634–1716) went on to describe what it must have been like to acquire knowledge in paradise:

> Study was not then a Duty, night-watchings were needless; the light of Reason wanted not the assistance of a Candle. This is the doom of faln man to labour in the fire, to seek truth in *profundo*, to exhaust his time and impair his health, and perhaps to spin out his dayes, and himself into one pittiful, controverted Conclusion. There was then no poring, no strugling with memory, no straining for Invention. His faculties were quick & expedite: they answered without knocking, they were ready upon the first summons, there was freedom, and firmness in all their Operations.[49]

Many of the early modern philosophies of knowledge acquisition, from Lullism to Cartesianism to Ramism to Bacon's empirical approach, had been conceived with a view to recovering (in some part) the lost mind of Adam and his world of effortless knowledge. Protestant thinkers were active participants in this quest, particularly the Calvinists of central Germany and New England.[50] For there was still a spark of Adam's original reason dormant in mankind that might be recaptured through prayer, penance, and obedience – along with a rigorous and systematic cultivation of the mind.

Contrary to the impression Luther's vitriol against what he termed that "whore" and "harlot" reason (*ratio*) may give on first reading, the reformer did reserve an important place for the rational faculty in the life of a Christian. Although he was never precise in distinguishing exactly what he meant by the term, Luther's general point was that reason, albeit a shadow of its prelapsarian self, was nevertheless a gift from God and the main method of perception in the sublunary world. Despite its many failings, of which its "sinful vanity" was perhaps the worst, reason was the final authority in all earthly affairs. But it had no place in the spiritual realm, for in its fallen state reason was unable to comprehend the higher mysteries of God. Any attempt to do so could only result in the dishonoring and debasing of the faith (hence the analogy to a harlot) and place the soul in jeopardy. Within its proper sphere, however, it was sovereign.[51] Calvin thought in similar terms, claiming it was an "absurd curiosity" that looked to probe the divine mysteries though the use of reason. But he was much more nuanced in his analysis of how the mind might perceive evidence of God in the visible world. Certain understanding of the divine came only through the Word, and yet God reveals traces of himself everywhere, "even in the smallest corners of the earth," and with the judicious use of reason it was possible to contemplate his works in this life. "In the whole architecture of this world," wrote Calvin, "God has given us clear evidence of his eternal wisdom, goodness, and power, and though he is invisible in himself he shows himself to us in some measure in his work. The world is therefore rightly called the mirror of divinity."[52]

Striking the right balance between reason and faith was a difficult and dangerous task, but for mainstream Protestants it was a vital balance to strike, for the only alternative was the radicals' idea of Spirit. Finding a place for reason in the Protestant mind thus became one of the principle concerns of the second and third generation of magisterial theologians. Theodore Beza, Calvin's successor in Geneva, conceded that the created order could provide some knowledge of the divine. He also claimed that there was a discursive dimension, in that observation of the terrestrial world called to mind the remnants of prelapsarian knowledge and therewith, if only briefly and imperfectly, made it possible for the individual to share in the "great tradition" reaching from Adam through Seth and Noah to the patriarchs, pharaohs and Greeks to the present day. But like Calvin, Beza did not think that this knowledge was sufficient to know God in any substantial way, and in fact he was quite clear on the distinction between *ante lapsum* and *post lapsum* epistemologies, concluding that in the latter "all the faculties of the soul are corrupted, the mind being given over to vanity, the senses being obscured by the thickest haze, the affections being gradually accustomed to evil, that they are finally delivered, devoid of judgement, into all uncleanliness."[53] Reason might shed some light on divinity, but it was a pale and deceptive reflection of higher knowledge, which for Beza and Calvin was acquired through the teachings of the church.

Similar arguments were made by the Calvinists of England. Actually, there were some outright champions of reason among the Anglicans, the most outspoken being Richard Hooker, who seemed to suggest that both reason and nature were required in order to grasp higher truths. But the Puritans were much more wary, and in general they took up Luther's ideas, including his view that the ability to reason was inescapably carnal and thus "a secret friend to Satan."[54] The main concern for the Puritans was to set limits on the exercise of reason, to keep it in check and within its proper bounds lest its vanity and self-glorification lead to the fatal corruption of religion. The result was a flood of works spelling out the proper balance between faith and reason, an approach that was frequently couched in the traditional dichotomies of enthusiasm versus order, spirit versus Word, and even law versus gospel. The sheer ingenuity of the Puritan effort to regulate the workings of the mind prompted Hooker to remark that "they never use Reason so willingly as to disgrace Reason."[55]

There was no better example of the Protestant effort to keep reason in check than the catechism, the pocket-sized "temples of the mind" designed to help the pastors imbibe necessary saving knowledge. Of course, the reformers did not invent the catechism, but they did afford it a role and a significance in the life of the church that had no parallel in medieval Catholicism – to the extent that it became the primary pedagogical means of indoctrinating the faith. Luther's two catechisms of 1529 were seminal, but most of the mainstream reformers, and indeed hundreds of local pastors as well, tried their hand at writing a catechism at some stage in their careers.

A number of early catechisms were written in dialogue form, including those penned by Balthasar Hubmaier and Wolfgang Capito, and there were some clergymen, like the

English poet-rector George Herbert, who used the catechism as a starting point for self-analysis and speculation. But the primary purpose of the catechism was to subdue curiosity, especially in children, and to move the believer away from self-analysis and implant fixed knowledge in the mind. This was necessary, as the Lutheran theologian Caspar Huberinus pointed out, because our fallen nature cannot be trusted to discover religious truth on its own.[56] By way of the catechism, the Protestant churches were able to impart right doctrine and proper belief in a one-way dialogue. It was not an exercise in open discourse or systematic learning. It was a rote, mechanical exercise in memory and diligence, and the purpose was not to engender knowledge but to complete it. The process was often described by way of metaphors such as grafting, striking, imprinting, heating, or even placing a knife blade to a whetstone. And the final aim was the memorization of certain words in a certain order. A successful performance required predetermined answers. "What is it to *repeat* them [words]," remarked Samuel Crooke, "but to make them as it were a *proverbe* in every one's mouth . . . that they might the better fasten both on . . . memory and conscience."[57]

In Saxony, catechizing the young became one of the main marks of the evangelical movement from the very beginning, and the practice quickly spread to the rest of Germany. Johannes Brenz (1499–1570), who himself published a popular synthesis of Lutheran teachings, spoke for hundreds of other pastors when he remarked on how the catechism served as "a short synopsis of all of Scripture, containing for us everything necessary for true and eternal salvation . . . so that the catechism can truly be termed 'a small Bible.'"[58] In England as well, the catechism became the preferred tool of indoctrination. As laid down in the rubrics of the Edwardian, Elizabethan, and Caroline prayer books, each cure of souls in the English parishes was entrusted with the catechizing of the youth. By the seventeenth century there was a wide range of English catechisms available, thus making it possible for the native clergy to replace the English-language translations of works by continental reformers. The Edwardian catechism of 1549 remained the most popular, but there were others in circulation, including those by John More, Eusebius Paget, William Perkins, and John Ball. Moreover, by the late sixteenth century there was a more nuanced understanding of the levels of learning the catechumens were expected to reach under the pastors. Some degree of accommodation was required, for not all parishioners could comprehend the same texts. And yet the overarching purpose remained as before, namely the systematic indoctrination of ideas by way of a simple text divided up into sums, parts, heads of doctrine, and the "sum of saving knowledge" that the parishioners had to learn through rote memorization.[59]

The catechism was just one aspect of a general concern with education bound up with the early Reformation. Indeed, in some minds, the relationship between proper learning and proper faith was so close there could be no talk of true Christianity until the schoolroom and the household had been turned into quasi-seminaries. Even later generations acknowledged the close cousinage. Speaking in Altenburg during the 1617 centenary celebrations, the German clergyman Joseph Clauder (1586–1653) remembered the Reformation as more of a pedagogical than a theological event, and he singled out Luther as the prefigured champion of education, the German Hercules who knocked down the walls of papal and scholastic ignorance and paved the way for a pedagogical revolution.[60]

For modern historians, however, the effect of the Reformation on education in the Protestant lands has long been a source of contention.[61] Did the Reformation effect a revolution in learning or simply build on the innovations already in place? A book of this kind is not the place to weigh up the various historiographical debates and propose a balanced solution. But neither is it necessary to take sides. Suffice it to say that both sides of the argument have valid points to make. Well before the rise of the evangelical movement and Luther's early endorsement of primary and secondary schooling there had been marked changes in the methods and means of learning, including an increase in the number of lower rural and upper urban (Latin) schools, a rise in university matriculation rates, an extension of lay involvement – which ranged from founding and funding schools, hiring teachers, to generally promoting the need for education – and a small-scale revolution in the nature of the curriculum: not only did the texts themselves become more complex, but the range of valid disciplines increased. At the same time, the Protestant recognition that learning was instrumental to the secular and the sacral welfare of church and commonwealth gave rise to a reform of the schooling system without precedent in European history.

In the lands of Germany, for instance, where two of the greatest preceptors of the age, Philipp Melanchthon and Johannes Sturm (1507–89), laid the foundations, the Protestant elite quickly stepped in to reform the local systems. In the sixteenth century alone, there were over 100 new school ordinances introduced, all mandating regular attendance, rationalizing and systematizing the curriculum, regulating the training and income of the schoolmasters, and overseeing the creation of vernacular and Latin schools, often built on the ruins (actual and metaphorical) of the monastic foundations.[62] Nor should we overlook the number of new Protestant universities of the period. Within the Lutheran lands of Germany, there was Marburg (1529), Jena (1548), and Helmstedt (1576), within the Reformed lands, Herborn (1584), Gießen (1606), and Rinteln (1610). The same sort of developments occurred in the other Protestant lands of northern Europe.

But rather than count bottoms on school seats, perhaps the best way to survey the relationship between Protestantism and pedagogy is to examine its intentions. And if we are looking for a philosophy that captures the essence of the Protestant approach to education there are few more instructive or ambitious examples than the pansophic vision of Jan Amos Comenius (1592–1670). Born in southern Moravia, and baptized in the church of the Bohemian Brethren (*Unitas Fratrum*), Comenius attended the Latin school in Prerov before pursuing advanced studies in Herborn and Heidelberg, the two German citadels of Reformed thought. Forced into exile along with thousands of other Moravian Protestants by the Habsburg advance after the battle of White Mountain in 1620, Comenius eventually found refuge in Leszno, Poland, where he began work on the discursive and pedagogical theory of knowledge acquisition he termed "pansophy." Though a profound visionary, Comenius was less a philosopher than a systematizer of ideas. Even the word pansophy was not his own, but taken from an epitome of Aristotelianism by the Rostock professor Peter Lauremberg (*Pansophia*, 1638), a work Comenius rated poorly because "it contained nothing appertaining to divine wisdom and the mysteries of salvation."[63] His own pansophic system, however, was much more fixed on the divine, and as such it is particularly revealing of Protestant attempts to reform Christian education.

Comenius worked at the intersection of two intellectual traditions. As a minister of the Bohemian Brethren, the radical branch of the Hussites, he was raised in a religious culture that accepted revelation and the providential nature of enlightenment. But the final authority in matters relating to higher wisdom was Scripture. Comenius spoke of theology as the first of the sciences and insisted that Scripture, if read in the proper light, agreed in all ways with the truths revealed by natural reason (though at times, he admitted, it did stretch the talents of man, which might explain why he preferred the more metaphorical texts such as Proverbs, Ecclesiastes, and the Song of Songs).[64] At the same time, Comenius was among the growing number of scholars who recognized the need for a panharmonic system, a type of unified theory of knowledge, that could effect universal reform by applying the fruits of philosophical thought. A number of different traditions fed into this enterprise, from the didactic theories of Melanchthon and Sturm, the Neoplatonism of thinkers such as Paracelsus and Campanella, to the encyclopedism of Johann Heinrich Alsted (1588–1638) (who was at Herborn when Comenius was a student) and the scientific empiricism of Francis Bacon. Comenius drew on all of these traditions as he worked up his pansophic system, and by doing so invited criticism from thinkers who believed that two traditions should be kept apart. Descartes, for instance, upbraided Comenius for letting too much theology press in on his system, while the Brethren in Poland feared the effects of placing so much trust in the profane.

While never challenging the axiom of unearned grace, and while speaking in familiar terms about the damaging effects of the Fall and the suffocating coils of sin, Comenius, like all Protestant theorists of education, had to grant some redemptive power to reason. If education were to play a role in universal reform, the theorists had to concede that mankind was "educable" and that learning could contribute to the making of a Christian soul. Comenius was particularly generous in this respect, claiming that postlapsarian Christians still retained the seeds of divine wisdom and so, aided by the grace of God, were able to recover some of the pure and perfect knowledge enjoyed by Adam. Learning was thus not just enlightenment in a utilitarian sense, but a renewal of the whole individual in preparation for eternal life.[65] This was a common enough idea in the century of Andreae and Alsted, but where Comenius surpassed his contemporaries was in his ability to build an entire system of pedagogical reform around this principle. Dismissing the sterility and lethargy of scholasticism and the compartmentalization of learning common to his day, Comenius's pansophic approach was aggrandizing and completely holistic. There was no science, no subject, and no source of knowledge that did not somehow factor into necessary wisdom, the "necessary" in this context being that which convinces the intellect to accept the "sovereignty of faith." As Comenius wrote: "The senses minister to reason, and reason ministers to faith, and therefore none of these things can be absent from the perfect Light, or else we shall certainly be deprived of the instruments for illuminating the mind."[66]

To substantiate the broader program, and to guard against the teaching of the radicals and their claims to Gnostic wisdom and direct revelation, Comenius spelled out in detail exactly how knowledge was acquired. He spoke of the three books or theaters of God: the natural world (*mundus*) perceived by our senses; the rational soul or conscience (*mens, conscientia*), perceived by reason and introspection; and Holy Writ (*scriptura*), perceived by faith. Through a gradual process of epistemological ascension,

Comenius taught that the human mind, if properly directed, could acquire knowledge of Christ. It begins, he wrote, with the close observation of the natural world (for the world itself is nothing less than the image of the divine), continued through the understanding of ourselves (for the seed of the divine was within us), and finished with the contemplation of Scripture, which oversees the other two forms of knowledge in that it interprets the natural world and guides the conscience. Scripture itself, however, cannot be grasped by man; it can only be comprehended through faith.[67] And in fact the whole purpose of pansophy was to lead the Christian toward a knowledge of Christ and thereby prepare him or her for eternal life. In this pilgrimage, Comenius insisted, all things stood revealed, and all things were significant.

The pansophic model of universal education was Protestant in the magisterial mold. Defined in the first instance by its criticisms of the traditional Catholic methods of instruction, and above all the dogmatism, didactics, and disputations of scholasticism, the pansophy of Comenius claimed to represent a much more inclusive and holistic approach, drawing "all nations and tongues of men" into the community of learning and thereby, as he put it in *Pampaedia*, enfranchising all of humanity in a vernacular dialogue with the divine.[68] But this new-found freedom was closely controlled. Pansophy was not just a theory of education but a very precise method of indoctrination. All aspects of teaching in the classroom were supervised and maintained by a hierarchy of approved teachers who were themselves exemplars of the pansophic ideal. And while the methods of instruction were adapted to accommodate the students, the end result was to be a member of society who stood in a right relationship with the church and the state. Comenius believed that too much freedom would lead to anarchy and disorder and that the role of education, and the educator, was to impose and internalize restraint.

Comenius argued that proper learning must take in all aspects of the human condition, not just the disciplines that made up the various fields of study but the practical dimensions of life as well – the actual exercise of virtue, for instance, or the dilemmas of moral choice faced by Christians each day. Moreover, pansophy relied on more than just rote learning. Comenius encouraged all modes of knowledge acquisition, from close study of the natural world to intense bouts of prayer. And all were directed towards the same end: proper knowledge of God. As he wrote in the *Great Didactic*: "Whatever is taught to the young in addition to the Scriptures (sciences, arts, languages etc.) should be taught as purely subordinate subjects. In this way it will be made evident to the pupils that all that does not relate to God and the future life is nothing but vanity."[69]

Like Calvin and Bucer before him, Comenius assumed that the shaping of the Christian soul would necessarily lead to the shaping of a Christian society. Universal education, he believed, would fashion a world rooted in charity, tolerance, and morality: the *regnum Christi* united in the Word. This sentiment was evident in his efforts to create a higher college of learning, such as the Universal College of Light, which would "call men back to the ancient ways of God."[70] But like all Protestant projections of this kind, the end result often fell short of original intentions, and it proved very difficult, even in theory, to maintain a balance between freedom and constraint. Convinced of the inherent harmony of all things, Comenius never really addressed the dilemma. But for those Protestant reformers with a less pansophic cast of

mind, the dilemma of the right balance between freedom and constraint was fundamental to the entire process of reform. Attempts made to control the soul as well as the
mind made this especially apparent.

The biblical soul

Historians have long considered the centrality of the Bible to Protestantism one of
the identifying features of the faith. The basic theory goes as follows: since the
evangelical principle of *sola Scriptura* did away with religious intermediaries and
referred believers directly to the Bible, salvation was no longer dependent upon the
medieval cycle of salvation and its various ritual and sacramental observances. With
grace mediated by the Word, there was no need for the sacramental formulae of the
medieval Church. As a consequence, the essence of belief became "verbal, non-
sensual communication" – by which is meant a faith that sought religious meaning in
thoughts and words rather than rites and rituals. It also meant that the individual had
become religiously empowered at the expense of the church, for with the rise of
Protestantism, "a man's subjective faith, his 'internal' religious attitude, came to
occupy the centre of religious and ecclesiastical life for the first time."[71] The Bible had
become an open book for all believers, and it was now the responsibility of every
Christian to find his or her own way to a right relationship with God. Luther had said
as much at the very start of the Reformation, when he advised the Wittenberg
parishioners that no Christian would die for another: we must shift for ourselves. This
was a profound change of perspective, and not just in theological terms (though it was
certainly that). Shifting for ourselves meant thinking for ourselves, or at least thinking
for ourselves through the prism of Scripture, and it provoked a range of interior
changes that, taken together, made up a Protestant mode of thought. Whereas
medieval Catholicism had been the sum total of ancient authorities, unwritten
verities, commentaries, glossaries, and spoken and unspoken tradition, all of which
were preserved in the communal memory, the religion of Protestants primarily relied
on the published and the spoken Word. Knowledge of saving faith had been reduced
to the surface of a freshly printed page.[72]

Whole fields of research have been built around this idea, and thus it is not feasible to
examine the full range of arguments and insights within the space of a single chapter.
Suffice it to say that if we adopt as our starting point the Protestant turn toward the
typographical, we could move in any number of different directions, from the rise of
individualism and the privatization of religion in the late seventeenth and eighteenth
centuries to the relationship between faith and reason and the making of the modern
conscience.[73] What follows below is a rather more modest inquiry into how the
Protestant devotion to the word, both the Word in the sense of God's Word and the
profane word as articulated in print, empowered the believer and influenced the nature
of religious perception. To what extent did subjective faith, the "internal" dimensions
of religiosity, come to the fore?

Let us begin with the visual. During the early phase of the evangelical movement, first
in Wittenberg under the influence of Karlstadt, then in those southern cities under the
spell of Swiss iconophobia, and finally in the later civic Reformations of northern
Germany and the Dutch Republic, the destruction of medieval art was one of the first

casualties of the Protestant disavowal of Catholicism.[74] At its most thorough it was a two-pronged attack, starting with popular bursts of uncontrolled iconoclasm and then passing over to the more ordered and measured magisterial dismantling of church interiors. In Strasbourg, for instance, after an early phase of unrestrained destruction that saw many objects taken from the churches and trampled underfoot or consumed in bonfires, the process of "cleansing" was taken in hand by the councils. In place of the altars, statuary, medieval paintings, and eucharistic equipage integral to late-medieval worship, a church interior emerged that had been shorn of its sacral semiotics. Images now had to be conjured in the mind through weekly sermons, pulpit readings, psalm-singing, and communal prayers, all closely regulated by the clergy.[75]

At the same time, however, many reformers, beginning with Luther and Bugenhagen and continuing up to the early Pietist Johann Arndt, encouraged the use of icons and images in Protestant worship. As long as the images themselves did not somehow deflect the faithful from proper Christ-centered contemplation, visual aids were harmless and might even benefit historical faith. We know that many church interiors in Protestant Europe retained much of the pre-Reformation paraphernalia, irrespective of the relentless condemnations of the theology that had created it. In the churches of the Dutch Republic, despite the Calvinist injunction to cleanse the interiors of Catholic idolatry, windows full of stained glass, paintings, organs, and altars remained in place well into the eighteenth century. Similarly, the Lutheran rejection of Catholic mate-rialism did not hinder massive artistic projects in late-sixteenth-century Dresden, where the churches were fitted with altar ornamentation, font reliefs, funerary monuments, pulpit friezes, crucifixes, and pictures of the evangelists and Old Testament typologies.[76]

But there was a difference in the way Protestants were meant to *see* religious art, a shift one art historian has described as a "triumph of the verbal over the visual."[77] Medieval theology had empowered icons and images, teaching that, as all forms somehow embraced the divine essence, not only was something of God revealed by them but contemplation of the appropriate objects could actually contribute to the state of grace. Drawing on the same rationale that had supported their arguments against the Mass, the reformers rejected this way of seeing religious objects. Calvin argued that the entire practice was based on deception and error, for God could not be contained within the compass of a created thing. Any attempt to mimic or represent God, even in the realm of the imagination, was a form of idolatry, for it was diminishing his majesty and forcing the infinite and the perfect to conform to the finite and the corrupt. To do so, as the Puritan Thomas Bilson put it, meant "you worshippe not the similitude of our saviour, but the conceite of this maker."[78]

Protestant seeing was not subject to this type of deception for, having rejected the idea that the divine could be captured in earthly things, it did not effect visual, emotional, or sacramental sympathy between a viewer and an object. Rather, it viewed art as important for what it could convey about the truth behind the façade of representation. Protestant art functioned as fact and reference, and what it referred to was the only truth available to the Christian believer – the Word of God. As a consequence, Protestant artists generally did away with images, themes, or metaphors that postulated interaction with the divine or derived their strength from the religious imagination. In their place they created a fixed visual world that continually referred the viewer back to Scripture. This could be done in a fairly transparent manner, as in Türkheim, a parish near Ulm in Germany, where in 1606 they painted 195 quotations from the Bible on the church walls, or in the Church of St Jacobi in Hamburg, which in 1649 had 229 biblical sayings. But it could also be done more subtly, as when Lucas Cranach the Elder turned saints into exemplars or draped Mary's mantle around the shoulders of Christ, not to incorporate the viewer in a realization of mediated grace but to present a visual metaphor of salvation through faith alone. With Protestant art, the dynamism of the medieval image disappeared; there was no attempt to effect an existential relationship between object and viewer. Instead, the imagery was static and referred to historical events – one-time events – such as the crucifixion of Christ.[79] Every icon and image was intended to refer beyond itself to the deeper truths of Scripture. Religious art had become the glossary of a text.

Ideally, then, every image, even every mental image, should refer back to Christ as revealed to us through Scripture. This type of mimesis was only feasible because the theologians expected the parishioners to have such an easy familiarity with a text they could conjure the right mental images from written and spoken words. And in fact by the end of the sixteenth century there was some basis for this assumption. Heralded by the reformers as the last gift of God before the end time, print quickly emerged as the most powerful agency in the rise of the Reformation. Not only did it emerge as the primary medium for the dissemination of evangelical thought, it also contributed to the historical shaping of the movement, especially in the early period when there was still a great deal of uncertainty and fluidity at work. Luther, for instance, the most ambidextrous of all Protestant theologians, simultaneously used the printed text as a means of gathering support for the Wittenberg movement, shaping and defining the boundaries between the new faith and the old, creating a distinction between the true and the false church, and even writing the history of the Reformation while experiencing it in the here-and-now – as he did with the publication of the *Acta Augustana* (1518), which was in effect a higher form of reportage that quickly assumed the status of historical truth.[80]

Through seminal texts and rhetorical strategies of this kind, Protestants were able to construct a sense of imagined community. And while the initial love affair cooled with later generations, the importance of the book remained one of the defining features of Protestantism well into the modern age. In so far as historians can take the measure of such things, the parishioners of Lutheran and Calvinist lands seem to have been more "bookish" than their Catholic counterparts. In the northern Netherlands, the Reformed authorities generally considered the development of reading skills one of the prerequisites of orthodoxy, and it seems to have had an effect: by the eighteenth century, up to 90 percent of the urban populace was literate, a quota that provoked their Catholic neighbors to associate reading with heresy.[81] In the German lands, although Bible-induced literacy did not arise during the lifetimes of the first few generations of reformers, by the late seventeenth century, as the Pietists began to place renewed stress on the need for the laity to read and understand Scripture, most Protestant parishioners would have had a fair degree of familiarity with print culture. In some school ordinances in the 1720s Bible reading became mandatory, a necessary skill for any man who wanted to rise in the public sphere.[82]

Statistics relating to literacy generally support the theory that Protestants were a people of the book, even if they do not satisfactorily answer questions concerning the causal nexus between the quality of faith and the ability to read. But perhaps even more telling of the Protestant relationship with the holy book was their devotion to the object itself. Bibles were treasured possessions, frequently given as gifts or passed on in probate wills, even to those who could not read, to sanctify the bonds within a community or confirm the lines of succession within a pious family. The French Huguenot noble-woman Anne de Mornay, for instance, having spent her days leafing through its pages and absorbing its imagery and meter, thought of her personal Bible as a relic of the family faith:

> This Bible was given to me by M. du Plessis, my most revered father. I wish that after me it shall be for Phillipe des Nouhes, my firstborn son, and that he shall read it diligently in order to learn to know and serve God in the Holy Trinity and that he shall bring to mind, in order to take courage from it, the example of his grandfather, from whom he received nourishment, and that he shall always remember the vows that I, his mother, have made for him.[83]

It was common for Protestant nobles to venerate family Bibles in this way, edging them with gold and silver, enfacing them with jewels, and placing them beside other objects of high value such as portraits, clocks, and globes. The same held true for the middling classes (though, of course, on a more modest scale), whose inventories often revealed at least one Bible among the household goods. And these were heirlooms that were put to good use. Dog-eared and foxed through years of close reading, Bibles served as private and public chronicles, the spaces between the printed text filled with the dates of births, deaths, and important family events; they worked as objects with a quasi-sacramental efficacy, invested with the power to ward off injury and harm; and they were utilized as a means of divination, as congeries of spells, cures, or snippets of gnostic wisdom.[84] From the earliest days of the evangelical movement, Protestants had treated Bibles as relics and talismans, as objects that were both symbolically and substantially vehicles of the divine, and this continued well into the eighteenth century. Both the English Puritans and the German Pietists fostered legends relating to Bibles that demonstrated supernatural characteristics, ranging from the ability to heal the sick to powers of immutability and incombustibility. Beliefs of this kind have little to do with the rationalized "verbal, non-sensual communication" of Protestantism in the Weberian mold, but it is powerful testimony of the place of the text in the religious imagination.

But we must not make too much of the Protestant love affair with the Bible. To begin with, some radicals delved so deeply into the gospel they moved beyond the text altogether, claiming that their insight flowed directly from the Spirit and required no mediation by commentaries or the "dead letter" of Scripture. Spiritualists of this cast had emerged as early as the Reformation itself, as we have seen in the discussion of wheats and tares, and the thought of the Silesian nobleman Caspar von Schwenckfeld and the Lutheran mystic Jakob Boehme (1575–1624) remained influential throughout the seventeenth century. But the tendency to kick over the traces of textual authority need not be reduced to a particular thinker or a radical sect. Prominent preachers of the Spirit tended to surface in numbers during periods of heightened dialogue or disorder. The first few decades of the Reformation in Germany and Switzerland was just such an epoch, as was the period of the Civil War in England, when numerous sects were claiming direct inspiration through prophecies, visions, and dreams while disparaging

Scripture as (at best) a book of history and (at worst) an idol of the Antichrist. Confronted by the claims of the radicals preaching free grace in the streets of London, Richard Baxter thought he was witnessing the reincarnation of the "madmen of Münster in Germany," and even the original Quaker, George Fox, feared that the Ranters had "fled the cross."[85]

But nothing in principle separated Baxter or Fox from the ideas they were condemning; it was only a matter of degree. For the very essence of the "Puritan impulse" – which was just a variation of the Protestant impulse – was to look beyond the "outward and imposing forms" to the truths that lay behind. By rejecting the need for a text to guide them in the matters of the Spirit, the radicals were simply following this impulse to its logical conclusion. Thus, whereas men like Baxter insisted that God had bound his Spirit to the Word and the sacraments, the only revelations being those that had been vouchsafed to the apostles, the Spiritualists (and their close kin) declared that the Spirit, the only certain source, was still at work in the modern age, speaking to men and women of faith without the need of text or sacrament. According to the radical Puritan John Saltmarsh (d.1647), this was nothing more than acknowledging that

> the great and excellent design of God in all these things, is only to lead out his people, Church, or Disciples from age to age, from faith to faith, from glory to glory, from letter to letter, from ordinance to ordinance, from flesh to flesh, and so to Spirit, and so to more Spirit, and at length into all Spirit.[86]

As in so many aspects of Protestant history, it was in large part the threat posed by the radicals that prompted the magisterial churches to embark on a campaign of self-definition. And once again it was a question of balance, internal to Protestantism because it was internal to Scripture. Outraged by the radicalism of the early Reformation, Luther drew back from his earlier recommendation that the Bible be placed in the parish schools to ensure that the common man "will not be looking for commandment and law where he should instead look for gospel and promise" and subsequently recommended that his reading be limited to the rote-drills, set-rhymes, and stock-answers of the catechism. In a similar manner, the conservative Puritans of England were quick to distance themselves from an unchecked hermeneutics, some making use of the medico-theological discourse about the effects of over-enthusiastic reading on the body and the mind, the point being that too much untutored familiarity with Scripture led to fantasy, visions, madness, and "disaffected brains."[87] As early as the 1520s the reformers recognized that the notion that Scripture would interpret itself was a dangerous proposition in the hands of a lay readership, and they reacted by reintroducing many of the authorities claimed by the Catholic magisterium, including the weight of tradition and the assembled wisdom of the church, even if they did not associate this higher wisdom with particular men or a specific succession of offices. What this meant in practical terms was that Protestant parishioners were encouraged to cultivate a Bible-based understanding of the faith, "if they possess[ed] the necessary competences which have to be mediated and practised catechetically and homiletically."[88]

Any number of examples might be used to illustrate the efforts made to impose what the radicals termed a legal or "book" religion on the parish mind, but a particularly suitable one in this context is the history of the first few editions of the English-language Bible. When the English reformer William Tyndale (circa 1494–1536) published his New Testament translation in 1526 his aim was to break down the barriers that kept Christians from the living Word. Famously, he conjured the Erasmian image of ploughboys better versed in Scripture than priests, and he believed that all men and women might approach the simple, plain Word of God for themselves. When Archbishop Thomas Cranmer prepared a preface for the Great Bible of 1539, he too believed that it should be made accessible to all parishioners, much in the sense conveyed in the title page woodcut of the 1539 version, where there is the image of a Bible (*verbum Dei*) being passed from hand to hand. But Cranmer, like other clergymen, was rapidly moving away from the idea of the Bible as an open text that might be subject to the fancies of a ploughboy. Following Luther's example, Bibles now came with prefaces encouraging the parishioners to rely on authorities in order to make sense of the text. Readers were warned against frivolous speculation or needless disputation, and they were admonished to approach the Bible with the appropriate sense of fear and trembling. A proper reading, Cranmer advised, should *confirm* a man in his (Anglican) faith.

At the same time, the church provided readers with the interpretative aids to help them reach the proper conclusions, first with the Great Bible and then with the Bishops Bible of 1567. Alongside the Book of Common Prayer and a book of homilies, both of which came with prefaces with notes on right interpretation, the authorities placed copies of Erasmus's New Testament paraphrases in the parish churches for the "unlearned multitudes." Little wonder that the Puritan authors of the *Second Admonition* came to the conclusion that the church, by way of textual commentaries and preaching restrictions, was burying the gospel beneath modern glossaries. "It is so circumscribed and wrapt within the compasse of suche statu[t]es," they wrote, "suche penalties, suche injunctions, suche advertisements, suche articles, suche canons, suche sober caveats ... that in manner it doth peepe out from behinde the screene."[89] It is worth noting that one of the reasons why James I was so quick to agree to a new authorized Bible translation was his fear of the effect of the Geneva Bible of 1560, which he termed "untrue," "seditious," and "traitorous" precisely because it presented Scripture as such an open text, encouraging the reader to react with its marginal notes and examine passages that traditionally had one established meaning.[90]

However, to draw attention to the fact that mainstream Protestantism kept a tight rein on its readers is not to deny the importance of Scripture in the lives of Protestants. For many of the English and American Puritans raised on the Bibles mentioned above, the *sola Scriptura* imperative of Reformation theology was a living impulse. Their thoughts were saturated by the language and imagery of the English Bible; it was their guide to interpreting the world, whether on the scale of the grand narrative arc of creation, redemption, resurrection, and the pending Last Days or at the more mundane level of pious conduct and religious practice. It is worth noting how many consciences were pricked during this period by a sentence or an image buried somewhere in the Bible, such as those of the clerical opponents of vestments in Elizabethan England who were willing to set themselves against church and state because the prophets and apostles wore "simple apparel."[91] Lay parishioners were just as likely to turn to Scripture when they were in need of advice or wanted to make sense of recent events. Among the Puritan gentry, it was common to draw parallels between the present and the past by leafing through the Bible and hashing out enigmatic passages. And there are numerous examples of bakers and artisans whose thought and conduct were deeply influenced by the word of Holy Writ. John Bunyan (just one such pious tinker) gave a sense of this in his work *Grace Abounding* (1666):

> Now about a week or fortnight after this, I was much followed by this Scripture, *"Simon, Simon, behold, Satan hath desired to have you,"* (Luke 22.31). And sometimes it would sound so loud within me, yea, and as it were call so strongly after me, that once above all the rest, I turned my head over my shoulder, thinking verily that some man had, behind me, called to me.[92]

Of course, not all souls were as biblical as Bunyan's, but historians of English Puritanism have unearthed more than enough material to suggest that the more pious parishioners had a close familiarity with the contents of the Bible, on a factual as well as an emotional and imaginative level.

But it is one thing to suggest that Scripture was a prism for the religious imagination; it is quite another to suggest that this is evidence of the fact that, to return to the theory discussed above, "a man's subjective faith, his 'internal' religious attitude" had become the main subject of Protestant religiosity. In practice, far from being a catalyst for self-reflection or self-understanding, this intense reverence for the Word of God tended to work against the tendency to think in independent terms or derive personal meaning from an encounter with the text.

To make the point let us remain with the example of the English Puritans, perhaps the most self-conscious of all early-modern Protestants. Many Puritans penned diaries or autobiographies, but in doing so they tended to think of themselves as exemplars or types derived from Scripture rather than *sui generis* personalities. They borrowed the characteristics of biblical figures and projected them back onto themselves, or they abstracted ideas of the religious conscience by looking for the various signs marked out for them by the Puritan theologians. Whatever method was adopted, the end result generally said more about Scripture than it did about the self. Of course, there were some profoundly original and perceptive Puritan voices, and these men and women were empowered by their close engagement with the Word.[93] But for the majority of pious Protestants, the discourse of the religious self was primarily a literary construct, drawing on the same paradigms, the same metaphors – the imprisoned body, the erring mind, the entrapped spirit, the *homo viator* – and even the same language in order to derive an orthodox version of what one contemporary termed the appropriate "rare and wonderful example" of a Christian believer. Religious understanding was equated with the models derived by Puritan theologians, and in fact it was their syllogisms of Reformed divinity that ordered the various personal stages of spiritual growth into the morphology of salvation. "Fear and trembling," for instance, was a requisite stage.[94] It is interesting to note how many victims of the new disease of religious melancholy were driven to such extremes of desperation precisely because, when confronted by the remorseless logic of predestination and reprobation, they were unable to find a "rare and wonderful example" of themselves in the textual descriptions of the elect. And it is also interesting to note how literary the clerical reaction was to this despair, using all manner of rhetorical tools, from trope and simile to metaphor and myth, in order to the make Calvinist teaching on predestination more palatable to the parish mind.[95]

There is no better example of this type of book religion (as it was denounced by the radicals) than Puritan practical divinity, the programmatic theology of self-analysis that sought to "link and coordinate *sola fides* with rule, duty and the Deuteronomic ideal."[96] Concerned more with moral amendment than passive faith, practical divinity emphasized the need to prove the state of grace by living a life in line with the conditions set down by Scripture. Faith could thus be demonstrated by certain "needful dispositions," and this is why it became so important for believers to search for the signs that they were among the elect and could count themselves members of the godly covenant. Practical theology of this type required pitiless self-analysis and furious self-scanning, for nothing less than salvation was at stake, and indeed the process was often described in aggressive terms such as ripping, ransacking, battering, and billowing. The questions reached to the very depths of the human condition. Was there sufficient evidence of a Christian disposition? Was there daily testimony to the "needful dispositions"?

Answering these questions would seem to require a measure of self-awareness merging on modern psychoanalysis, and yet in the end it turned out that a matter as crucial as personal salvation was too important to leave to the parishioners. Only the clergyman, "God's sounding board," with his orthodox understanding of Scripture and his hermeneutical and exegetical expertise, had the ability to determine whether or not the believer was among the elect. To bring home the point, practical theologians began to publish works such as Nicholas Byfield's *The Spiritual Touch-Stone; or, the Signes of a Godly Man* (1619) listing, in a series of intricate divisions and sub-divisions, the distinct marks of the visible saint alongside the proper ways to spot the signs.[97] In works of this kind, everything was spelled out for the reader. In essence, the books had already done the act of reading for the parishioner, and they worked as a powerful check on the ways that Scripture might be used and interpreted. For even though, as spiritual directors like Arthur Dent had written, Christians were expected "to fetch the warrant of our salvation from within ourselves," orthodox practice assumed that this could not be achieved without the intervention of the minister and his semiotics of signs and syllogisms. Only the clergyman, as interpreter, comforter, diagnostician of the soul, and champion of the visible saints, could lead the sure fight against the forces ranged against the pure conscience. For beneath the conscience, the clergy taught, on a battlefield unseen to the untrained eye, were the so-called hidden sins of guile, deception, assuredness, dissimulation, and the other "fair glosses for foul intentions" that could defeat the most searching soul.[98]

The examples could be multiplied, up to and including the famous conversion narratives of the New World Puritans, who frequently recycled the same narratives or drew on the same paradigms of religious experience in order to offer up proofs of election. In fact, there is reason to think that the public conversion testimony, although one of the few occasions when average Protestants left behind memorials of their beliefs, was so heavily scripted and so conscious of audience expectations that it was little more than a literary construct. Massachusetts theologians such as John Cotton may have viewed the testimony as a chance for the American Protestant to "fashion himself to a new mould,"[99] but the words themselves were so reliant on the authority of Scripture and the approbation of the worshipping community that very little of the individual soul was on display. Once again, however, this is not to deny the importance of the Bible to the mental world of early modern Protestants. On the contrary, the overwhelming presence of Scripture in the parish mind was why the conversion narratives reveal so little.

But acquaintance with a text and its surrounding commentaries is not the same thing as engagement or dialogue. No magisterial Protestant church of the confessional age ever encouraged its followers to approach the Bible as wholly free readers, with the warrant to draw their own conclusions, plot their own salvific histories, or derive their own idea of personal religious truth irrespective of orthodox teaching. Historically, within the mainstream tradition, there never was the plethora of heroic individual interpreters of Scripture posited by Luther (and quickly withdrawn) and then conjured by later theorists. In their ongoing campaign to order the world in accordance with specific religious ideas, the Lutheran and Reformed churches of the sixteenth and seventeenth centuries kept a very close check on the Word of God and how it might be understood. If late-medieval Catholicism had been half as effective in this regard, it is unlikely Protestants would have emerged when they did.

Protestant Environments

Liturgy and architecture

Look closely at some of the buildings of Valois France and it is possible to see signs of a Calvinist aesthetics pressing through traditional architectural codes. It is evident in the excessive ornamentation and swirling designs of the work of Bernard Palissy and Philibert de L'Orme, for instance. While Catholic art, ordered and well-proportioned, reflected a church secure in its sense of its historical trajectory, their deliberate over-elaboration was a challenge to this neatness, a symbolic reminder of the distortions and contortions of a world where the true faith (as they saw it) had been pressed back to the edge of existence.[100] And what was true for secular buildings was true for the churches or "temples" as well. Beliefs left their mark on the exteriors and the interiors of the buildings in which Protestants worshipped, on the spaces and places where they gave outer expression to their inner convictions. This is far too large a theme to address in any detail in a single chapter, but by adopting two different perspectives it is possible to reveal something of the Protestant ordering of space. The first is the interior of the church, the second the surrounding landscape.

Although there was no consensus about how a church should look, most of the reformers agreed that it was not a sacrosanct structure set upon hallowed ground in the manner of the Catholic foundations. It was not a holy place. Its sanctity was derived from its function: the preaching of the Word and the administering of the sacraments. Churches, as Calvin wrote in the *Institutes*, did not have an inherent holiness, no secret sanctity of their own. Similar views had been held by first-generation reformers. They were clearly present in Luther's early works, and made with some force by the Swedish reformer Olaus Petri (1493–1552), who ridiculed the idea that God could dwell in any building made by the hands of men.[101] And while the ideas of the church tended to vary considerably among the different shades of belief, the underlying principle of mainstream Protestant ecclesio-architectonics – that the church was a house built to accommodate a community at worship (*domus ecclesiae*) rather than a repository of the sacred – remained a basic principle of belief.[102] According to the Swiss reformer Rudolph Hospinianus (1547–1626), who wrote on this issue in *De templis* (1603), it was the different views on the idea of presence that led to different types of churches. While the Catholic buildings sheltered an interior alive to the touch of sacrality, hence the altars, the images, the relics, and the chancels, the Protestant churches were built to accommodate the worshipping community, hence the unencumbered space, the large windows, the stacked galleries, and the elevated pulpits.[103]

Inwardly, Protestant churches were "cleansed" of all objects that violated the reformers' reading of Scripture. We should not imagine, however, that fidelity to Scripture left the church interior a symbolically neutral space. The Lutherans purged much of the sacramental paraphernalia, but the main altars generally remained in place, and that holds true for many of the paintings and statues as well. In the absence of side altars, choir screens, and murals of saints' lives, other forms of church decoration evolved to take their place, including altar friezes, epitaph memorials, and historical panel paintings. One particularly effective Lutheran genre was the art of pulpit design, which combined biblical scenes with theological dialectics and often used the entire construct to fill out the narrative, from the steps to the door to the sounding boards and canopy. The favored iconographical program generally moved from fallen man to Christ as *salvator mundi* while privileging figurative images of the Old Testament and scenes from the gospels illustrating the life of Christ. Often the artists would work together with clergymen to ensure that the theological details were right, and on occasion, as Hieronymus Theodoricus, pastor of Sommerhausen found, the iconography of the pulpit itself was rich enough to serve as a backdrop to a sermon – provided, as Theodoricus warned his listeners, that we view such things "not with the vacant stare of beasts, but with vision tempered by faith."[104]

Even in the Reformed churches of the Dutch Republic, where the process of "purification" was perhaps the most orderly and comprehensive in all of Europe, Catholic objects survived the cull, from stained-glass windows and minor masterpieces of medieval painting to the highly crafted, and highly contentious, church organs. Moreover, Calvinists did not just strip the interior of ornamentation, they replaced Catholic items with objects of their own. Altars and monstrances, crucifixes on rood screens and alabaster retables made way for simple communion tables and modest stone fonts, while on the whitewashed walls, along with guild crests and coats of arms, calligraphic text-boards of biblical passages in both Latin and the vernacular oversaw the congregation.[105] Even in the austere surroundings of the Puritan meetinghouse there was symbolism on show, with doves carved into sounding boards and copies of the Bible and the *Book of Martyrs* next to the domestic plates and cups used for the Communion service. Even bare space was symbolic space. The clergy often used their sermons to refer to the allegories below the surface – the windows casting the purity and promise of light, for instance, or the plain pillars and white walls suggesting a cleansing and rebirth of the spirit, the corner stones and foundations comprising the "living rock" of the church.[106] The Protestant interior was not void of all objects and images that might evoke symbolic thought. What was different was how the objects sat in relation to the idea of liturgical space.

Outwardly, the first Protestant churches looked essentially the same as Catholic churches, necessarily so as the existing buildings were simply taken over by the evangelicals. The first Lutheran churches of northern Germany had little in terms of form, layout, or outward display to distinguish them from their late-medieval predecessors. The same trends were evident in Sweden and Denmark, where the Lutheran churches of the seventeenth century borrowed freely from medieval convention, replete with gothic exteriors, pointed arches, flying buttresses, and rose windows. Nor were the established Calvinist communities overly concerned with altering the basic design. In the Dutch Republic, the Reformation brought little in the way of architectural innovation. Although there was a switch in spatial emphasis from the longitudinal to the transversal as the pulpit was often placed beside the middle pillar of the nave, architects such as Hendrik de Keyser still borrowed the basic layout and design from gothic and classical tradition.[107] And there were reasons for this conservatism. Architecturally, there was no pressing need to abandon or rework the outward form if the inner necessities could be met. Protestants reconfigured the space where the service took place, but this could be done without radically transforming the outer structure. The main purpose of the Protestant church was to accommodate the worshipping community and nothing more.

Within the more plain of the Protestant traditions, little trace of Catholic design remained. The first steps in this direction were taken by the Calvinists in France. Recalling the utopian blueprints of architects such as Jacques Perret and Philibert de l'Orme, the Huguenot churches were monumental in scale but fairly austere in form: they looked more like amphitheaters and assembly halls than houses of God. The intention was to build a church that could best provide for the community at worship, but without the vanity and ostentation of the Catholic buildings. Even Charenton, the prototype basilical temple built for the Huguenots of Paris, had little to please the eye beyond a small bell-tower at one end of the roof. Minimalism of this kind was the corollary of religious belief, a point perhaps best illustrated with reference to the nature of the first Puritan churches in England and America. Generally termed "meetinghouses" rather than churches, they were of necessity rather bare and insubstantial, built in stealth and with basic materials. The American versions were little different from the civic buildings in the towns, most being squat, horizontal, readily-accessible brick and timber-framed constructions in the domestic styles of the day, the only sign of their inner function being the tombstones grouped outside. This plain and unadorned style was a deliberate aesthetic, a conscious attempt to construct a building for worship that reflected the simple truths of the faith.[108] Conceived as the antithesis of the (as they saw it) artificial, wasteful, vaunting, and insincere architectonics of the churches of Catholicism, where artificial frontiers interposed between God and man, the meetinghouse of the Puritans and the Quakers was just simple space, uncontrived and unconstrained, unifying at once the believer with God and the parishioners with each other.

Of course, the extent to which the different Protestant communities honored the ideal of plain style, or indeed thought plain style necessary, varied considerably. There was significant difference between the look of a Lutheran or an Anglican church and the log cabins of the Pennsylvanian Mennonites. But most Protestants shared the same basic ideas about how the interior space of the churches should be used. Now that the preaching of the Word had become the centerpiece of the service in the majority of Protestant settings, the pulpit became the prime focus, which meant that the senses converged on this point. In most Lutheran churches, which were not built from scratch, this meant placing the pulpit before the altar or against one of the central piers so that the majority of the congregation could see and hear. Within the double-chambered layout of nave and chancel, this might entail moving the body of worshippers to the centre of the church, as happened in Lutheran Hesse as early as 1526 when the pastors were instructed that the service "shall be performed with due decorum in the midst of the church so that all people . . . may learn to sing in harmony and with one heart may glorify God's name, for all have become priests in Christ."[109] In the Reformed churches of the Dutch Republic, a similar spatial convergence occurred, with the use of church interiors centered around the pulpit, the pulpits often set off from the encroaching congregations by a bay (*dooptuin*) reserved for baptisms, confessions, and the presentation of the clergy.[110] In the Puritan meetinghouse, the centrality of the pulpit was emphasized to an even greater extent, though the logic was the same: to fill the space with the Word of God. Sir Christopher Wren made the general point:

> The Churches must therefore be large; but still in our reformed Religion, it should seem vain to make a Parish-church larger, than that all who are present can both hear and see. The *Romanists*, indeed, may build larger Churches, it is enough if they hear the Murmur of the Mass, and see the Elevation of the Host, but ours are to be fitted for Auditories.[111]

Protestant churches were not the first to privilege the sermon. Renaissance builders also anchored their designs around the pulpit, with no less an architect than Leonardo da Vinci suggesting that the perfect church would be circular so that all ears might be equidistant from the Word.[112] But Protestants went one step further by collapsing the space into this single point. In the late-medieval church, the divine was communicated through the use of the interior, simultaneously reconfirming or restoring its presence (cleansing, purifying), delineating the boundaries between the sacred and the profane (ritual, processions), or simply utilizing the interior for the liturgy. The larger churches were designed to accommodate these presumed fields of sacral energy, not only acting as a horizontal and vertical span for the senses invoked in worship, but also making it possible, through choirs, chantries, chapels, and altars, for multiple services to take place simultaneously. The Protestant liturgy, however, configured space in a different way. Although attention still had to be paid to the altars, communion tables, and baptismal fonts, the primary focus of the service was now firmly on the pastor in the pulpit. There was nothing happening above, behind, or beside the congregation that might pull the parishioners in different directions. To use a phrase common in the Netherlands, the believers were gathered together in a "ring of prayer," an idea often captured in metaphoric terms by referring to the people attending worship as the body of Christ unified by the Word. The sacral energy in this setting was centripetal, drawing the believer in the direction of the clergyman and his text. Architectonically, the most appropriate design was one that could best facilitate this idea of liturgical space, hence the emphasis placed on the size of the windows or the clarity of the glass, the acoustics of the interior, and the configuration of the seating plan along with the placement of the pulpit. If a church were too large, wrote Wren, the result was "noise and confusion."[113]

Of course, clearing a line of sight straight to the sermon did not always have the intended result. In Protestant churches, no less than in medieval churches, there was plenty of non-devotional noise along with a general absence of piety and religious zeal. People still gossiped, daydreamed, and slept, babies still cried, children still ran about, and dogs still barked. Indeed, in the large urban churches of the Dutch Republic there was a space beyond the inner sanctum for secular pastimes such as strolling with partners or settling business affairs. Such activity was not only backhanded confirmation of Calvin's belief that the "secret sanctity" of the church would and should go the same way as the medieval images and reliquaries; it also drew attention to the fact that the main focus of the Protestant interior had become the congregation itself. In place of the filtered light, the smoke-filled naves, and the sacramental nooks and crannies of the Catholic interior, the church was now filled by the sound of the sermon and the body of the congregation. And while reformers such as Calvin may have taught that this austere interior, clear, pure, and infinite, was not just a metaphor but an actual manifestation of the divine, most parishioners would have been more aware of the surrounding humanity. For it may have been the case, as the architect Joseph Furttenbach imagined, that the Lutheran church was permeated with the "dear Word of the Lord our God, echoing with pleasure within," but most people must have found the divinity of sound and light difficult to capture with the senses.[114] Instead, they saw each other.

The integrative rites of medieval Catholicism had been replaced by a space devoted to a new type of spiritual communion. The former rituals that promoted devotional intimacy, such as the feasts, the *pax*, or the rites of integration, had been supplanted by an empty space given up to the gospel, with the only markers of community being the congregation gathered on pews and benches.[115] And now that the parishioners were seated in fixed rows and subject to sermons lasting several hours, they became much more aware of the human face behind the worshipping community. It would have been difficult to avoid the gaze of the elders in a Dutch church, for instance, who often sat at the foot of the pulpit; and it would have been all but impossible, and in fact against the spirit of the faith, to fail to take note of neighbors in the foursquare Quaker meetinghouse. Often, no doubt, the hearts of some parishioners would have thrived on this, with feelings of brotherly love and community strengthened by the sense of closeness. In the hotter types of Protestant, in contrast, a heightened awareness of humanity may have awakened stronger feelings of despair. But for the majority of parishioners, the close press of neighborhood would probably have roused more worldly concerns. One of the constant refrains of the Protestant sermon was the criticism of the congregation's inability to focus on the Word of God and their penchant instead for using the time in the church to think on more earthly matters. The religious writer Richard Younge epitomized this general sense of clerical despair when he spoke of "those blocks who go to Church as dogs do, only for company and can hear a powerful Minister for twenty or thirty years together, and minde no more what they hear then the seats they sit on."[116]

We need not take Younge's verdict at face value. There was room enough for all kinds in the Protestant church, some were pious and some were not. Yet there seems little doubt that social reality became much more "present" in the ordered interior of the Protestant church, especially in the Lutheran and Anglican settings, where seating arrangements often mirrored the particularities of the local population. In the Anglican churches of Virginia, for instance, seating was arranged according to status, dignity, age, militia rank, and tax burden. While the majority of parishioners sat on backless benches far from the pulpit and communion table, the elite gathered in bespoke pews, framed, wainscoted, and raised, that not only kept the community separate but confirmed the hierarchical distinctions through complexity of design or proximity to the pastor. In England it was not uncommon for quarrels to break out within the church over who sat where and why as instincts of possession and proprietorship momentarily eclipsed Christian fellowship.[117]

This creeping in of humanity was in large part a consequence of the Protestant campaign to divest the church of its "secret sanctity." It was also further grist for the mill for radicals such as the Quaker George Fox, who constantly warned against the dangers of mixing flesh and spirit and confessed openly that "the steeple houses and pulpits were offensive to my mind because both priests and people called them 'the houses of God,' and idolised them, reckoning that God dwelt there in the outward house. Whereas they should have looked for . . . their bodies to be made temples of God."[118] The conclusion was inescapable: remove all trace of the divine from the space where Christians gathered to worship and there was nothing left but plain humanity. Not all Protestants pushed the idea to the same extremes as Fox, as the variety of church architecture demonstrates, but all were faced with the same dilemma: how to effect a balance between an environment purged of the constraints of medieval sacrality and a community of believers seeking some sort of open commerce with the divine. It was a dilemma that Protestants faced outside of the churches as well.

Christianography

In March 1538, acting on the orders of Thomas Cromwell, the Italian military engineer Giovanni Portinari set to work demolishing the Cluniac Priory of St Pancras in Lewes, England. Joining Portinari was a team of demolition experts. Alongside smiths, carpenters, masons, and general laborers, there was a specialist for the dismantling of walls, a technician who attached gunpowder to the piers, and a smelter to reduce the lead roof tiles. Within a few months the team had effectively leveled the priory, having pulled down the vault, which had stood 93 feet high, and shipped off most of its fabric. Other English foundations suffered similar fates: stripped, gutted, and razed. And these were the dignified endings. More common was the fate of the monasteries in Lincolnshire. Because of the cost of demolition, these foundations were often only partially destroyed. Once the plundering was complete, they were left as a simulated quarry for the neighboring villages and towns, gradually picked apart and reduced to shapeless ruins.[119] Occasionally, the monasteries were converted into homes. Some of the Henrician and later Elizabethan courtiers revamped the emptied foundations and turned them into multi-courtyard palaces. Leez in Essex was an example of this type of conversion, as was Titchfield in Hampshire. Others were integrated into the surrounding architecture, as was the Cluniac priory in Reading. But the majority of the buildings just stood for centuries as they had been left by the wrecking crews, as the "grand and imposing ruins" of a Catholic past poised rather awkwardly on a Protestant landscape.

The dissolution of the monasteries in England, though perhaps unique in its bureaucratic efficiency, followed on the heels of similar events in the lands of northern Germany and Scandinavia. In Germany, the complex legal and political topography meant that each prince had to deal with the Catholic foundations in his territory according to the local circumstances of rule. There were too many patrons, ranging from the emperor down to the petty nobility, and too much political interest, to make the type of dissolution process carried out by Cromwell a possibility. But the same logic was at work. As long as the foundation wealth was used for religious purposes and not squandered on needless wars or court fêtes, it fell within the purview of the right of reformation. This meant that the vast majority of the assets, whether the buildings themselves, the valuables, or the endowments and annuities, went into the making of the Protestant state. As the monasteries, chantries, and chapels either closed their doors or were turned to other purposes, the universities, schools, and hospitals grew in size and number. In the provinces of Germany, for instance, Luther's own order of Augustinians suffered a reduction in the number of cloisters from 160 at the start of the Reformation to 96, Thuringia and Saxony alone losing 35 of them. This was not on the scale of destruction experienced in England, but it was certainly substantial enough to give the impression that the monastic world was falling away.[120]

But let us return to England. With the Henrician dissolution of the monasteries, the English landscape was suddenly home to a new range of objects: the ruins of a once-venerated Christian church. Tripping over the remnants of former religions was nothing new to the English: most counties were dotted with megaliths, cromlechs, and mysterious mounds. But the monastery ruins were different in kind, for they were the outer forms, the "architectural fossils," of a religion that had been intimately bound up with English sense of identity for so long there was no other living cultural memory. And it was a religion with a foothold in the present, for it would be many decades before Protestantism would press out Catholicism in the parish mind. The dissolution thus made for some soul-searching. Faced with the remains of a church they had helped to topple, but not yet so convinced of their cause to strike the final blow, the first few generations of English Protestants tended to view the ruins with something of a bad conscience.

Sixteenth-century authors often wrote with a sense of repentance and near contrition when describing the violence done to the monastic world, denouncing the "fatal survey" of the king and its ruination of buildings that had once been "the Glory of our English nation." Henry Spelman bewailed how "the axe and the mattock ruined almost all the chief and most magnificent ornaments of the kingdom," while John Aubrey could only view the ruins with the image in his mind of "their magnificence as they were when in perfection."[121] In the works of the antiquarians and historians of the late seventeenth century, however, this pining for the medieval past tended to lose its early tones of self-reproach and pass over into nostalgia and romanticism. Gothic chapels and the remains of monastic buildings were, after all, the stock-in-trade of the Restoration garden. But not all Protestant authors let their readers escape the pricks of conscience. John Bale and John Leland could not forgive the crimes done to the chapter libraries; they considered this a reproach to the national character. Nor did later commentators overlook the moral message that inhered in the abandoned cloisters. An example of this is the work of the Kent historian William Lambarde (1536–1601), who drew attention to how the just judgment of God had laid even Canterbury low, it passing "soudenly from great wealth, multitude of inhabitaunts, and beautiful buildings, to extreme povertie, nakednes, and decay."[122] None of these writers necessarily agreed on what the ruins had to say. Spelman and Lambarde would not have viewed the remains from the same perspective. But there was a general sense in all of their writing that the Catholic buildings had a message to relate to the people of Protestant England. It was just a matter of seeing them in the proper light.

Viewing the ruins on the landscape from a Protestant point of view was thus an act of reinterpretation, and one that not only required making sense of absence but called for the inscription of new meaning on the fixed and familiar. This applied to the natural terrain as much as it did to the buildings. To begin with there could be no place in the Protestant environment for the sacralized landscape of late-medieval religion.[123] In Catholic England there had been places considered extraordinarily holy. Whether natural phenomena such as wells and springs or manmade structures such as wayside chapels and pilgrimage shrines, there were certain spaces that had a heightened sanctity and were set off from the profane world. Protestantism, however, rejected the conceit that some places might be holier than others. The world was uniformly blessed, and in any case it was not possible for humans to conjure the divine through their own efforts in time or space.

Cleansing the parishes of such "monuments of superstition and idolatry" remained central to the Protestant mission until well into the seventeenth century. The reformers set out to uproot the holy thorns and stop up the sacral springs, in effect exorcising the landscape of its Catholic demons. At its most literal it was a case of simple substitution. Perhaps the best known examples of this practice occurred when the English Protestants first encountered the topography of America, where they simply overwrote the land in the language of their faith. Both time and space were named or renamed to remove all traces of native and, if the Spanish had been there before them, Catholic belief. As all days were "homogeneously sacred," the privileging of holy days, including Christmas and Easter, fell away. Similarly, as all places were equally holy, the Puritans desacralized the locations considered hallowed or sacrosanct and gave them deliberately profane designations, hence the emergence of places such as Beaver Brook, Spot Pond, Adam's Chair, and Cheese Rock.[124] The Massachusetts's governor John Winthrop, one of the most industrious of the Puritan onomatologists, offered the example of a pious man (himself) who could not rest easy knowing there was a place on the continent named Hue's Cross. "In respect," wrote Winthrop, "that such things might hereafter give the Papists occasion to say that their religion was first planted in these parts, [he] changed the name, and called it Hue's Folly."[125]

Yet Protestants also invested their landscapes with religious meaning. In New England it was common to build the meeting house in a location considered sanctified in some way. Similarly, certain spots cut out of the surrounding wilderness were held to be more holy than others, places where prayer was thought to be especially efficacious.[126] But there was a difference, and it was in the message that the landscape was thought to relate. Unlike the sacral geography of Catholicism, which promised direct access to the divine *in actu*, the Protestant horizon only offered divine intervention *in potentia*, and this usually in the form of punishment and wrath. God was not present in the landscape, at least not in sacramental form. Rather, God revealed himself to the faithful through the meaning he inscribed onto the environment and preached through the natural world. Earthquakes, winds, unrelenting floods, water pools that rose in times of crisis, wells that suddenly dried up, trees that twisted into human shapes – all had a divine message to relate if understood in the proper way. And in place of the rooted sacramentalism of the medieval environment, where boughs could heal goitre and springs recover sight with *ex opere operato* ease, the natural wonders of the Protestant world were explained with reference to Scripture. Were not the River Jordan and the Pool of Bethesda thaumaturgic waters? Viewing the landscape as a religious landscape thus required a sense of God's purpose rather than his proximity. The environment was not shaped by his immediate presence but by what one English Puritan termed the "disposing and digitating hand of Providence."[127]

The New England clergyman Cotton Mather had a name for this theology of the natural world: Christianography. Writing from the perspective of the second and third generation Puritans, Mather viewed the wilderness of America as a mirror on the mind of a God who had "spied out" the land as a refuge for the Reformed church. This would be the space where all things would converge in the millennium, where New Jerusalem would find its place on earth. The proofs in the landscape were not local but universal, the biblical metaphors and Scriptural typologies that revealed the place of America in the divine order. For Mather, to view the land as a Christian space was a visionary exercise, one that required more than just a sense of geography or powers of description. As he wrote in *Magnalia Christi Americana* (1702), "The *Church* of God must no longer be wrapp'd up in *Strabo's* Cloak: *Geography* must now find work for *Christiano-graphy* in Regions far enough beyond the Bounds wherein the *Church* of God had through all former Ages been circumscribed. Renown'd *Churches* of Christ must be gathered where the Ancients once Derided them that look'd for any *Inhabitants*."[128] Of course, Mather could add that whereas the ancients did not have Scripture to point the way, the moderns were surrounded by signs. Aside from all of the parallels between the history of this New Jerusalem in America and events in the Bible (wanderings, wilderness, crossings, covenants), there was also Philippians 2:10–11 that spoke of the bowing of knees of "things under the earth." But the most compelling of the antitypes was the image of the wilderness, which not only conjured notions of exile and temptation but provided the simile for interpretations that sought out signs of providence. This land had the potential blessing of God. It was, as Mather wrote, "a land not sown."[129] And yet at the same time, it had fallen out of the memory of man and had long been in thrall to the devil. In addition to being a refuge for the godly, it was also a place of temptation and sin.

By situating the landscape within the narrative of Christian history and drawing on ancient metaphors that related the idea of grace and covenant, the Puritans turned the errand into the wilderness into a type of homecoming. It was *terra cognita*. There was every reason to believe, as John Winthrop and Cotton Mather insisted, that the wilderness was "a shelter and a hiding place" for the faithful and a refuge from the general destruction that had overwhelmed Europe. And more than this, all the signs suggested that the very land had been set aside by God as the stage for the final act of providential history.[130] This did not mean that the landscape was sacred in the sense that the English landscape had been sacred to medieval eyes, a place where God was actually present and accessible. But it did imply that the divine purpose inhered in the wilderness and that it could be revealed by way of the proper exegesis. In doing this, most interpreters stuck to metaphor and typology. Only a few went as far as Edward Johnson (circa 1599–1672), surveyor, trader, and clerk of writ, whose interpretation in *The Wonder-Working Providence of Sion's Saviour in New England* (1653) detailed a program of environmental reform that enjoined the settlers to build up (or rather cut down) the land into the New Jerusalem.[131] Expediting the millennium entailed a literal deforestation, a task the settlers could best bring about through the proper balance of toil, prayer, and technology.

But the wilderness had another side to it as well, one less emblematic of God's blessings and more attune to his displeasure. Storms, winds, earthquakes, crop failures, epidemics, plagues of grasshoppers, shipwrecks, rogue wolves – all could quite easily be interpreted as heralds of pending wrath. Of course, there was nothing particularly Protestant about the idea of a natural world sensitive to divine displeasure. But the New World was an especially dangerous environment, partly because it meant (in fact and fiction) living in close proximity to just about every quasi-scientific species, Christian bogeyman, and Breughelian monstrosity possible for the early-modern mind to imagine. William Bradford spoke of a rattlesnake that could fly, its breath alone deadly enough to kill a man. Moreover, overseeing all of this chaos was the devil himself, a presence so familiar that Cotton Mather referred to him as "that old usurping *landlord* of America."[132] According to Mather and other Puritan historians, the devil had had the run of the continent for years, well before the English arrived. Lurking somewhere in the wilderness, he was always looking for opportunities to wreak havoc or turn the world upside down.

Thus, when the Protestant imagination took in the American landscape, it conjured up signs of both grace and wrath, and it evinced different reactions, some looking for more law and some for more gospel. The nature of the reading depended on how the symbols and signifiers sat within the projected course of Christian history. It also depended on the inner disposition of the exegete, for there was no doubt that the world outside was often just a projection of the world within. For some Puritans, viewing the raw and bestial in nature led to thinking about the raw and bestial in man. Hence the efforts made at the start of the colony to gather the settlers together and fence off the towns and villages from the surrounding rough country. Too much contact with, and too close a proximity to, the "howling wilderness" and the soul of man would regress to its savage state.[133] There was proof enough of this danger in the behavior of the colonists, especially in the later years of declension. But there was an even more obvious reminder of the wages of sin just beyond the walls of the towns: the American Indians.

In the beginning, the native peoples were embraced by the New England Puritans, and not just as the obvious targets of missionary zeal but as actors in the Protestant drama of salvation. Scholars speculated about Indian origins, some tracing their roots back to Adam or Noah, some claiming they were the cursed brood of Hamm, others concluding they were descendents of the lost tribes of Israel. The most sophisticated case in favor of the lost tribe theory was Thomas Thorowgood's *Jewes in America* (1650), which established the historical connections between Israelite and Algonquin by listing the similarities in their religious cultures.[134] This Hebraic genealogy was crucial for Puritan theories of the end time, for it was well known that the Jews had to be converted before the millennial timetable could run its course. Moreover, the idea of the Indians as a heathen but nonetheless innately virtuous people was the supreme counterpoise to the idea of the wilderness as evil run riot. Roger Williams was quick to exploit this notion in his war of words with the Bay Puritans, putting the following ditty in the mouths of the Narragansett:

> We weare no Cloaths, have many Gods,
> And yet our sinnes are lesse:
> You are Barbarians, Pagans wild,
> Your Lands the Wildernesse.[135]

But the image of the Indians as noble and pious savages did not last very long. Having failed in their attempts at mass conversion, and with warfare with the natives becoming more frequent and brutal over the course of the century, the New England Puritans abandoned their theories about lost tribes and innate virtues and discovered new Indian ancestors in Tartars and Scythians and new prefigurations in Amelikites and the armies of Gog and Magog. Second- and third-generation clergy tended to view the Indians as "devil-driven" with no hope of salvation. By the seventeenth century, most Bay Protestants would have agreed with William Hubbard when he wrote in his *General History of New England* (1680) that "here are no footsteps of any religion before the English came, but merely diabolical."[136]

This pessimism was partly engendered by native intransigence and partly by the difficulties Protestants were having transposing their faith on a foreign land. But it was certainly not unique to the Puritans of America. If the history of early-modern missionary activity is anything to go by, most European Protestants thought along the same lines.

The Missionary Turn

Few of the Catholic arguments against the authenticity of Protestantism had a more manifest historical basis than the charge that it was a religion without any measure of missionary success. For Catholics, the obligation to spread the faith throughout the world had been invested in the church by the resurrected Christ. It thus followed that the Spanish and Portuguese advance in the New World, where tens of thousands of aboriginal souls had been baptized, was a sure sign of divine favor. Protestant inertia, in contrast, confirmed it as heresy. At one level the Protestants could dismiss this as Jesuitical sophistry. Had not the Reformation itself been brought into being in order to fill the world with the light of the gospel and take Christ to the corners of the earth? While Luther had not raised the idea of a specific mission to foreign lands, he had taught that spreading the Word was the first duty of the true church, and one that was perpetual.[137] Some Protestants answered with actions rather than words. There were sporadic attempts to spread the faith among peoples beyond Latin Europe. Swedish Lutherans went among the Laplanders, German Lutherans targeted the Turks and the Slavs, while English Congregationalists worked to convert the American Indians. But these isolated instances aside, no general sense of missionary awareness featured in early Protestantism.

Recognizing the problem, critical voices were raised, calls came for more overseas engagement and even theologies of mission. In England, Adrianus Saravia (circa 1532–1613), a refugee from the Low Countries who ended his days as a deacon of Westminster, published a series of works in the 1590s on the need for the church to take up Christ's Great Commission. In the Dutch Republic there was no shortage of thinkers willing to point up the lack of missionary zeal, among them Peter Plancius, Justus Heurnius, Willem Teellinck, and Gottfried Cornelius Udemans. The first substantial systematizations of the theme came from the pens of Jean Taffin (nephew of his more famous namesake, Huguenot chaplain to William the Silent), whose ideas filtered down through the popular works of Teellinck, and Gisbertus Voetius (1589–1676), the latter developing a theology of mission while a professor at Utrecht. Although he borrowed much from Catholic missiology, Voetius was one of the first thinkers to contextualize the idea of Protestant evangelization, understanding that it had to work differently to the Catholic process, through different channels using different means.[138]

But the most important of the early critics was Justinian von Welz (1621–68). Born in Counter-Reformation Carinthia to Lutheran parents and forced to flee to Germany as a youth, Welz became a passionate voice in favor of Protestant mission. He had a conversion experience himself, prompting him to write *De vita solitaria* (1663), a work that detailed the inner transformation that leads a soul to Christ. Projecting this personal experience onto the world at large, Welz published tract after tract on the need to take the faith to the New World. He even developed a detailed scheme for the creation of a society devoted to overseas work. Many of the arguments of the later Protestant missiology first surfaced here, among them the idea of the eternal commission and the need for faith and love to quicken in the embrace of foreign peoples. And there were ecclesiological reasons as well, not the least of which was the need for the Protestant church to counter Catholic expansion in the New World. But the work of Welz, like that of Saravia and Voetius, had no substantive impact on its age. Frustrated and despondent, Welz eventually gave up the idea of convincing the Protestant authorities and set off on his own to convert the natives of South America. He died in 1668 near the banks of the river Serena, where it was reported that his body had been ripped to pieces by wild animals.[139]

Orthodox resistance to missions says much about the nature of magisterial Protestantism. It was a religion embedded in the secular and spiritual conditions that first cultivated it and was extremely reluctant to pull free of its intellectual and institutional inheritance. The idea of mission conjured up the fear of forces – peripheral, improvised, centrifugal – that threatened the ordered constitution of the Protestant church. Arguments against were generally twofold in nature: historical and theological. Throughout the sixteenth and seventeenth centuries, the authorities could answer with good conscience that Protestants were still in a fight for survival. By 1648 rights had been secured for Lutherans and Calvinists, but confessional warfare in Europe remained a constant reality. There was enough to do building the church at home without going abroad. Moreover, Protestantism by its nature was a localized phenomenon, rooted in the relations of state rule and legitimated by the imperial legal maxim *cuius regio, eius religio*. Both Voetius and Welz encountered rigid opposition to any suggestion that the Protestant mission should work within a transnational sphere. Drawing on arguments developed by Melanchthon, the authorities rejected the idea on the grounds that the spreading of the gospel was the prerogative of the state and that it would grant the laity too much power and autonomy.[140]

At this stage the historical merged with the theological. In arguing that the state alone had the right to send out missionaries, Lutherans such as Johann Heinrich Ursinus (who wrote a critical report on the proposals of Welz) raised the issue of the Great Commission (Matthew 28:19–20). Did not a desire to embark on missions suggest a lack of faith in the work of the Word and the apostles? And did it not imply a sense of hubris and misplaced prophecy, a sort of meddling with providence? This was the central plank of the orthodox rejection of the idea of mission, the belief that the command to teach and preach to all nations referred to the apostles alone.[141] Occasionally the orthodox might add to this by pointing out that even before the apostles the Word had been planted by Adam and Noah, but in general it was proof enough that the gospel had already been spread to all corners of the globe and that no individual had the right, and no church the need, to take on this commission. Such logic also made it easier to accommodate the natives into the Protestant scheme of providence and redemption, for now they became complicit in their guilt. If the natives did not recognize or respond to the preaching of the gospel, this was the proof of their state of damnation and the pastors need not exert themselves overmuch. Thus John Cotton could argue that the best strategy in bringing the Bay Algonquians to the faith was not to use compulsion "but to permit them either to believe willingly or not to believe at all."[142]

Of course, even in the absence of a systematic agenda or a developed missiology, Protestants still preached the gospel to the native peoples. The founding charters of the English colonies stipulated that (to cite the Virginian charter of 1606) "the true word, and service of God and Christian faith be preached, planted, and used, not only within every of the said several colonies, and plantations, but alsoe as much as they may amongst the Salvage people which doe or shall adjoine unto them, or border upon them."[143] The very seal of Massachusetts Bay Company bore the image of an Indian in a palm-leaf breechclout with the words "Come over and help us" written on a scroll. In 1646 the General Council directed the clergy to select two preachers to go among the Indians of Martha's Vineyard, Nantucket, and the Elizabeth Islands. This was followed in 1649 by an agency founded by the parliamentarians to gather and disburse funding for missionary activity.[144] Such initiatives registered momentary success, but in general the most successful English missionaries tended to be men driven by a private impulse rather than public directives. Roger Williams, John Eliot (1604–90), and Thomas Mayhew (1593–1682) were the best known of these Puritan apostles. Eliot was particularly devoted, writing a dictionary and grammar of the Massachuset tongue, translating the New Testament and other Christian texts, and gathering thousands of Indians together in the Bay Colony "praying towns," which at one time may have accounted for 10 percent of the local native population. But English Protestantism did not embark on a program of evangelization until Thomas Bray established the Society for the Propagation of the Gospel in Foreign Parts in 1701. And even this scheme, although entrusted with the conversion of "heathens and infidels," devoted most of its resources to the care of Anglicans overseas.

Other Protestant powers had similar histories. A case in point is the colony of New Netherlands. Although the Dutch never sought to establish a substantial presence in America, the directors nevertheless considered it a duty of the Reformed clergy to preach to the aboriginals. Even before the Dutch took possession of the American lands in 1624, the East Indian Company had already set up a seminary in Leiden (*Seminarium Indicum*) for the training of clergymen bound for Indonesia and Ceylon. But the seminary soon closed its doors and left no lasting impression. Dominie Bernardus Freeman, pastor of the Reformed church of Schenectady, worked among the Iroquois and translated the Bible into Mohawk, but he was not representative of the church as a whole. Most clergy were more in the mold of Johannes Megapolensis or Jonas Michaëlius. Both were pious men who went overseas with the mandate of the Amsterdam Classis in mind ("the edification and instruction of the inhabitants and indians"), but once faced with the strange customs and incomprehensible language of the natives, they quickly became disillusioned. By the end of his stay, Michaëlius thought the Algonquin as thick as garden stakes and full of evil.[145]

Historians sometimes refer to the ill-fated colony of French Huguenots planted off the Brazilian coast in 1555 as the first Protestant mission to America, primarily because it had the backing of the Reformed admiral of France, Gaspard de Coligny, and it was peopled with French Huguenots by Calvin in response to a letter sent to Geneva by the leader of the expedition, Nicolas Durand de Villegagnon (circa 1510–71), vice admiral of Bretagne (and fair-weather Protestant). At its point of origin, however, the expedition was never conceived as an evangelical mission or a refuge for Huguenots in the New World. The idea that Fort Coligny was the first Protestant errand into the American wilderness was projected onto events retrospectively by Reformed authors such as Jean de Léry, Marc Lescarbot, and Jean Crespin after the colony had fallen into Portuguese hands. Indeed, Crespin effectively canonized the expedition by claiming that three of the Huguenot colonists had been murdered "for the truth of the Gospel" by the apostate and arch-dissembler Villegagnon.[146] But their crimes, as Villegagnon saw it, were secular, as was the undertaking itself.

The colony was prefigurative in one sense, though, and that was in what it revealed about early Protestant perceptions of indigenous peoples. In his published report of the expedition, the *Histoire d'un voyage faict en la terre du Brésil* (1578), the Reformed minister Jean de Léry (1536–1613) described his encounters with the Tupinamba Indians. While sympathetic in many respects, Léry had difficulty finding a place for native religion within his categories of thought. To make it comprehensible, he used two modes of discourse: the carnivalesque and the theological. The first, the carnivalesque, was a common enough device among Protestant authors, especially when the purpose was to expose Catholicism to ridicule. Léry's ethnography partly worked in this way. In describing the body paints of the Tupinamba, Léry discerned the leggings of a priest, in their hairstyles he spied a tonsure, in the feathered headdress the papal tiara, in their rituals he made out traces of Catholic liturgy. Most damning by far were the parallels he drew between the ritual cannibalism of the natives and the Catholic Eucharist. At least the Tupinamba cooked the flesh, he remarked.[147]

Once he turned to the theological aspects of their culture, Léry became less Rabelaisian and more severe. The obstacle to thought was the fact that the Tupinamba belief system lacked all of the features that defined a church in early modern Europe: no cult, no temples, no priest. And as it was inconceivable to assume that the Indians practiced a faith that sat at the same level as Christianity, Léry was led to conclude that the sheer otherness of the Tupinamba religion was evidence of their damnation. Since the apostles had taken the Word to all peoples, it could be proved that they had turned their backs on God by the fact that they had forgotten the faith – as evidenced in the absence of writing and social memory (only the myth of a deluge remained) – and regressed to carnival and cannibalism. And isolation was no excuse. As Calvin himself had written, even if the Bible were not available there were enough signs of the divine in the book of the world to convince even the "plus simples idiotz" of the existence of God.[148] Little wonder that Léry, perhaps the prototypical missionary of early magisterial Protestantism, could not think of a single theological reason why he should try to convert them.

A referential theology and a substantial ecclesiology: both were difficult to transplant among peoples and places so far removed from the intellectual and institutional traditions of Europe. The problems are well illustrated by the colonial enterprise of the Dutch Republic in the East. By the middle of the seventeenth century, the Dutch were on the way to empire, solidly entrenched on the Indian subcontinent, the Malay peninsula, and the Indonesian Archipelago. The controlling interest in all of this was the East India Company (VOC), and the omnipresent motive was economic. Nevertheless, the Company was bound by its charter to promote and protect the Dutch Reformed church, and this included campaigns of evangelizing among the natives similar to missionary work.

During its two centuries of expansion, the Company may have sent as many as 1,000 clergymen to the East, not to count the myriad lay-readers and schoolmasters dispatched in support. By 1730, Batavia had more Reformed preachers than any other Dutch city save Amsterdam. And yet the ultimate impact of the Reformed church on the local populations was modest. Generally speaking, the clergy had most success among peoples who had already been converted to Catholicism by the Portuguese, such as the local populations of Ceylon, Amboina, and Taiwan. In Amboina, the Company requisitioned one of the Portuguese churches and turned it over to the Reformed minister, who offered services in both the Dutch and Malay communities. As more clergy arrived, they began to work among the natives, preaching, baptizing, and destroying the local temples and idols. In Formosa similar efforts were made, in particular by Georgius Candidius, the first preacher to arrive, who led a missionary movement on the island that numbered 32 clergymen and left behind traces of the faith that remained as late as the nineteenth century.[149]

In the majority of instances, however, the Reformed religion disappeared as soon as the Dutch withdrew. In part, this was because of impediments the clergy were not equipped to overcome. Few had been trained in languages such as Tamil or Sinhalese, and there was little an ill-prepared pastor could do to eradicate local customs or the complex belief systems of Islamism, Hinduism, and Buddhism when there was no common ground for dialogue. Add to this the fact that the local populace was continually in motion and the chances for conversion were few. But the deeper problem was ecclesiological. The church in the colonies was completely subordinate to the Company. Any attempt to invest the church with independent powers, as the preacher Philip Baldaeus set out to do in Ceylon, was met with immediate resistance and harsh reprimands. When rumors reached him that the church sought greater autonomy, the governor-general of Batavia placed restrictions on clerical movement, ordered that church correspondence must first pass through his hands, and deprived the clergy of all independent decisions in matters relating to discipline and doctrine.[150] No missionary work of any scope could operate under such conditions.

Many of these problems were first worked out in East India between 1706 and 1730 by the leaders of the Danish mission to Tranquebar when the combined efforts of the Danish monarchy and the Lutheran theologians of Halle created a program for overseas evangelization that served as model for later Protestantism. The issue of legitimacy was overcome by the involvement of the Lutheran king of Denmark Frederik IV (1671–1730), who considered it his duty as a Christian prince not only to provide for the spiritual welfare of his subjects abroad, but the "Jews and heathens" as well.[151] The legal basis for the princely initiative was orthodox Lutheran; it was simply an extension of the principle of right of reformation, now applied to lands overseas. However, there was an additional dimension to the royal order that made it more than just an issue of territorial aggrandizement. Frederik was personally involved in overseeing the mission; he considered it part of his obligation as a Protestant prince. He pushed through the ordination of the missionaries despite the resistance of the bishops and in 1714 established a missionary college that sought to propagate the gospel "as far and as wide as at all possible" within and beyond the bounds of Danish sovereignty.[152]

But the crucial dimension of the Danish mission was not derived from its magisterial order. It was rooted in a deep and unyielding personal conviction. In his first efforts to find suitable missionaries, the royal chaplain had approached the Lutheran bishops of Denmark, only to come up against orthodox resistance. Thus he turned instead to August Hermann Francke and the University of Halle, and there he found two extremely competent and dedicated men: Bartholomäus Ziegenbalg (1683–1719) and Heinrich Plütschau (c.1675–1752). Both had worked closely with Francke in Halle, and both were deeply influenced by the teachings of Lutheran Pietism. Ziegenbalg in particular had been inspired by the movement; it was this that had impelled him to embark on the Danish mission and work so closely with the people of Tranquebar. And it was this same devotion that brought Ziegenbalg into conflict with the Company officials. At one stage, Governor Hassius compared him to Thomas Müntzer.[153]

Ziegenbalg was a typical product of Pietism, one of the growing number who were convinced that sincere faith was on the decline, that the church was in need of reform, and that true Christianity was more interior than exterior and demanded total devotion in faith *and* deed to the teachings of Christ. For Ziegenbalg, the highest calling of the clergyman was to lead people to this type of faith (*pietas*), and that meant all people, within and without the church. By the early decades of the eighteenth century, Francke and his followers in Halle had managed to translate this private impluse into a missionary program that sent preachers to Russia, Estonia, Latvia, Poland, Lithuania, Bulgaria, North America, and even Constantinople. Orthodox Lutherans followed these developments with suspicion, especially once the Halle missionaries were joined in their efforts by enthusiastic laymen from independent groups such as the Moravian Brethren. But there was nothing the bishops of Denmark or the theologians of Wittenberg or indeed any orthodox Lutheran or Reformed authorities could do to put an end to the impulse. Despite powerful opposition, it would transform the nature of Protestant Christianity.

5

Revivals

During the first half of the seventeenth century, American Protestants looked on with horror as the Lutheran, Reformed, and Catholic armies of the Thirty Years' War (1618–48) marched through the parishes of Europe, and above all the parishes of Germany, and laid waste to the secular and spiritual order. Contemplating the waning piety of his own religious community, the Boston preacher John Norton (1606–63) asked his parishioners to think on the state of religious life in the Old World: "Many Churches in Europe, since the Reformation ... [in]Saxony, Bohemia, Hungaria, Poland, France, and other places [are] Unchurched and Dissipated."[1] For once, the prophecies and jeremiads were not far from the mark: Europe had indeed been devastated by warfare. In some places, up to half of the population had died from hunger, disease, or violence. Whole villages lay abandoned, the fields untilled and the houses razed, and even in the larger towns and cities the war had left its mark in the form of pillage and destruction. In such a climate of disorder and devastation, the religious culture of Europe necessarily suffered. In addition to the existential impact of the war, which raised questions about the orthodox interpretation of God and his plan for the world, there were the material effects of decades of conflict. Churches had been abandoned, visitations had been suspended, the clergy had been reduced in number – in short, the machinery of magisterial rule had ground to a halt.

Out of the ruins of the war, new Protestants emerged. And in fact in many ways the Protestant culture of the late seventeenth and early eighteenth centuries was stronger and more dynamic than anything that had existed before. Reform-minded clergy in the mainstream churches, recognizing that the idea of reformation had not yet been brought to completion, began to cultivate a new theology of piety that would complete the earlier reform of doctrine with a reform of life. Following in the footsteps of the English Puritans, Reformed theologians in the Netherlands and northern Germany and Lutheran pastors in the German lands began to replace the emphasis on doctrine with a concern with inner piety and the fruits of faith. What the Christian did outside the church was becoming just as important as what he or she did within under the tutelage of the clergyman.

Protestants: A History from Wittenberg to Pennsylvania 1517–1740   By C. Scott Dixon
© 2010 C. Scott Dixon

As a consequence of this, Protestant culture was reinvigorated in the late seventeenth century. But it was at the expense of the original magisterial paradigm of reform. Confessional culture started to lose its hold on the Protestant world. In place of the state churches and formal confessions of the previous era, new forms of spiritual life emerged. It was, in effect, the rebirth of the radical tradition, and it gave rise to a transformation in Protestant culture that reached from Germany, Silesia, and Sweden to the woodlands of the Delaware Valley.[2] In part it grew from within, the result of Puritan and Pietist reform initiatives by the ordained, and orthodox, clergy of the church. But it was also a movement with its own dynamic beyond the control of the magisterial system, the steady emergence, and re-emergence, of marginalized Protestant communities that broke through the former constraints of the confessional age and established a new trajectories in Protestant history.

To an extent this period represents the end phase of the Reformation, for with the Pietist turn we see the final coming-into-being of many of the principles that had either been abandoned by the reformers or relegated to the radical margins. And it was also the period when new cultural and intellectual forces, secular as well as spiritual in nature, begin to undermine the magisterial order. One of the most eccentric voices of this new impulse, the mystic German Pietist Johannes Kelpius (1673–1708), claimed that all of this was part of a "new reformation" and that the "ecstasies, revelations, apparitions, changings of minds, transfigurations, translations of their bodys" that Protestants were now experiencing were the harbingers of a new religious age.[3] Indeed, so certain was Kelpius of the changes to come that he took himself to the Pennsylvanian wilderness and lived an eremitical existence in a small cabin. While there he spent much of his time peering through a telescope fixed to his roof, looking for heavenly signs of the coming Christ.

Signs of the Times

Histories

In early 1617 the Protestants of Germany drew up a proposal for a day of tribute to mark the Reformation centenary. The express purpose of the event was to bring together Protestants in commemoration of their deliverance from papal captivity. The sermons thus played up the extremes, beginning, as in Reformed Heidelberg, with a preliminary discussion on the papal Antichrist before turning to the history of the rediscovery of the gospel. And yet in all of this triumphalism there was a clear note of anxiety as well. The same preachers who projected a sense of origins by alluding to the trumpet blasts of Jericho or Joshua's upbuilding of the Temple also warned about the many enemies still camped around, and within, the city walls. The Lutherans of Württemberg, for instance, were not only told to keep on guard against Jesuits, Calvinists, Zwinglians, Epicureans, and other "wild spirits," but the growing number of speculative thinkers who weakened the faith from within: Antinomians, Synergists, Majorists, Osiandrians, Adiaphorists, Crypto-Calvinists.[4]

In response to the perceived dangers, the clergy demanded greater devotion from the faithful and advised them to avoid speculation and remain true to the symbolic works.

Magisterial Protestantism generally reacted to threats in this way: the best defense was
the least defense. Parishioners were not encouraged to explore the Bible for themselves;
they were instructed to stick to the formal confessions of the church, which were in any
case, the clergy added, founded upon the Word of God. Too liberal an approach, as the
Book of Concord (1580) put it, would open up the faith

> to restless, contentious individuals, who do not want to be bound by any certain formula of
> pure doctrine, to start scandalous controversies at will and to introduce and defend
> monstrous errors, the only possible consequence of which is that finally correct doctrine
> will be entirely obscured and lost and nothing beyond uncertain opinions and dubious,
> disputable imaginations and views will be transmitted to subsequent generations.[5]

This captured a common concern. By the seventeenth century, all of the magisterial
traditions had an established corpus of belief that spelled out in detail exactly what
pastors and parishioners were expected to think and believe. The impulse to preserve
a closed canon of thought, to withdraw from speculation or dialogue and pay strict
adherence to an approved corpus of belief, was the essence of seventeenth-century
magisterial Protestantism during the age of orthodoxy.[6] In comparison with the first
century of reform, this latter period has been viewed by scholars as a sterile phase, more
concerned with safeguarding order than creating it anew.

Representative of the theological system-building of the second century was the digest
of necessary doctrine (*Epitome credendorum*, 1625) by the Wittenberg professor
Nicolaus Hunnius (1585–1643). Like his father Egidius before him, Hunnius divided
most of his time between composing learned Latin tracts in defense of Lutheranism and
writing polemical works against Crypto-Calvinists and Socinians. In the *Epitome*,
Hunnius arranged the Lutheran articles of faith according to the fundamental and the
non-fundamental, the former further subdivided into the primary and the secondary,
with the primary being those which, as the theologian Johann Wilhelm Baier put it, "we
not only cannot deny if we are to retain our faith and salvation, but that we cannot be
ignorant of."[7] Baier's double-negatives did little to help readers understand an already
confusing scheme, but in any event the distinctions were academic, as all of the articles,
whatever their place in the soteriological chain of being, were equally relevant in keeping
the dogmatic structure in place and guarding against innovation.

But it would be wrong to view works of this kind or the religious ideas they were meant
to synthesize as historical artifacts captured in time. Like most writers, Hunnius was
endlessly revising, adding passages, reworking his text. And like most readers, his
orthodox colleagues were constantly reviewing his ideas, particularly with reference to
what he meant as foundational. By this stage in Protestant history, not only was
confessional belief bound up in the culture of the age, it had become (to varying
degrees) a framework for perception and interpretation. Consequently, no matter how
fixed, formed, and dogmatic the principles may have seemed to the authors, the ideas
were gradually altered according to media, context, personality, and intention. Lutheran
ideas of Christology, for instance, were cast differently for a tractate than a hymn,
presented differently for a Catholic opponent than a Calvinist, and conceived differently
in a disputation and a sermon. Sermons were especially fertile settings for the adaptation
of ideas and intentions, many of the preachers realizing that the norms of the faith had to

be translated into comprehensible terms before they could have an impact on parish life. Theology had to speak down to reality, but without compromising essentials. Capturing complex theological concepts in language that the parishioners could grasp was a difficult task, especially when we remember that the pastors were speaking to particular historical situations with specific people and their sins in mind.[8]

But even when the dialogue was between scholars, where there was a clear affinity between medium, context, and intention, orthodox Protestantism changed with the times. Take, for example, the shift in focus and approach in the academic disputations in Wittenberg from the 1570s to the 1690s. When the Lutheran disputations began in earnest in the 1580s they were essentially basic affirmations of the principles of belief. In the following century the dialectic opened up, with candidates drawing on a range of disciplines, from history to geography to poetics, in order to engage the enemies of the faith. Freshly minted neologisms were required in order to accommodate the spectrum – *historico-theologica, exegetico-theologica,* and other mumbo-jumbo terms.[9] And this was just one symptom of a general trend. Throughout the period of classical Lutheran orthodoxy, the theologians of the church extended the dialogue, and stretched the language and the concepts, in order to keep pace with intellectual developments. The thought at the end of the period was different in kind from the thought at the start, and this despite the fact that the basic purpose of the orthodox movement had been to preserve the core teachings of the faith.

Lutheranism was especially predisposed to systematization. In the massive syntheses of Johann Gerhard, Martin Chemnitz, and Jacob Heerbrand we can see the efforts made to bring the symbolic teachings of the church into harmony with the historical teachings of Christianity, an exercise that was necessarily dialogic as the creeds, the church fathers, and the medieval authorities were re-examined in the midst of disputes with Catholics and Calvinists. By the mid-seventeenth century, orthodox Lutheranism was excessively discursive and referential, often proving points by amassing huge numbers of authorities in the footnotes or (as with Hunnius) simply paraphrasing established texts. The culmination of this trend was Johann Andreas Quenstedt's *Didactic, Polemical, or Systematic Theology* (1685), a massive, all-embracing work of dogmatics that set out to address every possible point of doctrine and place it in its historical context, ranging from the teachings of the ancient church to the works of contemporaries, Lutheran, Catholic, and Reformed. Contrary to the intentions of their authors, which was to preserve the legacy unaltered and intact, works of this kind tended to open up the discourse. Lutheran thought constantly refashioned itself through the modes of its own reproduction.[10]

In essence, the issue of orthodoxy was historical rather than doctrinal, the central problematic of Protestant origins. How can a religion that is derived from timeless absolutes be so closely bound up with human history? The constant need to justify Protestantism and set it off from Roman Catholicism, which reached fever-pitch during the age of orthodoxy, was in large part in response to this question, and most of the apologists answered in the same vein: that there is a deeper history, the history of the true church, which has been buried for centuries beneath papal accretions. This approach provided the magisterial Protestants with a plausible account of origins, and it inverted the charges of error and innovation and cast them back at the Catholics. And yet even this narrative changed over time.

The founder of Protestant historiography was Philipp Melanchthon, who was the first to invest the discipline with a theological imperative. Early histories of the movement, taking their cue from the anti-papalism of the humanists, had generally been moral or secular in approach. The Reformation was projected as the response of Christian men against the fallacies and corruptions of Rome, a reading that sat well within the history of the struggles between the German emperors and the popes. But Melanchthon introduced an additional dimension, the idea that there had been a continual line of true teaching running throughout Christian history, a body of belief preserved and taught by the teachers of the faith that had been taken up by the reformers. With this, the two aspects of the magisterial narrative were established: on the one hand, the idea that the faith had been preserved among select Christian men and women despite the efforts of the papacy; and on the other, that the history of Christianity – that is, the history of the Catholic church – had been a history of decline, an enduring retreat from the purity of the apostolic faith.[11]

The most influential histories in this vein were the works associated with the Lutheran Matthias Flacius Illyricus, a former student of Melanchthon and one-time professor of Hebrew at Wittenberg, whose two mid-century projects, the *Catalogus testium veritatis* (1556) and *Magdeburg Centuries* (1559–74), established an interpretative template that informed Protestant historiography for over a century. Central to the analysis in the *Catalogus* was the idea of the witnesses to the faith (*testes veritatis*), the men and women in the Christian past who had testified to the teaching of Christ despite the dangers of exclusion or persecution.[12] That they had been persecuted for their beliefs was the outcome of the Roman Catholic Church having started to fall away from the true faith from around AD 300, and thus the history of Christianity according to the *Catalogus* was essentially a trajectory of decline marked by the ineluctable rise of the papal Antichrist. Flacius went beyond Melanchthon in a number of respects, the two most significant being the emphasis he placed on the anti-papalism of the witnesses to the faith and the notion that Protestant history was not just an account of the past but a study in prophecy. For the line of continuity represented in the witnesses has an obvious terminus in the rise of Luther, particularly within the context of Flacius's apocalyptical reading of the past, and this invested the work with a logic not featured in Melanchthon's work. All of history becomes a battleground for the coming of Protestants.

Flacius placed so much emphasis on the coming of the Protestants in general that his work had a broad appeal. It was easily appropriated by Calvinists and Anglicans, for instance, to serve their agendas. The idea of the *testes veritatis* in particular became a central concept in Protestant history, especially once it was adopted by the martyrologists. Both Foxe and Crespin drew from the *Catalogus*, for instance. By the age of orthodoxy, however, this notion of proto-Protestants rather than proto-Lutherans or proto-Calvininsts was proving problematic. It was allowing for too broad a church and thus undermining the authenticity of the witnesses in the process.[13] By the late seventeenth century orthodox historians were already drawing back from the idea of a catalog of "reformers before the Reformation" in the general sense and looking more specifically for precursors of their distinct confessions. But there was a more serious challenge to the Flacian art of history than the debates over the authenticity of the sources.

At the turn of the century a survey of Christianity appeared that completely undermined the historiographical paradigm established by magisterial historians such as

Melanchthon and Flacius. Similar in approach to the *Catalogus*, but fundamentally different in intention, was the *Nonpartisan History of the Church and of Heretics* (1699–1700) by the Lutheran Gottfried Arnold (1666–1714), the most eloquent voice of the radical Pietists in the German lands. What distinguished Arnold's work from the magisterial narrative was his insistence that all church history was *necessarily* a story of decline, and that included the history of the Protestant church as well as the Catholic. Like Sebastian Franck before him, Arnold located the essence of Christianity in the individual rather than the institution, feeding his spiritualism into his analysis and projecting the history of Christianity among all modern strands of organized religions as an inversion of aspostolic origins. Arnold suggested that the objectification of religion, the forms, institutions, and dogmas of the confessions, was the very reason why Christianity had fallen away from the apostolic ideal. His dichotomies were similar in kind to those of Cranach's *Passional Christi et Antichristi* (1521), only now it was not pope versus Christ but any of the magisterial reformers versus the Christ of the New Testament. The general point was this: in place of a religion based upon the teachings of Christ and a piety inspired by the Spirit and enacted in the praxis of communal life, an externalized, formalized type of religion had taken shape and the idea of orthodoxy had emerged. From that point forward, Arnold believed, the religion of Christ had been perverted and manipulated to suit human nature. Ceremony and ritual replaced piety; symbols and confessions replaced an inner spiritual understanding; force and coercion replaced Christian freedom; and a state church and a bureaucratic ministry replaced a community of saints.[14] With this vision in mind, Arnold went on to argue that true religion survived not in the church but in the faith and conduct of a few enlightened souls who had surfaced on occasion in the narrative of Christian history – the alienated, the persecuted, the heretics, the radicals.

Orthodox Lutherans were not slow to realize that Arnold's approach to history was not just revisionism but a direct challenge to the order and authority of the church. History had been turned back on the faith. Ernst Solomon Cyprian (1673–1745), vice-president of the Gotha consistory, believed that Arnold's purpose in writing the work had been precisely this, to undermine organized religion to the benefit of radical religiosity. "To spread this opinion," wrote Cyprian, "and to bombard the evangelical church and its symbolic books with allegations of sectarianism, endless quarreling over words, the fabrication of heretics, and similar accusations, indeed, to overthrow our church constitution – that is why Arnold wrote the *History of Heretics*."[15] Another damning response came from the desk of Valentin Ernst Löscher (1673–1749), pastor, superintendent, professor, polemicist, poet, and perhaps the last of the great orthodox Lutheran theologians in Germany. Like Cyprian, Löscher considered the *History of Heretics* falsely conceived and dangerous in its intentions. Not long after reading the work, he founded a journal devoted to the defense of confessional Lutheranism. In its final form, it would prove to be a bastion of doctrinal purity, a vehicle for the orthodox response to the flood of journals and texts threatening the livelihood of the church. And like all of Löscher's work, it was directed to one specific end: the conservation of the magisterial tradition and the safeguarding of ecclesial order.[16]

Löscher identified three main threats to the Lutheran understanding of the Christian past common in his own day. First, and least menacing, or so he thought, was the rise of Pietist historiography. Although sympathetic at first, Löscher soon recognized that the

History of Heretics was a serious threat to the integrity of organized religion. Not only did it challenge the assumption that salvation was, and always had been, bound up with the church, but its detailed recreation of the history of apostolic Christianity provided the radicals with the historical foundations to support their theological teachings.[17] Second, Löscher was convinced that the thought and temper of the early Enlightenment was corruptive of true faith and godly order. And he saw all of the evils of the movement neatly bound up in its chief exponent in the German lands, Christian Thomasius, the Halle philosopher, whom we shall meet in a subsequent section of this chapter. In his elevation of reason above revelation, his calls for speculation in place of tradition, the moral in place of the spiritual, and the subordination of the church to the powers of the state, Thomasius represented all that was most threatening to the magisterial tradition. And finally, Löscher believed that the Christians of his age had become indifferent to the articles of the faith, that it was enough to have a vague commitment to an idea of Christianity without worrying too much about the specifics of confessional belief. Naturally, this type of laissez-faire religiosity undermined orthodox teaching, and thus we can understand why Löscher equated the problem of indifference in his time with the anomalous behavior of enthusiasts in Luther's day.[18] But in fact the real threat posed by the spirit of indifference was a lack of religious conviction rather than the overindulgence of the 1520s. The result, however, was the same. By the late seventeenth century, as Löscher observed, the magisterial tradition was beginning to lose its hold over the Protestant world.

Prophecy and wrath

As early as 1525, Martin Luther advised the Elector of Saxony that "unless your Electoral Grace will agree to undertake a great housecleaning, ... God's word and divine service will soon have vanished from the earth." By housecleaning Luther meant upbuilding, the creation of the first Protestant church, and the advice was offered in the context of a discussion regarding the means through which the elector, "God's faithful instrument," might best implant the faith in the land.[19] Of paramount importance in this undertaking was the visitation, the most direct intervention of the church into local affairs. As a yearly inventory of the state of religion in the parishes, the visitation enabled the clergy to address the practical issues of ongoing reform at the local level while at the same time providing a forum for the living voice of Protestantism.

But if we may judge by the results at the end of the century, the general opinion of the clergy seems to have been that there were not many years of Protestant life left. Throughout the parishes of central and northern Germany, the general lack of piety among the parishioners was considered to be the "misery of the whole German nation." Despite decades of Lutheran confessionalization, the visitors concluded that the parishioners remained as sinful and godless as their medieval ancestors had been. Not only were they subject to the same sins and superstitions, but what was worse, they actively resisted the attempts of the pastors to teach them the rudiments of the faith in the sermons and catechism sessions. The visitors of Zinna in the archbishopric of Magdeburg spoke for hundreds of others with their remarks of 1584:

Godlessness, open scorn for God's word and doctrine, for the gospel and the sacraments, contempt for pastors, disobedience, gross incivility and defiance have so gained the upper hand over the common people in this district, not to mention fornication, adultery, and every other sort of vice, especially blaspheming, fraud and deception, and swinish drinking, that it is not possible to give a sufficient description of it.[20]

It is no accident that the clergyman Michael Stiefel, who was entrusted with going over the results of the first Saxon visitation, spent much of the next four years preparing a work on the apocalypse.[21]

Visitation reports from English parishes in Gloucester, Chichester, and Salisbury read more or less the same: towns full of "atheists, epicures, libertines, worldings, neuters," a general disrespect of the clergy and the Word of God, absence from church and catechism sessions, lewd behavior, sexual indiscretions, drunkenness, disregard of the Sabbath, a chronic lack of morality, and a parish faith that is perhaps best described as a hybrid – a mix of Catholicism, Book of Common Prayer Calvinism, and a less reflexive, low-humming devotion to traditional parish folk beliefs. As an English bookend, as it were, to the judgment of the visitors of Zinna, we can cite the words of Edward Topsell from *The Reward of Religion* (1613): "Such pollution of sabbaths as never was, yea even in this time of dearth and famine, drinking and drunkenness, dancing and riot, feasting and surfeiting, chambering and wantonness, swearing and forswearing, accounting gain for godliness and godliness to be the burden of the world, with a thousand greater and more grievous calamities."[22]

Even during the years of the Civil War and the Interregnum, when Puritans reformed the festive calendar, simplified the liturgy, privileged the sermon to an even greater extent, and pushed through strict disciplinary measures and harsher sentences against blasphemy, adultery, and popular pastimes such as cock-fights, horse-race meetings, bear-baitings, and stage plays, the general tenor of conduct at the parish level did not improve markedly. The same moral crimes were committed; the same lackluster approach to religion remained. Partly it was because of the turmoil of the times, for as John Evelyn noted, in place of pastoral theology, the clergy outside London preached "but high and speculative points and straines"; partly it was because of the reluctance of the officials to cooperate in the disciplining and punishment of headstrong parishioners; and partly it was because of the general disinterest and unwillingness of the English parishioners to embrace, as the single and exclusive body of religious truth, the teachings of Reformed theology.[23] Whatever the reason, the point to take from this is that even after a period of intense evangelical activity, the clergy still believed that the number of people who might count themselves as truly Protestant remained very small.

There is no mistaking the sense of melancholy in the sermons and pastoral works of the seventeenth century. In place of the optimism of the early movement or the resolution guiding the confessional phase, a profound intellectual and psychological anxiety emerged rooted in the conviction that the parishioners had failed to meet the demands of the covenant and that the wrath of God would surely result. Although particularly important for the self-perception of the American Puritans, this rhetoric was common to all Protestant cultures of the seventeenth century.[24] For all clergymen could agree that there was a discrepancy between the vision of the early movement and later historical reality, and this necessarily had implications for a people conditioned to believe that they were the chosen few in a providential scheme of history. Failure could only mean one thing: mankind had fallen short of divine expectation (again). The result was the preaching of guilt and relentless calls for repentance, both of which were symptoms of a tendency, particularly prominent in Protestant culture, to mark the "failures" of the present in order to explain why the prophecies had not come to pass.

Listening in on the sermons delivered at St Paul's Cathedral in London gives something of the sense. Heavily laden with figures and types from Old Testament readings, and projecting a clear typological similitude between ancient Israel and modern England, the sermons hammered home the notion that England was in danger of forfeiting its covenant with God. There was no faith, honor, or charity in the land, and no knowledge that should mark out a Protestant people, just sloth, unholiness, backsliding, and a general failure to pay heed to the Word. England was a land mired in sin and guilt – a state of affairs, the clergy insisted, that the Lord would not tolerate for long.[25] And yet, even in the face of such a terrible reality, all was not lost, for as preachers like Thomas Hooker insisted in their closing appeals, if the nation humbled itself before the Lord, repented, and honored the faith, it was not too late to preserve its place in the providential scheme. Most Protestant jeremiads carried this mixed message of confidence and doom: they could liberate and paralyze in equal measure. The Massachusetts clergyman Increase Mather captured the paradox in a sermon of 1674. "The Lord hath been whetting his glittering Sword a long time over New England," wrote Mather. "The Sky looketh red and lowring. The clouds begin to gather thick in our Horizon. Without doubt . . . the Lord Jesus hath a peculiar respect unto this place, and for this people. This is Emmanuel's Land."[26]

As we have seen in the discussion of the Puritan soul, searching for the signs of divine displeasure was a particularly Protestant pastime. The supernatural was no longer as accessible as it had been in the medieval age, but the world was still suffused with sacred power and events were still shaped by divine intervention. For the Lutherans, God was *ubique et nullibi*, "everywhere and nowhere," both in the Eucharist and the world at large.[27] Thus it is mistaken, as historians have recently pointed out, to suggest that the Protestant earth was somehow desacralized and turned into a leaden mold of natural phenomena. On the contrary, Protestants, no less than Catholics, abstracted divine messages from comets, earthquakes, floods, strange deformities, fantastical creatures, and unnatural events, felt the nearness of God in places marked out as holy such as ancient oaks, springs, or sites of pilgrimage, and feared ghosts, goblins, witches – and, of course, the devil – as their ancestors had done before them. If anything, the Protestant psyche was even more attuned to the idea of a "moralized universe" than the Catholic had been, for they inhabited a world where both the micro and the macro were thought to reflect the same direct messages from God.[28] There was no sudden storm or flaming comet in later Protestantism that was not somehow a harbinger of divine displeasure. Perhaps this heightened sensitivity was because Reformation theology, with its reduction of the sacraments and its purging of sacramentals, had taken the supernatural out of the pastors' arsenal and so, deprived of that religious modality, they had to draw more attention to the natural world around them.[29] Perhaps it was simply the result of the success of the jeremiads they preached from the pulpits. At a certain point, the anxiety sought its own confirmation. Whatever the reason behind it, many Protestants were convinced that God was constantly broadcasting his message through the natural world, and that this message spoke of divine wrath and the judgment to come.

From the very outset, Protestant thought had been shaped by ideas of pending judgment. Having abolished the idea of purgatory and exploded the notion that salvation was acquired through a series of gradual works, Luther in effect "actualized" the theme of eschatology by claiming, on the one hand, that the end time had already occurred with the crucifixion and the resurrection and, on the other, that salvation was obtained solely through faith while in this life. The momentous struggle at the end of time between good and evil was thus not an event located at some stage in the future but in the "*hic et nunc* of the Word."[30] There was no interval between death and judgment. Needless to say, this tended to sharpen the prophetic senses, and indeed many Lutheran clergymen became obsessed with finding the evidence of this final struggle, an exercise which necessarily gave rise to heightened anxiety as the proofs mounted. Neither Zwingli nor Calvin placed the same emphasis on the end time as Luther did, and neither man thought that it stood so near (each spoke of future renewal). But both reformers, like Luther, located the final conflict in the present-time struggle that every Christian must face as he or she works to overcome sin and despair by way of faith.

Later generations of Protestant thinkers took these basic principles and turned them into a pseudo-science. Orthodox Lutherans in particular built on the expectancy and anxiety that followed Luther's death. By the 1550s, anthologies of Luther's predictions began to appear, and the central message was that the world was awash in sin, decadence, relentless conflict, and religious indifference, and that God's final judgment could not be far off. Later scholars became more exact in their predictions, devising methodologies for their predictions, not just turning to Scripture and other writings such as the Sibylline Oracles, Hermetic literature, or Jewish apocalypticism, but looking to the world of experience as well. Hiob Fincel, for instance, published a book of wonders and miraculous signs; David Chytraeus wrote closely observed prophetic histories; Adam Nachenmoser gathered different prophecies and predictions of the end; Leonard Krentzheim worked out exact reckonings of the coming apocalypse; while Georg Caesius published yearly almanacs that took note of the heavenly signs.[31] Others speculated on what would happen to the world at the end time. Would it be recast? Would it burn? Would it be completely annihilated?

Reformed theologians were generally more reluctant to probe so precisely for predictions of the end, though they too drew freely on eschatology and apocalypticism when censuring the godless nature of the world. Only with the rise of the German Pietists in the late seventeenth century did the orthodox Lutherans meet their match in the field of end-time speculation, with men such as Johann Albrecht Bengel (1687–1752) drawing up detailed chronologies of the apocalypse that were in effect algorithms of salvation. But the Pietists brought something new to the discourse as well. Not only did they further develop the twin themes of prophecy and wrath, they adopted some of the teachings of the radical tradition and merged them with the language of late-medieval mysticism. Pietists spoke of an age that would commence before the end time, the period of 1,000 years when God's reign would be established on earth and a union with Christ would be effected in the present.[32] Although much less militant, this was in effect the appropriation of the chiliasm and millenarianism of the early radicals.

On this note, it is worth emphasizing the extent to which Protestant prophecy could move between the poles of law and gospel. Orthodox Lutherans preached the same sorts of jeremiads as the early radicals and the later Pietists and threatened the parishioners with the same images of fire and brimstone, but the solution was always a formal one: return to church, read the catechism, heed the sermons, obey the pastor, and faith would follow. Thinking in this formal sense, the Wittenberg professor Leonhard Hutter drew the following conclusion: "Whoever believes, he will be saved; whoever does not believe, he will be damned."[33] The Lutheran theologian and pedagogue Johann Matthäus Meyfart wrote *The Last Judgment* (1632) in order to convey a similar point. If mankind was heading to destruction, it was because there was too much heresy, indifference, and epicureanism in the world. People had to throw themselves on the mercy of the church.[34]

The Pietists, however, although they were Lutheran or Calvinist in their theological essentials, preached eschatology and apocalypticism in order to shake believers free of the traditional forms and structures of corporate worship. As Philipp Jakob Spener wrote in *Pia Desideria* (1685), the only hope for better times was for the faith to move beyond the caesaropapism of orthodox Protestantism, the moribund ecclesiastical institutions, the stultified scholasticism of the schools, and the half-hearted, formalistic religion of the confessions, and allow for the Word to take root once again in the hearts of the common believer. The prophecies of Pietists such as Spener thus tended to speak of preparation and renewal instead of immediate wrath, and they emphasized the need for a living faith to develop within pious individuals. There was no better testimony to the radical implications of this teaching than the number of female prophets who emerged in seventeenth-century Germany. The most renowned was perhaps Rosamunde Juliane von der Asseburg, who had the patronage of the theologian Johann Wilhelm Peterson, but there were numerous influential prophetesses scattered throughout the empire, including local celebrities such as Katherina Reinecke and Anna Margaretha Jahn in Halberstadt, Anna Maria Schuchart and Maria Graf in Erfurt, and Magdalene Elrich and Anna Eva Jakobs in Quedlinburg.[35] Their ideas were generally derivative, popular renderings of the more abstract millennialism of Thomas Brightman, Alsted, and Comenius, but they were important because they were evidence of the rise of German Pietism, the most significant movement to emerge in Protestant culture since the onset of the Reformation. In their attempts to deal with the problems that faced seventeenth-century Protestantism – the lack of religiosity, the dead hand of orthodoxy, and the power of the state – the Pietists created a new synthesis that did not just want to supplement but to complete the Reformation.

True Christianity

Pietists

By the early seventeenth century, the flow of Protestant ideas had shifted course. The citadels of Lutheran and Reformed theology remained as before in continental Europe, but they now faced a steady influx of works on practical theology by the Puritans of England, the land Dutch clergymen were referring to as the home of piety. Puritan literature had become popular in the Netherlands and northern Germany, circulating in both English-language originals and print and manuscript translations. William Perkins, Paul Bunyan, Lewis Bayly, Joseph Hall, Richard Baxter, John Tillotson, Edward Stillingfleet – all became popular authors in pious Dutch households. Lewis Bayly (d.1631) in particular had a wide readership, with his *Practice of Piety* (1613) going through multifold German and Dutch editions as well as Hungarian, Romanian, French, and Italian translations.[36] Nor was it simply a one-way textual exchange. English Protestants had been migrating to the Netherlands since the 1580s and continued to do so well into the Golden Age. The most prominent migrants were the early separatists Henry Ainsworth, John Smyth, and John Robinson, but they were soon joined by a range of other Protestant émigrés, from the theologians William Ames and Thomas Hooker to merchants, scholars, authors, after-hours preachers, and other "fringe" Puritans such as the wax and candle salesman Humphrey Bromley, one of the founding members of the English church in Amsterdam, whose expertise ran from biblical scholarship to angelology, and who was said to have a box "wherin was mans flesh cut from a mans heart on the gallowes, wherin wormes did creepe."[37] English exiles often worked in close cooperation with Dutch printers, providing both home and foreign shores with a steady flood of Bibles, pastoral and theological works, scholarly tracts, and pamphlets. Even when there was no apparent English interest involved, Dutch printers, recognizing the profits they could make from English devotional works, did not wait on foreign initiative. Johannes Janssonius, for instance, had money on his mind when he published the *Opera Omnia* of Ames in 1658, and it was said that he printed copies of Bayly's *Practice of Piety* 10,000 at a time.

The Netherlands was fertile ground for Puritan thought, for even though orthodoxy had been strengthened by the Arminian controversy, the Dutch Reformed church never enjoyed a monopoly on belief. Religious diversity was too deeply rooted in the Republic's make-up for that. Moreover, by the mid-seventeenth century, many Dutch Calvinists, who were perhaps the most cosmopolitan peoples in all of Europe, were starting to think that their religion had grown stale and outdated when compared to the dynamic religiosity of English practical divinity. And it was not just the patricians. Gisbertus Voetius (1589–1676), Utrecht's high priest of Calvinist orthodoxy, came to the same conclusion: Dutch Reformed Protestantism was in need of a reform of life to match the reform of doctrine. Years of complacency had left the parishioners weak in faith and strong in superstition, the patricians mired in luxury and easy prey to the philosophies of Descartes and Spinoza, and the clergy ineffective, slack in discipline, and negligent in office.

Voetius represented the orthodox voice of what historians have termed the further Reformation (*nadere Reformatie*), a movement generally moderate in its theology, conservative in its ecclesiology, and precisianist in the Puritan mold, "precisianist" in this context meaning that it placed great stress on disciplinary exactitude and elaborate devotional routines. Yet this did not prevent its most vocal advocates from stressing the need for individuals to find the living faith within themselves and cultivate a piety outside the ministrations of the church. One of Voetius's followers, the Utrecht pastor Jodocus van Lodenstein (1620–77), went so far as to suggest that parishioners supplement regular services with conventicles. And neither Voetius nor van Lodenstein was the first to speak of the need for reform of this kind or to look to Puritanism for inspiration. Jean

Taffin and Arent Cornelisz. Croese, two practitioners of ascetic Protestantism, had been active years before, as had Willem Teellinck (1579–1629), sometimes referred to as the father of Dutch Pietism, who had spent time in the Puritan haven of Banbury in England at the feet of Puritan divines before returning to Middelburg. In 1627, in an effort to illustrate the scale of indifference, Teellinck published a catalog of sins, and he proposed a program of Christian reform that could be met within the household, starting with prayer and catechism sessions up to and including the Puritan regime of temperance, moderation, inner piety, and constant self-analysis. Godfrey Cornelius Udemans, pastor of Zierikzee, taught a similar message, and was one of the first in the Dutch context to emphasize rebirth and the rise of the "new creature."[38]

Both Puritanism and the Dutch Reformed variant spread into the lands of northern Germany. Peter Streithagen (1591–1653), for instance, court preacher to the Elector Palatine in the Haag, spent time in Caroline England and brought Puritan texts and reforming ideas with him when he returned to Heidelberg in 1650. Once back in Reformed Germany, he published tracts on the rebirth and the transformation of the Christian life. But the most influential of all German Reformed theologians schooled in the Dutch tradition was Theodor Undereyck (1635–93), a student of both Voetius and van Lodenstein. While in the Dutch Republic, Undereyck read deeply in Puritan literature, to the point that he became a Puritan in the style of Voetius. In 1660 he was appointed pastor in the parish of Mühlheim, a Reformed commune in a Lutheran land, and almost immediately introduced the brand of religiosity he had picked up in the Netherlands. He preached the new birth, held catechism and bible-reading sessions on the model of the English and Dutch conventicles, and stressed the need for the reform of life. Hearing word of this, the Lutheran lord of the parish condemned Undereyck for introducing "forbidden novelties and English Quakerism" into the parish, and as a consequence he was forced to leave. From Mühlheim he moved to Kassel, where from 1668 to 1670 he was the court preacher to Countess Hedwig Sophia, and from 1670 until his death in 1693 he was *Pastor primarius* in Bremen. In Bremen as well, despite the resistance of the ministry, who held him for a separatist, Undereyck staged conventicles and welcomed all pious Christians who sought a deeper, and a more personal, understanding of the faith.[39]

To speak of Pietism or Pietists before the end of the seventeenth century is imprecise and partly anachronistic, for the terms themselves only really acquired fixed meaning in the 1690s. Until then, the word "Pietist," like the name "Puritan" or the later sobriquet "Methodist," was generally used as an insult. "Pietism" became a common term of disdain when the orthodox clergy started to write about the new "sect" taking root in the cities. As ever, the natural reflex of magisterial Protestants was to equate the practitioners of alternative forms of the faith with the enthusiasts of Luther's day, and indeed for standard-bearers of orthodoxy such as Valentin Ernst Löscher and Johann Benedikt Carpzov some aspects of Pietist thought were reminiscent of the Anabaptists and the Münsterites. Pietists tended to gather in secret meetings outside the bounds of regular church services, they engaged in Bible readings with parishioners regardless of social standing or educational background, and they affected habits of piety that were held up as faithful renderings of apostolic Christianity. Viewing themselves as gatherings of the elect, they spoke in mocking and critical terms of the public church and its clergy. And more than this, Pietists, wittingly or not, had embraced ideas that could easily lead Protestants into error. Samuel Schelwig (1643–1715), an orthodox opponent of the movement, published two works, *Bedencken von der Pietisterey* (1693) and *Synopsis controversiarum* (1701), with lists of Pietist principles of thought and practice that ran into the hundreds. Nor was he the first. Two years earlier, the Halle archdeacon Albrecht Christian Roth (1651–1701) had written a pamphlet entitled *Imago Pietismi* that also denounced the "errors" and "abuses" of the Pietists, paramount being their indifference to the established Lutheran church, their ideas of perfectionism and chiliasm, their belief that Scripture requires the indwelling of the Spirit in order to be understood, and the general tendency to confuse law and gospel.[40]

German Pietism was not a novelty, as Undereyck's Lutheran patron had implied, but the gradual foregrounding of ideas and impulses that had lain just beneath the surface of public religion throughout the confessional age. The most articulate expression of this can be found in the work of the figure some scholars hold up as the father of the movement, Johann Arndt (1555–1621). Born in the duchy of Anhalt, Arndt had studied in Helmstedt, Wittenberg, Strasbourg, and Basel before taking up clerical posts in Berneburg, Quedlinburg, Braunschweig, Eisleben, and Celle. While at university, Arndt had been educated by prominent orthodox theologians, and until his death he considered himself a conventional Lutheran. In reality, however, his thought incorporated a broad range of different ideas, some of which were hallmarks of the radical tradition. (Arndt himself described his work *True Christianity* as an exercise in *colligere*, "connecting" or "combining.") While in Quedlinburg, where he began to rethink his long-standing interest in mysticism, his influences ranged from German, Spanish, and Italian mystics, Catholic and Reformed soteriologies, to the pansophic philosophies of radicals such as Weigel, Boehme, and Paracelsus.

Despite his broad knowledge of other traditions, Arndt was never primarily concerned with doctrine. On the contrary, the substance of this message was derived from a deep supraconfessional distress related to the sheer lack of Christianity he saw around him. By this he meant the lack of a living faith, the absence of any apparent godliness in the parishes despite generations of Protestant preaching. Arndt was not the first to make this point. The Lutheran theologians Johann Gerhard, Stephan Praetorius, and Philipp Nicolai had already written books of consolation stressing the need for a living faith to match the doctrinal renewal of Luther's Reformation. Gerhard's *Meditationes Sacrae* (1606) was in part an exercise in "therapeutic theology" designed to help the believer overcome religious anxiety by way of a more active faith. Nor should we forget that Arndt was living at a time when many Protestants had become disenchanted by the constant theological polemics, and with Lutheranism as an established rather than a revolutionary faith, they had come to feel less empowered or inspired by the doctrine of justification.[41] Pious Lutherans were looking for a religion to lift them out of the malaise. Arndt provided this, though not by merely reflecting on the concerns of his day or building on the thoughts of his predecessors. With *True Christianity*, he provided German Protestants with a new religious paradigm and set the framework for the next phase of Reformation.

The first book of *True Christianity* appeared in 1605. By 1610 four books in total were in print, comprising more than 1,000 pages. Though a pastoral rather than a theological work, it became the most influential Lutheran publication since the Small Catechism of 1529. And it opened as a jeremiad. As Arndt wrote:

the only things that still remain are the title of the gospel and the mere name of Christianity! Where are the fruits of righteousness? Where is the demonstration of living active faith, which alone makes a true Christian? Where is true repentance? Where is brotherly love? If we do not change our lives then true Christianity will eventually be entirely extinguished among us.[42]

In order to bring religion back into the parishioners' lives, *True Christianity* offered a threefold scheme of renewal, rebirth, and praxis. It was a vernacular handbook to spiritual awakening. Arndt never questioned the primacy of justification as taught by Lutheran orthodoxy, but he did shift the emphasis in the direction of sanctification and regeneration and thus turned it into a much more ethical doctrine. According to Arndt, the process was as follows: Christ first comes to us through the Word; once within, the Spirit works through the individual soul and gives rise to a state of genuine godliness; the result is a renewal or rebirth of the believer as evidenced by signs of an inner transformation, such as brotherly love or acts of piety. Unlike the medieval mystics, Arndt did not teach that Christians became one with God; but he did suggest that they might move a bit closer, and he did make the drama of salvation into a private rather than a corporate affair. *True Christianity* proposed that each baptized Christian had the power to seek his or her closer union with God.

Few of the ideas in *True Christianity* were new, as was proven in the eighteenth century when scholars began to dissect the work and extract the textual borrowings. But its very patchwork polysemy may have been the most revolutionary aspect of the text. Certainly contemporaries read it in this way. Christians of all stamps appealed to the work in support of their own agendas. To the magisterial thinkers, it was an endorsement of the existing tradition and a clarion call for a return to Reformation origins. To the radicals it was the blueprint for a religion that went beyond confessional Lutheranism. It was eminently adaptable. Christoph Besold (1577–1638) once justified his conversion to Catholicism with reference to the work, both Weigelians and Jesuits freely recommended it, and Schwenckfelders considered Arndt one of their own.[43]

Arndt never intended to write a book that could be used for or against Lutheranism in this way. He wrote as a Lutheran pastor, and he made corrections to the text in response to the criticism of the first edition, changing or removing passages that could be interpreted as too Catholic, too radical, or not Lutheran enough. Tinkering with the text was not enough for orthodox critics like Lukas Osiander (1534–1604), who considered *True Christianity* a nest of potentially poisonous doctrines, ranging from Catholic works-righteousness to Schwenckfeldian spiritualism. But most Protestants were not concerned about the relative orthodoxy of the work. They were simply inspired by its message and its appeal to further reform – and indeed inspired enough to make it the best-selling devotional work of the seventeenth century. The Nuremberg pastor Johann Saubert (1592–1646) was "Arndtian" in this sense. Although a mainstream orthodox Lutheran who did not think salvation was possible without the Word and the sacraments of the established church, Saubert became a tireless supporter of Arndt and his call for a heightened inner piety. In his work *Geistliche Flämmlein* (1620), Saubert spoke in similar terms about the need for a living faith, citing Arndt on numerous occasions. He even encouraged his listeners from the pulpit to read *True*

Christianity for themselves. Lutherans of the present age, declared Saubert, should be thankful for Arndt and the message he preached, for like the apostle James he had the courage to reveal the depth of sin and depravity and rip the masks from time-serving Christians.[44]

True Christianity would exercise Lutheran minds for the rest of the century, and yet there never was an Arndtian movement in any meaningful sense. It was not until the 1670s that the Pietist vision became a historical force, and the man responsible was the Alsacian Lutheran Philipp Jakob Spener (1635–1705), chief pastor of the imperial city of Frankfurt. Like the Puritans and the Pietists before him, Spener had grown convinced that there was need for further reform. "I have never been of the opinion," he wrote, "and am not so now, that the Reformation of Luther was brought to completion as one might hope."[45] A close study of Luther and Arndt had led him to this conclusion, but so too had his knowledge of other strands of Protestant thought. Although he had studied at Strasbourg with orthodox Lutherans, he was thoroughly familiar with the works of Tauler, Lütkemann, Belkius, Bayly, Baxter, and Labadie (whose ideas he encountered while in Geneva). And yet for all of his reading, Spener's importance was not to do with his range as a theologian. It was his skills as a religious practitioner that prompted contemporaries, and later historians, to speak of him as the founder of German Pietism.[46] During his time in Frankfurt (1666–85), Spener not only broadcast the Pietist message of repentance and reform from the pulpit as others were doing, he started to introduce practical measures designed to bring about the Protestant revival.

Within a few years of his arrival, Spener's efforts had brought both him and the Frankfurt movement considerable renown. Opinions were divided, however, as to how the movement should be understood in relation to the established church. Some Lutheran pastors, impeccably orthodox in outlook, embraced Spener's initiative and made their own attempts to introduce reform along the lines of the Frankfurt model. But others were less enthusiastic. August Pfeiffer (1640–98), for instance, the super-intendent of Lübeck, who had battled successfully against his own "nest" of Pietists, not only accused Spener of exegetical and doctrinal ignorance, but a latitude bordering on indifference, and an approach to religion so subjective in its modalities it was easily confused with enthusiasm. Johannes Deutschmann (1625–1706), a senior in Witten-berg, published a work in 1695 that accused Spener of making no less than 284 errors, paramount being his tendency to speak of the spiritual priesthood rather than the church as the locus of religious reform. This battle between orthodoxy and Pietism continued throughout Spener's lifetime, though without having too detrimental an effect on his career. Although his 1686 appointment as court chaplain to the Elector of Saxony ended prematurely because of his campaign against the "satanic" culture of the court, his role as rector in St Nicholas in Berlin in 1691 proved more successful, and he remained there until his death in 1705.[47]

Spener's *Pia Desideria* (1675), first published as a preface to the sermons of Arndt, was the platform of mainstream German Pietism. Similar to Luther's *Address to the Christian Nobility*, it was a vernacular call for reform. Unlike the *Address*, however, it did not place its hopes in the secular or spiritual authorities but rather in a renewal of faith within the individual Christian. By this, the *Pia Desideria* was not suggesting that pious Lutherans should separate from the church. Its program was set firmly within the ecclesial, theological, and clerical framework of orthodox Lutheranism. But Spener did not think that the Lutheran rulers had the requisite sense of Christian mission, nor did he believe that the impulse would come from the clergy, most of whom, he charged, had become comfortable office-holders in caesaropapist states. Owing to this lack of spiritual leadership, the faith of early Lutheranism had been replaced by over-complex theories of forensic justification and the actual practice of piety had been supplanted by a type of mechanical religion. Many Protestants, Spener claimed, still thought in terms of a quasi-Catholic approach to the sacraments and the Word. What was required was a turn to an inner religiosity. "Our entire Christianity," declared Spener, "exists in the inner or new man, whose soul is faith and its effects are the fruits of life."[48]

Spener's first steps in the direction of the living, active, and creative faith encouraged by Luther in his preface to Romans (the proof text for all mainstream Pietists) were the traditional methods of preaching, catechizing, and discipline. But in all aspects he went beyond set forms. In his cycle of sermons, Spener preached long and loud on the need for a more active piety, and he encouraged his listeners to bring their Bibles to church. He wrote his own catechism and reformed the methods of catechesis; he tightened up discipline and demanded stricter observance of the Sabbath; he saw through welfare reforms, including a new orphanage and a poor house; and he introduced additional days of prayer. But Spener's central innovation, and one of the main features of the Pietist movement inspired by the Frankfurt paradigm, was the *collegium pietatis*, the small assembly of religiously-minded men who started to meet in his study from 1670 onward. Although it began as a fairly closed session led by theologians and joined by select pious patricians, by 1677 Spener could describe it as a fellowship of people of all ages and social estates in which no distinctions were made of standing.[49] Within 12 years there were up to 100 members, a group so large they were forced to gather at a neighboring church. Indeed the sheer size of the *collegium*, not to mention the rumors that started to circulate about the subversive nature of the gatherings (some true and some false), eventually led to the intervention of the Frankfurt authorities. Spener, who consistently asserted his orthodoxy, distanced himself from the more radical elements, some of whom proved the instincts of the orthodox correct by forming conventicles of their own. By 1682 only a rump of the original *collegium* remained, and when Spener left for Dresden it was discontinued altogether.

An important historical demonstration of how moderate Pietist reform could potentially threaten the magisterial order was provided by events in Leipzig. In 1686, two resident theology students, Paul Anton (1661–1730) and August Hermann Francke (1663–1727), founded a *collegium philobiblicum*, a small gathering of biblical adepts engaged in translation and exegesis. Within a year, on the heels of a visit by Spener, who had encouraged the two young men to cultivate a more personal piety, the meeting started to open its doors to more people and move away from learned exegesis to general discussions in German on the Bible and popular pious works. This drift in the direction of the Spenerian *collegium* was given a further fillip in 1687 following Francke's return to Leipzig from a stay in Lüneburg, where he claimed to have had a conversion experience. Always of pious disposition (he had been reading Puritan literature since the age of 10), Francke became a preacher of the New Birth, and the meetings started to take on a different form.

Francke now asked the parishioners to read the Bible for its insights on the living of a Christian life; he admonished them to transform what they read and heard into an active Christianity; and he stressed the importance of the inner faith, the personal turn to God, in place of a reliance on external forms. The message was eagerly received. Soon the Leipzig students were being pressed out by bakers, merchants, goldsmiths, apothecaries, book peddlers, and large numbers of women. Meanwhile the Pietists became a much more self-aware group, dressing alike and following Francke through the streets as he went to his lectures and sermons. Pietist students began to speak critically about the teachings of orthodox Lutheranism – a stance no doubt strengthened by the actions of some sympathetic professors, who publicly burned some standard philosophy texts.[50] By 1690, orthodox thinkers such as Johann Benedikt Carpzov (1639–99) (Francke's one-time patron) and Albrecht Christian Roth, who disparaged the movement in his *Imago Pietismi*, could claim that the meetings had become a threat to the secular and the spiritual order. In response, the Leipzig authorities oversaw a formal inquisition, and it ended, as it had in Frankfurt, with an interdict on private meetings and the effective suspension of the meetings founded by Francke and Anton. But by that stage it must have been clear to Carpzov and everyone involved that events in Leipzig were just one localized example·of a much wider phenomenon.[51]

After the interdict of 1690, the roads leading out of Leipzig became the main arteries of a Pietist exodus. Francke moved to Erfurt and then on to Halle, which, as we will see, became the most important peregrination of the movement; Paul Anton, the co-founder of the *collegium*, settled in Rochlitz and held meetings in his home; Johann Caspar Schade (1666–98) joined Spener in Berlin, where he offered private tutorials; Andreas Achilles (1656–1721) became a pastor in Halberstadt and met privately with parishioners; Heinrich Julius Elers (1667–1728) followed Francke to Erfurt, worked as a tutor to a pious noblewoman in Arnstadt, and eventually moved on to Halle; and Clemens Thieme, another original member of the *collegium,* founded a conventicle in Wurzen while serving as chaplain to the Elector of Saxony. And then there were the Leipzig sympathizers, the people who attended the sessions. Among them we might single out Christoph Tostlöwe, a smith from Böhlitz, near Leipzig, who held devotional meetings in his house, and Johann Heinrich Sprögel, the deacon of Quedlinburg, who became an important point of contact for both mainstream and radical Pietists. Meanwhile the reform initiatives of Frankfurt and Leipzig took root independent of direct influence. Scholars and burghers in Jena and Gotha established Bible-reading groups, laymen in Giessen, Hamburg, and Lübeck founded *collegia* without waiting for clerical help, while the students of Leipzig and Erfurt went on quasi-missions to Weimar, Coburg, and the towns of Pomerania. It also reached beyond the cities and surfaced in territories as distant from each other as the Wetterau counties and the Baltic states.[52]

Equally as important as the geographical spread of Pietism was its emergence as a movement with a sense of identity and place. Spener and Francke had established networks of correspondence comparable to those of Bullinger and Calvin. Indeed, in the early years Spener's letter-writing habits held the disparate movement together, and they proved even more crucial after his move to Berlin, when he started to take on the mantle of patrician, consultant, and sympathetic ear. Similarly, between 1690 and 1693 Francke was in constant contact with followers in Magdeburg, Helmstedt, Quedlinburg, Halberstadt, Lüneburg, Lauenburg, Lübeck, and Wolfenbüttel. In part, the

Hallesche Zeitungen (1708), Pietism's first regular newsletter, was established in order to alleviate Francke's epistolary duties.[53] As a network evolved, Pietists started to think of themselves as members of a unique community, a group of the elect within the broader Protestant church.

Needless to say, this did not necessarily lead to greater harmony or fellowship in the parishes, and it was not only the orthodox clergy who set themselves against the movement. Most parishioners were not interested in the reform programs of Spener or Francke. They were quite content to continue as confessing Christians within the magisterial mold. Consequently, when men such as Justinus Töllner (1656–1718), the Pietist pastor of Panitzsch, set out to make godly neighbors by prohibiting dancing and drinking, condemning gambling and blasphemy, and denouncing popular customs such as the Whitsun Ale, he quickly faced the wrath of the parishioners.[54] In this case the pastor failed: Töllner was dismissed from office and made his way to Halle. But it did not always end in the parishioners' favor. More frequently there was a state of stalemate in the town or parish as the Pietists, often led by at least one clergyman and supported by prominent burghers, pushed for godly reform and the conversion, as they put it, of time-serving Christians. No doubt this sense of election rubbed many of the parishioners up the wrong way, and if we keep this in mind it makes it easier to sympathize with the actions of the congregation of St Moritz in Halle in 1693. One Sunday in that year, the self-proclaimed Pietist prophet Johann Heinrich Siegfried entered the church and shouted down the pastor as he preached from the pulpit, adding for good measure that the church of St Moritz was a house of the devil and had to be destroyed. According to one eyewitness, immediately after Siegfried's rant,

> there arose such a great tumult in the church that the deacon, who up to this point had continued to preach, had to cut his sermon short. The mob (*Pöbel*) was so incensed that it looked as though the enthusiast (*Schwärmer*) would not leave with a single bone in his body still intact. Some shouted: "Beat him to death." Others: "Let him live, for he had earned an even worse punishment." And still others: "Cut from his throat the tongue that has blasphemed God."[55]

Not all prophets were welcome, not even in Halle.

One of the reasons for the tensions provoked by Pietism was the lack of clear meaning surrounding the term. It had a broad enough range of reference to accommodate just about every virtue or vice. This lack of precision is a problem that modern scholars have not been able to overcome. In the search for origins, some historians trace the movement back to Arndt, others to Spener or Francke, and still others claim it is best conceived as one strand of a gradual unfolding of religious renewal that stretched from Puritanism and the *nadere Reformatie* to the Moravianism and Methodism of the eighteenth century.[56] Moreover, even if one grants that German Pietism was unique in both place and time, there is still the issue of *types* of Pietism, running from the radical strain, which will be discussed in the next section, to the mainstream variants of Spener and Francke and everything in between – which would include clerical and patriarchal forms, spontaneous lay gatherings, missionary evangelicalism, and the numerous prophets and their disciples.[57] Little wonder that the parishioners of St Moritz may have felt threatened by a man who thought of himself as a Pietist.

On this, however, there seems to be fairly widespread agreement: Pietists generally taught that the Reformation was not yet complete, that there was still need for a reform of life to match the earlier reform of doctrine. The overarching concern was with Christian renewal, not just with piety, and thus the emphasis was on the ethical dimensions of religion rather than the doctrinal or liturgical concerns of the confessional age. As Johann Arndt put it, "Our worship in the New Testament is no longer external in figural ceremonies, statues, and obligations, but rather inward in spirit and truth, that is, in faith in Christ."[58] This meant that there was a heightened concern with piety and godliness and less with the doctrinal aspects of magisterial Protestantism. However, since the majority of Pietists still considered themselves to be orthodox Lutherans, it also meant that it was a precariously balanced affair, for it did not take much for a religiosity that placed so much stress on the workings of the Spirit to pass over to the radical tradition. Commenting on the problems that faced the Puritans of England, one scholar has suggested that their central dilemma was the ongoing struggle to establish "a more or less stable equilibrium out of a balancing of polar parts,"[59] and we may think of the Pietist dilemma in similar terms.

Pietists pushed the magisterial order to the breaking point, and sometimes beyond. In their stress on the need for an interior faith, for instance, on the need for the believer to think of religion in personal rather than communal terms, Pietists ran the risk of shepherding the faithful out of the established church altogether. For if the essential matters were piety rather than doctrine, Spirit rather than office, and personal faith rather than forms or institutions, where did that leave the Lutheran church and its ordained clergy? At the very least, this approach introduced a degree of subjectivism into parish religion, and in extreme cases it openly questioned the efficacy of sacramental forms, as in the teaching of the Rostock pastor Heinrich Müller (1631–75), who labelled the baptismal font, the pulpit, the confessional, and the altar "the four dumb idols of the church."[60] There was a similar balancing act with the Pietist use of the Bible. Of course, all Protestants had looked to Scripture as the theological source, but the Pietists made it an essential part of the religious life. Not only were the new translations cheap enough for all parishioners to afford, which in itself was a breakthrough in Protestant culture, but in the cosseted surroundings of the *collegia* and the intimate devotional meetings in the home, the Bible became an open text for the first time since the rise of the Reformation. One of the corollaries of this embodied biblicism was the change in the practice of prayer. With this turn towards a religion of the heart, there was no longer a place for the formulaic prayers of the confessional age. Arndt had emphasized the virtues of using prayer as a means of establishing a direct relationship with the divine. Spener too preached the need for more spontaneity in the act of praying, and as if on cue, sales of prayer books plummeted after 1675.[61]

One of the distinguishing features of German Pietism were the *collegia pietatis*. Although central to the history of the movement, the nature of these meetings remains fairly imprecise. They could take on a variety of forms, from informal prayer meetings and Bible-study groups to extended sessions in exegesis and interpretation. In an effort to point up the potential dangers of these private assemblies, orthodox critics tended to associate the *collegia* with the separatist tradition. But the use of conventicles had been a fairly common phenomenon in the Reformed tradition, and there was a long history to draw on. Lutheran Pietists generally preferred to cite the apostolic precedent

(1 Corinthinans 14) rather than justify their actions with Reformed arguments, and they did so in the conviction that it was fully in keeping with the teachings of mainstream Lutheran thought. Years before Spener had gathered his group in Frankfurt, the clergy in Butzbach, Strasbourg, Hamburg, and Görlitz had thought in these terms while founding conventicles of their own.[62]

In setting up the *collegia*, early Pietists did not presume to challenge the authority of the church or the special functions of the clergy. On the contrary, men like Spener first thought of the meetings as a supplement to the sermons, services, and sacraments of orthodox worship. They were not conceived as para-ecclesiastical institutions, but as helpmeets to the clergy in their efforts to remedy the perceived decline in piety that had set in since the Reformation. In some ways they were analogous to the secular societies of the day, for here too it was a question of finding a place for interests and motives that no longer fit within traditional forms. But there were tensions and contradictions built in.

In Frankfurt, for instance, although they began under the auspices of Spener himself, once Johann Jakob Schütz (1640–90), Spener's co-founder, moved closer to the radical tradition, the meetings became more openly critical of the church. The former distinctions between the clergy (or the theologically aware) and the laity fell away, with each man and woman granted an equal voice in interpretation. At the same time the meetings became more frequent and less accountable. One week they might meet at the Saalhof, the next at the house of Schütz or a Dr Kißner, another at the residence of a tailor on the Fahrgasse.[63] Similarly, in Lübeck there was a conventicle movement as early as the 1660s. Led by two pious laymen, one of whom was a trained theologian, the meetings were a way for select parishioners to meet in small groups and cultivate a more personal faith. And although, as in Frankfurt, the meetings were not originally intended to replace or supplant the service, in time leaders began to impinge on the rights of the church, going so far as to offer the Lord's Supper in private sessions. On receiving word of this, the ministers and magistrates of Lübeck condemned it as Quakerism and the conventicles were suppressed, the ringleaders either imprisoned or expelled.[64] A final example is provided by the history of events in Halberstadt. Founded in 1690 by Andreas Achilles, one of the Leipzig exiles, the Halberstadt conventicle soon turned into a forum for the reading and interpretation of radical ideas. Notions of rapture and prophecy replaced prayer and exegesis, and within a few years the conventicle became infamous for the ecstatic visions of Anna Margaretha Jahn, whom Achilles considered a prophetess. As in Lübeck, the authorities intervened, and in this instance with the full backing of the Halberstadt parishioners, who feared that their town was on its way to becoming the new Münster.[65]

Regardless of the type of community taking shape, whether the fellowship of radicals in Halberstadt or the early exegetical workshop in Leipzig, Pietistism invested the laity with a greater role in religious affairs. The Reformation had promised the same thing in the early years, Luther himself projecting a return to the apostolic notion of the royal priesthood – what he termed the priesthood of all believers – and an elimination of the strict separation between the clergy and the laity. And in so far as Protestant theology taught that all men and women were spiritually equal in the eyes of God and that all shared in the ministry of the gospel, this goal had been realized. In practical terms, however, after the disaster of the Peasants' War and the rise of the radicals, the

Protestant churches returned to a powerful culture of clericalism. Presbyteries, as Milton famously put it, became old priests writ large. Spener wanted to reverse this balance, to restore some remnant of the apostolic vision in the form of a "spiritual priesthood" (his version of the paradigm). While still maintaining that the clergy alone had the authority to initiate and oversee reform, Spener granted the laity a heightened spiritual role, not just expecting them to foster an inner piety and a living faith, but to admonish others and help to spread the Word.[66] In effect, they became pastors on a very small scale, if not prophets then pundits of the Word. This principle, in combination with the Pietist tendency to turn away from corporate religion and privilege private or group worship, was a threat to the magisterial order for it fostered a new idea of priesthood that was based on an inner calling rather than an external confirmation.

The best proof of the Pietist empowering of the laity was the role assumed by women. In the early phase, female members of the *collegia* were restricted in what they might do. In Frankfurt, for instance, they sat behind a dividing wall without the right to speak. But their impact was substantial beyond the conventicles, when pious women became active as writers, teachers, promoters, and patrons of the movement. Within the radical tradition, women were not only active participants in the group meetings, they emerged as leaders, prophets, and theologians with large regional and interregional followings. Indeed, according to Johann Heinrich Feustking, author of the *Gynaeceum Haeretico Fanaticum* (1704), Pietism itself was the creation of women, enthusiasts and visionaries such as Rosamunde Juliane von der Asseburg and Johanna Eleonora von Merlau (Petersen), who had encouraged the local prophetesses of Erfurt, Quedlinburg, and Halberstadt, who had then preached their visions and written their books and led the parishioners away from the church.[67]

What made the Pietist invocation of the priesthood of all believers so revolutionary was its teaching on the rebirth (*Wiedergeburt*). Spener once termed this the central matter or substance (*materia*) of Christianity, and even though it remained a vague concept in theological terms, most Pietists knew what they meant when they used it. Like the majority of Pietist thought, it was borrowed. Karlstadt and Müntzer had preached rebirth and renewal over a century before. But German Pietists preferred to look to Luther for their origins, and they were able to find confirmation in his theories on grace, especially in the preface to Romans, to consider the idea of rebirth an orthodox development. In its effects, however, it represented a radical departure from traditional Lutheranism, for even though the first cause was, as ever, faith alone in Christ, to the Pietists the important matter was not so much the moment of justification as what happened afterwards.[68]

In working up a morphology of salvation, Pietist theologians moved Protestant religiosity away from theories of forensic justification towards a concern with sanctification and renewal. As a consequence, the orthodox idea that the believer was a passive participant in the drama of salvation, or that mankind's status as both sinner and justified at the same time meant that questions of moral renewal had no bearing on the existence of the individual Christian, was partially superseded by a very personal concern with the cultivation of a pious life. In the words of the church historian Carter Lindberg, "The Reformation's theocentric and eschatological orientation becomes anthropocentric and historical."[69] The general scheme went like this: after faith is planted in the heart by the gift of grace and the believer is justified, the Christian takes on a new nature. Enabled by the Spirit residing within, the reborn Christian is able to effect a partial restoration of humanity to its prelapsarian state and go some way towards restoring the lost divinity in man. Such was the theological rationalization for the Pietist idea of a living faith, and it postulated the same signs and proofs from the believer as the morphologies of the New England Puritans – beginning with doubts, anxieties, and *Anfechtungen* and graduating to assurance, love, and other pious acts that spoke of the workings of the Spirit. What this meant in practice was that Pietists thought of salvation in very personal terms. The best evidence of this was the rise of the conversion experience in Lutheran culture, starting with Franck's own paradigmatic event, which made it possible for the faithful to date exactly when the new birth began. The Erfurt jurist Georg Heinrich Brückner could remember it to the minute: "And then it happened, at the very moment I was reading Arndt's *True Christianity*, it came like a lightning bolt in my heart and changed me completely, and indeed I was moved to the point that I thought I would ascend to heaven."[70]

Placing such stress on personal experience or teaching that faith required completion through rebirth and the cultivation of an affective Christianity necessarily devalued the importance of doctrine, the sacraments, and ecclesial authority. And while mainstream Pietists did not directly challenge the Lutheran doctrine of justification or posit that Christians might reach a state of moral perfection in this life, ultimately the turn towards rebirth and renewal weakened the integrity of the magisterial system. No one realized this better than the guardians of orthodoxy. Valentin Ernst Löscher, for instance, perhaps the last of the great Lutheran scholastics, had a long list of reasons why Spener's form of Pietism was more harmful than it may have seemed. But his main concern was with the idea of Christian renewal and above all the premise that it might be brought about independently of the forms and formulas of the Lutheran church. Löscher was convinced that this impulse, however honest in its intentions, could only lead to heresy.[71]

Each of these Pietist innovations – the *collegia pietatis*, the spiritual priesthood of all believers, and the ideas of rebirth and renewal – was the enacted principle of a religious movement that developed from within the magisterial tradition as an *ecclesiola in ecclesia*, that is, as a smaller church within a church. Indeed, if one were searching for a single concept to sum up the Pietist impulse, the idea of a church within a church is probably closest to the mark. For what was revolutionary about Pietism, even in its conservative guise, was that it did not project itself as an alternative to the Lutheran or the Reformed confessions, but rather as a native, and necessary, growth. Thus, unlike the radicals, who, historically speaking, had made little headway since the Reformation precisely because their professed aim was to overturn the existing order, the Pietists were able to transform the nature of Protestant religiosity from within the fold. Spener was insistent that this was the only sure remedy for an ailing church. "Certainly," he wrote, "if we do not establish smaller churches within the church – though while doing so make certain, of course, that we do not give rise to schism – then there is hardly any chance that we will achieve what is incumbent on all of us to achieve.'[72]

And yet there was no avoiding the fact that these *ecclesiolae in ecclesia* were symptomatic of ideas and impulses that threatened the magisterial order. Instead of a comprehensive church gathered by doctrine, discipline, and the Sunday service, the Pietists spoke of a smaller community of the pious who distinguished themselves from the mass of time-serving Christians; instead of a religion enacted by routinized doctrine and clerical oversight, the Pietists spoke of a living faith based on the devotion of its members; and instead of the church that emphasized Word and sacrament, the Pietists spoke of witness and example.[73] If all of this sounds like the thought and language of radical Protestantism, it is because many of the ideas central to Pietism, and in particular the teaching on rebirth and renewal, were the hallmarks of this tradition. Of course, this did not turn all self-professed Pietists into radicals, but it did mean that radical ideas had now found their way into the orthodox order and were bringing about a gradual transformation of the confessional state. Evidence of this, as we will see, was demonstrated by the impact of Pietism in Brandenburg-Prussia. However, before we turn to the influence of Pietism within the magisterial synthesis, it is necessary to trace the rise of the self-professed Pietists who *did* think of themselves as radicals outside of the mainstream tradition. For in the history of Pietism, as in all Protestant history, the taxonomy of types moved along a sliding scale.

The radical rebirth

On October 21, 1694, Conrad Bröske (1660–1713), court preacher to the Reformed count of Offenbach, took part in the baptism of a young Turkish servant girl, and it confirmed him in his belief that the kingdom of Christ was near. More particularly, it confirmed him in his belief that the apocalyptical writings by the Philadelphian Thomas Beverley were soon to be proved true, including Beverley's prophecy that the heathens and the Jews would convert and the saints would reign for 1,000 years. Beverley spoke of this as the Philadelphian age, thus making reference to the sixth church in Revelation – the one that would replace the Sardic church (the magisterial church) of the confessional age. For end-time prophets such as Beverley, the mainstream Protestant churches were mired in "form and ceremony" and vitiated by "regimental and synagogal" constitutions. The Philadelphian church, in contrast, would be a church of the gospel ruled by Christ.

What is noteworthy about Bröske's interest in the works of Beverley is that he was an ordained minister within the very Sardic church the Philadelphians condemned. He remained the court preacher of Offenbach even as he published his own commentaries on Revelation suggesting that the Reformed church was "still not completely free of the yoke of Antichrist."[74] This created problems. Being a Philadelphian sympathizer raised the suspicions of the church authorities, and Bröske was reproached by the Elberfeld Classis on more than one occasion. But it also raised the ire of full-scale radicals such as Johann Konrad Dippel (1673–1734), who had separated completely from established Protestantism. Dippel accused Bröske of being a court Pietist, a charge he leveled at Spener as well, by which he meant they were ready to compromise by remaining within the orthodox church while preaching rebirth and renewal. Dippel claimed that Bröske "has sought till now to stand at once on both sides, and through the power of his own intellect to combine old and new, good and bad with each other."[75] For Dippel the matter was rather more straightforward. Like the Swiss Anabaptists almost two centuries before, he proclaimed that there could be nothing in common between Christ and Belial, and true to this logic, he separated from the church.

Radical Pietism, as this case suggests, was partly a question of perspective. To be "radical" did not necessarily mean adhering to a corpus of thought or practicing an alternative form of Protestant Christianity. It meant that in one or more respects an individual or a group had gone far enough beyond the bounds of orthodoxy to be classified as heterodox and/or separatist.[76] A Pietist could be radical *by degrees*, and that is why the movement was so significant, for it was not only the revival of the marginalized radical tradition but an incremental impulse from within. Most of the radical Pietists were thus hybrids. In some (perhaps most) respects they honored the orthodox order; but in others they transgressed. There was no such thing as an archetypical radical Pietist. Different groups stressed different aspects of the faith, though usually within the compass of the following themes: the experience of conversion; direct and affective communion with God; love as the central message of the faith and the consequent need for a heightened morality; the importance of scriptural norms for the Christian life; freedom from theological and ecclesiastical compulsion; and the belief that faith will effect a transformation of the individual, a rebirth or "new birth" that will distinguish the elect from the mass of time-serving Christians.

Perhaps the best example of a radical Pietist was the Frankfurt jurist Johann Jakob Schütz. Though an affluent burgher, widely respected scholar, and prominent practitioner of law, the co-founder of Spener's *Collegium* had been an early adept of post-Arndtian affective religiosity, his need for a deeper sense of inner faith being strengthened, on the recommendation of Spener, by his reading of Tauler.[77] From the beginning, Schütz was eager to use the *Collegium* as a forum for an emotive lay spirituality. As a consequence, around 1674, the meetings became less structured and more spontaneous, and they often took place in private houses rather than the parsonage or the church. Despite these developments, however, Schütz drew back from the *Collegium* in the mid-1670s, claiming that there was still too much reason and not enough heart, and he began to work out the implications of his evolving beliefs. In 1675 he published a devotional work on the need for an active faith. This was followed two years later by *Rules for a Christian Life* (1677), which was primarily a compendium of New Testament sayings, but explicit enough in its stress on righteousness over justification to earn the disapproval of Spener. And in 1684 Schütz published *Discurses*, an explicit defense of separation on the premise that the church did not have the inner resources to reform itself. Though published anonymously, the authorship of the *Discurses* was an open secret, for Schütz had withdrawn from Communion in 1676 and church services in 1682, and he had long expressed his distaste for the Lutheran church in Frankfurt. Moreover, since the late 1670s he had been in regular contact with separatists in Germany and the Netherlands, as well as Quakers and Labadists, and his fame was such that people often referred to the Frankfurt Pietists as Schützians (*Schützianer*).[78] Indeed, in his ability to mediate and consolidate, there is reason to think of Schütz as the founder of the radical German Pietist movement, much in the same way that Spener was the founder of the mainstream branch.

Writing in 1677, Schütz gave the impression that his drift towards radicalism was not only the result of his own spiritual inclinations but a consequence of the rigid party lines. As he wrote,

There are still a number of well-meaning spirits in Germany, but they refuse to budge an inch from their revered formulas. Years can go by, and still scarcely any progress will be made distinguishing the best from the most absurd of things. One can have an ironclad and abiding allegiance to the main articles of their orthodoxy, and yet as soon as one begins to suggest even a little bit that it is incumbent on Christians to deny themselves and follow the way of Christ, he is defamed by his colleagues in every way possible and held up as a Socinian, a Papist, a Weiglian, a Quaker, and so on.[79]

Schütz may have been within his rights to argue that the orthodox were so inflexible they were forcing the pious from the fold, but it was certainly stretching the truth to suggest there was no substance to the charge. There was a flourishing culture of radical Protestants in the late seventeenth century – some were the descendants of the Reformation radicals, some emerged during the Pietist period of spiritual rebirth – and Schütz himself, for all of his special pleading, was one of the central contacts in this radical matrix. He was in close communication with the Sulzbach court in the Upper Palatinate, for instance, and its college of mystics, hermeticists, and pansophists; he exchanged texts and ideas with radical thinkers in Nuremberg, including Loth Fischer, one of the first German translators of the Philadelphian Jane Leade; he received Reformed devotional texts from a Heidelberg professor, a one-time student of Gisbertus Voetius, and recommended Quaker and Labadist works in return; and he posted letters to radical apothecaries and spice traders in Cologne, updating them on occasion on the affairs of the Labadists in Hamburg-Altona. Quakers, too, were among his contacts, William Penn having visited Frankfurt in 1677 while recruiting for his colony.[80]

That Schütz was able to establish such a broad range of contacts is testimony to the scale of the radical matrix. Despite the efforts of the magisterial churches, Europe's marginalized Protestants had not been swept aside. Even after the defeat at Münster in 1535, Anabaptists in the Netherlands and northern Germany endured in biblically grounded voluntary fellowships held together by a precarious mix of the unchecked Spirit and the literal Word.[81] Four core groups emerged: the Münsterites, who settled in Oldenburg; the Batenburgers, who took up the sword after the defeat; the Melchiorites, who exchanged violence for visions; and the Obbenites, named after Obbe Philips, who spread throughout Holland and Friesland. Though none of these groups recognized a single confession, small-scale forms of confessionalism did take place. New leaders emerged as well, the first being Menno Simons (1496–1561), the inheritor of the Münsterite legacy, who changed the course of Anabaptist history by consolidating a tradition based on non-violence, separation from worldly affairs, and the semblance of a fixed ecclesiological order. Simons taught rebirth and sanctification, but he also stressed the need for the sacraments of baptism and the Lord's Supper. Above all, he set the framework for a dialogue within Anabaptism about the need for public confessions and ecclesial forms that continued to shape Anabaptism long after his death.

This emphasis on order was too much for some Anabaptists, and in mid-century a group in Friesland separated from the main body of the Mennonites. This was the first stage of a process of segregation that would continue into the seventeenth century. Beginning with the Waterlanders of western Friesland, who were termed *Doopsgezinden* to distinguish them from the Mennonites, Anabaptist communities began to go their separate ways over questions of discipline, preaching, and the use of excommunication. Periods of conflict and tension were followed by attempts at reconciliation, as when the Flemish and Frisian groups came together under the *Olive Branch Confession* (1626). Thus, by the time Schütz was looking for radical allies in the 1670s, there were numerous Anabaptist communities in the Netherlands, East Friesland, and the north of France that had survived over a century of exclusion and persecution. In fact, by the late seventeenth century many of the Dutch Mennonites had distinguished themselves as "good citizens" during the wars against England, and in any event they seemed much less of a threat to the Christian order than Collegiants, Spinozists, Cartesians, and other practitioners of the new philosophies spreading throughout the northern lands and challenging the very foundations of magisterial religion.[82]

A similar story can be told of the Swiss Brethren. Following the initial separation from Zwingli, the dissenting groups moved into the Tyrol, Alsace, the Palatinate, and the Rhine Valley.[83] Like the Dutch Anabaptists, the history of the Swiss Brethren was impacted by the emergence of a unifying figure in mid-century, in this case the lay theologian Pilgram Marpeck (d.1556). Having escaped the persecution of the Habsburg Tyrol and settled in southern Germany, where he pursued a career as a hydro-engineer in Strasbourg and Augsburg, Marpeck became the first of the Swiss Brethren to establish a theological reputation substantial enough to unite the scattered communities. And like Menno Simons, Marpeck was, in relative terms, a moderate: he wrote against the Spiritualists and defended the idea of a visible church with methods of discipline and the sacraments of baptism and Communion. But he rejected pedobaptism, endorsed non-violence, and as he detailed in his major work *Elaboration of the Testaments* (1547), his main emphasis was on regeneration and sanctification rather than justification. For Marpeck, the core article of the Christian faith was the incarnation, for this was the point of division between the Old Testament and the New and the revelation of God's will for humanity. By necessity, all reborn believers strive to walk in the footsteps of Christ, to honor his words, deeds, and spiritual gestures. Just over 20 years later further consolidation was provided when representatives of the Swiss Brethren met in Strasbourg and worked up the *Strasbourg Discipline* of 1568, which provided guidelines for the ethical and ecclesiological constitution of the communities. Many of the distinct public features of the Brethren – how they dressed and conducted themselves in public, for instance, and how they regulated local churches – were settled for over three centuries on the basis of this document.

Further divisions followed, the most notable being the separation of Jakob Ammann (circa 1656–1730) and his followers (later termed the Amish) because of his insistence on stricter discipline. But by the seventeenth century, though still an outlawed and persecuted faith, the Swiss Brethren had been able to spread throughout the German and Swiss lands, with Alsace and the Palatinate being particularly important for their survival, as was the New World once emigration became an option. Some lived by subterfuge, attending Reformed or Lutheran services, baptizing their children in the parish church, and even attending Communion. Once back in the private sphere, however, they would practice their own piety. And most parishioners left them in peace. Indeed, as confessional culture waned in the late seventeenth century and persecution became sporadic, the Swiss Brethren emerged as exemplars of a deep and inspirational faith. In 1693 the Swiss Reformed pastor Georg Thormann remarked that the rural parishioners "have the notion that a ... Christian and an Anabaptist are one and the same thing, and that you could not be a ... true Christian unless you were – or became – an Anabaptist."[84]

The radical rebirth of the seventeenth century was thus the confluence of two separate streams. In addition to the already existing communities, such as the Swiss Brethren and the post-Münster Anabaptists, there was now a powerful radical impulse within the Pietist movement as well, as exemplified by Schütz. Overstepping orthodoxy no longer required a total break with praxis or community. It could be effected in stages, as a critique or rejection of one aspect of the public church that either continued to gather momentum until it ended in an alternative form of Protestantism or remained as one article of radicalism within an otherwise mainstream religious profile. Yet even the more conservative of the radicals – Conrad Bröske, for instance – were ultimately contributing to the fragmentation of the magisterial systems, for by appropriating radical ideas, if only piecemeal, they were undermining the church. And two themes in particular proved especially corrosive: ideals of separation and theories of the end time.

The radicals of the Pietist age revived the idea of separatism, elevating it from a principle exclusive to the Protestant underground to a constituent feature of the spiritual rebirth. In principle, even Spener's idea of an *ecclesiola in ecclesia* was an act of separation, recognition that there was a body of elect distinct from the run of time-serving Christians. But Spener never went so far as to suggest that the act of separation impinged on salvation. The radicals did, however, and in particular the "father of separatist Pietism" Jean de Labadie (1610–74), whose works Spener had read while in Geneva.[85] Born into a Catholic family in Bordeaux, Jesuit educated, Labadie's spiritual leanings eventually took him from Oratorianism to Jansenism before converting to the Reformed faith in 1650. After spending time in Geneva, where he was hailed as a second Calvin, he settled in Middelburg in Holland with a group of followers and pursued a new pattern of Christian worship. Paramount for Labadie was what he termed "l'union de l'âme à Dieu," which meant, in practical terms, close fellowship with pious Christians, group study of the Bible, conventicles, and a theology that emphasized the mystic and chiliastic aspects of Protestantism while demanding that Christians observe a strict self-regulated regime. Thus, while Labadie preached the necessity of church and clerical reform, he also taught that the true church was the community of the elect, the born again, and that worship was a personal matter between the individual and God. All true believers were on the same level as part of a prophetic ministry, and only these elect members of the church should partake of Communion.[86] In 1669, having raised the suspicions of the Middelburg authorities, Labadie moved to Amsterdam with a core group of followers, and then to Altona, where he died in the year 1674. The Labadist community, relocated in Wieuwerd in Friesland, outlived its founder for a few decades, however, serving as a beacon of the separatist revival and a model of New Testament Christianity.

Labadism provided a pattern for the separatist turn, inspiring, for instance, though in different ways, both Spener and Schütz as they developed their respective ideals of the *collegium* in Frankfurt.[87] But separatism was not specific to one particular group. Wherever radical Pietists gathered in numbers, there were *de facto* separatist communities, even if the teaching and the types may have varied. Wandering preachers and pious seekers could gather and pursue their dissenting visions of Protestant Christianity in the counties of Wittgenstein in eastern North Rhine Westphalia where there was a high concentration of separatists. The most influential was Ernst Christoph Hochmann von Hochenau (1670–1721), a missionary of separatism, who took refuge near Schwarzenau. A mystic, convinced that religion was purely a matter of the "inner word," Hochenau eschewed the outer forms and formulas of the "external Babylonian sect" and spread his message of private Christianity, free of church orders, human institutions, sacraments and formal worship, throughout the Wittgenstein counties and into Saxony, Franconia, Hesse, the Palatinate, and the Lower Rhine.[88] Other separatists settled in the county of Ysenburg, where two ruling counts, Karl August and Ernst Casimir, themselves Pietists, were willing to grant toleration for all peoples "who due to scruples of conscience do not hold to any external religion."[89] Ysenburg became a refuge for separatists who could not yet develop their own communities in safety, attracting radicals from the Palatinate, Württemberg, Swabia, Alsace, and Switzerland. But a formal community was not always the main goal. The "inspired ones" of the Wetterau, for instance, a spiritualist group that emerged in the belief that all confessional churches represented the New Babylon, devoted themselves to traveling through the German lands gathering followers and preaching the coming millennium. Johann Friedrich Rock (1678–1749), a saddler, emerged as the most prominent of these prophetic leaders, undertaking over the course of his lifetime at least 94 missions across the Wetterau, Württemberg, Switzerland, Alsace, and Silesia.[90]

The "inspired ones" was a prophetic sect, preaching the Spirit in the end times, and in this they were representative of another central principle of revived radicalism: the concern with eschatology. The foundations for the rethinking of orthodox apocalypticism had been laid by Spener with his notion of the "hope of better times." Whereas the Lutheran church had taught the Augustinian schematic, which held that the biblical prophecies had been fulfilled and that the current age was the final age, Spener argued that the 1,000-year reign of Christ was still to pass before the end time. Since neither the conversion of the Jews nor the Fall of Rome had yet taken place, Spener rejected the theory that the end was nigh and spoke instead of a time of preparation for the coming of Christ, which in practical terms entailed more preaching of the Word, the formation of spiritual priesthoods, more piety and less dogma, and a general reform of Christian society.[91] It was an important revaluation of the Protestant scheme of salvation history, for it not only removed the ever-present threat of a pending apocalypse, but it invested pious Protestants with a new sense of Christian mission.

Spener expected this new sense of urgency to feed into the upholding of the Lutheran church in the form of sermons, Bible study, *collegia*, clerical reform, and charity. For the radical thinkers, however, chiliast theories of this kind could be turned against public religion, used as a form of critique or a type of higher knowledge to expose the weaknesses of orthodoxy. And the apparent urgency was only heightened by historical circumstance. Surveying the panorama of recent events, which included the advance of the Turks and the devastation wrought by the Catholic armies of Louis XIV, most radical thinkers sensed the approaching end of days: Gottfried Arnold collated the signs, Johann Heinrich Horch announced the millennium, and Johann Konrad Dippel spoke of the golden age that would commence at the turn of the century.[92]

But the most articulate and influential of the radical voices in this vein were those of Johann Wilhelm Petersen (1649–1726) and his wife Johanna Eleonora Petersen, née von Merlau (1644–1724), both of whom became prolific speculators on the meaning of Revelation and the ideas associated with radical chiliasm or millennialism – that is, the theory of the 1,000-year golden age on earth during which Satan will be chained and Christ will reign – thereby taking Spener's basic notion of a hope of better times and adapting it to radical thought. Their most important "discovery," which they derived from the writings of the English Philadelphian sect, was the theory of universal salvation, a concept that rejected Protestant teaching on eternal damnation and postulated instead that all subjects of God, Satan included, would ultimately be comprehended by the "everlasting gospel" and taken up in the purification process. Taken together, the Petersens' speculations about Revelation and the final phase of Christian history represented a direct challenge to orthodox ideas on sin, salvation, and the place of the Lutheran church in God's plan. And they found a wide readership. Johann had been preaching the coming end time since soon after he took up the post of Superintendent of Lüneburg, where both he and Johanna published works devoted to the study of eschatology while supporting and publicizing the prophecies of female visionaries. Inevitably, this created tensions between the Petersens and the Lutheran clergy of Lüneburg, and in 1692 the couple were forced to leave the duchy and embark on careers as beneficiaries of noble patronage and missionaries of apocalypticism, gathering followers in cities such as Quedlinburg, Halberstadt, Halle, and Erfurt and spreading the message as far afield as Franconia, Württemberg, Silesia, and Bohemia.[93]

To get a sense of how radical eschatology could lead parishioners to challenge the authority of the established church we need look no further than the example of Heinrich Kratzenstein (1649–96), a goldsmith of Quedlinburg. For over 20 years a quiet, respected, and reputable husband and regular churchgoer, around 1689 Kratzenstein began to attend a Pietist conventicle. Two years later, while on his sickbed, Kratzenstein had a conversion experience, with dreams, inner voices, and emotive episodes, and thereafter he claimed to be a prophet, announcing that God had spoken to him directly about the coming 1,000-year kingdom and the need to find faith and do penance before the end.[94] Empowered by the need to set the world right in preparation for the coming kingdom, Kratzenstein began to speak openly against those aspects of the faith that stood in the way of salvation, almost all of which were fundamental attributes of orthodox Lutheranism. He railed against the clergy, calling them "priests of Baal," lacking in insight, piety, and any trace of the Spirit. Nor did Kratzenstein think the institutional church, which he once termed "the spiritual Babylon, the mother of whoredom and all anathema on earth," was necessary for salvation. Pedobaptism and Communion were purely external ceremonies with no deeper import, and all doctrine, unless it was strictly true to the Word of God, was nothing more than "lies" and need not be honored by true Christians. Indeed, he went so far as to suggest that true Christians should avoid all association with churchgoers unless there was sufficient proof they were numbered among the elect. After a few years of such preaching, Kratzenstein was condemned to be flogged and sent into exile, but he died in prison before these measures could be imposed.[95]

Radical Pietism was generally the sum total of men and women like Heinrich Kratzenstein and Johanna Eleonora Petersen. It was not a synchronized movement or a confessional stance, but rather a disposition that stirred different people in different ways. And yet it did impact Protestant culture in a general sense. Perhaps the best evidence of this can be found in Württemberg, where the works and ideas of Spener had found a receptive audience in the 1680s. Numerous higher clergy proved sympathetic to the Frankfurt reform program, including Tübingen professors, Stuttgart super-intendents, and indeed the Consistorium Director himself.[96] But in Württemberg, as elsewhere, some thought that Spenerian Pietism did not go far enough. Conventicles emerged in towns and cities with a marked focus on discipline, prophecy, revelation, and the enactment of the priesthood of all believers – all distinct features of the radical turn. Prominent clergymen started to broadcast radical ideas. Ludwig Brunnquell, pastor of Löchgau, who preached the coming 1,000-year reign of Christ and ques-tioned orthodox theories of justification, gathered followers before being dismissed from office. Johann Jakob Zimmermann, another clergyman out of office because of his radical millennialism, worked up chronologies of the coming end time, as did Johann Albrecht Bengel, a distant relative of the Schwäbisch Hall reformer Johannes Brenz, whose salvation history was based on a painstaking deconstruction of Revelation.[97]

But the radical impulse in Württemberg was not limited to the circles of the clerical elite. It found a following among the Imperial Knights, especially among prominent noblewomen, such as Amalia Hedwig von Leiningen and Johanna Katharina von Gaisberg, who became patrons of separatists. It was embraced by the urban magistracy, both in the smaller demesne towns and larger cities, where jurists, merchants, court-regulars, doctors, and a range of other citizens gathered in conventicles in order to pursue a type of religiosity that could not be satisfied by orthodox Lutheranism. In some conventicles, the participants signed their names to a book, proof of their personal "act" of separation. And like the Puritans and the Quakers of England, over time the Württemberg radicals developed a subculture that distinguished them from the run of their fellow Protestants. In religious terms, the obvious radical traits were an osten-tatious piety, a refusal to baptize their children, and a rejection of the institutional or sacramental aspects of public religion. Socially, as well, there was a habitus that distinguished them as a group. The radical Pietists of Württemberg tended to avoid traditional greetings, honorary titles, or any gesture meant to flatter or deceive. They lived moderate lives, eschewed luxury and excess, and wore plain-colored clothes made of inexpensive cloth. The only self-indulgence was a star or a comet stitched on their shirts and jackets, emblems of their election before the pending apocalypse.[98]

In Württemberg, as elsewhere in Germany, the radical impulse waned in the second and third decades of the eighteenth century. Radical Pietists still existed, of course, but no substantial church or transregional community emerged and many dissenters eventually returned to the magisterial fold. But the teachings remained in circulation, and the ideals continued to captivate Protestants who sought a more affective religi-osity, a more pious society, or a greater role within the church. During the early eighteenth century, it became easier to realize these ideals within the context of mainstream Protestantism, and this was in large part because of the influence of the radical tradition. Indeed, to an extent, Pietism had become the victim of its own success, for even though Pietists were retreating from the historical stage, the ideals they had practiced and popularized remained a living force and were gradually appropriated by the mainstream. And at the start of the eighteenth century, they would contribute to the transformation of Protestantism in two settings: that of the mainstream church itself, as in Brandenburg-Prussia, where the old confessional order established by the Reformation began to relinquish its hold; and that of the New World, Pennsylvania in particular, which became a haven for radical Protestants and a crucible for new syntheses.

The End of Reformation

Politics and piety

From April to July 1732, over 20,000 Protestants, mostly cattle farmers, left their scattered farmsteads in the Alpine districts of Salzburg and set off on a long trek through Germany for a new life in the eastern marches of Ducal Prussia. The land the refugees were leaving was the diocese of Salzburg, recently subjected to the rule of the Jesuit-educated Archbishop Leopold Anton, Freiherr von Firmian (1679–1744). Soon after his election in 1727, Archbishop Firmian pledged to root out the Alpine Lutherans, and he was prepared to use all manner of means, from the missionary to the military, to do so. In the end, he settled on expulsion. On November 11, 1731 the archbishop issued an edict that declared his intention to "extirpate and uproot these unruly, seditious, and rebellious folk wholly and henceforth." Those without fixed abode were to leave "with bag and baggage" within a week.[99] The land in which the refugees were settling was located at the far north-eastern corner of the empire on the coast of the Baltic Sea. And they had been invited. In February 1732, Friedrich Wilhelm I, Elector of Brandenburg-Prussia, had issued a formal patent of invitation to the Salzburg Protestants and thereby, to the very public relief of the Protestant world, provided them with a place of refuge. To the elector, it was not only an act of Christian charity but a gesture that made good political sense. For with the publication of the patent, Friedrich Wilhelm confirmed his status as Europe's leading Protestant ruler, while at the same time he was able to contribute to the *retablissement* program and repopulate the debilitated towns and villages of East Prussia.

Although ostensibly a religious conflict, the Salzburg emigration is actually most valuable for what it reveals about the relatively minor role played by faith in this very public drama. By 1731, most European powers considered Firmian's heavy-handed intolerance a relic of the confessional past, and if there was a moral to be learned, it was not in the martyrdom of the Protestants but rather in the measured *politique* of the elector. But this was nothing new. The electors of Brandenburg had been subverting religion to reason of state since the introduction of the Reformation in the 1540s. Home to a very mild form of Lutheranism to begin with, Brandenburg did not experience a concerted process of confessionalization until the 1570s, and this was cut short in 1613 when the regnant elector, Johann Sigismund (1572–1619), converted to Calvinism and published a credal statement the following year detailing his reasons as well as his intention to have the rest of the land join him in the fold. Despite the best efforts of the government, however, the populace would not be converted, and as a consequence Brandenburg became a bi-confessional state. Followers of the Reformed faith tended to be limited to the court, the military, and the University of Frankfurt an der Oder, while Lutherans made up the bulk of the population, from nobles and patricians to townsmen and peasants.[100]

Brandenburg, or Brandenburg-Prussia as it became, was able to preserve a degree of religious plurality in the midst of confessional Germany without compromising the power of the state. And indeed, by subverting confession to the interests of the state, the electors strengthened the political and economic standing of the land. Friedrich Wilhelm (1620–88), for instance, the Great Elector, did not try to enforce his own Reformed beliefs on the subject population, but he did use religion as a tool of statecraft, privileging Calvinists at court, creating Calvinist interest groups, and forming alliances with Calvinist powers, including Silesia, the Palatinate, Anhalt, Scotland, and England. In 1685, decades before the Salzburg emigration, he had arranged for thousands of Huguenot refugees to settle in Brandenburg. By 1700, over one-quarter of Berlin inhabitants spoke French.

The confessional imperative that shaped the relations between church and state in so many other German states during this period never really took hold in Brandenburg-Prussia. In the beginning, this relative latitude was not the product of a theory of tolerance but the outcome of practical politics by rulers who, though often deeply religious, had learned to place the interests of the state above the interests of the church.[101] And yet, if pragmatic at first, by the seventeenth century it had become a more principled stance, and by the early eighteenth it had emerged as the rationale of rule.

To some degree, then, it was a odd quirk of fate that German Pietism reached full flower in the lands of Brandenburg-Prussia. Numerous Pietists had followed Spener to Berlin and the surrounding area in the 1690s, and they all did their part to seed the movement. But it was August Hermann Francke (1663–1727) who ultimately secured Pietism its place in Protestant history.[102] After the exodus from Leipzig in 1690, Francke moved on to Erfurt, where he set up Bible-study groups and tutored theology students. The fateful move, however, came in 1691, when Spener brokered him a transfer to the parish of Glaucha, just outside the walls of Halle. In Glaucha, Francke was able to translate his theories of spiritual renewal into a program of active pastoral care.

As in Leipzig and Erfurt, Francke founded a *collegium* to provide the laity with a forum for the discussion of Scripture. On a broader scale, he increased the frequency and intensity of the sermons and followed these up with catechism sessions, and he continued to cultivate the need for a living Christianity, going so far as to test the standards of faith by imposing stricter discipline and limiting access to Communion. While doing this, Francke skirted the edges of radical Pietism. Not only were his sermons and writings markedly anti-orthodox, constantly emphasizing the need for conversion and piety while taking the clergy to task for their lackluster sermons and reliance on set forms and formulas, he was also drawn to the mystical side of the movement and indeed when he first arrived in Halle he was censored by the orthodox for his association with a group of female visionaries. Unlike Schütz, however, this did not lead Francke to separation. On the contrary. After Spener had denounced the women and the Berlin officials had launched an investigation, Francke began to distance himself from the radicals and channel his spiritual energies into the institutional consolidation of Pietism in Halle. He never abandoned the mystical elements of his thought, and he continued to believe that the converted were distinct from the mass of time-serving Christians, but he no longer associated with individuals or groups the authorities considered a threat to the sacral or social order of Brandenburg-Prussia. Instead, Francke spent his career devising ways in which the Pietist impulse could be accommodated within that very sacral and social order.[103]

No Protestant clergyman since Martin Luther had been so effective at promoting himself or his theological vision as August Hermann Francke. Like Luther, Francke made use of university colleagues sympathetic to his cause, the two most important being Joachim Justus Breithaupt (1658–1732), professor of theology and author of dogmatic works in the spirit of Pietist thought, and Paul Anton, who had followed Francke from Leipzig and continued the conventicle tradition in Halle. "Who knows," wondered Johann Albrecht Bengel in 1713, "whether Christianity could ever again see such men brought together as has occurred in Halle with Breithaupt, Anton, and Francke."[104] And yet Francke's success at the university paled in comparison to his accomplishments in the public realm. Within 10 years of his appointment, he had revolutionized the social and cultural world of Halle. In 1695, primarily on the basis of donations, he founded a school for boys, an establishment where orphans and the children of the poor could be educated for minimal cost while learning a craft. This modest foundation was followed by a Latin school, and eventually by a third place of learning, a *Paedagogium* intended for the children of the elite. In 1698, Francke oversaw the construction of a new orphanage, an imposing multistory stone building that became the administrative and symbolic heart of the movement. It also became the headquarters for two further important initiatives. First, in 1699 the orphanage set up its own publishing house, a venture that proved so successful that branches were established in Berlin, Leipzig, and Frankfurt. Between 1717 and 1723 alone the printing house sold more than 35,000 tracts – a rate of production that justified the purchase of a paper mill. Second, Francke set up a pharmacy. Well-wishers throughout Europe sent cures and prescriptions to Halle, and these were turned into medicines, nostrums, and counteractants and then shipped throughout Germany and eventually Europe. By 1701 the pharmacy had its own wonder-working panacea – the gold-tinctured *essentia dulcis* – that provided a steady stream of income. And all of this wealth fed straight back into the upkeep of the foundations. None of the founders profited personally or used the foundations for ends other than those intended by Francke. When Heinrich Julius Elers, the long-term director of the publishing house, died, in 1728, he left behind a single piece of property, a Wittenberg Bible, and he bequeathed it to the orphanage.[105]

The rise of Francke's version of institutionalized Pietism was only possible because it was supported by the state. Both of the electors who ruled during Francke's career, Friedrich III/I (1657–1713) and Friedrich Wilhelm I (1688–1740), were patrons to Francke. Each ruler had personal reasons for this, ranging from the political to the religious, though historians have often found it easier to associate the austere and melancholic Friedrich Wilhelm with Pietism than Friedrich. Any man whose first acts on the throne included sacking the *chocolatier*, castrato singers, cellists and organ-builders, and shipping off the lions of the royal menagerie to the King of Poland, as was the case with Friedrich Wilhelm, would seem a good fit with men like Francke and Elers.[106] But Friedrich III was at least as important. It was Friedrich who first extended the invitation to Spener and approved the appointment of other Pietists at the newly founded Halle

University. Once Francke was in Glaucha, the elector and his Berlin ministers supported his efforts, defending him against the orthodox clergy and the local nobles and patricians, granting him privileges to help with the building of the foundations and providing a range of gifts and exemptions that made it possible for the self-funding enterprise to grow.

Friedrich Wilhelm I, whom Francke had courted before his accession, confirmed these privileges once on the throne and subsequently did even more to integrate Halle Pietism into the running of the land. By the 1720s, at least two semesters' study with the Pietists of Halle University was required for state service. But this patronage came at a price. Francke recognized early on in his Halle career that he would have to disavow those aspects of Pietism that were potential threats to the social and political order. In fact, one of the selling points of Halle Pietism, as Francke reminded Elector Friedrich in 1701, was that Pietists made better subjects, for it was not the external constraints that compelled them to conform to the law, but rather an inner compulsion nurtured by the strength of their faith.[107]

But Brandenburg-Prussia was not a Pietist land in any meaningful sense, for unlike the situation in the Protestant polities of the sixteenth century, where religion had shaped the social and political world, Halle Pietism was subordinate to the interests of the state. Francke was only able to realize his program of reform in so far as it was in sync with reason of state, and this was no longer primarily confessional in its logic. Pietists were generally more irenical than orthodox Protestants, and in a land where a Reformed ruler reigned over a Lutheran populace it was an advantage to have clergymen who could speak in generic terms about faith and piety without crossing theological divides.[108] Politically, as well, Pietists sat above the fray. By sending them into lands of entrenched Lutheran resistance, such as East Prussia or the duchy of Magdeburg, the electors were able to use the Pietists as leverage for undermining the resistance of the local populations. Whether up against the magistracy of Königsberg or the estates of Magdeburg, the Berlin government recognized that by placing Pietists into positions of influence and having them teach and preach to the locals it was able to effect a domestic colonization that tied the periphery to the core. And, above all, Pietism spoke the language of political obedience. The terms and concepts were meant in another sense by men such as Francke, of course, and yet all of the central values at the heart of the Halle project – from the virtues of duty, industry, humility, and diffidence to the ideals of honor, sacrifice, and the common good – could be applied without much distortion to the philosophy of rule as it was articulated in Berlin. In terms of the language used there was little difference between the description of Christian piety and an upright devotion to the state, a point made by Elector Friedrich William when he demanded of each prospective state-servant that he

> besides God prize nothing more highly than the grace of his king, serve the latter out of love and more out of honor than for monetary remuneration, and seek in all his conduct of affairs purely and simply the interest and service of his king, shunning all intrigues.[109]

Pietism in Brandenburg-Prussia represented "a new form of orthodoxy, a new style of state religion" different in kind from the mainstream Protestant state-churches of the confessional age.[110] For even though Pietism developed within the framework of the state, it did not have the ordering function of the public religions of the previous

century. By the reign of Friedrich Wilhelm I (1713–40), the confessional imperative
had largely been pressed back by secular concerns, and this meant that for Halle Pietism
to make an impact beyond the role marked out for it by the state it had to rely on its own
inner resources. In short, it had to take a leaf from the book of the radicals and cultivate
a faith that was rooted in spontaneity, insight, voluntary association, an affective rather
than a sacramental religiosity, personal familiarity with Scripture, and lay involvement in
religious affairs.

In Brandenburg-Prussia, this was feasible because the electors had effectively given
Francke and his followers their stamp of approval. On each occasion (1692 and 1700)
that a Berlin commission was sent to investigate the unrest in Halle between Francke
and the Lutheran clergy it concluded that, if not taken to enthusiastic extremes,
Pietist teaching on rebirth, sanctification, revelation, and private edification were in
keeping with the Word of God. Beyond its utilization in the army or the academy,
however, which was the main value of Pietism to the state, the actual development of
religious reform was left to the clergy and their parishioners. Consequently, we see the
first signs of the evangelicalism of the eighteenth century pressing through traditional
ecclesiastical forms, as Francke and other Pietists began "to mediate between the
world of ecclesiastical precision, and the world of spiritual nutriment."[111] Pastors
now preached the importance of a living, experiential faith. Leading clergymen such
as Johann Adam Steinmetz (1698–1762), superintendent of Magdeburg, published
devotional tracts, catechisms, spiritual guidebooks, homiletics, and prayer calendars
to help their congregations foster an inner spirituality. Ministers facilitated lay
involvement, encouraged the parishioners to bring their Bibles to church, nurtured
faith in the household, and generally supported the development of an active
spirituality outside of the church, stressing, for instance, conversion, sanctification,
and spiritual self-examination. These were the central themes of Pietism, as we have
seen, and taken together represented an impulse that moved the believer away from
reliance on doctrine to a more spontaneous, personal type of faith.[112] In Brandenburg-Prussia, Francke and his followers were able to weave these impulses into the
fabric of the magisterial system.

Religion was withdrawing into the private sphere. The overly affective and self-
conscious type of Protestantism cultivated by the Halle Pietists was now reserved for the
household, a state of affairs that actually worked to the advantage of the movement in
Brandenburg-Prussia as it acquired something of a monopoly over the turn towards the
privatization of faith.[113] The state itself, however, was heading in a different direction. If
the concerns of the Reformation prince had been creating and maintaining the
conditions appropriate to the confessional state as delineated by the theologians, they
now tended to be those aspects of statecraft that historians have associated with
secularized forms of rule. Order remained the paramount concern, but the logic and
the methods used to enforce it had changed. Instead of looking to the theologians,
rulers turned to experts on military and economic affairs, the emerging practitioners
of public law, or the professors of the cameral sciences taking up newly created
university chairs. Cameralism, the German version of mercantilism, was essentially
a science devoted to discovering the most effective ways to fill up the coffers of the
prince. The economic order rather than the moral order topped the agenda, and it led
to speculation on issues ranging from trade, industry, fiscal systems, and national

economics to minting, mining, and water wheels. And all was justified with reference to the necessity (*necessitas*) of state.[114]

In Brandenburg-Prussia, as increasingly in the rest of the Protestant world, Enlightenment thought was dismantling the confessional state. Secular theorists such as Samuel Pufendorf (1632–94), Christian Thomasius (1655–1728), and Justus Henning Böhmer (1674–1749) were developing theories of rule based exclusively on natural law principles. Whereas Reformation theology had invested the institutional church and its ministry with some degree of sovereign power, the new philosophies rejected the idea that the clergy had any claims on rule. The use of force, elemental to the exercise of power, was not among the attributes of the church, and in fact the church had no independent powers beyond what was accorded to it as a *collegium* or a corporation within the broader framework of state sovereignty. This did not mean that the ruler had the right to force his will on the church. On the contrary, the purpose of the state was the opposite. In tune with the discourse of the European Enlightenment, the Brandenburg philosophers argued that the central purpose of the state was to preserve freedom of conscience and guarantee the exercise of religion without fear of persecution. According to Thomasius, the central mandate of a prince with reference to the *circa sacra* was to tolerate dissenters and protect them against persecution.[115] The enforcement of godly order was not within the mandate of rule.

One by one the theocratic pillars of the confessional state began to fall away. The Lutheran theory of the three estates, which had made it possible for the clergy to claim a distinctive sphere of power, was rejected in favor of a simplified model of social and political relations that subjected the church to the power of the state. The orthodox distinction between the internal and external dominion of the church – the former referring to matters such as the sacraments and preaching – was overwritten by new notions of rationalized sovereignty that claimed that *all* authority was derived from, and limited to, the territory itself. As Böhmer wrote, the territorial law was sufficient as a basis for the rights of the prince, and it made no place for an alternative sovereign power such as the church. And finally, the premise, so central to Melanchthon's thought, that the prince as the first member of the church had an elevated religious role, or indeed some sort of dual sacral/secular status, was rejected outright by the theorists. In these new political philosophies, all sovereign authority was derived from secular (natural) law. The only political role left for the church was to support the policies of the prince and help to maintain the peace – which was often best served by less rather than more religion.[116]

The most relentless German voice in defense of the desacralized Protestant state was the jurist and philosopher Christian Thomasius, an Enlightenment thinker who served as professor of jurisprudence at the University of Halle. For Thomasius, the relationship between church and state was purely a question of practical politics. It had nothing to do with salvation or the approximation of a godly order. Basing his ideas on the historical perspective acquired through a close reading of Gottfried Arnold, Thomasius argued that the coercion of public religion was actually a threat to the peace and order of the realm. With more than just a casual allusion to the Electorate of Saxony, he described how the confessional imperative, with its imposition of fixed doctrine and legislated orthodoxy, tended to undermine the integrity of the Christian commonwealth, which in its pure form should be a single sovereign entity with all power vested in the prince.[117]

Thomasius spent much of his university career establishing the secular foundations of the state he described. And he began by rejecting the revelatory character of Protestant theories of state. Instead, he established a body of political thought that was based on the use of reason as applied to history, philosophy, and natural law. Thomasius was able to encroach upon the sacral enclaves of the Protestant polity by stretching the idea of adiaphora, or "middle things," until all aspects of the external church fell within the purview of the secular arm. Because, as a Pietist sympathizer, he believed that true Christianity was all about inner faith, and because he had learned from reading Arnold that there were no external forms in the apostolic church, he rejected the idea that there was a sphere reserved for the church in the political realm. All aspects of public religion, from the calendar, to music, vestments, images, and ceremony, were middle things and subject to the jurisdiction of the state. Nothing essential to salvation was political. Thus the Christian virtue of the Protestant prince was not demonstrated by his efforts to effect the godly realm, as Bucer and Melanchthon had taught, but on the contrary, by the degree of tolerance and religious freedom he was willing to observe, which was the only proper state of affairs for preserving peace and order in the realm. Anything else, argued Thomasius, ran the risk of either making dutiful Christians the martyrs of tyrant kings or pious kings the "lickspittles" of tyrant priests.[118]

Of course, we should not take the thought of Christian Thomasius as a mirror on political developments. Yet as a scholar of jurisprudence, like his older contemporary Samuel Pufendorf, he was at the very center of the fight for the soul of the state, and as such he does provide a unique and particularly relevant perspective on developments. What Thomasius was trying to do was remove theology altogether from the emerging philosophies of rule. In its place, he turned to natural law theory and presented it as the "modern" solution to the question of order. Devoid of the sacralism and providentialism of the confessional model, it was quintessentially rational and scientific, and its overriding purpose was to serve the interests of men and women in their social and political compacts.[119] And yet this did not mean there was no place for religion. Thomasius had been an early convert to Pietism, and for many years he was an open supporter of Francke in Halle. When he speculated on the need to remove theology from the public realm, it was only possible because he had a view of religion conditioned by Pietist thought. True Christianity, he argued, was a personal bond with God; it was voluntary rather than forced, nurtured within the individual, and expressed within the framework of the pious group or worshiping congregation. And it had very little to do with the forms, ceremonies, and dogma of the orthodox churches. Thus, although Thomasius still believed that the state was a Christian creation, and that the rulers served as the "prefects and vicars of the Kingdom of God," the type of Protestant Christianity he wanted to see preserved in the state was the non-confessional private "religion of the heart" practiced by the Pietists.[120]

August Hermann Francke died in 1727. At that point, the teachings and methods of Halle Pietism were being emulated in places as far apart as Silesia and New England. In England, in particular, the influence of what they termed *Pietas Hallensis* was deeply felt. A generation of Protestant missionaries was inspired by the writings of Halle, among them George Whitefield, who would leave England to become a preaching sensation in America. But as Francke himself remarked a few years before his death, the spiritual impulse of the 1690s and early 1700s was starting to wane.

The number of dedicated, activist Pietist clergy in the parishes was falling away, and the students in Halle were less interested in devoting themselves to the study and the practice of gospel teaching and spent rather more time attending the lectures and reading the works of Enlightenment thinkers such as Christian Wolff. In part, as mentioned earlier, this was a consequence of the very success of the Pietism movement. It had taken root within the magisterial order, creating the space for a more personal and non-doctrinal type of religion, more lay involvement, and a church that derived much of its direction and inspiration from the local congregation.[121]

But the Pietist impulse was not just waning of its own accord; it was being absorbed by other historical developments as well. In the Prussia of Friedrich II (1712–86) (known as Frederick the Great by English historians) there would be other objects of devotion and solidarity for the subject population. The strength of religious identity was ceding ground to patriotism, with more and more people speaking of their love for the "fatherland" rather than their love for the faith. At the same time, Enlightenment thought was creating a new world of thought and language that provided an alternative space for the intellectual and social energies behind the success of Halle Pietism. As Thomasius and Pufendorf had demonstrated, it was now possible to imagine a Christian order without reserving a place for an institutional church. We should not conclude from this that Pietism, its few victories intact, no longer had a role to play. The effects of the Pietist impulse, with the importance it placed on social engagement and its elevation of the virtues of duty, suffering, and obedience, would be felt well into the early nineteenth century as the discourse of nationalism reconfigured notions of identity.[122] But to the pious Protestants of the early eighteenth century, Francke among them, it must have seemed as if the movement was coming to an end. That is why so many Pietists joined the emigration of marginalized Protestants to America during this period. It seemed to be the final opportunity to realize a vision of godly order that no longer had a place in Europe.

Mixed multitudes

Once America had become a republic, it was common for European observers to extol the virtues of its religious liberties, many claiming, like the English reform publicist William Cobbett (1763–1835), that "all is harmony and good neighborhood . . . Here are no disputes about religion; or, if they be, they make no noise."[123] Cobbett was not the first to speak in this way. Years earlier the minor French nobleman Hector St John de Crèvecoeur (1735–1813) had been saying similar things while living in Orange County, New York as a naturalized citizen. In 1782 he published *Letters from an American Farmer*, a collection of narrative vignettes, and he too remarked on the heterogeneity of American culture, going so far as to speak of "a new race of men" who had broken free of European prejudices. Crèvecoeur made his point with an imaginary account of a stroll through the American countryside, where a prosperous Catholic, a "good honest plodding German Lutheran," a "seceder" from the Church of England, and a profit-minded Calvinist are met in succession, each one going about his business without a care for the religion of the other.[124] Like other reports in this vein, *Letters* was part fiction. Surely Crèvecoeur must have known, for instance, that Catholics were the subjects of lingering prejudice and civil disabilities. But there is much truth there as well, and it reminds us that religious diversity was a reality of American life. It may not have been the "harmony and good neighborhood" described by men like Cobbett and Crèvecoeur, but it was a new phenomenon, a fresh synthesis, and it gave rise to new types of Protestants.

As we have seen, in its accommodation of religious diversity, New Netherland worked as both a catalyst and an archetype for the Protestant communities in the mid-Atlantic regions. Even after the colony was captured by the English in 1664 and renamed New York after James Stuart, Duke of York, who administered it, it remained religiously pluriform. The duke preserved liberty of conscience, guaranteeing that none who professed Christianity would be disturbed in their faith. Indeed, in his desire to secure political stability and economic prosperity in the region, James Stuart went even further than the pragmatic Dutch and published a series of laws that encapsulated something of a charter of tolerance, the most fateful consequences for the actual practice of religion being the inclusion of the right of the communities to determine the faith of the local church and the exclusion of any confessional norms beyond the proof of Protestant ordination.[125] In most things the Dutch Reformed community was left to practice as before, though now without the support of the state and, effectively, the classis of Amsterdam. Forced to gather incomes made up of beaver pelts, wampum, and multifarious silver coins, and faced by the babel of religious opinions, it was little wonder that many of the ministers feared for the future of the church. Dominie Dellius predicted that "soon some marvelous kind of theology will develop here; ministers will be self-created, and the last will be the first, and the first will be the last."[126]

Yet Dutch Calvinists did not fare any worse than the other religions of New York, which at the start of the English takeover included Dutch and Swedish Lutherans, Anglicans, Catholics, English Puritans, French Huguenots, and a growing Jewish community. The famous observation made in 1687 by the Catholic governor summed up the confessional culture of the area: "Here bee not many of the Church of England; few Roman Catholicks; abundance of Quakers preachers men and women especially; Singing Quakers, Ranting Quakers; Sabbatarians; Antisabbatarians; some Anabaptists [;] some Independents; some Jews; in short of all sorts of opinions there are some, and the most part [are] of none at all."[127] Other parts of the Middle Colonies were similar. Maryland, for instance, Lord Baltimore's Catholic refuge, had no ecclesiastical structure to speak of during the first 60 years of its existence. Despite the fact that they practiced the public religion, Catholics tended to worship in their homes and private chapels, and they had even pushed through an act of toleration in 1649 as an exercise in self-preservation. Over time they would be pressed back by Quakers and Independents; and because, as the clergyman John Yeo observed, there was no care or provision made for the building up of the Protestant religion (by which he meant Anglicanism), the communities continued to fragment and diversify.[128]

By the early eighteenth century, the mainstream churches were making concerted attempts to turn back the clock on colonial religion, to bring the New World in line with the Old World tradition. Time and place made this an impossible task, and yet the magisterial countermarch was not without its effects, even if the consequences were not as originally planned. The Church of England was further consolidated in Virginia; moreover, it was established in Maryland, the two Carolinas, North and South, and planted amid the sectarians in New Jersey and Massachusetts. Inspired by the leadership of the commissary James Blair, the confession experienced something of a renaissance. The number of churches in Virginia doubled, new parishes emerged, the quality of the clergy and their conditions of office improved, and the liturgy and the surroundings of worship became more elaborate. But in order to make these gains, the church had been forced to compromise and adapt. Wherever Anglicanism was the public church, Virginia included, it had to learn to share the land with dissenters. In Maryland, for instance, Anglicans were surrounded by Independents, Presbyterians, Baptists, and Quakers. In such a setting, the idea of a comprehensive national church was not feasible, nor was imposing the faith on the colonists in the manner of confessionalization or insisting that they maintain a pastor against their wills. The best approach, as the governor of New Jersey remarked in 1711, was to take a leaf out of the book of the radicals – that is, take up the gospel and try to win them voluntarily.[129]

Similar histories can be told of the Lutheran and the Reformed communities in the Middle Colonies. No doubt many of the parishioners would have been sympathetic to the views of the Swiss widow who declared that "this country is a house of refuge for all expelled sects, a confused Babel, a repository of all impure spirits, a dwelling-place of devils, a first world, a Sodom."[130] Mounting the only defense they knew, the Reformed authorities responded by relying on ordained pastors, published confessions, and orthodox services. The Lutherans also turned to the pastorate, appointing recent graduates from the universities in Germany and Sweden, tightening up the hierarchy of the church, and organizing the parishes in a quasi-presbyterial manner. But even as they worked to patch together the magisterial system, the differences were exposed. When the Dutch Reformed congregations could not find an orthodox clergyman from within the fold they would turn to Presbyterians or Anglicans – any Protestant would do. Lacking preachers altogether, they might recruit schoolmasters or even pious tailors. So too with the Lutherans. In Tulpehocken, a parish in Pennsylvania, the Lutheran community went without a pastor for years. During this period they would meet in houses or a defensive fort and, when Lutheran or Reformed clergy were not available, rely on lay readers of the congregation for the service – or perhaps a passing hedge-preacher, some of whom doubled up as bloodletters, dentists, or soothsayers. It was a different type of community with different ideas about the church. When the Lutheran pastor Henry Mühlenberg (1711–87) arrived to take up his post in Pennsylvania, he soon realized that he would make no progress lording over the congregation in the manner expected by graduates of Göttingen and Halle. Too many sermons, too much discipline, or too fine a theology and the parishioners would withhold the tithes and trek to another church. Mühlenberg made his point with reference to a colleague who returned to Germany in disgust: "He imagined that one could bend and force the people here … as in Germany with the secular or consistorial arm of the law. But … experience proves something different."[131]

The Puritans of New England also made attempts to shore up the ecclesial system, the most ambitious being the introduction of the half-way covenant. But other steps were taken, including the creation of a more effective territorial scheme of parishes, the emergence of consociations of ministers that worked in spirit (and sometimes in name) like presbyterial systems, a general shift of emphasis from the congregations to the pastors and the magistrates, and closer control of education and the licensing laws.

Despite their best efforts, however, the Puritan divines no longer maintained a monopoly on religious practice. Parishioners could now just as easily attend a Presbyterian, Anglican, or Quaker service as a Congregationalist – or indeed no service at all, as Deists and rationalists later demonstrated. A good measure of this new religious economy was the establishment of the Brattle Street Church in 1699. Founded by a group of Boston merchants along "broad and catholick" lines, it welcomed all professors of the Christian faith and rejected the idea of a covenanted congregation. In 1691, this trend had been given further encouragement by the Crown when a new royal charter legislated tolerance for dissenting groups and abolished the requirement of church membership for political enfranchisement, which had been one of the pillars of the New England Way.[132]

Some clergy reacted to this diversity by making the faith more appealing to the parishioners – shorter sermons or more elaborate ceremonies, for instance. Many others, however, responded in the manner of John Norton, who held that liberty and innovation were the death-knell of godly order when taken too far, regardless of whether it came from inside or outside of the church. "Israel must stand to this," he wrote; "if it be in matters of Religion, there is the Priest; if in matters Civil, there is the Magistrate, and he that stands not, or submits not to the Sentence of these, *let him be cut off from Israel*; so requisite a thing is Order."[133] The problem facing New England Puritans like Norton, however, was that there were by this time more than enough parishioners who would willingly separate from a Church of Israel built in the image of his beliefs. They might opt to join up with the Quakers, Anglicans, or Baptists, or perhaps the more lenient forms of Bay Congregationalism that had emerged after the introduction of the half-way Covenant. It was no longer feasible to preserve order through the traditional magisterial means.

Realizing this, Puritan divines preached jeremiads claiming that God had fallen out with the colony and that his wrath was everywhere to see. Look around, they enjoined, in addition to famine, disease, shipwrecks, Indian wars, and fires in Boston there were the divisive effects of social and economic change, the rise of luxury and commerce and English fashion, the creeping atheism of European thought, and the breakdown of community brought on by the sale of cheap land to immigrants in search of quick profit. Historically, these secular developments were probably more important than the shifts in religious thought; but for Puritan divines like Norton, it was the sins of desertion and declension that would leave New England in the same state as post-war Europe, unchurched and dissipated.[134]

In at least one respect the jeremiads were wide of the mark: New World Protestants were not falling away from Christianity. None of the colonies, not even the infamous Babel (as the Bay Puritans saw it) of Rhode Island, was an experiment in secularism. The problem in America was not too little religion but too much, and in their efforts to come to terms with the diversity, all of the communities, magisterial and radical alike, borrowed from the techniques of confessional age Europe. The process was more politically diffuse and less theologically driven than the European variant, but the Protestant communities in America also acquired much of their shape in a race to exploit the resources of the state. Moreover, even where the state was not involved, the churches generally reacted to plurality by tightening up the confessional bonds. This was a natural enough reflex in the mainstream tradition, which is why Ulster

Presbyterians in the backwoods of Pennsylvania were so quick to establish presbyteries, visitors, court sessions, and demand subscription to the Westminster Confession; but even the Quakers introduced disciplinary institutions along with yearly, quarterly, and monthly sessions, while the Baptists in the Delaware Valley began to form broad interregional associations, appointing and approving ministers from above.[135] One consequence of this was further religious fragmentation, so Baptists became Keithian Baptists, Particular Baptists, Seventh Day Baptists, and so on. Another was the heightened sense of confessional community or a readiness to affirm religious identity. Through their sheer plainness of dress and speech, for instance, their lack of pockets and buckles and their white and lead-colored clothes, this was exactly the route taken by the Mennonites of Pennsylvania. And we might even view the mahogany Communion tables of the Bay Puritans, the carved pews of the Anglicans, or indeed the sacral skylines of Boston or Charleston in the same light – all testimony to the importance of religion to the sense of identity and community.[136]

But this was an altogether different type of confessionalism than the European variant. For even in the 1740s, when the magisterial resurgence was in full swing, the essential energy of Protestant development was no longer derived from the public church or the state but rather from the parishioners themselves. Year after year American Protestants, regardless of type, had been engaging directly with religious affairs in order to preserve Christian order in the relative anarchy of America. Of course, for the radicals who flourished in the New World, this was nothing other than true Christianity; but even within the mainstream tradition, there was now an irreversible trend towards greater lay involvement, personal faith, charismatic preaching, communal forms of ecclesial governance, and a broader-based, voluntary approach to religion. To observers like the governor of North Carolina it seemed as though the foundations of religion were being undermined, and that if the churches of Europe did not send out reinforcements very soon "the very footsteps of religion will, in a short time, be worne out."[137] But in truth this loosening of confessional ties was not leading Protestants to their destruction, just changing the nature of the relationship between the believers and the church. And it was not simply a question of whether the reinforcements of the magisterial tradition would provide the remedy, for the radicals were doing exactly the same thing. What was happening, in fact, was that new types of Protestant communities were emerging, new syntheses that fed on the revival of the radical tradition.

Firstborn of these syntheses was Pennsylvania, the brainchild of the English Quaker William Penn (1644–1718), son of an admiral who had taken part in the restoration of Charles II. The colony of Pennsylvania was given to Penn in lieu of a debt owed to his father by the Crown, and it was this grant of land in the Delaware Valley that would be site of his "holy experiment" in Quaker religiosity. Pennsylvania was a refuge for people whose inward faith and ability to live according to the will of God would create a society not seen on earth since the days of the apostles. As he wrote in a letter to Thomas Janney, "Mine eye is to a blessed governmt, and a virtuous ingenious and industrious society, so as people may live well and have more time to give to ye L[or]d then in this Crowded land. God will plant Americka and it shall have its day in ye Kingdom."[138] The hub of the colony was to be Philadelphia, named after the one city in Revelation that was not rebuked. Its layout was organized on a grid pattern, two miles long and one mile wide, bound by the Schuylkill and Delaware rivers. Penn planned the city with his surveyor-general Thomas Holme, a Quaker acquaintance from his days in Ireland, and together they mapped out a cityscape that encapsulated the plain style of dissenting Protestants. No doubt questions of social and economic utility, along with memories of the London's Great Fire of 1666, played a role in the design, but the sparse functionalism of the layout, what Thomas Hamilton later described as "a sort of habitable problem – a mathematical infringement on the rights of individual eccentricity," is clearly reminiscent of utopias like *Christianopolis* and their desire to contain fallen man by way of Christian order.[139]

By its very foundation Pennsylvania transformed Protestant development, for here was an entire colony rooted in the radical tradition, namely the Quakers, the most successful of the sects to emerge out of the English Civil War. Historians traditionally trace Quaker origins back to George Fox (1624–91), the son of a Leicestershire weaver from Drayton-in-the-Clay. Although a cobbler with no theological training, Fox began to preach a message of Christian comfort based on the idea of the Inner Light or Spirit. And he soon gathered followers, first in Nottinghamshire, Leicestershire, and Derbyshire, and then in Yorkshire, Lancashire, and Durham as he took his message north. Moreover, his inspired preaching attracted disciples as well. Proselytizers such as William Dewsbury, James Naylor, and James Parnel embarked on their own preaching missions on the Inner Light, the latter claiming that his words were as infallible as those of the prophets. Quaker techniques were similar to those of the early evangelicals. In order to win converts, they would interrupt sermons, shout down clergymen, hold public debates with Puritan divines, and even stage public rituals, the most infamous being Naylor's Bristol re-enactment of Christ riding into Jerusalem on the back of an ass.[140] As the number of converts grew, Quakers became the objects of sustained persecution, especially after the Restoration. Prominent leaders were fined, imprisoned, and exiled, meetings were dispersed and meetinghouses pulled down, while local parishioners, who did not much like Quaker shows of sanctity even if they could stomach their faith, smashed the windows of their homes, attacked them in the streets, or just informed on them to the authorities. One estimate has suggested that up to 15,000 men and women may have been dealt with in this way.[141] Persecution of this kind tended to lessen after the Toleration Act (1689), and indeed one sign of this was that Quakers became less zealous and more willing to compromise their principles in order to accommodate the state. Writing in 1734, Voltaire claimed this was because a less ardent generation had arisen who were happy with honors, buttons, and cuffs and were content just to call themselves Protestants. But for the first generation, there was no compromise, and consequently the history and experience of their faith was marked out by suffering and intolerance. These were the men and women encountered by William Penn.

The guiding principle of Quaker faith was the Inner Light or Spirit, an idea with obvious antecedents in the thought of medieval mystics such as Johannes Tauler and radicals such as Thomas Müntzer, and one that was integral to the religious discourse of the Interregnum: Winstanley spoke of Spirit and nature, for instance, Cromwell of Spirit and Providence. And there were scriptural proofs as well, beginning with John 1:9 ("That was the true light, which lighteth every man that cometh into the world"), a passage that captured the Quaker conviction that the Light resides within *every* man. According to Fox and his followers, the path to salvation was solely within the individual. There was no need for the ordinances and forms of the outer church or its dogmas relating to heaven, hell and salvation. The essential struggle was within, and this was the war between the gospel, that is the ways of Christ (or the Lamb), and the world, the world being anything that turned the believer away from Christ, whether the sinful nature of man or the legalistic aspects of orthodox religion. The quest for salvation thus entailed a struggle to overcome the self, and this could only be effected by turning to the Spirit and gaining an awareness of sin profound enough to destroy the bestial and carnal in man. In this process, the Light both judged and condemned, and in doing so it created new men and women whose godly conduct moved them, as Naylor put it, "nearer to God, and into his Likeness and Nature" and bound them closer together in Christian fellowship.[142]

Quaker leaders were quite open in their belief that the Spirit led human beings in the direction of perfection, that the flesh with all of its temptations could be overcome. Fox himself went so far as to describe his own conversion experience as a return to Eden through the fiery sword of Genesis where all things began anew. His was a higher state, higher than that of Adam, for it was one that could resist temptation. This was the return of the radical idea of sanctification with a vengeance, and one that raised Puritan hackles. Even the devil, wrote Richard Baxter, had less pride.[143]

It is easy to see why this teaching was considered such a threat by the mainstream Protestants, for it taught a doctrine of direct revelation open to every man and placed the Spirit, the "ingrafted Word," above Scripture and all other confessional texts. This was the voice of the German radicalism reborn, as the orthodox revealed in calling them Anabaptists and Münsterites, and the goal was nothing less than the dismantling of the magisterial system. His purpose, as Fox explained while in Leicestershire, was "to bring people off their old ways, . . . from their churches, . . . from all the world's religions, . . . from all the world's fellowships, and prayings and singings, . . . from heathenish fables, and from men's inventions and windy doctrines, . . . all their images and crosses, and sprinkling of infants, with all their holy days . . . and all their vain traditions."[144] Quaker worship, accordingly, lacked liturgical and ecclesial forms; there was no ceremony, ritual, or sermonizing. Indeed, because they bound the believer to the world, words were generally avoided. Instead, the worshippers gathered in silence and waited for the Spirit to speak directly through them. Only in this way, they believed, by searching in silence for the Inner Light and avoiding all of the "mumming and dumming" of an Anglican service, could they reach a true understanding of God. There were moments in the Quaker meetinghouse when the Spirit, through "openings" and "motions," moved individuals to speak, and there were the famous emotive gestures as well, the raised eyes, the tears, the sudden shaking and quaking (what they termed the "convincements") that marked out the Quaker form of worship. But above all there was silence, a predilection to "retire inward, and sink down into the pure stillness, and keep in the Valley."[145]

Here was a people at odds with almost all of the traditional forms of Protestant Europe. Rejecting the overuse of words in the church, they turned away from Bibles, fixed confessions, and liturgical texts to the silence within. And it was not just the sacral aspects of words, but any usage that tied the believer to the carnal realm, including insincere greetings and vain salutations. Only "Thee" and "thou" were in keeping with the Quaker idea of plain language and the honesty of a regenerated soul. They also avoided the use of oaths, not only because there was a clear biblical injunction against it, but also because it was formula designed to compensate for the lies and dishonesty of fallen man, and there was no need for that among true Christians. Plainness and sincerity also enjoined them to refuse to doff their hats, give way in the streets, or greet passers-by with the customary honorific titles – all was vanity and hypocrisy. Their clothes were basic, no lace, ribbons, cuffs, or buttons, hats with bands or skirts with bones. Sometimes they wore sackcloth – or when going naked as a sign, nothing at all. Although they did not separate from the world in the manner of the Swiss and German radicals, they encouraged one another to avoid it and remain within the Society of Friends. Becoming a Quaker might mean a total break in the personal histories of the people who joined the faith. Sons and daughters abandoned their families, townsmen and villagers abandoned their communities, parishioners abandoned their church. Moreover, given that the Inner Light begat a new creature, it also implied that individual believers had to break free of their own past and, in essence, become new people. Solomon Eccles was just such a convert. Once a respected music teacher, on becoming a Quaker he renounced his former profession and sold his spinets and viola. Still burdened by guilt, however, he bought them back and buried them in the ground.[146]

With the foundation of Pennsylvania, William Penn created a refuge for Quakers in the New World. It was not the first time that Quakers had thought of America as a possible safe haven. Small groups had been risking the passage to the Chesapeake as early as the 1650s, but most had been imprisoned, fined, exiled, put to death, pushed back to the swamps of Albemarle Sound, or shipped off to Barbados. In the 1670s, an attempt was made to create a Quaker colony in western New Jersey, with Penn himself as a trustee.[147] But nothing on the scale of Pennsylvania had ever been ventured before. It was the first attempt by radical Protestants to plant the "seed of a nation" fully within the juridical and political framework of colonial expansion in full view of Protestant Europe. Indeed, one of the reasons for the colony's rapid success was Penn's talents and energies as a promoter. Previous to the grant of the charter, he had traveled through northern Europe promoting relations between the Pietists and the Quakers. He had spent time in Frankfurt, for instance, convincing men like Johann Jakob Schütz of the need to migrate. He published advertisements in numerous languages, sent letters to friends and public figures throughout Europe, and dispatched recruiting agents to London, Dublin, Edinburgh, Rotterdam, and the Rhineland. Penn proclaimed that he was looking for men and women of "ingenious spirits" who were willing to seek freedom in Pennsylvania, living together in industrious communities in piety, sobriety, and loving neighborhood. Unlike the Puritan experiment in Massachusetts Bay, this was not projected as a temporary refuge of the true church until such time as it could be replanted back in England. Pennsylvania, the Quakers proclaimed, was conceived "not to make Colonys for her, but from her, for our Selves."[148]

Thousands of Quakers answered the call and migrated to Pennsylvania and its surrounds in the late seventeenth century. Quakers began to land en masse in the early 1680s, one estimate counting at least 90 shiploads of immigrants between 1682 and 1685. If we include the early Quaker settlers to West New Jersey, many of whom later moved to Pennsylvania, the number of new immigrants to the Delaware Valley before 1715 may have been as high as 23,000. By 1750, Quakers made up the third

largest denomination in the British Colonies, just behind Anglicans and Congregationalists. Once there, they spread out and diversified, settling throughout Pennsylvania proper but also pushing into West Jersey, north-east Maryland, through the Ohio
Valley and the southern back country. Even among the Quakers, the communities were
diverse. There were Friends from different English counties as well as Ireland, Wales,
Scotland, and Ulster.

But the exodus did not end with the Quakers. Pennsylvania became a refuge for all
kinds of "ingenious spirits," a place where all pious peoples might go in search of
freedom of conscience (or whatever freedoms they sought – political, economic,
social).[149] There was a massive influx of Lutherans and Reformed from the Rhineland
and the Palatinate, Presbyterians from Scotland and Ulster, Schwenckfelders from
Saxony, Baptists from Wales, and Labadites and Mennonites from the Dutch Republic.
In 1727 alone, five ships arrived from Rotterdam with 1,300 settlers ranging from
Dutch Mennonites, Palatine Calvinists, northern Catholics, Swedish Lutherans, and
Anglicans. One estimate has suggested up to 15,000 Rhineland Calvinists settled in
the Delaware Valley by the year 1730.[150] But again, what was really unique about the
exodus was not so much the numbers as the nature of the communities involved. This
was an exodus of the radical tradition, an opportunity for the marginalized Protestants
of England and continental Europe to develop their visions of Christian order without
having to worry about discrimination or persecution. For the orthodox back home in
England, this was exactly the type of colony both feared and ridiculed in work's like
Joseph Hall's *The Discovery of a New World* (1609) at the start of the colonial period.
Here indeed was Hall's nightmare vision of Sectarouria, the second province of
Fooliana, a land completely overrun by the radicals.[151]

Pennsylvania was Penn's holy experiment in liberal Protestantism, an attempt to
establish, and then to preserve, a religious order that enabled individuals to worship
God as they saw fit. The only conditions placed on conscience were that the colonists
recognize the monotheistic deity of Christianity, profess faith in Christ, and live
reasonably and peaceably with others. What this meant in practice, according to one
historian of American religion, was that the colony became "a populous antecedent
of America's pluralistic society."[152] From the beginning, none of the methods or means
of magisterial control was in force. Even though the Quakers dominated, there was no
state church; nor was there a fixed orthodoxy, a test for office holders, or a general
church tax. Religion was voluntary and institutional control was negligible. In such
a setting, first principles of the Reformation such as Scripture alone or the priesthood of
all believers had the power to transform whole religious communities. And since every
colonist had the right to worship free of the restraints of civil and ecclesiastical law
(within reason and basic Christian expectation), it may have seemed, as Adam Smith
remarked, that Pennsylvania had no church rule to speak of.

And yet Penn did not want to do away with order. Like the mainstream reformers
before him, he held that government was a necessary evil. As he put it in the *Frame of
Government* (1682), it was part of religion itself, sacred in its institution and in its end.
Unlike Luther and Calvin, however, he did not hold that earthly institutions could
contribute to Christian order. Only the Inner Light, if given the freedom to work within
the believer, was able to create virtuous men who could then create virtuous states.
"Governments," he wrote, "like clocks, go from the motion men give them, and as

governments are made and moved by men, so by them they are ruined too . . . Let men be good, and the government cannot be bad; if it be ill, they will cure it."[153] There was no other cure, neither for the state nor for the church, than the Inner Light itself. No dogma, no orthodoxy, no fixed liturgy or sacraments, and no seat of church governance could enforce Christian order, just the Spirit working through men and women of faith. This was Penn's remedy to the same dilemma of order faced by Luther at the start of the Reformation, and indeed Penn defined it in similar terms: "liberty without obedience is confusion, and obedience without liberty is slavery."[154] His solution to the paradox, however, was completely different in kind.

It is difficult to offer a general description of the type of Protestant communities that emerged in the Delaware Valley, for each group responded to developments in a different way. In so far as it is traceable by the historian, it does seem as if Penn's vision of a colony beyond confessional boundaries did become something of a reality. Many Protestants were willing to share churches and pastors or move from one denomination to another to take in services. In their personal lives as well, they grew accustomed to a degree of religious diversity unmatched in Europe. The domestic servants of Francis Daniel Pastorius, for instance, a Lutheran Pietist who helped to settle Germantown in Pennsylvania, included Lutherans, Catholics, Anabaptists, Anglicans, and at least one Quaker.[155] This type of embodied diversity was bound to weaken the hold of traditional orthodoxies. Penn's experiment in cross-pollination gave rise to new dialogues about Christian order and Protestant belief, and the sheer variety of possibilities meant that no single model was able to emerge triumphant out of the mix.

By way of example we might look at the community of Ephrata, a breakaway group of radical Protestants who set up a type of monastic congregation on the banks of Cocalico Creek outside of Germantown. Ephrata was founded by Conrad Beissel (1691–1768), a baker's apprentice from Germany whose spiritual journey had taken him from the Reformed faith of the Palatinate to the radical Pietism of Heidelberg and Frankfurt and eventually, after he had migrated to America, to the faith of the Dunkers (or Church of the Brethren), the spiritual descendents of the Swiss Anabaptists, many of whom had traveled to Delaware from Schwarzenau, their point of origin in Germany. Before long Beissel left the Dunkers as well, both theologically and literally: he went into the wilderness, taking up residence in the cabin of a former Mennonite preacher. There he was able to create the community of Ephrata, a monastic settlement of celibate brothers and sisters who spent their days giving proofs of their faith while contributing to the communal economy. Beissel and his followers were indicative of the syncretisms that emerged in Pennsylvania. Part Reformed, part Anabaptist, infused by the teachings of mystics like Tauler and Boehme, and inspired by the historiography of the radical Pietist Gottfried Arnold, Ephrata left little of the old order in place. The emphasis was on personal faith, inward illumination, a pious or sanctified life, and perfect fidelity to godly laws. And there was no formal confession, no creed but the gospel and the revelations of the Inner Light.[156]

The heterogeneity of religious praxis in Pennsylvania was not mirrored in its religious thought. Until the mid-eighteenth century, both the mainstream and the radical traditions remained faithful to the teachings that they had brought with them from the Old World.[157] And in truth, even with reference to praxis, much of the Old World order gradually crept back in. In political terms, although the colony had been envisioned as an example of godly order and "loving neighborhood" held together by the Inner Light, the realities of a propriety system in the hands of William Penn and his Quaker favorites was bound to give rise to tensions. Political freedoms, so tightly bound to religious freedoms, were easily transgressed in a polity that was overseen by a man such as Penn, whose providential sense of purpose prompted Algernon Sidney to say of him that he was more absolute than the Turk. It was natural for other confessions within the Quaker-dominated colony, especially the Lutherans and the Anglicans in the lower counties, to view the holy experiment as an exercise in religious absolutism, and they could even use the principles of tolerance and religious freedom in their defense. Were not the injunctions against cockfights and stage plays, the lax marriage laws, or the rejection of oaths a violation of the Anglican conscience?

But religion was not the only force pulling politics apart. Even among the Quakers themselves, spurred on by merchant interests, property grievances, and political discontent, factions evolved that divided the colony – ample proof, as one historian has remarked, of "the ingenuity of the Quaker mind in obstructing unwanted authority."[158] In religious terms, as was the case in the other colonies north and south, growing diversity and the freedom to proselytize often resulted in the closing rather than the opening of the religious mind. After an initial phase of cooperation and dialogue, many Presbyterians and Baptists fell out over theological issues and stopped sharing churches. Baptists in the Delaware Valley tightened up the relations between the various communities, while Presbyterians founded the Synod of Philadelphia in 1716, which exercised control over congregations, tested the orthodoxy of its members, controlled ordination, examined candidates, and settled local disputes. Among the Quakers, the quest for greater order eventually led to a schism after George Keith, the surveyor-general of East New Jersey, made calls for more doctrine and law and less Inner Light. In 1691 the Yearly Meeting rejected Keith's proposals, but this did not deflect him from his purpose and he continued to rail against the dominant Quaker faction, terming them hypocrites, heretics, popes, and cardinals, and condemning them for ruling over the faith in closed sessions "with their Magistratical Robes."[159]

But we should not confuse this turn to law and order with the Protestantism of confessional Europe. Too many changes had occurred for a return of that kind. Incremental steps away from established forms in the direction of heightened spiritual inwardness, individual and congregational participation, degrees of confessional relativity, and affectional piety had laid the foundations for the religious culture that would emerge with the evangelicalism of the eighteenth century. When George Whitefield landed on the Delaware coast in 1739, he was able to embark on his mission of "trafficking for the Lord" among Protestant communities that had never existed before.

Epilogue
Modern Protestants

At the start of the eighteenth century there was a general quickening of Protestant religiosity as the various strands of piety and spirituality began to feed into one another. While the Puritan and Pietist impulse effected a transformation of the magisterial churches in Europe, the radical tradition, with its stress on lived religion rather than doctrine and its notions of a less formal, more experiential, inward, and voluntary type of faith, surfaced in the public realm and, for the first time in history, became a viable alternative to the mainstream forms of Protestantism. This did not mean that Lutherans, Calvinists, or Anglicans suddenly became Anabaptists, Hutterites, or Quakers, but it did mean that there was a much greater degree of borrowing and lending and general cross-pollination between the various traditions, with the result that the Protestants at the start of the eighteenth century were markedly different in kind from the Protestants that had lived during the age of Luther, Zwingli, and Calvin. Throughout continental Europe and the British Isles, and in the New World in particular, which became the crucible for the new forms of Protestant community, it was now commonplace for pastors, regardless of confession, to preach a capacious gospel in a more emotive fashion, looking to reach the heart rather than the mind. There was a growing indifference to dogmatic distinctions and the constraints of the institutional church. And there was a greater stress on the role of the parishioners, the best testimony to this being the rise of the lay-led initiatives for spiritual renewal, from Spener's *collegia* to the voluntary societies of Protestant England. The Protestant world had been transformed.

By 1740, a revivalist impulse had spread throughout Europe and America. And it was more than just a few isolated incidents. Joined by a network of preachers, scholars, pious laymen and laywomen, activists, publicists, and missionaries, a global community of evangelical Protestants emerged that, by preaching and practicing rebirth and renewal, began to transform the nature of traditional religion while "escaping confessional control."[1] Across the confessions, there was a growing spirit of irenicism and eclecticism, and a readiness to effect what was termed a "new reformation." In large part these Protestant revivalist movements were the final, and logical, denouement of the original reformations in Wittenberg, Zurich, and Geneva. But they were also conditioned by the age. For just as Pietists, latter-day Puritans, and emergent Evangelicals

Protestants: A History from Wittenberg to Pennsylvania 1517–1740 By C. Scott Dixon
© 2010 C. Scott Dixon

were preaching rebirth, renewal, and the need to cultivate an inner faith, Enlightenment thinkers were championing reason at the expense of faith and denigrating the traditional sacral bonds of Reformation Europe. As we have seen with reference to Brandenburg-Prussia, with the increasing secularization of the public sphere and the loosening grip of confessional religion, pious Protestants were forced to take refuge in the spaces and modalities that had been created for them by the Puritans and Pietists.[2]

The timeframe of this revival varied from place to place: in some locations it ran parallel with developments in Halle, in others it followed on from earlier developments. In the duchies of Silesia, for instance, where the Catholic Habsburgs had been systematically rooting out Protestants since the mid-seventeenth century, a mass awakening took hold of the land in 1708 that led to preaching movements and revivalist meetings. The reforming impulse traveled to northern Europe as well, reaching as far as Finland, where the idea of revival won over supporters and inspired isolated parishioners to meet for group worship in houses, barns, and boats. Within the German-speaking lands, although Pietism began to lose momentum after the deaths of Spener (d.1705) and Francke (d.1727), preachers and communities kept the original vision alive. In Pomerania, there was a widespread call for repentance and conversion in 1736. In Halberstadt, parishioners met regularly for prayer meetings and open-air services in 1739. In north-west Germany, although orthodoxy still had a strong hold on public religion, Pietists were able to practice, preach, and gather followers in substantial numbers. And, finally, in the Netherlands, the original crossroads of Puritan and Pietist religiosity, a revivalist movement gathered pace throughout the 1740s that stressed the importance of inner piety in place of outward conformity. Important in this regard was the pastor Willem Schortinghuis (1700–50), a preacher of revival and reform, whose work *Christianity Resting on Inward Experience* (1740) was a clarion call for many Dutch pastors.[3]

Emblematic of the type of reformer to emerge during the revivalist surge of the early eighteenth century was Count Nikolaus Ludwig von Zinzendorf (1700–60). As a young man Zinzendorf had been drawn to the world of Protestant spirituality, and he eventually decided to settle down on his estate in Berthelsdorf and look to his soul. While there, he cultivated his interest in mysticism and the need for a deeper, active, and more personal piety. In short order, Berthelsdorf became an enclave of Pietism, with Zinzendorf fostering a culture of sermonizing, conventicles, forms of Christian charity, and social benevolence modeled on the initiatives in Halle. Zinzendorf's aim was to create a community of awakened Protestants unencumbered by the forms and formulas of confessional Lutheranism. To this end, in the early 1720s, he welcomed emigrants from Moravia and Bohemia, members of the Church of the Unity of Brethren (the Church of Comenius) to seek asylum in Berthelsdorf. Once there, they founded Herrnhut, a safe-haven for the practice of their faith. By the year 1734 over 600 religious refugees had found shelter from persecution in Moravia, Bohemia, Hungary, parts of Germany, and eastern Europe. Herrnhut became a localized experiment in the type of Protestantism projected by the preachers of revival. Parishioners were encouraged to attend Bible classes and conventicles, to sit in on sermons and discourse with the pastor, to read the devotional literature of other traditions. Emphasis was placed on the universal truths of Christianity rather than specific confessional teachings, and tolerance was touted as an ideal, both in principle and in practice.

In effect, Zinzendorf was trying to foster a revivalist movement within Lutheranism in the hope that it would lead to a general reform or awakening of the church. He envisioned reform movements taking root in each denomination, the final goal being the establishment of an ideal universal church. What is unique about Zinzendorf and the Herrnhut Moravians, and what makes them important in the Protestant story, is that they not only pursued these ideals in the relative safety of Berthelsdorf (until expelled by the Saxon government in 1736) but throughout the world. Zinzendorf and his fellow Moravians became the first Protestant missionaries, not only spreading the faith within Europe but taking their mix of Brethren religiosity and Lutheran Pietism to the corners of the globe, including North and South America, Greenland, the West Indies, East India, Egypt, and the west coast of Africa.[4]

The Herrnhut Moravians were inspirational for many reform-minded Protestants, but the main setting for the first phase of eighteenth-century revivalism was not continental Europe but the British Isles and the colonies of North America. In England, for instance, where the Glorious Revolution and the Toleration Acts of 1689 had led to a general loosening of the corporate or magisterial aspects of public religion, there was a turn towards more informal, spontaneous fellowships and religious societies that fostered lay involvement and personal forms of piety within the framework of the Anglican establishment. More Protestants were becoming active believers, not only in the sense that they were more inclined to read the Bible for themselves, but also in the way in which faith was becoming bound up with daily life. As the English hymn writer Isaac Watts (1674–1748) put it, "True Christianity, where it reigns in the heart, will make itself appear in the purity of life … The fruits of the Spirit are found in the life and the heart together … Let us never content ourselves with any exercise of lively devotions unless we feel our corrupt affections in some measure subdued thereby."[5] This sentiment, fundamental to the Puritanism and the Pietism of the previous century, was becoming the common property of all Protestants.

In Wales, this message was spread by the revivalist preachers throughout the 1730s. Howell Harris (1714–73), for instance, a lay exhorter taken by the Spirit, traveled from parish to parish gathering supporters and preaching the Word, as did Daniel Rowland (1713–90), who worked together with Harris in converting Welsh Protestants to a more inward, personal form of religion while founding religious societies to help with the cultivation of the faith. The Anglican minister Griffith Jones (1684–1761) had embarked on a similar mission, preaching to parishioners in church yards and open fields, distributing vernacular Bibles, and, uniquely, creating circulating schools that provided basic religious knowledge in the Welsh language. In England there were similar movements afoot, especially in and around London where the agents of Halle and the Moravian Brethren had planted the seeds of German Pietism. The most prominent and successful of the English revivalist preachers was George Whitefield (1714–70), the "universal gospel salesman," who became a preaching sensation in both Britain and the New World. In 1737, while waiting to embark on his preaching mission to the native Americans of Georgia, Whitefield made a name for himself by taking up an itinerant ministry and spreading the revivalist message of the need for inner religion, a change of heart, and the affective cohabitation of the Spirit with a living faith. He preached to all pious parishioners, regardless of whether they were Anglican, Presbyterian, Congregational, Baptist, or otherwise. On occasion, it was claimed, the number of people who pressed into the churches to hear him was so great that condensation accumulated on the rafters and dripped on the faithful below.[6] From 1739 to 1740, Whitefield toured the American colonies, from Charleston and Savannah to Philadelphia, New York, and Boston, preaching to crowds that numbered in the thousands.

Whitefield, like all of revivalist preachers, had his own unique approach to the faith and a somewhat idiosyncratic approach to theology, and thus it would be stretching the historical record to suggest that there was a unified reform movement in this period joined by common teaching. But there certainly were common themes and emphases, paramount being the stress on regeneration and conversion, the importance of sermons, prayer, and Bible reading, the inclination to create smaller communities and societies of the faithful beyond the framework of the institutional church, and a general disregard for the traditional theological boundaries between the Protestant confessions. Whitefield, as he reminded the clergy of Boston in 1740, was not concerned with the *type* of Protestant he reached. He was only concerned with converting souls. "It was best to preach the new birth," he said, "and the power of godliness, and not to insist so much on the form: for people would never be brought to one mind as to that; nor did Jesus Christ ever intend it."[7]

Most significant of all for the Protestant revivalist movement were the colonies of the New World. This was well-tilled ground, as we have seen, because of the diversity of religions, the predominance of radical communities, and the Puritan legacy – for we should not forget that New England congregationalism was a regenerative faith. By the 1720s, there were isolated attempts at renewal and awakening, including the efforts of the Dutch minister Theodore Frelinghuysen (1692– circa 1747), who spread his brand of Pietism throughout the Raritan River Valley of New Jersey. Within the American lands, however, the most influential theoretician of Protestant revival was Jonathan Edwards (1703–58), the pastor of Northampton in Connecticut. Edwards was a congregational Calvinist in the New England mold, but he had come to believe that the American faithful had fallen away from the faith. In his search for a remedy he became an apologist for experiential religion. Edwards organized conventicle groups for his parishioners, encouraged Bible reading, and preached the need for conversion and rebirth. Eventually, responding to the request of a London clergyman, Edwards drew together his thoughts on the Northampton experience in *A Faithful Narrative of the Surprizing Work of God in the Conversion of Many Hundred Souls in Northampton* (1737), a work that became the paradigmatic relation of the revivalist experience in the English-speaking world. With the *Faithful Narrative*, pious Protestants in America and Britain (where the work was eagerly received) now had a template for ordering their thoughts and experiences in their search for a living faith.[8]

As a consequence of the efforts of men such as Edwards and Whitefield, not to forget the many other preachers of the "divine fire"who followed in their footsteps, Protestants in America experienced what was called a "great and general awakening" beginning around the year 1740. By its very nature it was a diverse phenomenon, and yet common threads did run through the movement. Most dramatic of all was the stress it placed on the role of the individual in the quest for salvation. Its protagonists preached a new birth that was not reliant on creeds, confessions, or clergy but was a matter between the individual and the divine. The laity were accorded a much greater stake in their own salvation and a much greater stake in the church, for not only did the parishioners have more control over their own spiritual destinies, they could now play a role in the destinies of other believers as well. Many of the preachers of the great awakening were laymen and laywomen, indeed even young girls and slaves. To orthodox Protestants, this seemed to be yet another episode in the rise of radicalism, the unleashing of "secret impulses" that could only lead to chaos and disorder and the ultimate overturning of "grave and serious sett forms."[9] And indeed, that is exactly what it was, though by this stage in Protestant history it was no longer an external threat to the magisterial order but an impulse resonating from within, powerful enough to transform Protestant development. In the words of the church historian Mark Noll,

> In the more general history of American religion, the Awakening marked a transition from clerical to lay religion, from the minister as an inherited authority figure to self-empowered mobilizer, from the definition of Christianity by doctrine to its definition by piety, and from a state church encompassing all of society to a gathered church made up only of the converted.[10]

Historians have labeled the developments of the early eighteenth century as the rise of evangelicalism, or more specifically the "Evangelical Revival" in Britain and the "Great Awakening" in America. The movement tended to vary from place to place, both in terms of religious ideas and historical forms assumed. Unlike the original Protestant Reformation, further reform was not necessarily bound up with a specific confession or an institutional church but was, rather, the sum total of the disparate parts of the revivalist impulse that followed on from the teachings of the Puritans and the Pietists. Over time, the movement "acted as a solvent for hard-edged definitions of the church," though without being directed at a specific church or particular theology.[11] And while there were certainly leading figures in the different settings, it was not the creation of a single reformer or a particular corpus of belief but a widespread impulse that took on local color and local forms.

Instructive in this regard is the history of John Wesley (1703–91) and his younger brother Charles Wesley (1707–88), who are generally held to be the founders of English Methodism. Both men were early converts to the idea that the English church was in need of some sort of revival or awakening, and yet there was no single or straightforward path to the type of reform they envisioned. Born to a household immersed in Anglican spirituality, in later life both John and Charles came into close contact with the Moravians and borrowed much from their teachings, and both men derived a sense of self and a sense of mission from the writings of Francke and the Halle Pietists. They were symptomatic of the Protestantism of the age, stirring and mixing and generally unsettled. Even in his most private of recollections – for instance, the moment of his conversion – John Wesley revealed something of the unease which prompted Protestants to search for further reform from within the framework of a Protestant church. In his case, he claimed that it occurred during a visit to a meeting of the Moravians in Aldersgate Street, London,

> where one was reading Luther's preface to the *Epistle to the Romans*. About a quarter before nine, while he was describing the change which God works in the heart through faith in Christ, I felt my heart strangely warmed. I felt I did trust in Christ, Christ alone, for

salvation; and an assurance was given me, that he had taken away *my* sins, even *mine*, and saved *me* from the law of sin and death.[12]

Moved by Luther's preface to the *Epistle to the Romans*, the proof text of German Pietism, and engaged with the very same book of Scripture that had prompted Luther to question Catholic teaching, John Wesley would go on to devote his life to the making of Methodism, a profound instance of the union of the evangelical impulse with the mainstream, or magisterial, church of the confessional age. Two centuries in the making, this was one of the first historical examples of the talent for synthesis that has become a defining trait of modern Protestants.

Endnotes

Because of restrictions on space, references have been kept to a minimum, with the endnotes generally limited to those texts that have provided the foundations for my analysis and the factual details for the narratives. On those occasions where quotations from the primary materials have been taken from secondary works, I have often cited a range of page numbers to make it clear to the reader that the quotation was part of a broader analysis and that this analysis has informed my own argument. I intend to treat the literature and the historiography of early modern Protestant history in a separate work, also to be published by Wiley-Blackwell, entitled *Contesting the Reformation*.

Abbreviations

Those texts to which I make frequent reference throughout this book are abbreviated as follows:

Martin Brecht (ed.), *Geschichte des Pietismus* (Göttingen, 1993).	*GdP*
Philip Benedict, *Christ's Churches, Purely Reformed* (New Haven, 2002)	*CC*
D. Martin Luthers Werke. Kritische Gesamtausgabe (Weimar, 1883–)	*WA*
Luther's Works (St Louis and Minneapolis, 1955–86)	*LW*
Pietismus und Neuzeit	*PuN*

Introduction

1. Joseph Leo Koerner, *The Moment of Self-Portraiture in German Renaissance Art* (Chicago, 1993), 368.
2. Joseph Leo Koerner, *The Reformation of the Image* (London, 2004), 43–6; Werner Hofmann (ed.), *Luther und die Folgen für die Kunst* (Munich, 1983), 355; for the theme in Lutheran art, see Heimo Reinitzer, *Gesetz und Evangelium* (Hamburg, 2006), i, 41–70.
3. Gerhard Ebeling considered the reformers' concern with law and gospel "the foundational formula of theological understanding" in the Reformation that ultimately led to "a new departure in the history of concepts." See Gerhard

Ebeling, "Luther: Theologie," in Kurt Galling (ed.), *Die Religion in Geschichte und Gegenwart* (Tübingen, 1960), iv, 502; Gerhard Ebeling, *Word and Faith* (Philadelphia, 1963), 256; Albrecht Peters, *Gesetz und Evangelium* (Gütersloh, 1981), 29–101, here 34.

4. For the differences between Lutheran and Reformed interpretations, see the contributions in Magne Stæbø (ed.), *Hebrew Bible/Old Testament* (Göttingen, 2008), 363–451, 691–757, 905–25.

5. Ebeling, *Word and Faith*, 262; Karl Barth, *God, Grace and Gospel* (Edinburgh, 1959), 3–27.

6. Carter Lindberg, *The Third Reformation* (Macon, 1983), 43–7.

7. Gerald Strauss, *Enacting the Reformation in Germany* (Aldershot, 1993), xv, 291–306.

8. *LW*, 31: 344; *WA*, 7: 21.

9. Peter W. Williams, *America's Religions* (Urbana, 1998), 3–4.

10. There have been a number of excellent histories of the Reformation in recent years, including: Hans Hillerbrand, *The Division of Christendom* (Louisville, 2007); Philip Benedict, *Christ's Churches, Purely Reformed* (New Haven, 2002); Diarmaid MacCulloch, *Reformation* (London, 2003); Ulinka Rublack, *Reformation Europe* (Cambridge, 2005); Carter Lindberg, *The European Reformations* (Oxford, 1996); Euan Cameron, *The European Reformation* (Oxford, 1991); James D. Tracy, *Europe's Reformations, 1450–1650* (Oxford, 1999).

11. Theodore K. Rabb, *The Struggle for Stability in Early Modern Europe* (Oxford, 1975), vii.

12. William James Bouwsma, *The Waning of the Renaissance, 1550–1640* (New Haven, 2002), 20–142.

13. Compare Alister McGrath, *Christianity's Dangerous Idea* (London, 2007); William G. Naphy, *The Protestant Revolution* (London, 2007); Steven Ozment, *Protestants: The Birth of a Revolution* (London, 1992).

14. McGrath, *Christianity's Dangerous Idea*, 443.

15. Hans-Christoph Rublack, "Reformation und Moderne. Soziologische, theologische und historische Ansichten," in Hans Guggisberg and Gottfried Krodel (eds), *The Reformation in Germany and Europe* (Gütersloh, 1993), 17–38; Mary Fulbrook, *Piety and Politics* (Cambridge, 1983), 1–18.

16. See the discussion in Harm Klueting, *Das konfessionelle Zeitalter* (Darmstadt, 2007), 15–33.

17. Friedrich Wilhelm Graf, *Der Protestantismus* (Munich, 2006), 7–19; Alister E. McGrath and Darren C. Marks, "Protestantism – The Problem of Identity," in Alister E. McGrath and Darren C. Marks (eds), *The Blackwell Companion to Protestantism* (Oxford, 2004), 1–19; Martin E. Marty, *Protestantism* (London, 1972), ix–xii.

18. See the literature and debates in Lori Pearson, *Beyond Essence* (Cambridge, MA, 2008), 125–62.

19. Adolf Laube, "Radicalism as a Research Problem in the History of Early Reformation," in Hans Hillerbrand (ed.), *Radical Tendencies in the Reformation* (Kirksville, 1988), 9–23, here 10–11; and in general, Hans-Jürgen Goertz, *Pfaffenhaß und groß Geschrei* (Munich, 1987).

20. For discussions of the distinctions between the radicals and the mainstream Protestants in history and historiography, see Michael Driedger, "Anabaptism and Religious Radicalism," in Alec Ryrie (ed.), *The European Reformations* (Basingstoke, 2006), 212–31; Geoffrey Dipple, "*Just as in the Time of the Apostles*" (Kitchener, ON, 2005), 17–30; Hans-Jürgen Goertz, *Religiöse Bewegungen in der Frühen Neuzeit* (Munich, 1993), 59–107; for the categorization of the radical groupings into Anabaptists, Spiritualists, and Evangelical Rationalists, and the further divisions within these groups, see George Huntston Williams, *The Radical Reformation* (Philadelphia, 1962), xxiii–xxxi.

Foundations

1. Berndt Hamm, "Einheit und Vielfalt der Reformation – Oder: was die Reformation zur Reformation machte," in Berndt Hamm, Bernd Moeller, and Dorothea Wendebourg (eds), *Reformationstheorien* (Göttingen, 1995), 57–127.
2. Michael M. Tavuzzi, *Prierias* (London, 1997), 1–131.
3. Ernest George Schwiebert, *Luther and his Times* (St Louis, 1950), 206; Helmar Junghans, *Martin Luther und Wittenberg* (Munich, 1996), 39–64.
4. Schwiebert, *Luther and his Times*, 199–221; Maria Grossmann, *Humanism in Wittenberg*, 1485–1517 (Nieuwkoop, 1975), 1–70.
5. See now Thomas Kaufmann, *Geschichte der Reformation* (Frankfurt/Leipzig, 2009), 9–299.
6. Robert Herndon Fife, *The Revolt of Martin Luther* (New York, 1957), 225.
7. *LW*, 34: 336–7; *WA*, 54: 185–6.
8. *LW*, 34: 337; *WA*, 54: 186.
9. Berndt Hamm, "What was the Reformation Doctrine of Justification?," in C. Scott Dixon (ed.), *The German Reformation* (Oxford, 1999), 79.
10. On the debates see Bernhard Lohse, *Luthers Theologie in ihrer historischen Entwicklung und ihrem systematischen Zusammenhang* (Göttingen, 1995), 97–110.
11. Leif Grane, *Martinus Noster* (Mainz, 2000), 9–44.
12. Jens-Martin Kruse, *Universitätstheologie und Kirchenreform* (Mainz, 2002), 42–112.
13. Hans-Georg Leder, "Luthers Beziehungen zu seinen Wittenberger Freunden," in Helmar Junghans (ed.), *Leben und Werk Martin Luthers von 1526 bis 1546* (Göttingen, 1983), i, 419–40.
14. Ulinka Rublack, *Reformation Europe* (Cambridge, 2005) and Kruse, *Universitätstheologie und Kirchenreform*.
15. Rublack, *Reformation Europe*, 30–6.
16. Kruse, *Universitätstheologie und Kirchenreform*, 237.
17. Wilhelm Borth, *Die Luthersache* (Causa Lutheri) *1517–1524* (Lübeck, 1970), 38.
18. Hans J. Hillerbrand, *Reformation in its own Words* (London, 1964), 44.
19. Heiko A. Oberman, "Wittenbergs Zweifrontenkrieg gegen Prierias und Eck," *Zeitschrift für Kirchengeschichte*, 80 (1969), 333.

20. Martin Brecht (trans. James L. Schaaf), *Martin Luther* (Minneapolis, 1994), i, 200–12.

21. Karl-Heinz Zur Mühlen, *Reformatorisches Profil* (Göttingen, 1995), 187; Bernd Moeller, "Das Berühmtwerden Luthers," *Zeitschrift für historische Forschung*, 15 (1988), 65–92.

22. Ronald J. Sider, *Andreas Bodenstein von Karlstadt* (Leiden, 1974), 71.

23. Brecht, *Martin Luther*, i, 324.

24. Brecht, *Martin Luther*, i, 317–22.

25. Kruse, *Universitätstheologie und Kirchenreform*, 214; Brecht, *Martin Luther*, i, 309–26; Josef Greving, *Johann Eck als junger Gelehrter* (Münster, 1906), 87–8.

26. Grane, *Martinus Noster*, 115–7; Joseph Lortz, "Die Leipziger Disputation," *Bonner Zeitschrift für Theologie und Seelsorge*, 3 (1926), 35.

27. Thomas Fuchs, *Konfession und Gespräch* (Cologne, 1995), 155–87.

28. Hillerbrand, *Reformation*, 80–4.

29. Armin Kohnle, *Reichstag und Reformation* (Gütersloh, 2001), 50–6; Brecht, *Martin Luther*, i, 404–11.

30. Heiko A. Oberman (trans. Eileen Walliser-Schwarzbart), *Luther* (London, 1989), 39.

31. Susan Karant-Nunn, "What was Preached in German Cities in the Early Years of the Reformation? " in Phillip Bebb and Sherrin Marshall (eds), *The Process of Change in Early Modern Europe* (Athens, OH, 1988), 84; Bernd Moeller and Karl Stackmann, *Städtische Predigt in der Frühzeit der Reformation* (Göttingen, 1996), 300–46.

32. Rudolf Mau, *Evangelische Bewegung und frühe Reformation 1521 bis 1532* (Leipzig, 2000), 40–51, 74–9, 89–92.

33. Bernd Moeller (trans. H. C. Erik Midelfort and Mark U. Edwards, Jr), *Imperial Cities and the Reformation* (Philadelphia, 1972), 29.

34. Grane, *Martinus Noster*, 1–58.

35. Heinz Thomas, "Die Deutsche Nation und Martin Luther," *Historisches Jahrbuch*, 105 (1985), 426–54; Georg Schmidt, "Luther und die frühe Reformation – ein nationales Ereignis?" in Stephen E. Buckwalter and Bernd Moeller (eds), *Die frühe Reformation in Deutschland als Umbruch* (Gütersloh, 1998), 54–75.

36. A. G. Dickens, *The German Nation and Martin Luther* (London, 1974), 35.

37. Walter E. Köhler, *Luthers Schriften An den Christlichen Adel deutscher Nation im Spiegel der Kultur- und Zeitgeschichte* (Halle, 1895), 86–287.

38. Andrew Cunningham and Ole Peter Grell, *The Four Horsemen of the Apocalypse* (Cambridge, 2000), 50–1.

39. Hans Preuss, *Die Vorstellungen vom Antichrist im späteren Mittelalter* (Leipzig, 1906), 83–144; Matthias Pohlig, *Zwischen Gelehrsamkeit und konfessioneller Identitätsstiftung* (Tübingen, 2007), 86–9.

40. Peter Martin, *Martin Luther und die Bilder zur Apokalypse* (Hamburg, 1983), 104–12.

41. Philipp Schmidt, *Die Illustration der Lutherbibel: 1522–1700* (Basel, 1977), 13–28.

42. Heimo Reinitzer, *Biblia deutsch* (Hamburg, 1983), 207.

43. Herbert Wolf, *Martin Luther* (Stuttgart, 1980), 68–74; Birgit Stolt, *Martin Luthers Rhetorik des Herzens* (Tübingen, 2000), 1–41.

44. Werner Besch, *Die Rolle Luthers in der deutschen Sprachgeschichte* (Heidelberg, 1999), 17–20.

45. Lutz, "Die deutsche Nation," 546–7.

46. Besch, *Die Rolle Luthers*, 35.

47. Robert W. Scribner, *For the Sake of Simple Folk* (Oxford, 1994), 14–36; Moeller, "Das Berühmtwerden Luthers," 65–92.

48. C. Scott Dixon, "The Princely Reformation in Germany," in Andrew Pettegree (ed.), *The Reformation World* (London, 2000), 146–68, here 155–6.

49. Eike Wolgast, "Die deutschen Territorialfürsten und die frühe Reformation," in Buckwalter and Moeller, *Die frühe Reformation*, 407–34.

50. Theodore G. Tappert (ed.), *The Book of Concord* (Philadelphia, 1959), 25.

51. G. R. Potter, *Zwingli* (Cambridge, 1978), 1–46, 111.

52. Much of the following discussion is based on Bruce Gordon, *The Swiss Reformation* (Manchester, 2002), 46–85.

53. Robert C. Walton, *Zwingli's Theocracy* (Toronto, 1967), 77.

54. Benedict, *CC*, 19–32.

55. Heiko A. Oberman, *Werden und Wertung der Reformation* (Tübingen, 1977), 237–303.

56. Gottfried Locher, *Die Zwinglische Reformation im Rahmen der europäischen Kirchengeschichte* (Göttingen, 1979), 83–122, here 15.

57. Oskar Vasella, *Reform und Reformation in der Schweiz* (Münster, 1958), 49–71.

58. C. Arnold Snyder, "Word and Power in Reformation Zurich," *Archiv für Reformationsgeschichte*, 8 (1990), 263–85, here 269.

59. On this theme, see Berndt Hamm, *Zwinglis Reformation der Freiheit* (Neukirchen-Vluyn, 1988), 2–99; Christoph Dahling-Sander, *Zur Freiheit befreit* (Frankfurt, 2003), 100–71.

60. Martin Sallmann, *Zwischen Gott und Mensch* (Tübingen, 1999), 198–226; Hamm, *Zwinglis Reformation*, 83–97.

61. Peter Blickle (trans. Thomas Dunlap), *Communal Reformation* (London, 1992), 12–25, 99–103, 131–6; Locher, *Die Zwinglische Reformation*, 226–35.

62. Gordon, *Swiss Reformation*, 6–45.

63. Thomas Maissen, *Die Geburt der Republik* (Göttingen, 2006), 299–303.

64. Gordon, *Swiss Reformation*, 6–45; Locher, *Die Zwinglische Reformation*, 452–501.

65. Gordon, *Swiss Reformation*, 139.

66. On this theme, see Dorothea Wendebourg, *Essen zum Gedächtnis* (Tübingen, 2009); Lee Palmer Wandel, *The Eucharist in the Reformation* (Cambridge, 2006); Cameron, *The European Reformation* (Oxford, 1991), 161–6.

67. Gottfried Locher, *Zwingli's Thought* (Leiden, 1981), 223.

68. Wandel, *Eucharist*, 46–93.

69. Moeller and Stackmann, *Städtische Predigt*, 281–340.

70. Blickle, *Communal Reformation*, 98–110; Franziska Conrad, *Reformation in der bäuerlichen Gesellschaft* (Stuttgart, 1984), 97–9.

71. Blickle, *Communal Reformation*, 12–53.
72. Peter Blickle, *Der Bauernkrieg* (Munich, 1998), 41–103.
73. Peter Blickle (trans. Thomas A. Brady and H. C. Erik Midelfort), *The Revolution of 1525* (Baltimore, 1981), 185.
74. Thomas Hohenberger, *Lutherische Rechtfertigungslehre in den reformatorischen Flugschriften der Jahre 1521–22* (Tübingen, 1996), 199–235.
75. Gerd Haendler, *Amt und Gemeinde bei Luther im Kontext der Kirchengeschichte* (Stuttgart, 1979), 35–42.
76. C. Scott Dixon, *The Reformation in Germany* (Oxford, 2002), 77–8.
77. Blickle, *Communal Reformation*, 12–53; Conrad, *Reformation*, 91–7.
78. Michael G. Baylor, *The Radical Reformation* (Cambridge, 1991), 232.
79. James M. Stayer, The *German Peasants' War and Anabaptist Community of Goods* (Montreal, 1991), 45–60; Baylor, *Radical Reformation*, 103; Blickle, *Der Bauernkrieg*, 35–69.
80. Bernd Moeller, "Die Rezeption Luthers in der frühen Reformation," in Hamm, Moeller, Wendebourg, *Reformationstheorien*, 9–29.
81. J. Samuel Preus, *Carlstadt's Ordinaciones and Luther's Liberty* (Cambridge, MA, 1974), 85; Haendler, *Amt und Gemeinde bei Luther*, 50–9.
82. W. P. Stephens, *The Theology of Huldrych Zwingli* (Oxford, 1986), 260–70, at 270.
83. Ernst Troeltsch (trans. Olive Wyon), *The Social Teaching of the Christian Churches* (Louisville, 1992), ii, 469–515, at 479.
84. See Günther Wartenburg, *Wittenberger Reformation und territoriale Politik* (Leipzig, 2003).
85. Karl Burckhardt, *Geschichte der sächsischen Kirchen- und Schulvisitation von 1524 bis 1545* (Leipzig, 1879), 1–39.
86. Tom Scott and Bob Scribner, *The German Peasants' War* (London, 1991), 330–1.
87. C. Scott Dixon, *The Reformation and Rural Society* (Cambridge, 1996), 26–32.
88. Susan Karant-Nunn, *The Reformation of Ritual* (London, 1997), 192.
89. Compare John Bossy, *Christianity in the West, 1400–1700* (Oxford, 1985), 11, 91–104, 115–26.
90. Günther Franz, *Der deutsche Bauernkrieg* (Munich, 1933), 87.
91. Matthew C. Harrison, "Liturgical Uniformity and Church Polity in the Augustana and the Formula of Concord: The Church Orders as Hermeneutical Key," *Lutheran Theological Journal*, 36 (2002), 71–83.
92. Tappert, *Book of Concord*, 460.
93. Luise Schorn-Schütte, *Evangelische Geistlichkeit in der Frühneuzeit* (Gütersloh, 1996), 20–40, 390–429; Thomas Kaufmann, *Universität und lutherische Konfessionalisierung* (Gütersloh, 1997), 178–232.
94. See Frank Fätkenheuer, *Lebenswelt und Religion* (Göttingen, 2004), 195–298.
95. Gordon Rupp, *Patterns of Reformation* (Philadelphia, 1969), 138.
96. Baylor, *Radical Reformation*, 73.
97. Hans-Jürgen Goertz, "Karlstadt, Müntzer and the Reformation of the Commoners, 1521–1525," in John D. Roth and James M. Stayer (eds), *A Companion to Anabaptism and Spiritualism, 1521–1700* (Leiden, 2007), 5–20.

98. Günter Vogler, "Reformation als Alternative – Alternativen der Reformation. Eine Einleitung," in Günter Vogler, *Wegscheiden der Reformation* (Weimar, 1994), 11–18; Rupp, *Patterns of Reformation*, 273.

99. Tom Scott, *Thomas Müntzer* (New York, 1989), 60; Richard van Dülmen, *Reformation als Revolution* (Munich, 1977), 39–55.

100. Baylor, *Radical Reformation*, 11–32; Hans-Jürgen Goertz, *Ende der Welt und Beginn der Neuzeit* (Mühlhausen, 2002), 13–15.

101. George Huntston Williams, *The Radical Reformation* (Philadelphia, 1962), 96.

102. Gordon, *Swiss Reformation*, 191–201; Werner O. Packull, *Hutterite Beginnings* (Baltimore, 1995), 15–32, 21; Williams, *Radical Reformation*, 185–93.

103. Andrea Strübind, *Eifriger als Zwingli* (Berlin, 2003), 131–46.

104. Franklin H. Littell, *The Anabaptist View of the Church* (Boston, 1958), 1–45, here 19.

105. Geoffrey Dipple, "*Just as in the Time of the Apostles*" (Kitchener, Ont., 2005), 63–116.

106. Claire Gantet, "Dreams, Standards of Knowledge and Orthodoxy in Germany in the Sixteenth Century," in Randolph C. Head and Daniel Christensen (eds), *Orthodoxies and Heterodoxies in Early Modern German Culture* (Leiden, 2007), 78–9.

107. Hans-Jürgen Goertz (trans. Trevor Johnson), *The Anabaptists* (London, 1996), 50.

108. Heinz Schilling, "Alternative Konzepte der Reformation und Zwang zur lutherischen Identität," in Vogler, *Wegscheiden der Reformation*, 277–308; Hans-Jürgen Goertz, "Eine 'bewegte' Epoche. Zur Heterogenität reformatorischer Bewegungen," in Vogler, *Wegscheiden der Reformation*, 23–56.

109. Packull, *Hutterite Beginnings*, 43–5; Fritz Blanke, *Brüder in Christo* (Zurich, 1955), 21–55.

110. James Martin Estes, *Peace, Order and the Glory of God* (Leiden, 2005), 190.

111. Paul Wappler, *Inquisition und Ketzerprozesse in Zwickau zur Reformationszeit* (Leipzig, 1908), 1–69, 85–95, 61; Troeltsch, *Social Teaching*, ii, 493.

112. Goertz, *The Anabaptists*, 127–8.

113. Norman Cohn, *The Pursuit of the Millennium* (London, 1970), 272; Albert Fredrik Mellink, *De wederdopers in de noordelijke Nederlanden 1533–41* (Groningen, 1954), 25–38.

114. Karl Heinz Becker, *Die Reformation und das "Reich Christi zu Münster" 1535* (Munich, 1939), 29–34.

115. Ernst Laubach, 'Das Täuferreich zu Münster in seiner Wirkung auf die Nachwelt,' *Westfälische Geschichte*, 141 (1991), 123–50.

116. Bruce Gordon, *Calvin* (New Haven, 2009), 1–47; Alister E. McGrath, *A Life of John Calvin* (Oxford, 1990), 21–78.

117. William J. Bouwsma, *John Calvin* (Oxford, 1988), 32–65, here 34.

118. Bouwsma, *John Calvin*, 24.

119. Bouwsma, *John Calvin*, 46–7.

120. Gordon, *Calvin*, 64–5.

121. Jean-Luc Mouton, *Calvin* (Paris, 2009), 223–30.

122. William G. Naphy, *The Protestant Revolution* (London, 2007), 73.
123. See William G. Naphy, *Calvin and the Consolidation of the Genevan Reformation* (Manchester, 1994).
124. Randall C. Zachman, *John Calvin as Teacher, Pastor and Theologian* (Grand Rapids, 2006), 231–42; Randall C. Zachman, "John Calvin," in Justin S. Holcomb (ed.), *Christian Theologies of Scripture* (New York, 2006), 114–33.
125. Richard A. Muller, *The Unaccommodated Calvin* (Oxford, 2000), 101–39.
126. Bouwsma, *John Calvin*, 219.
127. Felix Emil Held, *Christianopolis* (London, 1916), 27–8.
128. E. William Monter, *Calvin's Geneva* (New York, 1967), 125–43, here 137.
129. John Witte Jr and Robert M. Kingdon, *Sex, Marriage, and Family in John Calvin's Geneva* (Grand Rapids, 2005), 62–79, 70.
130. Michael F. Graham, *The Uses of Reform* (Leiden, 1996), 4–27, here 22.
131. Benedict, *CC*, 460–89; Graeme Murdock, *Beyond Calvin* (Basingstoke, 2004), 76–101; Diarmaid MacCulloch, *Reformation* (London, 2003), 591–607.
132. Paul Helm, *John Calvin's Ideas* (Oxford, 2004), 93–128, here 106; Christian Link, *Prädestination und Erwählung* (Neukirchen-Vluyn, 2009), 33–96.
133. William R. Stevenson, *Sovereign Grace* (Oxford, 2007), 59–86, 105–48, here 122, 64, 120.
134. Alexandra Walsham, *Providence in Early Modern England* (Oxford, 1999), 2–3.
135. Werner Schenck, *The Concern for Social Justice in the Puritan Revolution* (London, 1948), 26.
136. See Denis Crouzet, *La genèse de la réforme Française, 1520–1562* (Paris, 1996), 266–83; Michael Walzer, *The Revolution of the Saints* (London, 1965), 231, 256–8.
137. Benedict, *CC*, 49–114; MacCulloch, *Reformation*, 237–69.
138. Murdock, *Beyond Calvin*, 31–53, here 34.
139. Heiko Oberman, *The Two Reformations* (New Haven, 2003), 111–16.
140. Benedict, *CC*, 281–91.
141. Benedict, *CC*, 125–51; Crouzet, *La genèse*, 452–6.
142. The following is based on Keith C. Robbins, *City on the Ocean Sea* (Leiden, 1997), 107–83; Judith Pugh Mayer, *Reformation in La Rochelle* (Geneva, 1996), 71–138.
143. Graeme Murdock, *Calvinism on the Frontier 1600–1660* (Oxford, 2000), 11–45, 46–76, here 53–4.

Kingdoms

1. Wolfgang Reinhard, "Die lateinische Variante von Religion und ihre Bedeutung für die politische Kultur Europas," *Saeculum*, 43 (1992), 250.
2. William D. J. Cargill Thompson, *The Political Thought of Martin Luther* (Brighton, 1984), 16–35; Gustav Törnvall, *Geistliches und weltliches Regiment bei Luther* (Munich, 1947), 69–116.
3. Ralph Keen, *Divine and Human Authority in Reformation Thought* (Nieuwkoop, 1997), 121–2.

4. *LW*, 44: 127; *WA*, 6: 407.
5. *LW*, 44: 130; *WA*, 6: 409.
6. *LW*, 44: 136–7; *WA*, 6: 413–15.
7. John Witte, *Law and Protestantism* (Cambridge, 2002), 5–23, 87–117; Volker Mantey, *Zwei Schwerter – zwei Reiche* (Tübingen, 2005); Cargill Thompson, *Political Thought*, 36–61; Hans Joachim Gänßler, *Evangelium und weltliches Schwert* (Wiesbaden, 1983), 52–124.
8. Steven Ozment, *Protestants: The Birth of a Revolution* (London, 1992), 128.
9. Joshua Mitchell, *Not by Reason Alone* (Chicago, 1993), 19–45, 39.
10. Gottfried Hammann, *Entre la secte et la cité* (Geneva, 1984), 103–72.
11. Martin Greschat, "The Relation between Church and Civil Community in Bucer's Reforming Work," in D. F. Wright (ed.), *Martin Bucer* (Cambridge, 1994), 31.
12. Max Weber, *The Protestant Ethic and the "Spirit" of Capitalism* (Harmondsworth, 2002), 75.
13. Greschat, "Church and Civil Community," 17.
14. Andreas Gäumann, *Reich Christi und Obrigkeit* (Bern, 2001), 159–243.
15. Constantin Hopf, *Martin Bucer and the English Reformation* (Oxford, 1946), 99–130.
16. Wilhelm Pauck, *Das Reich Gottes auf Erden* (Berlin, 1928), 1–67; Gäumann, *Reich Christi und Obrigkeit*, 131–256.
17. Euan Cameron, *The European Reformation* (Oxford, 1991), 210–66; Olaf Mörke, *Die Reformation* (Munich, 2005), 93–100.
18. Eberhard Isenmann, "Norms and Values in the European City, 1300–1800," in Peter Blickle (ed.), *Resistance, Representation and Community* (Oxford, 1997), 185–213.
19. Bernd Moeller (trans. H. C. Erik Midelfort and Mark U. Edwards, Jr), *Imperial Cities and the Reformation* (Philadelphia, 1972), 41–115; Peter Blickle, *Die Reformation im Reich* (Munich, 1992), 87–105.
20. Peer Friess, "Die Bedeutung der Stadtschreiber für die Reformation der süddeutschen Reichsstädte," *Archiv für Reformationsgeschichte*, 89 (1998), 96–124.
21. Thomas A. Brady Jr, *Ruling Class, Regime, and Reformation at Strasbourg: 1520–1555* (Leiden, 1978), 199–235.
22. Brady, *Ruling Class*, 215–38, 218.
23. Eberhard Isenmann, *Die deutsche Stadt im Spätmittelalter: 1250–1500* (Stuttgart, 1988), 146–221.
24. Tilman Schröder, *Das Kirchenregiment der Reichsstadt Esslingen* (Esslingen, 1987), 222–360; Cameron, *European Reformation*, 246–61.
25. Thomas A. Brady Jr, "In Search of the Godly City," R. Po-Chia Hsia (ed.), *The German People and the Reformation* (Ithaca, 1988), 14–31; Berndt Hamm, *Bürgertum und Glaube* (Göttingen, 1996), 51–140.
26. Hamm, *Bürgertum und Glaube*, 143–78; Gunter Zimmermann, *Prediger der Freiheit* (Mannheim, 1999), 171.
27. Gerald Strauss, "Protestant Dogma and City Government: The Case of Nuremberg," *Past and Present*, 36 (1967), 46.

28. Kristin Eldyss Sorensen Zapalac, *In His Image and Likeness* (Ithaca, 1990), 27–91; Stephan Albrecht, "Gute Herrschaft – Fürstengleich. Städtisches Selbstverständnis im Spiegel der neuzeitlichen Rathausikonographie," in Heinz Schilling, Werner Heun, and Jutta Götzmann (eds), *Heiliges Römisches Reich Deutscher Nation* (Dresden, 2006), ii, 206–9.

29. Susan Tipton, *Res publica bene ordinata* (Hildesheim, 1996), 131–57.

30. Schorn-Schütte, *Evangelische Geistlichkeit*, 390–433.

31. W. P. Stephens, *The Theology of Huldrych Zwingli* (Oxford, 1986), 306–8, here 308.

32. Christine Kooi, *Liberty and Religion* (Leiden, 2000), 12.

33. Joke Spaans, *Haarlem na de Reformatie* ('s-Gravenhage, 1989), 128–39; the idea of "a-confessional" comes from Benjamin J. Kaplan, *Calvinists and Libertines* (Oxford, 1995), 291–4.

34. First coined by A. G. Dickens, *The German Nation and Martin Luther* (London, 1974), 182.

35. Denis Crouzet, *La genèse de la réforme Française, 1520–1562* (Paris, 1996), 523–31.

36. Benedict, *CC*, 22.

37. Stephens, *Theology of Huldrych Zwingli*, 307–8.

38. Gottfried W. Locher, *Zwingli's Thought* (Leiden, 1981), 3.

39. Heiko A, Oberman, *Werden und Wertung der Reformation* (Tübingen, 1977), 237–95.

40. Oliver Bangerter, *La pensée militaire de Zwingli* (Bern, 2003), 38–64.

41. Benedict, *CC*, 25; Bruce Gordon, *The Swiss Reformation* (Manchester, 2002), 59–61, 75–81.

42. Brigitte Brockelmann, *Das Corpus Christianum bei Zwingli* (Breslau, 1938), 5–64; Berndt Hamm, *Zwinglis Reformation der Freiheit* (Neukirchen-Vluyn, 1988), 114–16.

43. Robert C. Walton, *Zwingli's Theocracy* (Toronto, 1967), 115.

44. Benedict, *CC*, 29–32.

45. J. Wayne Baker, *Heinrich Bullinger and the Covenant* (Athens, OH, 1980), 107–40, here 116.

46. Benedict, *CC*, 49–65, here 55; Gordon, *Swiss Reformation*, 228–60.

47. James Martin Estes, *Peace, Order and the Glory of God* (Leiden, 2005), 53–133.

48. Francis Oakley, "Christian Obedience and Authority, 1520–1550," in J. H. Burns (ed.), *The Cambridge History of Political Thought 1450–1700* (Cambridge, 1991), 160–92, here 174.

49. Oakley, "Christian Obedience", 174.

50. See Axel Gotthard, *Der Augsburger Religionsfrieden* (Münster, 2004).

51. Witte, *Law and Protestantism*, 53–105.

52. The following discussion is based on the chapters by Ole Peter Grell, Martin Schwarz Lausten, and Thorkild Lyby in Grell (ed.), *The Scandinavian Reformation* (Cambridge, 1995).

53. Martin Schwarz Lausten, "König und Kirche. Über das Verhältnis der weltlichen Obrigkeit zur Kirche bei Johann Bugenhagen und König Christian III von

Dänemark," in Hans-Georg Leder (ed.), *Johannes Bugenhagen* (Berlin, 1984), 154.

54. Schwarz Lausten, "König und Kirche," 156–8; Grell, *Scandinavian Reformation*, 141–3.

55. The following paragraph is based on C. Scott Dixon, "The Politics of Law and Gospel," in Bridget Heal and Ole Peter Grell (eds), *The Impact of the European Reformation* (Aldershot, 2008), 37–62.

56. Schwarz Lausten, "König und Kirche," 150–6.

57. Paul Kléber Monod, *The Power of Kings* (New Haven, 1999), 96–103.

58. Harro Höpfl, *The Christian Polity of John Calvin* (Cambridge, 1982), 152–71; Denis Müller, *Jean Calvin* (Paris, 2001), 42–6.

59. William J. Bouwsma, *John Calvin* (Oxford, 1988), 204–13, here 212–13.

60. Ruth Wesel-Roth, *Thomas Erastus* (Lahr/Baden, 1954), 90–125.

61. Benedict, *CC*, 202–29; Heinz Schilling, *Religion, Political Culture, and the Emergence of Early Modern Society* (Leiden, 1992), 247–301.

62. Thomas Klein, *Der Kampf um die zweite Reformation in Kursachsen 1586–91* (Cologne, 1962), 98; Volker Press, *Calvinismus und Territorialstaat* (Stuttgart, 1970), 181–266.

63. Eike Wolgast, *Reformierte Konfession und Politik im 16. Jahrhundert* (Heidelberg, 1998), 33–64.

64. Henry Cohn, "The Territorial Princes in Germany's Second Reformation, 1559–1622," in Menna Prestwich (ed.), *International Calvinism, 1541–1715* (Oxford, 1985), 135–65, here 151; Paul Münch, *Zucht und Ordnung* (Stuttgart, 1978), 125–62.

65. Benedict, *CC*, 220; Kaspar von Greyerz (trans. Thomas Dunlap), *Religion and Culture in Early Modern Europe* (Oxford, 2007), 69–77.

66. James D. Tracy, "Public Church, *Gemeente Christi*, or *Volkskerk*: Holland's Reformed Church in Civil and Ecclesiastical Perspective," in Hans Guggisberg and Gottfried Krodel (eds), *The Reformation in Germany and Europe* (Gütersloh, 1993), 487–510.

67. Andrew Pettegree, "Coming to Terms with Victory: The Upbuilding of a Calvinist Church in Holland 1572–90," in Andrew Pettegree, Alistair Duke and Gillian Lewis (eds), *Calvinism in Europe 1540–1620* (Cambridge, 1994), 160–80, here 172, no. 58.

68. John Calvin (trans. Ford Lewis Battles), *Institutes of the Christian Religion* (London, 1960), i, 847.

69. Eike Wolgast, *Die Religionsfrage als Problem des Widerstandsrechts im 16. Jahrhundert* (Heidelberg, 1980), 9.

70. Quentin Skinner, *The Foundations of Modern Political Thought* (Cambridge, 1978), ii, 189–225; Robert von Friedeburg, *Self-Defence and Religious Strife in Early Modern Europe* (Aldershot, 2002), 37–90; Wolgast, *Die Religionsfrage*, 9–27.

71. Skinner, *Foundations,* ii, 205, 202.

72. Friedeburg, *Self-Defence and Religious Strife*, 56–90.

73. Thomas Kaufmann, *Das Ende der Reformation* (Tübingen, 2003), 192.

74. Michael Walzer, *The Revolution of the Saints* (London, 1965), 112; Graeme Murdock, *Beyond Calvin* (Basingstoke, 2004), 61.

75. Robert M. Kingdon, "Calvinism and Resistance Theory, 1550–1580," in Burns, *Cambridge History of Political Thought*, 194–200; Roger A. Mason, *Kingship and the Commonweal* (East Linton, 1998), 139–64.

76. Skinner, *Foundations*, ii, 228, 235–6.

77. Donald R. Kelley, *The Beginnings of Ideology* (Cambridge, 1981), 309.

78. Kelley, *Beginnings of Ideology*, 293–5; Skinner, *Foundations*, ii, 310–14; Ralph E. Giesey, "The Monarchomach Triumvirs: Hotman, Beza and Mornay," *Bibliothèque d'Humanisme et Renaissance*, 32 (1970), 46; Murdock, *Beyond Calvin*, 58–9; for the full range of public discourse, see Denis Crouzet, *Les guerriers de Dieu* (Seyssel, 1990), i, 495–637; ii, 186–236.

79. See the discussion on authorship in Hugues Daussy, *Les Huguenots et le Roi* (Geneva, 2002), 229–56.

80. Giesey, "The Monarchomach Triumvirs," 49–56; Skinner, *Foundations*, ii, 325–35.

81. See Denis Crouzet, "Calvinism and the Uses of the Political and the Religious (France, ca. 1560–ca. 1572)," in Philip Benedict (ed.), *Reformation, Revolt and Civil War in France and the Netherlands, 1555–1585* (Amsterdam, 1999), 99–114.

82. George Garnett (ed.), *Vindiciae, contra tyrannos* (Cambridge, 1994), 30.

83. Anne McLaren, "Rethinking Republicanism: *Vindiciae, contra tyrannos* in Context," *The Historical Journal*, 49 (2006), 23–52; Daussy, *Les Huguenots et le Roi*, 230–3; Kathleen A., Parrow, *From Defence to Resistance* (Philadelphia, 1993), 38–47, here 40.

84. Crouzet, *Les guerriers de Dieu*, i, 507–10.

85. Penny Roberts, "Huguenot Petitioning during the Wars of Religion" in Raymond A. Mentzer and Andrew Spicer (eds), *Society and Culture in the Huguenot World 1599–1685* (Cambridge, 2002), 62–77.

86. Crouzet, "Calvinism," 100–2.

87. Crouzet, *La genèse*, 470–3.

88. Elisabeth Labrousse, *Conscience et conviction* (Paris, 1996), 71–95.

89. Mason, *Kingship and the Commonweal*, 139–55, here 149.

90. Benedict, *CC*, 159.

91. Anthony D. Smith, *Chosen Peoples* (Oxford, 2003), 1–130; Jason A. Nice, "'The Peculiar Place of God:' Early Modern Representations of England and France,' *English Historical Review*, 493 (2006), 1002–18.

92. Alain Tallon, *Conscience nationale et sentiment religieux en France au XVIe siècle* (Paris, 2002), 27–53.

93. Smith, *Chosen Peoples*, 122.

94. Ulinka Rublack, *Reformation Europe* (Cambridge, 2005), 164–7; Helen Watanabe-O'Kelly, *Court Culture in Dresden* (Basingstoke, 2002), 5–36.

95. Carl C. Christensen, *Princes and Propaganda* (Kirksville, 1992), 92–101.

96. Patrick Collinson, *The Birthpangs of Protestant England* (Basingstoke, 1988), 5.

97. Jeffrey Knapp, *An Empire Nowhere* (Berkeley, 1992), 62–105; Richard Helgerson, *Forms of Nationhood* (Chicago, 1992), 254–68.

98. Simon Schama, *The Embarrassment of Riches* (New York, 1987), 51–125; for the longevity of the discourse, see Roelof Bisschop, *Sions vorst en volk* (Veenendaal, 1993).

99. Graeme Murdock, "Magyar Judah: Contructing a New Canaan in Eastern Europe," in R. N. Swanson (ed.), *The Holy Land, Holy Lands, and Christian History* (Woodbridge, 2000), 270.

100. Schama, *Embarrassment of Riches*, 98; Hendrik Smitskamp, *Calvinistisch nationaal besef in Nederland voor het midden der 17 de eeuw* ('s-Gravenhage 1947), 1–19.

101. Gerrit Groenhuis, *De predikanten* (Groningen, 1977), 89–90.

102. Schama, *Embarrassment of Riches*, 98.

103. Collinson, *Birthpangs*, 17; Smith, *Chosen Peoples*, 54–94.

104. Alexandra Walsham, Providence in Early Modern England (Oxford, 1999), 289.

105. Knapp, *An Empire Nowhere*, 68–70.

106. Walsham, *Providence*, 323.

107. William S. Maltby, *The Black Legend in England* (Durham, 1971), 30; Helgerson, *Forms of Nationhood*, 181–91.

108. Carol Z. Wiener, "The Beleaguered Isle: A Study of Elizabethan and Early Jacobean Anti-Catholicism," *Past and Present*, 51 (1971), 43–5.

109. See Peter Lake, "The Significance of the Elizabethan Identification of the Pope as Antichrist," *Journal of Ecclesiastical History*, 31 (1980), 168–9.

110. Patrick Collinson, "John Foxe and National Consciousness," in Christopher Highley and John N. King (eds), *John Foxe and his World* (Aldershot, 2002), 10–34; Murdock, *Beyond Calvin*, 120; Collinson, *Birthpangs*, 21–5; Walsham, *Providence*, 302.

Communities

1. Roland Bainton, "The Parable of the Tares as the Proof Text for Religious Liberty to the End of the Sixteenth Century," *Church History*, 1 (1932), 67–9.

2. On this theme in general, see Claus Bernet, *Gebaute Apokalypse* (Mainz, 2007).

3. Susan Groag Bell, "Johann Eberlin von Günzburg's *Wolfaria*: The First Protestant Utopia," *Church History*, 36 (1967), 122–39; Geofffrey Dipple, *Antifraternalism and Anticlericalism in the German Reformation* (Aldershot, 1996), 37–93; for doubts about the Protestant nature of Wolfaria, see Christian Peters, *Johann Eberlin von Günzburg, ca. 1465–1533* (Gütersloh, 1994), 16–51.

4. *Sämtliche Schriften. Johann Eberlin von Günzburg* (Ludwig Enders, ed.) (Halle, 1896), i, 117.

5. Bernet, *Gebaute Apokalypse*, 166–215; Richard van Dülmen, *Die Utopie einer christlichen Gesellschaft* (Stuttgart, 1978), 143–77.

6. Johann Valentin Andreae (trans. and ed. Edward H. Thompson), *Christianopolis* (Dordrecht, 1999), 142–282, 218; Christoph Neeb, *Christlicher Haß wider die Welt* (Bern, 1999), 129–57.

7. Andreae, *Christianopolis*, 234.

8. Andreae, *Christianopolis*, 281.

9. Ferdinand Seibt, *Utopica* (Munich, 2001), 82–104.
10. Hans-Jürgen Goertz, "Radical Religiosity in the German Reformation," in R. Po-Chia Hsia (ed.), *A Companion to the Reformation World* (Oxford, 2004), 77.
11. Michael G. Baylor, *The Radical Reformation* (Cambridge, 1991), 210–25; Carola Schelle-Wolff, *Zwischen Erwartung und Aufruhr* (Frankfurt/Bern, 1996), 133–299.
12. Hans-Jürgen Goertz, *Ende der Welt und Beginn der Neuzeit* (Mühlhausen, 2002), 9.
13. Roland Grahay, "L'Utopia pratiquée des Anabaptistes," in Jacques Marx (ed.), *D'Erasme à Campanella* (Paris, 1985), 119–31.
14. Bob Scribner, "Practical Utopias: Pre-modern Communism and the Reformation," *Comparative Studies in Society and History*, 36 (1994), 756.
15. C. Arnold Snyder, "The Birth and Evolution of Swiss Anabaptism, 1520–1530," *The Mennonite Quarterly Review*, 80 (2006), 532; Hans-Georg Tanneberger, *Die Vorstellung der Täufer von der Rechtfertigung des Menschen* (Stuttgart, 1999), 32–76.
16. For the points of separation, see the concluding articles in Anselm Schubert, Astrid von Schlachta, and Michael Driedger (eds), *Grenzen des Täufertums* (Gütersloh, 2009), 395–416.
17. Bruce Gordon, *The Swiss Reformation* (Manchester, 2002), 193.
18. Werner O. Packull, *Hutterite Beginnings* (Baltimore, 1995), 30.
19. Steven Ozment, *The Age of Reform* (New Haven, 1981), 342. I have included Ozment's interpolations.
20. Carter Lindberg, *The Third Reformation* (Macon, 1983), 55–130.
21. Rufus Matthew Jones, *Spiritual Reformers in the Sixteenth and Seventeenth Centuries* (London, 1914), 49.
22. Thomas Kaufmann, "Nahe Fremde – Aspekte der Wahrnehmung der 'Schwärmer' im frühneuzeitlichen Luthertum," in Kaspar von Greyerz *et al.* (eds), *Interkonfessionalität – Transkonfessionalität – binnenkonfessionelle Pluralität* (Gütersloh, 2003), 182–5.
23. Claire Gantet, "Dreams, Standards of Knowledge and Orthodoxy in Germany in the Sixteenth Century," in Randolph C. Head and Daniel Christensen (eds), *Orthodoxies and Heterodoxies in Early Modern German Culture* (Leiden, 2007), 78–84.
24. Martin Brecht, "Das Aufkommen der neuen Frömmigkeitsbewegung in Deutschland," *GdP*, i, 113–30; Emmet McLaughlin, "Spiritualism: Schwenckfeld and Franck and their Early Modern Resonances," in Roth and Stayer, *Companion*, 119–61; Diarmaid MacCulloch, *Reformation* (London, 2003), 182–9.
25. Ekkehart Schraepler, *Die rechtliche Behandlung der Täufer in der deutschen Schweiz, Südwestdeutschland und Hessen 1525–1618* (Tübingen, 1957), 30–104.
26. Sigrun Haude, "Anabaptism," in Andrew Pettegree (ed.), *The Reformation World* (London, 2000), 250.
27. Kaufmann, "Nahe Fremde," 179–205, here 204.
28. Theodore G. Tappert (ed.), *The Book of Concord* (Philadelphia, 1959), 498.

29. James M. Stayer, The *German Peasants' War and Anabaptist Community of Goods* (Montreal, 1991), 61–92, 107–22; Gottfried Seebass, *Müntzers Erbe* (Gütersloh, 2002), 161–280.

30. Andrea Strübind, *Eifriger als Zwingli* (Berlin, 2003), 203–470; Gordon, *Swiss Reformation*, 191–227; George Huntston Williams, *The Radical Reformation* (Philadelphia, 1962), 212–45.

31. Packull, *Hutterite Beginnings*, 63; Snyder, "Birth and Evolution of Swiss Anabaptism," 623–9.

32. The encyclopedic overview remains Williams, *Radical Reformation*.

33. Williams, *Radical Reformation*, 1068–9; Packull, *Hutterite Beginnings*, 55.

34. To borrow a phrase from Leszek Kolakowski, *Chrétiens sans église* (Paris, 1987).

35. Snyder, "Birth and Evolution of Swiss Anabaptism," 564–5.

36. Claus-Peter Clasen, *Anabaptism* (Ithaca, 1972), 152–94.

37. Packull, *Hutterite Beginnings*, 177–80.

38. MacCulloch, *Reformation*, 166–71.

39. Williams, *Radical Reformation*, 644.

40. Andrea Chudaska, *Peter Riedemann* (Gütersloh, 2003), 216–55.

41. Stayer, *German Peasants' War*, 95–159; Packull, *Hutterite Beginnings*, 1–132.

42. Astrid von Schlachta, *Hutterische Konfession und Tradition* (Mainz, 2003), 192.

43. Goertz, *The Anabaptists*, 22–5.

44. Goertz, "Radical Religiosity," 71–5.

45. J. C. Davis, "Against Formality: One Aspect of the English Revolution," *Transactions of the Royal Historical Society*, 6 ser. 3 (1993), 265–88; Jonathan Scott, *England's Troubles* (Cambridge, 2000), 229–89; Klaus Deppermann, "Der englische Puritanismus," in Brecht (ed.), *GdP*, i, 26–32.

46. Diarmaid MacCulloch, *Tudor Church Militant* (London, 1999), 57–156, here 127–8.

47. Felicity Heal, *Reformation in Britain and Ireland* (Oxford, 2003), 357.

48. M. M. Knappen, *Tudor Puritanism* (Chicago, 1939), 163–246; Patrick Collinson, *The Elizabethan Puritan Movement* (London, 1967), 156–71.

49. Benedict, *CC*, 230–3.

50. Knappen, *Tudor Puritanism*, 187–216.

51. Collinson, *Elizabethan Puritan Movement*, 333–82, 364; Knappen, *Tudor Puritanism*, 283–302.

52. Parick Collinson, *Godly People* (London, 1983), 539.

53. Patrick Collinson, "Puritans," in Hans Hillerbrand (ed.), *Oxford Encyclopedia of the Reformation* (Oxford, 1996), iii, 369.

54. Heal, *Reformation in Britain and Ireland*, 373.

55. John Spurr, *English Puritanism 1603–1689* (Basingstoke, 1998), 58–93.

56. Nicholas Tyacke, *Aspects of English Protestantism, c. 1530–1700* (Manchester, 2001), 90–100; Spurr, *English Puritanism 1603–1689*, 28–58.

57. Heimo Ertl, *Die scheinheiligen Heiligen* (Frankfurt, 1997), 32–158; Collinson, "Puritans," 364–70.

58. Knappen, *Tudor Puritanism*, 258–64; Spurr, *English Puritanism*, 72–8.

59. Patrick Collinson, *The Birthpangs of Protestant England* (Basingstoke, 1988), 28–59.

60. David Underdown, *Fire from Heaven* (London, 1992), 90–130, here 90.

61. Patrick Collinson, "Hooker and the Elizabethan Establishment," in Arthur Stephen McGrade (ed.), *Richard Hooker and the Construction of Christian Community* (Tempe, 1997), 150–81.

62. Diarmaid MacCulloch, "Richard Hooker's Reputation," *English Historical Review*, 473 (2002), 778–9.

63. Scott, *England's Troubles*, 122.

64. Michael Walzer, *The Revolution of the Saints* (London, 1965), 130.

65. Scott, *England's Troubles*, 21–122.

66. Walzer, *Revolution of the Saints*, 1–183, here 33; Denis Müller, *Jean Calvin* (Paris, 2001), 20–30, 42–6.

67. See August Lang, *Puritanismus und Pietismus* (Darmstadt, 1941), 72–100.

68. J. C. Davis, "Religion and the Struggle for Freedom in the English Revolution," *The Historical Journal*, 35 (1992), 517–19.

69. Christopher Hill, *The World Turned Upside Down* (London, 1991), 57–150, here 129; David Cressy, *England on Edge* (Oxford, 2006), 211–47; Michael R. Watts, *The Dissenters* (Oxford, 1978), 77–220.

70. Watts, *The Dissenters*, 111–13.

71. Davis, "Against Formality," 273.

72. Hill, *World Turned Upside Down*, 100, 154, 193, 204, 210, 312.

73. Christopher Hill, *A Turbulent, Seditious, and Factious People* (Oxford, 1998), 188.

74. Hill, *World Turned Upside Down*, 151–230; Werner Schenck, *The Concern for Social Justice in the Puritan Revolution* (London, 1948), 82–96.

75. Hill, *World Turned Upside Down*, 167–8.

76. Collinson, 'Puritans,' 369.

77. Christopher Hill, *The Experience of Defeat* (London, 1994), 27–123, here 53–5; Spurr, *English Puritanism*, 131–52; Watts, *The Dissenters*, 221–41.

78. Sydney E. Ahlstrom, *A Religious History of the American People* (New Haven, 2004), 121–84.

79. Frank Lambert, *The Founding Fathers and the Place of Religion in America* (Princeton, 2003), 74.

80. David Cressy, *Coming Over* (Cambridge, 1987), 74–106; Virginia D. Anderson, *New England's Generation* (Cambridge, 1991), 12–46.

81. Edmund S. Morgan, *The Puritan Dilemma* (Boston, 1958), 91–101; Darrett Bruce Rutman, *Winthrop's Boston* (Chapel Hill, 1965), 3–9.

82. Andrew Delbanco, *The Puritan Ideal* (Cambridge, MA, 1989), 81–3.

83. Ahlstrom, *Religious History*, 149.

84. Francis J. Bremer, *The Puritan Experiment* (New York, 1976), 95.

85. Michael Winship, "Godly Republicanism and the Origins of the Massachusetts Polity," *William and Mary Quarterly*, 63 (2006), 427–62, 455; Ahlstrom, *Religious History*, 156.

86. Morgan, *Puritan Dilemma*, 91–109, here 96.

87. On the theological foundations, see David A. Weir, *The Origins of Federal Theology in Sixteenth-Century Reformation Thought* (Oxford, 1990), 1–147; 317–52, MacCulloch, *Reformation*, 179–9, 389–91, 540–1.

88. John von Rohr, *The Covenant of Grace in Puritan Thought* (Atlanta, 1986), 1–33, here 8; William K. B. Stoever, '*A Faire and Easie Way to Heaven*' (Middletown, 1978), 3–33.

89. Watts, *The Dissenters*, 7–76; Edmund S. Morgan, *Visible Saints* (New York, 1963), 33–63, here 57.

90. Perry Miller, *The New England Mind* (Cambridge, MA, 1982), 378.

91. Morgan, *Visible Saints*, 64–112; Stoever, "*A Faire and Easie Way to Heaven*," 81–118; E. Brooks Holifield, *The Covenant Sealed* (New Haven, 1974), 139–96.

92. Miller, *New England Mind*, 398–431, here 420.

93. Perry Miller, *Errand into the Wilderness* (Cambridge, MA, 1956), 190; Robert Middlekauff, "Piety and Intellect in Puritanism," *William and Mary Quarterly*, 22 (1965), 457–70.

94. Norman Pettit, *The Heart Prepared* (New Haven, 1966), 109.

95. Theodore Dwight Bozeman, *The Precisianist Strain* (Chapel Hill, 2003), 82–3, 139; Charles Lloyd Cohen, *God's Caress* (Oxford, 1986), 25–241.

96. Philip F. Gura, *A Glimpse of Sion's Glory* (Middletown, 1984), 155–84.

97. Michael P. Winship, *Making Heretics* (Princeton, 2002), 28–43, here 42.

98. Bozeman, *Precisianist*, 211–80; Morgan, *Puritan Dilemma*, 190.

99. Lambert, *Founding Fathers*, 94.

100. Miller, *New England Mind*, 451; Lambert, *Founding Fathers*, 90–6; Rutman, *Winthrop's Boston*, 120–34.

101. David D. Hall, *Worlds of Wonder, Days of Judgment* (Cambridge, MA, 1990), 109.

102. Robert Gardner Pope, *The Half-Way Covenant* (Princeton, 1969), 3–75, here 57; Stephen Foster, *The Long Argument* (Chapel Hill, 1991), 175–230.

103. Richard T. Hughes and Crawford L. Allen, *Illusions of Innocence* (Chicago, 1988), 36.

104. Edwin Scott Gaustad, *Liberty of Conscience* (Grand Rapids, 1991), 43; W. Clark Gilpin, *The Millenarian Piety of Roger Williams* (Chicago, 1979), 50–62.

105. Ahlstrom, *Religious History*, 166; Hugh Spurgin, *Roger Williams and Puritan Radicalism in the English Separatist Tradition* (Lewiston, 1989), 123–38.

106. Irwin H. Polishook, *Roger Williams, John Cotton and Religious Freedom* (Engelwood Cliffs, 1967), 18–36, 72.

107. Edmund S. Morgen, *Roger Williams* (New York, 1967), 95; Timothy L. Hall, *Separating Church and State* (Urbana, 1998), 83.

108. Thomas N. Ingersoll, "'Riches and Honour were Rejected by Them as Loathsome Vomit': The Fear of Leveling in New England," in Carla Gardina Pestana and Sharon V. Salinger (eds), *Inequality in Early America* (Hanover, 1999), 46–52; David D. Hall, *The Antinomian Controversy, 1636–1638* (Middletown, 1968), 275.

109. Theodore Dwight Bozeman, "Religious Liberty and the Problem of Order in Early Rhode Island," *The New England Quarterly*, XLV (1972), 54.

110. Joseph Lecler, *Histoire de la tolérance au siècle de la réforme* (Paris, 1955), 161–361.

111. Richard Reinitz, "The Separatist Background of Roger William's Argument for Religious Toleration," in Sacvan Bercovitch (ed.), *Typology and Early American*

Literature (Boston, 1972), 109–21; Andrew R. Murphy, *Conscience and Community* (University Park, 2001), 75–122.

112. Mark Noll, *The Old Religion in a New World* (Grand Rapids, 2002), 10–26.

113. Donald Skaggs, *Roger Williams' Dream for America* (New York, 1992), 86.

114. Willem Frijhoff, 'Religious Tolerance in the United Provinces: from "Case" to "Model",' in R. Po-chia Hsia and Henk van Nierop (eds), *Calvinism and Religious Toleration in the Dutch Golden Age* (Cambridge, 2002), pp. 27–52, here 33.

115. Willem Frijhoff, "Dimensions de la coexistence confessionnelle," in Christiane Berkvens-Stevelinck, Jonathan I. Israel, and G.H.M. Posthumus Meyjes (eds), *The Emergence of Tolerance in the Dutch Republic* (Leiden, 1997), 213–37.

116. Henry Méchoulan, *Amsterdam au temps de Spinoza* (Paris, 1990), 154. On the religious landscape of Amsterdam, see Jo Spaans, "Stad van vele geloven, 1578–1795," in Willem Frijhoff and Maarten Prak (eds), *Geschiedenis van Amsterdam II–1, Centrum van de wereld, 1578–1650* (Amsterdam, 2004), 393–404.

117. Willem Frijhoff, "The West India Company and the Reformed Church: Neglect or Concern?" *De Halve Maen*, 70 (1997), 67; Evan Haefeli, "The Creation of American Religious Pluralism" Princeton University PhD 2000, 48–81.

118. Albert Eekhof, *Jonas Michaëlius, Founder of the Church in New Netherland* (Leiden, 1926), 131.

119. George L. Smith, *Religion and Trade in New Netherland* (Ithaca, 1973), 173; Willem Frijhoff, *Wegen van Evert Willemsz* (Nijmegen, 1995), 543–801.

120. Smith, *Religion and Trade*, 190–237; Michael Kammen, *Colonial New York* (Oxford, 1975), 48–72; Henry Kessler and Eugene Rachlis, *Peter Stuyvesant and his New York* (New York, 1959), 169–96.

121. Haefeli, "American Religious Pluralism," 142–3; Oliver A. Rinck, *Holland on the Hudson* (Ithaca, 1986), 154–5; Kammen, *Colonial New York*, 37.

122. Kessler and Rachlis, *Peter Stuyvesant*, 181; Smith, *Religion and Trade*, 190–211.

123. J. H. Elliott, *Empires of the Atlantic World* (New Haven, 2006), 207–18; Noll, *Old Religion*, 10–26.

Dominions

1. See the discussion by Randolph C. Head and Daniel Christensen (eds), *Orthodoxies and Heterodoxies in Early Modern German Culture* (Leiden, 2007) pp. 1–24.

2. See the discussion in Thomas Kaufmann, *Konfession und Kultur* (Tübingen, 2006), 3–26.

3. Oliver K. Olson, *Matthias Flacius and the Survival of Luther's Reform* (Wiesbaden, 2002), 219.

4. Andrew Delbanco, *The Puritan Ideal* (Cambridge, MA, 1989), 125.

5. Brad S. Gregory, *Salvation at Stake* (Cambridge, MA, 1999), 139–96; Peter Burschel, *Sterben und Unsterblichkeit* (Munich, 2004), 51–157.

6. Jean-François Gilmont, *Jean Crespin* (Geneva, 1981), 165–90.

7. Yves Krumenacker, "La généalogie imaginaire de la Réforme protestante," *Revue Historique*, 130 (2006), 259–89; David El Kenz, *Les búchers ded roi* (Seyssel, 1997), 120–240.

8. Émile Léonard (trans. Joyce M. H. Reid), *History of Protestantism* (London, 1966), ii, 108; Benedict, *CC*, 134.

9. Mack P. Holt, *The French Wars of Religion*, 1562–1629 (Cambridge, 1995), 8–49.

10. Benedict, *CC*, 127–51.

11. Elisabeth Labrousse, *Essai sur la révocation de l'Édit de Nantes* (Geneva, 1985), 45–94.

12. Hugh Trevor-Roper, *Europe's Physician* (New Haven, 2006), 297.

13. Trevor-Roper, *Europe's Physician*, 300. Much of the following discussion is based on the contributions in Raymond A. Mentzer and Andrew Spicer (eds), *Society and Culture in the Huguenot World* 1599–1685 (Cambridge, 2002).

14. Léonard, *A History of Protestantism*, ii, 385.

15. Mark Greengrass, "Informal Networks in Sixteenth-Century French Protestantism," in Mentzer and Spicer, *Society and Culture in the Huguenot World*, 78–97, here 78.

16. Léonard, *A History of Protestantism*, ii, 371.

17. Barbara Dölemeyer, *Die Huguenotten* (Stuttgart, 2006), 50–80.

18. See Eckart Birnstiel and Chrystel Bernet (eds), *La diaspora des Huguenots* (Paris, 2001); Sabine Beneke and Hans Ottomeyer (eds), *Zuwanderungsland Deutschland* (Berlin, 2005).

19. Heiko A. Oberman, "Europa afflicta: The Reformation of the Refugees," *Archiv für Reformationsgeschichte*, 83 (1992), 91–111.

20. Graeme Murdock, *Beyond Calvin* (Basingstoke, 2004), 31–53.

21. Greengrass, "Informal Networks," 78–97.

22. Murdock, *Beyond Calvin*, 39.

23. Mark Greengrass, "Samuel Hartlib and International Calvinism," *Proceedings of the Huguenot Society*, 25 (1993), 464–75.

24. Trevor-Roper, *Europe's Physician*, 191–2.

25. Anne Goldgar, *Impolite Learning* (New Haven, 1990), 174–218, here 211.

26. See Ernst Walter Zeeden, *Die Entstehung der Konfessionen* (Munich, 1965).

27. Hans Preuss, *Die Vorstellungen vom Antichrist im späteren Mittelalter* (Leipzig, 1906), 240.

28. Volker Leppin, *Antichrist und Jüngster Tag* (Gütersloh, 1999), 206–92.

29. Geoffrey Parker, *The Thirty Years' War* (London, 19872), 45.

30. Robert von Friedeburg, *Self-Defence and Religious Strife in Early Modern Europe* (Aldershot, 2002), 91–154; Alexander Schmidt, *Vaterlandsliebe und Religionskonflikt* (Leiden, 2007), 290–358.

31. Wolfgang Harms, "Gustav Adolf als christlicher Alexander und Judas Makkabaeus," *Wirkendes Wort*, 35 (1985), 168–83, here 171; Sverker Oredsson, *Geschichtsschreibung und Kult* (Berlin, 1994), 26–34.

32. Thomas Kaufmann, *Dreißigjähriger Krieg und Westfälischer Friede* (Tübingen, 1998), 41.

33. Friedrich Wilhelm Kantzenbach, *Das Ringen um die Einheit der Kirche im Jahrhundert der Reformation* (Stuttgart, 1957), 119–47, 230–44.

34. See Maximilian Lanzinner, "Das konfessionelle Zeitalter 1555–1618," in Wolfgang Reinhard (ed.), *Gebhardt Handbuch der deutschen Geschichte* (Stuttgart, 2001), x, 79–125.

35. See the contributions in Hans-Christoph Rublack (ed.), *Die lutherische Konfessionalisierung in Deutschland* (Gütersloh, 1992).

36. William James Bouwsma, *The Waning of the Renaissance, 1550–1640* (New Haven, 2002), 233–4.

37. For discussions on the theme of confessionalization, see Stefan Ehrenpreis and Ute Lotz-Heumann, *Reformation und konfessionelles Zeitalter* (Darmstadt, 2002), 62–81; Kaufmann, *Konfession und Kultur*, 2–26; Heinrich Richard Schmidt, *Konfessionalisierung im 16. Jahrhundert* (Munich, 1992).

38. Hans Knapp, *Matthias Hoe von Hoenegg und sein Eingreifen in die Politik und Publizistik des Dreißigjährigen Krieges* (Halle, 1902), 12–47.

39. Karl Lorenz, *Die kirchlich-politische Parteibildung in Deutschland von Beginn des dreißigjährigen Krieges im Spiegel der konfessionellen Polemik* (Munich, 1903), 69–75, here 77.

40. Hans Leube, *Kalvinismus und Luthertum im Zeitalter der Orthodoxie* (Leipzig, 1928), i, 100–63.

41. Bodo Nischan, *Lutherans and Calvinists in the Age of Confessionalism* (Aldershot, 1999), 142–158, here 154.

42. Nischan, *Lutherans and Calvinists*, 209; Alexandre Ganoczy, "Schöpfung und Sakrament in der Kraft des Gottesgeistes. Calvins pneumatologisches Sakramentsverständnis," in Walter Brandmüller, Herbert Immenkötter and Erwin Iserloh (eds), *Ecclesia Militans* (Paderborn, 1988), ii, 193–208.

43. Nischan, *Lutherans and Calvinists*, 61.

44. See Irene Dingel, *Concordia controversia* (Gütersloh, 1996).

45. Harmut Lehmann, "Lutheranism in the Seventeenth Century," in R. Po-chia Hsia (ed.), *Cambridge History of Christianity* (Cambridge, 2007), vi, 56–72.

46. Joseph Leo Koerner, *The Reformation of the Image* (London, 2004), 171–251; Ulinka Rublack, *Reformation Europe* (Cambridge, 2005), 157–80.

47. Jörg Bauer, "Lutherische Christologie," in Rublack, *Die lutherische Konfessionalisierung*, 104–5.

48. Siegfried Müller, "Repräsentationen des Luthertums – Disziplinierung und konfessionelle Kultur in Bildern," *Zeitschrift für historische Forschung*, 29 (2002), 215–55; Carola Jaeggi and Jörn Staecker (eds), *Archäologie der Reformation* (Berlin, 2007), 3–25.

49. Anita Traninger, "Sündenfallstudie," in Johannes Süßmann, Susanne Scholz, Gisela Engel (eds), *Fallstudien* (Berlin, 2007), 195–208, here 199; Peter Harrison, "Original Sin and the Problem of Knowledge in Early Modern Europe," *Journal of the History of Ideas*, 63 (2002), 239–59.

50. See Anita Traninger, *Mühelose Wissenschaft* (Munich, 2001); Howard Hotson, *Commonplace Learning* (Oxford, 2007); Perry Miller, *The New England Mind* (Cambridge, MA, 1982).

51. Bernhard Lohse, *Ratio und Fides* (Göttingen, 1958), 55–126.

52. Randall C. Zachman, *John Calvin as Teacher, Pastor and Theologian* (Grand Rapids, 2006), 231–42, here 236.

53. Jeffrey Mallinson, *Faith, Reason, and Revelation in Theodore Beza* (Oxford, 2003), 99–141, here 117–18.

54. Theodore Dwight Bozeman, *To Live Ancient Lives* (Chapel Hill, 1988), 51–80; John Philip Morgan, *Godly Learning* (Cambridge, 1986), 41–78, Miller, *New England Mind*, 111–238.

55. Morgan, *Godly Learning*, 68.

56. Gerald Strauss, *Luther's House of Learning* (Baltimore, 1978), 151–75, 146, 164; Ian Green, *The Christian's ABC* (Oxford, 1996), 13–20; Stanley Fish, *The Living Temple* (Berkeley, 1978), 1–53.

57. Fish, *The Living Temple*, 18.

58. Christop Weismann, *Eine kleine Biblia* (Stuttgart, 1985), 10.

59. Green, *Christian's ABC*, 13–92.

60. Matthias Pohlig, *Zwischen Gelehrsamkeit und konfessioneller Identitätsstiftung* (Tübingen, 2007), 130–1.

61. See Ulrich Köpf, "The Educational System during the Confessional Period," in Sæbø, *Hebrew Bible*, 647–62.

62. See Anton Schindling, *Bildung und Wissenschaft in der frühen Neuzeit* (Munich, 1999).

63. Robert Fitzgibbon Young, *Comenius in England* (London, 1932), 33.

64. Daniel Neval, *Die Macht Gottes zum Heil* (Zurich, 2006), 29–46.

65. Olivier Cauly, *Comenius* (Paris, 2000), 4–80; Étienne Krotky, *Former l'homme* (Paris, 1996), 25–44.

66. Daniel Murphy, *Comenius* (Dublin, 1995), 79–135, here 85.

67. Daniel Neval, *Comenius' Pansophie* (Zurich, 2007), 125–63.

68. Murphy, *Comenius*, 79–135.

69. Murphy, *Comenius*, 164; Neval, *Die Macht Gottes zum Heil*, 252–71.

70. John Edward Sadler, *J. A. Comenius and the Concept of Universal Education* (London, 1966), 164–86, here 179.

71. Richard van Dülmen, "The Reformation and the Modern Age," C. Scott Dixon (ed.), *The German Reformation* (Oxford, 1999), 203; Friedrich Wilhelm Graf, *Der Protestantismus* (Munich, 2006), 70–9; this is also the underlying argument of Alister McGrath, *Christianity's Dangerous Idea* (London, 2007) and William G. Naphy, *The Protestant Revolution* (London, 2007).

72. Walter Ong, *The Presence of the Word* (New Haven, 1967), 262–86.

73. See Kaspar von Greyerz (trans. Thomas Dunlap), *Religion and Culture in Early Modern Europe* (Oxford, 2007), 187–226.

74. For a discussion of the literature and the themes, see Norbert Schnitzler, *Ikonoklasmus-Bildersturm* (Munich, 1996), 9–25.

75. Lee Palmer Wandel, *Voracious Idols and Violent Hands* (Cambridge, 1995), 106–44; Susan Karant-Nunn, *The Reformation of Ritual* (London, 1997), 91–102, 192.

76. Cornelius Albertus van Swigchem, Teunis Brouwer, and W. van Os, *Een huis voor het Woord* (s'Gravenhage, 1984), 269–85.

77. Koerner, *Reformation of the Image*, 46.

78. Stuart Clark, *Vanities of the Eye* (Oxford, 2007), 161–203, here 164; William A. Dyrness, *Reformed Theology and Visual Culture* (Cambridge, 2004), 49–89.
79. Koerner, *Reformation of the Image*, 41–2, 171–318.
80. Johannes Burckhardt, *Das Reformationsjahrhundert* (Stuttgart, 2002), 30–64.
81. Willem Frijhoff, "Calvinism, Literacy, and Reading Culture in the Early Modern Northern Netherlands: Towards a Reassessment," *Archiv für Reformations-geschichte*, 95 (2004), 252–65; in general, see Benedict, *CC*, 514–18.
82. Richard Gawthorp and Gerald Strauss, "Protestantism and Literacy in Early Modern Germany," *Past and Present*, 104 (1984), 31–55.
83. Janine Garrisson-Estèbe, *L'homme protestant* (Paris, 1980), 79.
84. Nadezda Schevchenko, *Eine historische Anthropologie des Buches* (Göttingen, 2007), 66–91, 230–61; David Cressy, *Literacy and the Social Order* (Cambridge, 1980), 48–52.
85. Nigel Smith, *Perfection Proclaimed* (Oxford, 1989), 23–9; Christopher Hill, *The World Turned Upside Down* (London, 1991), 257–305.
86. Geoffrey Nuttall, *The Holy Spirit in Puritan Faith and Experience* (Oxford, 19472), 20–33, 48–61, 90–133, here 106.
87. Gawthorp and Strauss, "Protestantism and Literacy," 34–8; Adrian Johns, "The Physiology of Reading in Restoration England," in James Raven, Helen Small, and Naomi Tadmor (eds), *The Practice and Representation of Reading in England* (Cambridge, 1996), 136–63.
88. Johann Anselm Steiger, "The Development of the Reformation Legacy: Hermeneutics and Interpretation of the Sacred Scripture in the Age of Orthodoxy," in Sæbø, *Hebrew Bible*, ii, 717.
89. John Knott, *The Sword of the Spirit* (Chicago, 1980), 13–41, here 33.
90. Robert Zaller, *The Discourse of Legitimacy in Early Modern England* (Stanford, 2007), 195.
91. Bozeman, *To Live Ancient Lives*, 30–50, here 42.
92. Smith, *Perfection Proclaimed*, 33; Hunt, *Puritan Moment*, 219–34.
93. Theodore Dwight Bozeman, *The Precisianist Strain* (Chapel Hill, 2003), 27.
94. Michael Mascuch, *Origins of the Individualist Self* (Cambridge, 1997), 55–96; Smith, *Perfection Proclaimed*, 36–40; Charles Lloyd Cohen, *God's Caress* (Oxford, 1986), 77–8.
95. Gerd Birkner, *Heilsgewissheit und Literatur* (Munich, 1972), 7–45.
96. Bozeman, *Precisianist Strain*, 27.
97. Cohen, *God's Caress*, 3–73, 162–200; Bozeman, *Precisianist Strain*, 134–6.
98. Bozeman, *Precisianist Strain*, 121–68, 139; David Como, *Blown by the Spirit* (Stanford, 2004), 117–37.
99. Patricia Caldwell, *The Puritan Conversion Narrative* (Cambridge, 1983), 92.
100. Catherine Randall, *Building Codes* (Philadelphia, 1999), 44–137.
101. Per Gustaf Hamberg (trans. Nancy Adler), *Temples for Protestants* (Gothenburg, 2002), 8.
102. I take this distinction from Harold W. Turner, *From Temple to Meeting House* (The Hague, 1979).
103. Richard Kieckhefer, *Theology in Stone* (Oxford, 2004), 24–32.

104. Peter Poscharsky, *Die Kanzel* (Gütersloh, 1963), 112–97, here 194; Kieckhefer, *Theology in Stone*, 84–96.

105. Van Swigchem, Brouwer, and van Os, *Een huis voor het Woord*, 269–85.

106. Graeme Murdock, "'Pure and White': Reformed Space for Worship in Early Seventeenth-Century Hungary," in Andrew Spicer and Sarah Hamilton (eds), *Defining the Holy* (Aldershot, 2005), 243–4; Hamberg, *Temples for Protestants*, 54–7.

107. Hamberg, *Temples for Protestants*, 47–124; Andrew Drummond, *The Church Architecture of Protestantism* (Edinburgh, 1934), 19–61.

108. Peter Williams, *Houses of God* (Urbana, 1997); 1–46; Anthony Garvan, "The New England Plain Style," *Comparative Studies in Society and History*, 3 (1960), 106–22.

109. Turner, *From Temple to Meeting House*, 215.

110. Hamberg, *Temples for Protestants*, 52–7; Judith Pollmann. "The Cleansing of the Temple. Church Space and its Meanings in the Dutch Republic," in José Pedro Paiva (ed.), *Religious Ceremonials and Images* (Coimbra, 2002), 177–89.

111. Martin S. Briggs, *Puritan Architecture and its Future* (London, 1946), 30.

112. André Biéler, *Liturgie et architecture* (Geneva, 1961), 67.

113. Bernard Reymond, *L'Architecture religieuse des protestants* (Geneva, 1996), 44–87; Briggs, *Puritan Architecture*, 31.

114. Poscharsky, *Die Kanzel*, 96.

115. John Bossy, *Christianity in the West, 1400–1700* (Oxford, 1985), 140–2.

116. Christopher Marsh, "Sacred Space in England, 1560–1640: The View from the Pew," *Journal of Ecclesiastical History*, 53 (2002), 308.

117. Dell Upton, *Holy Things and Profane* (Cambridge, MA, 1986), 175–96; Marsh, "Sacred Space," 298–311; Patrick Collinson, *The Religion of Protestants* (Oxford, 1982), 195.

118. Turner, *From Temple to Meeting House*, 229.

119. David Knowles, *Bare Ruined Choirs* (Cambridge, 1976), 266–72.

120. Christopher Ocker, *Church Robbers and Reformers in Germany 1525–1547* (Leiden, 2006), 17–48.

121. Margaret Aston, "English Ruins and English History: The Dissolution of the Sense of the Past," *Journal of the Warburg and Courtauld Institutes*, 36 (1973), 236, 251, 254.

122. Aston, "English Ruins," 247.

123. See now Alexandra Walsham, *The Reformation of the Landscape* (Oxford, forthcoming).

124. James P. Walsh, "Holy Time and Holy Space in Puritan New England," *American Quarterly*, 32 (1980), 79–85.

125. George R. Stewart, *Names on the Land* (Boston, 1967), 50.

126. Walsh, "Holy Time and Holy Space," 88–91.

127. Walsham, *Reformation of the Landscape*.

128. Cotton Mather (Kenneth B. Murdock, ed.) *Magnalia Christi Americana* (Cambridge, MA, 1977), 118.

129. George H. Williams, "The Idea of the Wilderness of the New World in Cotton Mather's *Magnalia Christi Americana*," in Murdock, *Magnalia Christi Americana*, 48–58.

130. Avîhû Zakai, *Exile and Kingdom* (Cambridge, 1992), 131–9.
131. Cecelia Tichi, *New World, New Earth* (New Haven, 1979), 37–66.
132. J. H. Elliott, *Empires of the Atlantic World* (New Haven, 2006), 190.
133. John Canup, *Out of the Wilderness* (Middletown, 1990), 88–148.
134. Ulrike Brunotte, *Puritanismus und Pioniergeist* (Berlin, 2000), 255–6.
135. Canup, *Out of the Wilderness*, 147.
136. Elliott, *Empires of the Atlantic World*, 190.
137. Werner Elert (trans. Walter A. Hansen), *The Structure of Lutheranism* (St Louis, 1962), 385–402.
138. Gustav Warneck, *Abriß einer Geschichte der protestantischen Missionen von der Reformation bis auf die Gegenwart* (Berlin, 1905), 16–29; James Tanis, "Reformed Pietism and Protestant Missions," *Harvard Theological Review*, 67 (1974), 68–71; Jan Jongeneel, "The Missiology of Gisbertus Voetius: The First Comprehensive Protestant Theology of Missions," *Calvin Theological Journal*, 26 (1991), 47–79.
139. Fritz Laubach, *Justinian von Welz* (Wuppertal, 1989), 7–32.
140. Laubach, *Justinian von Welz*, 26; Elert, *Structure of Lutheranism*, 399.
141. Warneck, *Abriß einer Geschichte*, 10–29.
142. Elliott, *Empires of the Atlantic World*, 75.
143. Alexander Browne, *The Genesis of the United States* (London, 1890), 67–8.
144. Elliott, *Empires of the Atlantic World*, 72–8.
145. Albert Eekhof, *Jonas Michaëlius, Founder of the Church in New Netherland* (Leiden, 1926), 132–5; Gerald Francis De Jong, "Dominie Johannes Megapolensis: Minister to New Netherland," *New York Historical Society Quarterly*, 52 (1968), 7–47.
146. Silvia Shannon, "Villegagnon, Polyphemus, and Cain of America: Religion and Polemics in the French New World," Michael Wolfe (ed.), *Changing Identities in Early Modern France* (Durham, 1997), 325–44.
147. Kirsten Mahlke, *Offenbarung im Westen* (Frankfurt, 2005), 141–95.
148. Frank Lestringant, *Jean du Léry ou l'invention du sauvage* (Paris, 2005), 117–46, here 133.
149. Gerrit J. Knaap, *Kruidnagelen en Christenen* (Leiden, 2004), 105–25; C. R. Boxer, *The Dutch Seaborne Empire 1600–1800* (London, 1972), 145–8.
150. Boxer, *Dutch Seaborne Empire*, 132–40; Sinnappah Arasaratnam, *Ceylon and the Dutch, 1600–1800* (Aldershot, 1996), 33–5.
151. On the mission, see the contributions in Andreas Gross (ed.), *Halle and the Beginning of Protestant Christianity in India*, 3 vols. *The Danish-Halle and the English-Halle Mission* (Halle, 2006).
152. Nørgaard, "The Mission's Relationship to the Danes," in Gross (ed.), *The Danish-Halle and the English-Halle Mission*, 180.
153. Nørgaard, "The Mission's Relationship to the Danes," 173.

Revivals

1. Harry S. Stout, *The New England Soul* (Oxford, 1968), 109; Edmund S. Morgan, *The Puritan Dilemma* (New York, 2006), 52.

2. W. R. Ward, *The Protestant Evangelical Awakening* (Cambridge, 1992), 1–53.
3. Ward, *Protestant Evangelical Awakening*, 51.
4. Hans Juergen Schönstädt, *Antichrist, Weltheilsgeschehen und Gottes Werkzeug* (Wiesbaden, 1978), 10–85, 106–200, here 114.
5. Theodore G. Tappert (ed.), *The Book of Concord* (Philadelphia, 1959), 13.
6. For general surveys, see Oliver Fatio, "L'Orthodoxie protestante," in Pierre Chaunu (ed.), *L'Aventure de la réforme* (Paris 1982). Johann Anselm Steiger, "The Development of the Reformation Legacy: Hermeneutics and Interpretation of the Sacred Scripture in the Age of Orthodoxy," in Sæbø, *Hebrew Bible*, 691–757.
7. Robert D. Preuss, *The Theology of Post-Reformation Lutheranism* (Saint Louis, 1970), i, 143–54, here 148; Hans Leube, *Kalvinismus und Luthertum im Zeitalter der Orthodoxie* (Leipzig, 1928), i, 138–42, 152–63.
8. Sabine Holtz, *Theologie und Alltag* (Tübingen, 1993), 314–76.
9. Kenneth G. Appold, *Orthodoxie als Konsensbildung* (Tübingen, 2004), 88–111.
10. Preuss, *Post-Reformation Lutheranism*, 15–71; see Carl Heinz Ratschow, *Lutherische Dogmatik zwischen Reformation und Aufklärung* (Gütersloh, 1964).
11. Matthias Pohlig, *Zwischen Gelehrsamkeit und konfessioneller Identitätsstiftung* (Tübingen, 2007), 270–389; Pontien Polman, *L'Elément historique dans la controverse religieuse du 16e siècle* (Gembloux, 1932), 157–78.
12. Pohlig, *Gelehrsamkeit*, 270–341; Olson, *Matthias Flacius and the Survival of Luther's Reform*(Wiesbaden, 2002), 233–79.
13. Pohlig, *Gelehrsamkeit*, 339–41.
14. Hermann Dörries, *Geist und Geschichte bei Gottfried Arnold* (Göttingen, 1963), 130–9; Juergen Büchsel, *Gottfried Arnold* (Witten, 1970), 76–132.
15. C. Scott Dixon, "Faith and History on the Eve of Enlightenment: Ernst Salomon Cyprian, Gottfried Arnold, and the *History of Heretics*," *Journal of Ecclesiastical History*, 57 (2006), 33–54, here 49.
16. Martin Greschat, *Zwischen Tradition und neuem Anfang*(Witten, 1971), 9–142, here 60.
17. Erich Seeberg, *Gottfried Arnold* (Meerane, 1923), 535–611.
18. Greschat, *Zwischen Tradition und neuem Anfang*, 144–219; and in general, Jonathan I. Israel, *The Radical Enlightenment* (Oxford, 2001), 628–63.
19. Gerald Strauss, *Luther's House of Learning* (Baltimore, 1978), 250–1.
20. Strauss, *Luther's House of Learning*, 249–308, here 276; on the success and failure debates in general, Geoffrey Parker, "Success and Failure during the First Century of the Reformation," *Past and Present*, 136 (1992), 43–82; C. Scott Dixon, *The Reformation and Rural Society*(Cambridge, 1996), 142–202; for the French context, Philippe Joutard, "Protestantisme populaire et univers magique: le cas cévenol," *Le monde Alpin et Rhodanien*, V (1977), 145–71; Raymond A. Mentzer, "The Persistence of 'Superstition and Idolatry' Among Rural French Calvinists," *Church History*, 65, (1996), 220–33; for the Dutch context, Wiebe Bergsma, *Tussen Gideonsbende en publieke kerk* (Hilversum, 1999), 344–404; Herman Roodenburg, *Onder Censuur*(Hilversum, 1990), 205–29, 321–82; for a general discussion of the effects of reform, see Kaspar von Greyerz (trans.

Thomas Dunlap), *Religion and Culture in Early Modern Europe, 1500–1800* (Oxford, 2008), 40–55.

21. Karl Burckhardt, *Geschichte der sächsischen Kirchen- und Schulvisitation von 1524 bis 1545* (Leipzig, 1879), 39.

22. Christopher Haigh, "Success and Failure in the English Reformation," *Past and Present*, 173 (2001), 28–49, here 27 and 32; Christopher Haigh, *The Plain Man's Pathway to Heaven* (Oxford, 2007), 145–80.

23. Derek Hirst, "The Failure of Godly Rule in the English Republic," *Past and Present*, 132 (1991), 23–66, here 45.

24. See Sacvan Bercovitch, *The Puritan Origins of the American Self* (New Haven, 1975), 72–108.

25. Alexandra Walsham, *Providence in Early Modern England* (Oxford, 1999), 281–325.

26. Bercovitch, *Puritan Origins*, 54–5; full citation in Frank Shuffelton's review of Bercovitch in *Eighteenth Century Studies*, 15 (1981/2), 233.

27. Werner Elert (trans. Walter A. Hansen), *The Structure of Lutheranism* (St Louis, 1962), 441.

28. Robert W. Scribner, "Reformation, Popular Magic, and the 'Disenchantment of the World,'" in C. Scott Dixon (ed.), *The German Reformation* (Oxford, 1999), 259–79; Alexandra Walsham, "The Reformation and the 'Disenchantment of the World' Reassessed," *The Historical Journal*, 51 (2008), 497–528.

29. C. Scott Dixon. "Popular Astrology and Lutheran Propaganda in Reformation Germany," *History*, 84 (1999), 403–18.

30. Erhard Kunz, *Protestantische Eschatologie von der Reformation bis zur Aufklärung* (Freiburg, 1980), iv, 3–22.

31. Robin Bruce Barnes, *Prophecy and Gnosis* (Stanford, 1988), 60–258; Volker Leppin, *Antichrist und Jüngster Tag* (Gütersloh, 1999), 206–92; Kunz, *Protestantische Eschatologie*, 43–67.

32. Ulrich Gäbler, "Geschichte, Gegenwart, Zukunft," in Hartmut Lehmann (ed.) *GdP* (2004), iv, 33–36; Kunz, *Protestantische Eschatologie*, 70–92.

33. Kunz, *Protestantische Eschatologie*, 61.

34. Harmut Lehmann, *Das Zeitalter des Absolutismus* (Stuttgart, 1980), 114–61.

35. Hans Schneider, "Der radikale Pietismus im 17. Jahrhundert", in Brecht, *GdP*, i, 400–2.

36. Ward, *Protestant Evangelical Awakening*, 10–13; for a list of early Puritan texts, see Willem Jan op 't Hof, *Engelse piëtistische geschriften in het Nederlands, 1598–1622* (Rotterdam, 1987), 169–406.

37. Keith L. Sprunger, *Trumpets from the Tower* (Leiden, 1994), 46–125, here 77.

38. Johannes van den Berg, "Die Frömmigkeitsbestrebungen in den Niederlanden," in Brecht, *GdP*, i, 57–112; Benedict, *CC*, 355–64.

39. To-Hong Jou, *Theodor Undereyck und die Anfänge des reformierten Pietismus* (Bochum, 1994), 136–76; Johann Friedrich Gerhard Goeters, "Der reformierte Pietismus in Deutschland 1650–1690," in Brecht, *GdP*, i, 240–77.

40. Martin Gierl, *Pietismus und Aufklärung* (Göttingen, 1997), 193–265; Klaus Deppermann, *Der hallesche Pietismus und der preußische Staat unter Friedrich III* (Göttingen, 1961), 73–4.

41. Martin Brecht, "Das Aufkommen der neuen Frömmigkeitsbewegung in Deutschland," *GdP*, 130–4; Johannes Wallmann, *Der Pietismus* (Göttingen, 2005), 28–47.
42. Johannes Wallmann, "Johann Arndt (1555–1621)," in Carter Lindberg (ed.), *The Pietist Theologians* (Oxford, 2005), 27.
43. Hans Schneider, *Der fremde Arndt* (Göttingen, 2006), 205–6.
44. Wolfgang Sommer, *Politik, Theologie und Frömmigkeit im Luthertum der frühen Neuzeit* (Göttingen, 1999), 239–62.
45. F. Ernest Stoeffler, *The Rise of Evangelical Pietism* (Leiden, 1965), 228–46, here 235.
46. Johannes Wallmann, "Die Anfänge des Pietismus," *PuN*, 4 (1979), 48–9; W. R. Ward, *Early Evangelicalism* (Cambridge, 2006), 24–39.
47. Martin Brecht, "Philipp Jakob Spener, sein Programm und dessen Auswirkung," in Brecht, *GdP*, i, 279–389, 364–5.
48. Carter Lindberg, *The Third Reformation* (Macon, 1983), 144–9, here 146; Wallmann, *Pietismus*, 66–102.
49. Hartmut Lehmann, "Der Pietismus im Alten Reich," *Historische Zeitschrift*, 214 (1974), 83; Johannes Wallmann, *Philipp Jakob Spener und die Anfänge des Pietismus* (Tübingen, 1970), 190–335; Gierl, *Pietismus und Aufklärung*, 211–12.
50. Martin Brecht, "August Hermann Francke und der Hallische Pietismus," in Brecht, *GdP*, i, 440–52; Ryoko Mori, *Begeisterung und Ernüchterung in christlicher Vollkommenheit* (Tübingen, 2004), 8–24.
51. Christian Peters, "Daraus der Lärm des Pietismi entstanden..." *PuN*, 23 (1997), 103–30.
52. See the overviews in Mori, *Begeisterung und Ernüchterung*, 8–100; Wallmann, *Pietismus*, 91–5; Brecht, "Philipp Jakob Spener," 333–52, 368–71; and for the broad framework, Ward, *Protestant Evangelical Awakening*, 54–92, 116–41, 160–85, 241–65, 310–16.
53. Manfred Jakubowski-Tiessen, "Eigenkultur und Traditionsbildung," in Lehmann, *GdP*, iv, 203–6.
54. Mori, *Begeisterung und Ernüchterung*, 60–2.
55. Mori, *Begeisterung und Ernüchterung*, 244–5.
56. See the discussion in Lindberg, "Introduction," in Lindberg, *Pietist Theologians*, 1–20; Johannes Wallmann, "Eine alternative Geschichte des Pietismus. Zur gegenwärtigen Diskussion um den Pietismusbegriff," *PuN*, 28 (2002), 30–79.
57. Hartmus Lehmann, *Transformationen der Religion in der Neuzeit* (Göttingen, 2007), 120–5.
58. Lindberg, "Introduction," 7.
59. Melvin B. Endy, jr, "Puritanism, Spiritualism, and Quakerism: An Historiographical Essay," in Richard S. Dunn (ed.), *The World of William Penn* (Philadelphia, 1986), 286.
60. Brecht, "Das Aufkommen," 174–5.
61. Johannes Wallmann, "Frömmigkeit und Gebet," in Lehmann, *GdP*, iv, 80–101.
62. Markus Matthias, "*Collegium pietatis* und *ecclesiola*," *PuN*, 19 (1993), 46–59; Wallmann, *Philipp Jakob Spener*, 253–82.

63. Andreas Deppermann, *Johann Jakob Schütz und die Anfänge des Pietismus* (Tübingen, 2002), 81–98.

64. Jonathan Strom, "Early Conventicles in Lübeck," *PuN*, 27 (2002), 19–52.

65. Douglas Shantz, "Politics, Prophecy, and Pietism in the Halberstadt Conventicle, 1691–1694," in Fred van Liedburg (ed.), *Confessionalism and Pietism* (Mainz, 2006), 129–47, 137.

66. Hans Otte, "The Pietist Laity in Germany, 1675–1750," in Deryck W. Lovegrove (ed.), *The Rise of the Laity in Evangelical Protestantism* (London, 2002), 51–2.

67. Ruth Albrecht, "Frauen," in Lehmann, *GdP*, iv, 522–55, 530.

68. See Martin Schmidt, *Wiedergeburt und neuer Mensch* (Witten, 1969), 169–94.

69. Lindberg, *Third Reformation*, 161–5, here 165; Markus Matthias, "Bekehrung und Wiedergeburt," in Lehmann, *GdP*, iv, 49–79.

70. Mori, *Begeisterung und Ernüchterung*, 84.

71. Greschat, *Zwischen Tradition und neuem Anfang*, 213–14.

72. Matthias, "*Collegium pietatis* und *ecclesiola*," 54.

73. See Wallmann, "Eine alternative Geschichte des Pietismus," 30–79; Wallmann, "Die Anfänge des Pietismus," 49–51.

74. Douglas H. Shantz, *Between Sardis and Philadelphia* (Leiden, 2008), 125–61, here 141.

75. Shantz, *Between Sardis and Philadelphia*, 196.

76. See Hans Schneider, "Der radikale Pietismus in der neueren Forschung," *PuN*, 8 (1982), i, 15–42; ii, 117–51.

77. Wallmann, *Philipp Jakob Spener*, 283–306.

78. Deppermann, *Johann Jakob Schütz*, 158–206.

79. Deppermann, *Johann Jakob Schütz*, 182.

80. Klaus Deppermann, "Pennsylvania als Asyl des frühen deutschen Pietismus," *PuN*, 10 (1984), 190–201; Deppermann, *Johann Jakob Schütz*, 222–334; Wallmann, *Pietismus*, 136–51.

81. See Piet Visser, "Mennonites and Doopsgezinden in the Netherlands, 1535–1700" in John D. Roth and James M. Stayer (eds), *A Companion to Anabaptism and Spiritualism, 1521–1700* (Leiden, 2007), 299–345; Samme Zijlstra, *Om de ware gemeente en de oude gronden* (Hilversum, 2000), 126–339.

82. Jonathan I. Israel, *Enlightenment Contested* (Oxford, 2006), 63–201.

83. See John D. Roth, "Marpeck and the Later Swiss Brethren, 1540–1700," in Roth and Stayer, *Companion*, 348–88; Packull, *Hutterite Beginnings*, 133–58.

84. Roth, "Marpeck and the Later Swiss Brethren," 381; compare Hanspeter Jecker, *Ketzer, Rebellen, Heilige* (Liestal, 1998), 406–528.

85. Stoeffler, *Rise of Pietism*, 162–80, here 169; Wallmann, "Eine alternative Geschichte," 56.

86. See Trevor John Saxby, *The Quest for the New Jerusalem* (Dordrecht, 1987).

87. Wallmann, "Eine alternative Geschichte des Pietismus," 56; Deppermann, *Johann Jakob Schütz*, 288–98.

88. Hans Schneider (trans. Gerald T MacDonald), *German Radical Pietism* (Lanham, 2007), 89–96;. Wallmann, *Der Pietismus*, 174–80.

89. Schneider, *German Radical Pietism*, 97.

90. Schneider, *German Radical Pietism*, 118–24; Wallmann, *Der Pietismus*, 178–9.

91. Kunz, *Protestantische Eschatologie*, 70–92; Wallmann, *Philipp Jackob Spener*, 307–35; Hartmut Lehmann, "Vorüberlegungen zu einer Sozialgeschichte des Pietismus im 17./18. Jahrhundert," *PuN*, 21 (1995), 69–74.

92. Gäbler, "Geschichte, Gegenwart, Zukunft," 19–21; Schneider, *German Radical Pietism*, 6–8.

93. Hans Schneider, "Der radikale Pietismus im 17. Jahrhundert," in Brecht, *GdP*, i, 402–6.

94. Mori, *Begeisterung und Ernüchterung*, 160–83.

95. Hans Schneider, "Der radikale Pietismus im 17. Jahrhundert," in Brecht, *GdP*, i, 402; Mori, *Begeisterung und Ernüchterung*, 174–8.

96. Hartmut Lehmann, *Pietismus und weltliche Ordnung in Württemberg vom 17. bis zum 20. Jahrhundert* (Stuttgart, 1969), 22–65.

97. Wallmann, *Der Pietismus*, 204–13; Kunz, *Protestantische Eschatologie*, 81–4.

98. Eberhard Fritz, *Radikaler Pietismus in Württemberg* (Epfendorf, 2003), 35–96, 257–360.

99. Mack Walker, *The Salzburg Transaction* (Ithaca, 1992), 31–68, here 62.

100. Bodo Nischan, *Prince, People and Confession* (Philadelphia, 1994), 5–131, 185–259.

101. Gerd Heinrich, "Religionstoleranz in Brandenburg-Preußen. Idee und Wirklichkeit," in Manfred Schlenke (ed.), *Preußen* (Reinbek, 1986), 83–120.

102. See Brecht, "August Hermann Francke," 439–539.

103. Mori, *Begeisterung und Ernüchterung*, 212–21.

104. Wallmann, *Der Pietismus*, 125.

105. Helmut Obst, *August Hermann Francke und die Franckeschen Stiftungen in Halle* (Göttingen, 2002), 55–74; Brecht, "August Hermann Francke," 473–96.

106. Christopher Clark, *Iron Kingdom* (London, 2006), 79.

107. Richard L. Gawthrop, *Pietism and the Making of Eighteenth-Century Prussia* (Cambridge, 1993), 200–69; Thomas Müller-Bahlke, "Protektion und Privilegien. Das Verhältnis zwischen den Franckeschen Stiftungen und dem Preußischen Staat," in Thomas Müller-Bahlke (ed.), *Gott zur Ehre und zu des Landes Besten* (Halle, 2001), 122.

108. Clark, *Iron Kingdom*, 127.

109. Gawthrop, *Pietism*, 244; Deppermann, *Der hallesche Pietismus*, 62–87; Mary Fulbrook, *Piety and Politics* (Cambridge, 1983), 153–73.

110. Fulbrook, *Piety and Politics*, 153.

111. Ward, *Protestant Evangelical Awakening*, 49.

112. Nicholas Hope, *German and Scandinavian Protestantism 1700–1918* (Oxford, 1995), 131–210.

113. Greyerz, *Religion and Culture*, 187–212.

114. Andre Wakefield, *The Disordered Police State* (Chicago, 2009), 1–25.

115. Matthias Fritsch, *Religiöse Toleranz im Zeitalter der Aufklärung* (Hamburg, 2004), 63.

116. Klaus Schlaich, "Der rationale Territorialismus. Die Kirche unter dem staats-rechtlichen Absolutismus um die Wende vom 17. zum 18. Jahrhundert,"

Zeitschrift der Savigny-Stiftung für Rechtsgeschichte KA, 54 (1968), 269–340; Ian Hunter, *Rival Enlightenments* (Cambridge, 2001), 234–73.

117. See Martin Kühnel, *Das politische Denken von Christian Thomasius* (Berlin, 2001), 153–73.
118. Ian Hunter, *The Secularisation of the Confessional State* (Cambridge, 2007), 21–167, here 189–90.
119. Israel, *Enlightenment Contested*, 194–200.
120. Thomas Ahnert, *Religion and the Origins of the German Enlightenment* (Rochester, 2006), 9–56; Kühnel, *Das politische Denken*, 159–65.
121. Hope, *German and Scandinavian Protestantism*, 131–210.
122. Gerhard Kaiser, *Pietismus und Patriotismus im literarischen Deutschland* (Wiesbaden, 1961), 32–57.
123. William R. Hutchison, *Religious Pluralism in America* (New Haven, 2003), 14.
124. Hutchison, *Religious Pluralism*, 11–14.
125. John Webb Pratt, *Religion, Politics, and Diversity* (Ithaca, 1967), 26–48; Evan Haefeli, "The Creation of American Religious Pluralism" Princeton University PhD (2000), 220–61.
126. David G. Hackett, *The Rude Hand of Innovation* (Oxford, 1991), 30; Randall Balmer, *A Perfect Babel of Confusion* (Oxford, 1989), 3–50.
127. Jon Butler, *Awash in a Sea of Faith* (London, 1990), 64.
128. Patricia U. Bonomi, *Under the Cope of Heaven* (Oxford, 1986), 21–3; Butler, *Sea of Faith*, 51–5.
129. Sydney E. Ahlstrom, *A Religious History of the American People* (New Haven, 2004), 214–29, 218–19; Butler, *Sea of Faith*, 98–128.
130. Peter Vogt, "Different Ideas about the Church . . ." in Hans-Jürgen Grabbe (ed.), *Halle Pietism, Colonial North America, and the Young United States* (Stuttgart, 2008), 38–9.
131. Bonomi, *Cope of Heaven*, 39–85, here 80.
132. Ahlstrom, *Religious History*, 158–65; Butler, *Sea of Faith*, 105–6; Bonomi, *Cope of Heaven*, 61–72.
133. Stephen Foster, *The Long Argument* (Chapel Hill, 1991), 186–206, here 196.
134. Stout, *New England Soul*, 109; Perry Miller, *The New England Mind* (Cambridge, MA, 1982), 463–91.
135. Patrick Griffin, "The People with no Name," *William and Mary Quarterly*, 58 (2001), 587–614; Butler, *Sea of Faith*, 116–23.
136. Cynthia G. Falk, *Architecture and Artifacts of the Pennsylvania Germans* (University Park, 2008), 130–1; Butler, *Sea of Faith*, 110–12.
137. Bonomi, *Cope of Heaven*, 72–85, here 84.
138. Edwin B. Bronner, *William Penn's "Holy Experiment"* (New York, 1962), 6–49, here 27.
139. George Bishop Tatum, *Penn's Great Town* (Philadelphia, 1961), 17–26, here 19; Irma W. Corcoran, *Thomas Holme* (Philadelphia, 1992), 112–15.
140. Hugh Barbour, *The Quakers in Puritan England* (New Haven, 1964), 33–71; Adrian Davies, *The Quakers in English Society, 1655–1725* (Oxford, 2000), 11–34.

141. John Miller, "'A Suffering People': English Quakers and their Neighbours c.1650–c.1700," *Past and Present*, 188 (2005), 71–103; Michael R. Watts, *The Dissenters* (Oxford, 1978), 221–62, 236.

142. Holmer L. Ingle, *First Among Friends* (Oxford, 1994), 41–52; Barbour, *Quakers in Puritan England*, 94–126, here 124.

143. Pink Dandelion, *An Introduction to Quakerism* (Cambridge, 2007), 22–3.

144. Ingle, *First Among Equals*, 62, Davies, *Quakers in English Society*, 19.

145. Richard Bauman, *Let your Words be Few* (Cambridge, 1983), 120–36, here 126.

146. Kathleen H. Thomas, *The History and Significance of Quaker Symbols in Sect Formation* (Lewiston, 2002), 19–84; Davies, *Quakers in English Society*, 35–90; Barbour, *Quakers in Puritan England*, 166–86, 167.

147. Thomas D. Hamm, *Quakers in America* (New York, 2003), 22–36.

148. Bronner, *Penn's 'Holy Experiment'*, 24–6; Sally Schwarz, *A Mixed Multitude* (New York, 1987), 81–119, here 40.

149. Even Penn admitted that "though I desire to extend religious freedom, yet I want some recompense for my trouble." Quoted in Gary B. Nash, *Quakers and Politics* (Princeton, 1968), 10.

150. David Hackett Fischer, *Albion's Seed* (Oxford, 1989), 419–67; Ahlstrom, *Religious History*, 230–59; see the articles in Jonathan Strom, Hartmut Lehmann, and James Van Horn Melton (eds), *Pietism in Germany and North America 1680–1820* (Farnham, 2009).

151. David S. Lovejoy, *Religious Enthusiasm in the New World* (Cambridge, MA, 1985), 44–5.

152. Ahlstrom, *Religious History*, 208; Jerry W. Frost, *A Perfect Freedom* (Cambridge, 1990), 10–43.

153. Bronner, *Penn's 'Holy Experiment'*, 11.

154. Frank Lambert, *The Founding Fathers and the Place of Religion in America* (Princeton, 2003), 108.

155. Schwarz, *Mixed Multitude*, 64–80; Ward, *Protestant Evangelical Awakening*, 249–51.

156. Jeff Bach, *Voices of the Turtledoves* (University Park, 2003), 3–97.

157. Mark A. Noll, *America's God* (Oxford, 2003), 19–30.

158. Nash, *Quakers and Politics*, 117, 48–126; Lambert, *Founding Fathers*, 110–23.

159. Nash, *Quakers and Politics*, 144–61, here 150.

Epilogue

1. W. R. Ward, *The Protestant Evangelical Awakening* (Cambridge, 1992), 1–53, here 49.

2. Kaspar von Greyerz (trans. Thomas Dunlap), *Religion and Culture in Early Modern Europe, 1500–1800* (Oxford, 2008), 187–222.

3. Ward, *Evangelical Awakening*, 54–240; for the discussions that follow, see also the contributions in Martin Brecht and Klaus Deppermann (eds), *GdP* (Göttingen, 1995), ii.

4. Ward, *Evangelical Awakening*, 116–59.

5. Mark Noll, *The Rise of Evangelicalism* (Downers Grove, 2003), 74.

6. Ward, *Evangelical Awakening*, 296–352; Michael R. Watts, *The Dissenters* (Oxford, 1978), 394–445.

7. Noll, *Rise of Evangelicalism*, 15.

8. Sydney E. Ahlstrom, *A Religious History of the American People* (New Haven, 2004), 280–329; Noll, *Rise of Evangelicalism*, 76–99.

9. Frank Lambert, *The Founding Fathers and the Place of Religion in America* (Princeton, 2003), 123–58, here 149.

10. Mark A. Noll, *America's God* (Oxford, 2002), 44.

11. Noll, *Rise of Evangelicalism*, 19, 34.

12. Watts, *Dissenters*, 402; on Wesley and Halle Pietism see Sung-Duk Lee, *Der deutsche Pietismus und John Wesley* (Giessen, 2003), 20–57, 81–102.

Index